Cram101 Textbook Outlines to accompany:

American Government : Power and Purpose

Theodore Lowi, 11th Edition

A Content Technologies Inc. publication (c) 2012.

Cram101 Textbook Outlines and Cram101.com are Cram101 Inc. publications and services. All notes, highlights, reviews, and practice tests are written and prepared by Content Technologies and Cram101, all rights reserved.

WHY STOP HERE... THERE'S MORE ONLINE

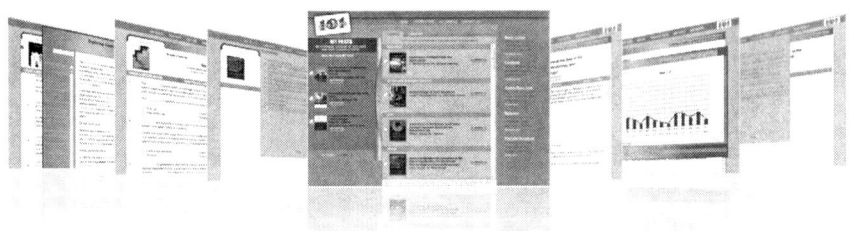

With technology and experience, we've developed tools that make studying easier and efficient. Like this Craml0l textbook notebook, Craml0l.com offers you the highlights from every chapter of your actual textbook. However, unlike this notebook, Craml0l.com gives you practice tests for each of the chapters. You also get access to in-depth reference material for writing essays and papers.

By purchasing this book, you get 50% off the normal subscription free!. Just enter the promotional code **'DK73DW17096'** on the Cram101.com registration screen.

CRAMI0I.COM FEATURES:

Outlines & Highlights
Just like the ones in this notebook, but with links to additional information.

Integrated Note Taking
Add your class notes to the Cram101 notes, print them and maximize your study time.

Problem Solving
Step-by-step walk throughs for math, stats and other disciplines.

Practice Exams
Five different test taking formats for every chapter.

Easy Access
Study any of your books, on any computer, anywhere.

Unlimited Textbooks
All the features above for virtually all your textbooks, just add them to your account at no additional cost.

TRY THE FIRST CHAPTER FREE!

Be sure to use the promo code above when registering on Craml0l.com to get 50% off your membership fees.

STUDYING MADE EASY

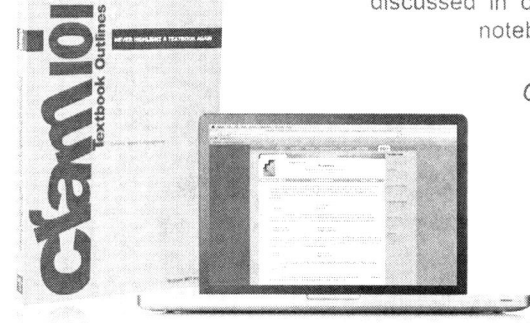

This Cram101 notebook is designed to make studying easier and increase your comprehension of the textbook material. Instead of starting with a blank notebook and trying to write down everything discussed in class lectures, you can use this Cram101 textbook notebook and annotate your notes along with the lecture.

Our goal is to give you the best tools for success.

For a supreme understanding of the course, pair your notebook with our online tools. Should you decide you prefer Cram101.com as your study tool,

we'd like to offer you a trade...

Our Trade In program is a simple way for us to keep our promise and provide you the best studying tools, regardless of where you purchased your Cram101 textbook notebook. As long as your notebook is in *Like New Condition**, you can send it back to us and we will immediately give you a Cram101.com account free for 120 days!

Let The *Trade In* Begin!

THREE SIMPLE STEPS TO TRADE:

1. Go to www.cram101.com/tradein and fill out the packing slip information.
2. Submit and print the packing slip and mail it in with your Cram101 textbook notebook.
3. Activate your account after you receive your email confirmation.

* Books must be returned in *Like New Condition*, meaning there is no damage to the book including, but not limited to: ripped or torn pages, markings or writing on pages, or folded / creased pages. Upon receiving the book, Cram101 will inspect it and reserves the right to terminate your free Cram101.com account and return your textbook notebook at the owners expense.

Learning System

Cram101 Textbook Outlines is a learning system. The notes in this book are the highlights of your textbook, you will never have to highlight a book again.

How to use this book. Take this book to class, it is your notebook for the lecture. The notes and highlights on the left hand side of the pages follow the outline and order of the textbook. All you have to do is follow along while your instructor presents the lecture. Circle the items emphasized in class and add other important information on the right side. With Cram101 Textbook Outlines you'll spend less time writing and more time listening. Learning becomes more efficient.

Cram101.com Online

Increase your studying efficiency by using Cram101.com's practice tests and online reference material. It is the perfect complement to Cram101 Textbook Outlines. Use self-teaching matching tests or simulate in-class testing with comprehensive multiple choice tests, or simply use Cram's true and false tests for quick review. Cram101.com even allows you to enter your in-class notes for an integrated studying format combining the textbook notes with your class notes.

Visit **www.Cram101.com**, click Sign Up at the top of the screen, and enter **DK73DW17096** in the promo code box on the registration screen. Your access to www.Cram101.com is discounted by 50% because you have purchased this book. Sign up and stop highlighting textbooks forever.

Copyright © 2011 by Cram101, Inc. All rights reserved. "Cram101"® and "Never Highlight a Book Again!"® are registered trademarks of Cram101, Inc. ISBN(s): 9781618120052. PUBE-3 .2011516

American Government : Power and Purpose
Theodore Lowi, 11th

CONTENTS

1. Five Principles of Politics 2
2. Constructing a Government: The Founding and the Constitution 23
3. Federalism and the Separation of Powers 49
4. Civil Liberties and Civil Rights 83
5. Congress: The First Branch 133
6. The Presidency as an Institution 166
7. The Executive Branch: Bureaucracy in a Democracy 207
8. The Federal Courts: Structure and Strategies 231
9. Public Opinion 264
10. Elections 293
11. Political Parties 331
12. Groups and Interests 364
13. The Media 390
14. Economic Policy 413
15. Social Policy 450
16. Foreign Policy 479

Chapter 1. Five Principles of Politics

Social security	Social security is primarily a social insurance program providing social protection, or protection against socially recognized conditions, including poverty, old age, disability, unemployment and others. Social security may refer to: • social insurance, where people receive benefits or services in recognition of contributions to an insurance scheme. These services typically include provision for retirement pensions, disability insurance, survivor benefits and unemployment insurance. • income maintenance--mainly the distribution of cash in the event of interruption of employment, including retirement, disability and unemployment • services provided by administrations responsible for social security.
Attack	In computer and computer networks an attack is any attempt to destroy, expose, alter, disable, steal or gain unauthorized access to or make unauthorized use of an asset. Definitions IETF Internet Engineering Task Force defines attack in RFC 2828 as: US Government CNSS Instruction No. 4009 dated 26 April 2010 by Committee on National Security Systems of United States of America defines an attack as: The increasing dependencies of modern society on information and computers networks (both in private and public sectors, including military) has led to new terms like cyber attack and Cyberwarfare. CNSS Instruction No. 4009 define a cyber attack as: Phenomenology

Chapter 1. Five Principles of Politics

An attack can be active or passive.

An attack can be perpetrated by an insider or from outside the organization;

> An "inside attack" is an attack initiated by an entity inside the security perimeter (an "insider"), i.e., an entity that is authorized to access system resources but uses them in a way not approved by those who granted the authorization.
> An "outside attack" is initiated from outside the perimeter, by an unauthorized or illegitimate user of the system (an "outsider").

Government	In the social sciences, the term government refers to the particular group of people, the administrative bureaucracy, who control a state at a given time, and the manner in which their governing organizations are structured. That is, governments are the means through which state power is employed. States are served by a continuous succession of different governments.
Adjustment	In law, the term adjustment may appear in varied contexts, as a synonym for terms with unrelated definitions: General Definition

Chapter 1. Five Principles of Politics

Adjust:

1. To settle or to bring to a satisfactory state, so that the parties are agreed in the result; as, to adjust accounts.
2. When applied to a liquidated demand, the verb "adjust" has the same meaning as the word "settle" in the same connection, and means to pay the demand. When applied to an unliquidated demand, it means to ascertain the amount due or to settle. In the latter connection, to settle means to effect a mutual adjustment between the parties and to agree upon the balance.

Common Uses

General Debt

- Debtor and creditor adjustment: As the term appears in an assignment for the benefit of creditors, "Creditor" means one who has a definite demand against the assignor, or a cause of action capable of adjustment and liquidation at trial. 6 Am J2d Assign for Crs § 109.
- Adjustable Rate Loan: Loan arrangement which permits the lender to change the interest rate based on a specific factor such as the prime lending rate charged by banks.
- Adjusting agency: In one sense, a collection agency; in another sense, an agency representing a debtor in making an arrangement with his creditors for the settlement of his obligations by modification of the indebtedness.

Allegiance

An allegiance is a duty of fidelity said to be owed by a subject or a citizen to his/her state or sovereign.

Etymology

From Middle English ligeaunce . The al- prefix was probably added through confusion with another legal term, allegeance, an "allegation" .

Chapter 1. Five Principles of Politics

Bush v. Gore	Bush v. Gore, 531 U.S. 98 (2000), is the landmark United States Supreme Court decision that effectively resolved the 2000 presidential election in favor of George W. Bush. Only eight days earlier, the United States Supreme Court had unanimously decided the closely related case of Bush v. Palm Beach County Canvassing Board, 531 U.S. 70 (2000), and only three days earlier, had preliminarily halted the recount that was occurring in Florida. In a per curiam decision, the Court ruled that the Florida Supreme Court's method for recounting ballots was a violation of the Equal Protection Clause of the Fourteenth Amendment.
Congress	A congress is a formal meeting of the representatives of different nations, constituent states, independent organizations (such as trade unions), or groups. The term was chosen for the United States Congress to emphasize the status of each state represented there as a self-governing unit. Subsequent to the use of congress by the U.S. legislature, the term has been incorrectly adopted by many states within unions, and by unitary nation-states in the Americas, to refer to their legislatures.
Court	A court is a form of tribunal, often a governmental institution, with the authority to adjudicate legal disputes between parties and carry out the administration of justice in civil, criminal, and administrative matters in accordance with the rule of law. In both common law and civil law legal systems, courts are the central means for dispute resolution, and it is generally understood that all persons have an ability to bring their claims before a court. Similarly, the rights of those accused of a crime include the right to present a defense before a court.
Election	An election is a formal decision-making process by which a population chooses an individual to hold public office. Elections have been the usual mechanism by which modern representative democracy operates since the 17th century. Elections may fill offices in the legislature, sometimes in the executive and judiciary, and for regional and local government.
Election Day	Election Day refers to the day when general elections are held. In many countries, general elections are always held on a Sunday, to enable as many voters as possible to participate, while in other countries elections are always held on a weekday. However, some countries, or regions within a country, always make a weekday election day a public holiday, thus satisfying both demands.

Chapter 1. Five Principles of Politics

Health association	A health association is a professional organization for health professionals. They are often based on specialty and are usually national, often with subnational or regional affiliates. Health associations usually offer conferences and continuing education. They often serve in capacities similar to trade unions, and often take public policy stances on medical issues.
Pledge	A pledge is a bailment or deposit of personal property to a creditor to secure repayment for some debt or engagement, The term is also used to denote the property which constitutes the security.
	Pledge is the ravi of Roman law, from which most of the modern law on the subject is derived. It differs from hypothecation and from the more usual mortgage in that the pledge is in the possession of the pledgee; it also differs from mortgage in being confined to personal property (rather than real property).
Veteran	A veteran is a person who has had long service or experience in a particular occupation or field; " A veteran of ..." . This page refers to military veterans, i.e., a person who has served or is serving in the armed forces, and has direct exposure to acts of military conflict, commonly known as war veterans (although not all military conflicts, or areas in which armed combat takes place, are necessarily referred to as "wars").
	Public attitude towards veterans
	Military veterans often receive special treatment in their respective countries due to the sacrifices they made during wars.
Break	In locksmithing, a break in the pins is a separation in one or more sections of the pin used to encode the lock for a specific key or set of keys in a master keying system.
Opposition	In politics, the opposition comprises one or more political parties or other organized groups that are opposed to the government, party or group in political control of a city, region, state or country. The degree of opposition varies according to political conditions - for example, across authoritarian and liberal systems where opposition may be repressed or welcomed.

Chapter 1. Five Principles of Politics

Outsourcing	Outsourcing or sub-servicing often refers to the process of contracting to a third-party. Overview A precise definition of outsourcing has yet to be agreed upon. Thus, the term is used inconsistently.
Constitutional convention	A constitutional convention is an informal and uncodified procedural agreement that is followed by the institutions of a state. In some states, notably those Commonwealth of Nations states which follow the Westminster system and whose political systems are derived from British constitutional law, most of the functions of government are guided by constitutional convention rather than by a formal written constitution. In these states, the actual distribution of power may be markedly different from those which are described in the formal constitutional documents.
National Convention	During the French Revolution, the National Convention, in France, comprised the constitutional and legislative assembly which sat from 20 September 1792 to 26 October 1795 . It held executive power in France during the first years of the French First Republic. It was succeeded by the Directory, commencing 2 November 1795. Prominent members of the original Convention included Maximilien Robespierre of the Jacobin Club, Jean-Paul Marat (affiliated with the Jacobins, though never a formal member), and Georges Danton of the Cordeliers.
Disabilities	Disabilities were legal restrictions and limitations placed on Jews in the Middle Ages. They included provisions requiring Jews to wear specific and identifying clothing such as the Jewish hat and the yellow badge, restricting Jews to certain cities and towns or in certain parts of towns (ghettos), and forbidding Jews to enter certain trades. Disabilities also included special taxes levied on Jews, exclusion from public life, and restraints on the performance of religious ceremonies.
Europe	Created by Romain Rolland and his associates, the magazine Europe began on 15 February 1923, and is still published by Éditions Rieder.

Chapter 1. Five Principles of Politics

René Arcos, one of the founders (along with Jean Guéhenno and Jean Cassou), explained the choice of title: "We speak of Europe because our vast peninsula, between the East and the New World, is the crossroads where civilisations meet. But it is to all the peoples that we address ourselves [...] in the hope of averting the tragic misunderstandings which currently divide mankind."

Up until 1939, when it was suspended on the announcement of the Molotov-Ribbentrop Pact, it followed the Communists in the anti-Fascist struggle.

Germany	Germany officially the Federal Republic of Germany, is a country in Western Europe. It is bordered to the north by the North Sea, Denmark, and the Baltic Sea; to the east by Poland and the Czech Republic; to the south by Austria and Switzerland; and to the west by France, Luxembourg, Belgium, and the Netherlands. The territory of Germany covers an area of 357,021 km^2 and is influenced by a temperate seasonal climate.
Insurance	In law and economics, insurance is a form of risk management primarily used to hedge against the risk of a contingent, uncertain loss. Insurance is defined as the equitable transfer of the risk of a loss, from one entity to another, in exchange for payment. An insurer is a company selling the insurance; an insured, or policyholder, is the person or entity buying the insurance policy.
Japan	Japan is an island nation in East Asia. Located in the Pacific Ocean, it lies to the east of the Sea of Japan, China, North Korea, South Korea and Russia, stretching from the Sea of Okhotsk in the north to the East China Sea and Taiwan in the south. The characters that make up Japan's name mean "sun-origin", which is why Japan is sometimes referred to as the "Land of the Rising Sun".
Khmer Rouge	The Khmer Rouge was the name given to the followers of the Communist Party of Kampuchea, who were the ruling party in Cambodia from 1975 to 1979, led by Pol Pot, Nuon Chea, Ieng Sary, Son Sen and Khieu Samphan. The regime led by the Khmer Rouge from 1975 to 1979 was known as the Democratic Kampuchea.
	This organization is remembered primarily for its policy of social engineering, which resulted in genocide.

Chapter 1. Five Principles of Politics

North Korea	North Korea officially the Democratic People's Republic of Korea (DPRK; Chosongul: ??????????), is a country in East Asia, occupying the northern half of the Korean Peninsula. Its capital and largest city is Pyongyang. The Korean Demilitarized Zone serves as the buffer zone between North Korea and South Korea.
Rights	Rights are legal, social, or ethical principles of freedom or entitlement; that is, rights are the fundamental normative rules about what is allowed of people or owed to people, according to some legal system, social convention, or ethical theory. Rights are of essential importance in such disciplines as law and ethics, especially theories of justice and deontology. Rights are often considered fundamental to civilization, being regarded as established pillars of society and culture, and the history of social conflicts can be found in the history of each right and its development.
Soviet	Soviet was a name used for several Russian political organizations. Examples include the Czar's Council of Ministers, which was called the "Soviet of Ministers"; a workers' local council in late Imperial Russia; and the Supreme Soviet of the Soviet Union. Etymology "Soviet" is derived from a Russian word signifying council, advice, harmony, concord.[trans 1] The word "sovietnik" means councillor.
Soviet Union	The Union of Soviet Socialist Republics, informally known as the Soviet Union, was a constitutionally socialist state that existed on the territory of most of the former Russian Empire in Eurasia between 1922 and 1991. The Soviet Union had a single-party political system dominated by the Communist Party until 1990. Although the USSR was nominally a union of Soviet republics (of which there were 15 after 1956) with the capital in Moscow, it was in actuality a highly centralized state with a planned economy.

Chapter 1. Five Principles of Politics

	The Soviet Union was founded in December 1922 when the Russian SFSR, which formed during the Russian Revolution of 1917 and emerged victorious in the ensuing Russian Civil War, unified with the Transcaucasian, Ukrainian and Belorussian SSRs.
Autocracy	An autocracy is a form of government in which one person possesses unlimited power. An autocrat is a person (such as a monarch) ruling with unlimited authority. The term autocrat is derived from the word autokrator (α?τοκρ?τωρ, lit.
Democracy	Democracy is a political form of government in which governing power is derived from the people, by consensus (consensus democracy), by direct referendum (direct democracy), or by means of elected representatives of the people (representative democracy). The term comes from the Greek: δημοκρατ?α - (demokratía) "rule of the people", which was coined from δ?μος (dêmos) "people" and κρ?τος (Kratos) "power", in the middle of the 5th-4th century BC to denote the political systems then existing in some Greek city-states, notably Athens following a popular uprising in 508 BC. Even though there is no specific, universally accepted definition of 'democracy', equality and freedom have been identified as important characteristics of democracy since ancient times. These principles are reflected in all citizens being equal before the law and having equal access to power.
Trade union	A trade union is an organization of workers that have banded together to achieve common goals such as better working conditions. The trade union, through its leadership, bargains with the employer on behalf of union members (rank and file members) and negotiates labour contracts (collective bargaining) with employers. This may include the negotiation of wages, work rules, complaint procedures, rules governing hiring, firing and promotion of workers, benefits, workplace safety and policies.
Oligarchy	The oligarchy is a form of power structure in which power effectively rests with a small number of people. These people could be distinguished by royalty, wealth, family ties, corporate, or military control. The word oligarchy is from the Greek words "?λ?γος" (olígos), "a few" and the verb "?ρχω" (archo), "to rule, to govern, to command".
Rationality	The term "rationality" is used differently in different disciplines.

Chapter 1. Five Principles of Politics

In philosophy, rationality is originally the exercise of reason, the way humans come to conclusions when considering things most deliberately. However, the term "rationality" tends to be used in the specialized discussions of economics, sociology, psychology and political science.

Redistricting

Redistricting, a form of redistribution, is the process of drawing United States district lines. This often means changing electoral district and constituency boundaries in response to periodic census results. In 36 states, the state legislature has primary responsibility for creating a redistricting plan, in many cases subject to approval by the state governor.

Stamp Act

A stamp act is a law enacted by government that requires a tax to be paid on the transfer of certain documents. The stamp act was considered unfair by many people. Those that pay the tax receive an official stamp on their documents.

Institution

An institution is any structure or mechanism of social order and cooperation governing the behavior of a set of individuals within a given human community. Institutions are identified with a social purpose and permanence, transcending individual human lives and intentions, and with the making and enforcing of rules governing cooperative human behavior.

The term "institution" is commonly applied to customs and behavior patterns important to a society, as well as to particular formal organizations of government and public service.

ARTHUR

ARTHUR is an abbreviation for mobile "Artillery Hunting Radar" system developed in Sweden. This field artillery acquisition radar was developed for the primary role as the core element of a brigade or division level counter battery sensor system. It can also be used for peace support operations.

Voting

Voting is a method for a group such as a meeting or an electorate to make a decision or express an opinion--often following discussions, debates, or election campaigns. It is often found in democracies and republics.

Reasons for voting

Chapter 1. Five Principles of Politics

	In a representative government, voting commonly implies election: a way for an electorate to select among candidates for office.
Agenda	An agenda is a list of meeting activities in the order in which they are to be taken up, beginning with the call to order and ending with adjournment. It usually includes one or more specific items of business to be considered. It may, but is not required to, include specific times for one OR more activities.
Bill	A bill is a proposed law under consideration by a legislature. A bill does not become law until it is passed by the legislature and, in most cases, approved by the executive. Once a bill has been enacted into law, it is called an act or a statute.
Delegation	Delegation is the assignment of authority and responsibility to another person (normally from a manager to a subordinate) to carry out specific activities. However the person who delegated the work remains accountable for the outcome of the delegated work. Delegation empowers a subordinate to make decisions, i.e. it is a shift of decision-making authority from one organizational level to a lower one.
Gatekeeping	Gatekeeping is the process through which information is filtered for dissemination, be it publication, broadcasting, the Internet, or some other type of communication. As an academic theory, it is found in several fields, including communication studies, journalism, political science, and sociology. Originally focused on the mass media with its few-to-masses dynamic, theories of gatekeeping also now include the workings of face-to-face communication and the many-to-many dynamic now easily available via the Internet.
Power	Power is a measure of an entity's ability to control its environment, including the behavior of other entities. The term authority is often used for power, perceived as legitimate by the social structure. Power can be seen as evil or unjust, but the exercise of power is accepted as endemic to humans as social beings.
Coalition	The Coalition in Australian politics refers to a group of centre-right parties that has existed in the form of a coalition agreement (on and off) since 1922. The Coalition partners are the Liberal Party of Australia (or its predecessors before 1945) and the National Party of Australia (known as the Australian Country Party from 1921-1975 and the National Country Party of Australia from 1975-1982). The Country Liberal Party in the Northern Territory and the Liberal National Party in Queensland are their equivalents in those states, while the National Party of Western Australia and The Nationals South Australia are not in any form of coalition and are separate parties. There is no National Party in the ACT or Tasmania.

Chapter 1. Five Principles of Politics

Speaker	The term speaker is a title often given to the presiding officer (chair) of a deliberative assembly, especially a legislative body. The speaker's official role is to moderate debate, make rulings on procedure, announce the results of votes, and the like. The speaker decides who may speak and has the powers to discipline members who break the procedures of the house.
Decentralization	Decentralization is the process of dispersing decision-making governance closer to the people and/or citizens. It includes the dispersal of administration or governance in sectors or areas like engineering, management science, political science, political economy, sociology and economics. Decentralization is also possible in the dispersal of population and employment.
News conference	A news conference is a media event in which newsmakers invite journalists to hear them speak and, most often, ask questions. A joint press conference instead is held between two or more talking sides. Practice In a news conference, one or more speakers may make a statement, which may be followed by questions from reporters.
George Washington	George Washington is a public artwork that is a copy of an original bust created by French artist and neoclassical sculptor Jean Antoine Houdon, displayed inside of the Indiana Statehouse, which is located in Indianapolis, Indiana, USA. The bust is made of white plaster and its dimensions are 25x18x18 inches. Description This piece is a bust of the first President of the United States, George Washington. It is made of white plaster, and its dimensions are 25x18x18 inches.

Chapter 1. Five Principles of Politics

Medicare	Medicare is a social insurance program administered by the United States government, providing health insurance coverage to people who are aged 65 and over, or who meet other special criteria. Medicare operates similar to a single-payer health care system, but the key difference is that its coverage only extends to 80% of any given medical cost; the remaining 20% of cost must be paid by other means, such as privately-held supplemental insurance, or paid by the patient. The program also funds residency training programs for the vast majority of physicians in the United States.
Tammany Hall	Tammany Hall, also known as the Society of St. Tammany, the Sons of St. Tammany, or the Columbian Order, was founded in 1786 and incorporated on May 12, 1789 as the Tammany Society. It was the Democratic Party political machine that played a major role in controlling New York City politics and helping immigrants, most notably the Irish, rise up in American politics from the 1790s to the 1960s. It controlled Democratic Party nominations and patronage in Manhattan from the mayoral victory of Fernando Wood in 1854 through the election of John P. O'Brien in 1932. Tammany Hall was permanently weakened by the election of Fiorello La Guardia on a "fusion" ticket of Republicans, reform-minded Democrats, and independents in 1934, and, despite a brief resurgence in the 1950s, it ceased to exist in the 1960s.
Collective action	Collective action is the pursuit of a goal or set of goals by more than one person. It is a term which has formulations and theories in many areas of the social sciences. In sociology As an explanation of social movements, an inquiry into collective action involves examining those factors that cause the setting of standards of social integration, as well as those factors which lead to standards of deviance and conflict.
Interest	Interest is a fee paid on borrowed assets. It is the price paid for the use of borrowed money, or, money earned by deposited funds. Assets that are sometimes lent with interest include money, shares, consumer goods through hire purchase, major assets such as aircraft, and even entire factories in finance lease arrangements.

Chapter 1. Five Principles of Politics

Treaty	A treaty is an express agreement under international law entered into by actors in international law, namely sovereign states and international organizations. A treaty may also be known as: (international) agreement, protocol, covenant, convention, exchange of letters, etc. Regardless of the terminology, all of these international agreements under international law are equally treaties and the rules are the same.
Abortion	Abortion is the termination of a pregnancy by the removal or expulsion of a fetus or embryo from the uterus, resulting in or caused by its death. An abortion can occur spontaneously due to complications during pregnancy or can be induced, in humans and other species. In the context of human pregnancies, an abortion induced to preserve the health of the gravida (pregnant female) is termed a therapeutic abortion, while an abortion induced for any other reason is termed an elective abortion.
Free riding	Free riding is a term used in the stock-trading world to describe the practice of buying shares or other securities without actually having the capital to cover the trade. This is possible when recently bought or sold shares are unsettled, and therefore have not been paid for. Since stock transactions usually settle after three business days, a crafty trader can buy a stock and sell it the following day (or the same day), without ever having sufficient funds in the account.
Issue	In law, issue can mean several things: - In wills and trusts, a person's issue are his or her lineal descendants or offspring. These are distinguished from heirs, which can include other kin such as a brother, sister, mother, father, grandfather, uncle, aunt, nephew, niece, or cousin. - In corporations and business associations law, issue can refer to areas involving stocks. - In evidence as well as civil and criminal procedure, there are issues of fact. Issues of fact are rhetorically presented by statements of fact which are each put to a test: Is the statement true or false?

Chapter 1. Five Principles of Politics

	Often, different parties have conflicting statements of fact.
Publics	Publics are small groups of people who follow one or more particular issue very closely. They are well informed about the issue(s) and also have a very strong opinion on it/them. They tend to know more about politics than the average person, and, therefore, exert more influence, because these people care so deeply about their cause(s) that they donate much time and money.
Public good	In economics, a public good is a good that is nonrival and non-excludable. Non-rivalry means that consumption of the good by one individual does not reduce availability of the good for consumption by others; and non-excludability that no one can be effectively excluded from using the good. In the real world, there may be no such thing as an absolutely non-rivaled and non-excludable good; but economists think that some goods approximate the concept closely enough for the analysis to be economically useful.
Commission	A commission is a physical document issued to certify the appointment of a commissioned officer by a sovereign power. The more specific terms commissioning parchment or commissioning scroll are often used to avoid ambiguity, due to "commission" being a homonym which directs the individual in carrying out their duty regardless of what authority or responsibility they may have at any time. However the document is not usually in the form of a scroll and is more often printed on paper instead of parchment.
The commons	The commons is terminology referring to resources that are collectively owned or shared between or among populations. These resources are said to be "held in common" and can include everything from natural resources and land to software. In some areas the process by which the commons are transformed into private property is termed enclosure.

Chapter 1. Five Principles of Politics

Poland	Poland officially the Republic of Poland - is a country in Central Europe bordered by Germany to the west; the Czech Republic and Slovakia to the south; Ukraine, Belarus and Lithuania to the east; and the Baltic Sea and Kaliningrad Oblast, a Russian exclave, to the north. The total area of Poland is 312,679 square kilometres (120,726 sq mi), making it the 69th largest country in the world and the 9th largest in Europe. Poland has a population of over 38 million people, which makes it the 34th most populous country in the world and the sixth most populous member of the European Union, being its most populous post-communist member.
Policy	A policy is typically described as a principle or rule to guide decisions and achieve rational outcome(s). The term is not normally used to denote what is actually done, this is normally referred to as either procedure or protocol. Whereas a policy will contain the 'what' and the 'why', procedures or protocols contain the 'what', the 'how', the 'where', and the 'when'.
Legislation	Legislation is law which has been promulgated (or "enacted") by a legislature or other governing body, or the process of making it. (Another source of law is judge-made law or case law). Before an item of legislation becomes law it may be known as a bill, and may be broadly referred to as "legislation" while it remains under consideration to distinguish it from other business.
New Deal	The New Deal is a programme of active labour market policies introduced in the United Kingdom by the Labour government in 1998, initially funded by a one off £5bn windfall tax on privatised utility companies. The stated purpose is to reduce unemployment by providing training, subsidised employment and voluntary work to the unemployed. Spending on the New Deal was £1.3 billion in 2001.
Caucus	A caucus is a meeting of supporters or members of a political party or movement, especially in the United States. As the use of the term has been expanded the exact definition has come to vary among political cultures. Origin of the term The origin of the word caucus is debated, but it is generally agreed that it first came into use in the English colonies of North America. A February 1763 entry in the diary of John Adams of Braintree, Massachusetts, is one of the earliest appearances of Caucas, already with its modern connotations of a "smoke-filled room" where candidates for public election are pre-selected in private

Chapter 1. Five Principles of Politics

	This day learned that the Caucas Clubb meets at certain Times in the Garret of Tom Daws, the Adjutant of the Boston Regiment.
Adolf Hitler	Adolf Hitler was an Austrian-born German politician and the leader of the National Socialist German Workers Party, commonly known as the Nazi Party. He was Chancellor of Germany from 1933 to 1945, and served as head of state as Führer und Reichskanzler from 1934 to 1945. A decorated veteran of World War I, Hitler joined the precursor of the Nazi Party (DAP) in 1919, and became leader of NSDAP in 1921. He attempted a failed coup d'etat known as the Beer Hall Putsch, which occurred at the Bürgerbräukeller beer hall in Munich on November 8-9, 1923. Hitler was imprisoned for one year due to the failed coup, and wrote his memoir, "My Struggle", while imprisoned.
Franklin D. Roosevelt	Franklin D. Roosevelt (January 30, 1882 - April 12, 1945) was the 32nd President of the United States (1933-1945) and a central figure in world events during the mid-20th century, leading the United States during a time of worldwide economic crisis and world war. The only American president elected to more than two terms, he forged a durable coalition that realigned American politics for decades. Franklin D. Roosevelt defeated incumbent Republican Herbert Hoover in November 1932, at the depths of the Great Depression.
Vietnam	Vietnam, officially the Socialist Republic of Vietnam is the easternmost country on the Indochina Peninsula in Southeast Asia. It is bordered by People's Republic of China (PRC) to the north, Laos to the northwest, Cambodia to the southwest, and the South China Sea, referred to as East Sea (Vietnamese: Bi?n Đông), to the east. With a population of over 86 million, Vietnam is the 13th most populous country in the world.
Identity	Identity is an umbrella term used throughout the social sciences to describe a person's conception and expression of their individuality or group affiliations (such as national identity and cultural identity). The term is used more specifically in psychology and sociology, including the two forms of social psychology. The term is also used with respect to place identity.

Chapter 1. Five Principles of Politics

Debate	Debate is a formal method of interactive and representational argument. Debate is a broader form of argument than logical argument, which only examines consistency from axiom, and factual argument, which only examines what is or isn't the case or rhetoric which is a technique of persuasion. Though logical consistency, factual accuracy and some degree of emotional appeal to the audience are important elements of the art of persuasion, in debating, one side often prevails over the other side by presenting a superior "context" and/or framework of the issue, which is far more subtle and strategic.
Executive	Executive branch of government is the part of government that has sole authority and responsibility for the daily administration of the state bureaucracy. The division of power into separate branches of government is central to the democratic idea of the separation of powers. In many countries, the term "government" connotes only the executive branch.
Executive order	An executive order in the United States is an order issued by the President, the head of the executive branch of the federal government.

Chapter 1. Five Principles of Politics

Chapter 1. Five Principles of Politics

Chapter 2. Constructing a Government: The Founding and the Constitution

American Revolution	The American Revolution was the political upheaval during the last half of the 18th century in which thirteen colonies in North America joined together to break free from the British Empire, combining to become the United States of America. They first rejected the authority of the Parliament of Great Britain to govern them from overseas without representation, and then expelled all royal officials. By 1774 each colony had established a Provincial Congress, or an equivalent governmental institution, to form individual self-governing states. The British responded by sending combat troops to re-impose direct rule.
Stamp Act	A stamp act is a law enacted by government that requires a tax to be paid on the transfer of certain documents. The stamp act was considered unfair by many people. Those that pay the tax receive an official stamp on their documents.
Congress	A congress is a formal meeting of the representatives of different nations, constituent states, independent organizations (such as trade unions), or groups. The term was chosen for the United States Congress to emphasize the status of each state represented there as a self-governing unit. Subsequent to the use of congress by the U.S. legislature, the term has been incorrectly adopted by many states within unions, and by unitary nation-states in the Americas, to refer to their legislatures.
Adjustment	In law, the term adjustment may appear in varied contexts, as a synonym for terms with unrelated definitions: General Definition

Chapter 2. Constructing a Government: The Founding and the Constitution

Adjust:

1. To settle or to bring to a satisfactory state, so that the parties are agreed in the result; as, to adjust accounts.
2. When applied to a liquidated demand, the verb "adjust" has the same meaning as the word "settle" in the same connection, and means to pay the demand. When applied to an unliquidated demand, it means to ascertain the amount due or to settle. In the latter connection, to settle means to effect a mutual adjustment between the parties and to agree upon the balance.

Common Uses

General Debt

- Debtor and creditor adjustment: As the term appears in an assignment for the benefit of creditors, "Creditor" means one who has a definite demand against the assignor, or a cause of action capable of adjustment and liquidation at trial. 6 Am J2d Assign for Crs § 109.
- Adjustable Rate Loan: Loan arrangement which permits the lender to change the interest rate based on a specific factor such as the prime lending rate charged by banks.
- Adjusting agency: In one sense, a collection agency; in another sense, an agency representing a debtor in making an arrangement with his creditors for the settlement of his obligations by modification of the indebtedness.

Americas

The Americas, are the lands of the western hemisphere, composed of numerous entities and regions variably defined by geography, politics, and culture.

The Americas are frequently recognised to comprise two separate continents (North America and South America), particularly in English-speaking nations. The Americas may also be recognised to comprise a single continent, in Latin America and in some European nations.

Chapter 2. Constructing a Government: The Founding and the Constitution

Court	A court is a form of tribunal, often a governmental institution, with the authority to adjudicate legal disputes between parties and carry out the administration of justice in civil, criminal, and administrative matters in accordance with the rule of law. In both common law and civil law legal systems, courts are the central means for dispute resolution, and it is generally understood that all persons have an ability to bring their claims before a court. Similarly, the rights of those accused of a crime include the right to present a defense before a court.
Federalist	The term federalist describes several political beliefs around the world. Also, it may refer to the concept of federalism or the type of government called a federation. In early United States history, the Federalist Party was one of the first political parties; its members or supporters called themselves Federalists.
James Madison	James Madison, Jr. (March 16, 1751 - June 28, 1836) was an American politician and political philosopher who served as the fourth President of the United States (1809-1817) and is considered one of the Founding Fathers of the United States. He was the principal author of the United States Constitution, and is often called the "Father of the Constitution".
New England	New England was a colony allegedly founded in the mid-to-late 11th century by English refugees fleeing William the Conqueror. Its existence is only attested in two sources, dating from the 13th and 14th centuries. Namely, the French Chronicon Universale Anonymi Laudunensis and the Icelandic Játvarðar Saga.
Territory	In international politics, a territory is a non-sovereign geographic area which has come under the authority of another government; which has not been granted the powers of self-government normally devolved to secondary territorial divisions; or both.

Chapter 2. Constructing a Government: The Founding and the Constitution

Types of administrative and/or political territories include:

- Many types of legally administered territories, each of which is a non-sovereign geographic area that has come under the authority of another government with varying degrees of local governmental control.

- This can include federated states which share authority with a central government such as the Länder of Germany or the Counties of a state within one of the States of the United States (those states being another example themselves that were sovereign and ceded rights to a central federated government),

- or alternatively, an administrative district established by a central nation-state as with the Bundesländer of Austria (which are now a federation),

- or the subnational entities constituting a unitary state such as France.

For example, American Samoa, Guam and Puerto Rico are all territories of the government of the United States with varying local autonomy. Similarly, with regard to the Canadian provinces and territories, the major difference between a Canadian province and a Canadian territory is that the federal government has more direct control over the territories, while the provinces are run by provincial governments empowered by the constitution.

Royalist	A royalist supports a particular monarch as head of state for a particular kingdom, or of a particular dynastic claim. In the abstract, this position is royalism. It is distinct from monarchism, which advocates a monarchical system of government, but not necessarily a particular monarch.
Sudan	Sudan officially the Republic of Sudan, Arabic: ??????? ???????? Jumhuriyat al Sudan, is a country in northeastern Africa. It is the largest country in Africa and the Arab world, and tenth largest in the world by area. It is bordered by Egypt to the north, the Red Sea to the northeast, Eritrea and Ethiopia to the east, Kenya and Uganda to the southeast, the Democratic Republic of the Congo and the Central African Republic to the southwest, Chad to the west and Libya to the northwest. The world's longest river, the Nile, divides the country between east and west sides.

Chapter 2. Constructing a Government: The Founding and the Constitution

Suffrage	Suffrage, political franchise, or simply the franchise is the civil right to vote, or the exercise of that right. In English, suffrage and its synonyms are sometimes also used to mean the right to run for office (to be a candidate), but there are no established qualifying terms to distinguish between these different meanings of the term(s). The right to run for office is sometimes called (candidate) eligibility, and the combination of both rights is sometimes called full suffrage.
John G. Adams	John G. Adams was the US Army's counsel in the Army-McCarthy Hearings. He was an Army veteran of World War II, and he worked in Washington, DC for the Defense Department before he became the US Army general counsel in 1953. From 1953 to 1955 he was the chief legal adviser to Army Secretary Robert Ten Broeck Stevens. Publications - Adams, John G. (1983).
Boston Tea Party	The Boston Tea Party is a U.S. political party named after the Boston Tea Party of 1773. Its ideology is libertarian. A group of former Libertarian Party (LP) members founded the party in 2006. They criticized the LP for its "abdication of political responsibilities", saying that "Americans deserve and desperately need a pro-freedom party that forcefully advocates libertarian solutions to the issues of today".
East India Company	The East India Company was an early English joint-stock company that was formed initially for pursuing trade with the East Indies, but that ended up trading mainly with the Indian subcontinent and China. The oldest among several similarly formed European East India Companies, the Company was granted an English Royal Charter, under the name Governor and Company of Merchants of London Trading into the East Indies, by Elizabeth I on 31 December 1600. After a rival English company challenged its monopoly in the late 17th century, the two companies were merged in 1708 to form the United Company of Merchants of England Trading to the East Indies, commonly styled the Honourable East India Company, and abbreviated, HEIC; the Company was colloquially referred to as John Company, and in India as Company Bahadur (Hindustani bahadur, "brave"/"authority").

Chapter 2. Constructing a Government: The Founding and the Constitution

	The East India Company traded mainly in cotton, silk, indigo dye, saltpetre, tea, and opium.
Articles of Confederation	The Articles of Confederation was the first constitution of the United States and specified how the Federal government was to operate, including adoption of an official name for the new nation, United States of America. The Second Continental Congress appointed a committee to draft the Articles in June 1776 and sent the draft to the states for ratification in November 1777. In practice, the Articles were in use beginning in 1777. The ratification process was completed in March 1781. Under the Articles, the states retained sovereignty over all governmental functions not specifically relinquished to the national government.
	On June 12, 1776, a day after appointing a committee to prepare a draft of the Declaration of Independence, the Second Continental Congress resolved to appoint a committee of thirteen to prepare a draft of a constitution for a confederate type of union. The last draft of the Articles was written in the summer of 1777 and the Second Continental Congress approved them for ratification by the States on November 15, 1777, after a year of debate.
Balkan Federation	The Balkan Federation was a project about the creation of a Balkan federation, based mainly on left political ideas.
	The concept of a Balkan federation emerged at the late 19th century from among left political forces in the region. The central aim was to establish a new political unity: a common federal republic unifying the Balkan Peninsula on the basis of internationalism, social solidarity, and economic equality.
Continental Congress	The Continental Congress was a convention of delegates called together from the Thirteen Colonies that became the governing body of the United States during the American Revolution. The Congress met from 1774 to 1789 in three incarnations. The first call for a convention was made over issues of mounting taxation without representation in Parliament and because of the British blockade.

Chapter 2. Constructing a Government: The Founding and the Constitution

Declaration	In law, a declaration is a binding adjudication of the rights or other legal relations of the parties which does not provide for or order enforcement. Where the declaration is made by a court, it is usually referred to as a declaratory judgment. Less commonly, where declaratory relief is awarded by an arbitrator, it is normally called a declaratory award.
First Continental Congress	The First Continental Congress was a convention of delegates from twelve of the thirteen North American colonies that met on September 5, 1774, at Carpenters' Hall in Philadelphia, Pennsylvania, early in the American Revolution. It was called in response to the passage of the Coercive Acts (also known as Intolerable Acts by the Colonial Americans) by the British Parliament. The Intolerable Acts had punished Boston for the Boston Tea Party.
Independence	Independence is a condition of a nation, country, or state in which its residents and population, or some portion thereof, exercise self-government, and usually sovereignty, over its territory.
	Attainment of independence should not be confused with revolution, which typically refers to the violent overthrow of a ruling authority. While some revolutions seek and achieve national independence, others aim only to redistribute power -- with or without an element of emancipation, such as in democratization -- within a state, which as such may remain unaltered.
Second Continental Congress	The Second Continental Congress was a convention of delegates from the Thirteen Colonies that met beginning on May 10, 1775, in Philadelphia, Pennsylvania, soon after warfare in the American Revolutionary War had begun. It succeeded the First Continental Congress, which met briefly during 1774, also in Philadelphia. The second Congress managed the colonial war effort, and moved incrementally towards independence, adopting the United States Declaration of Independence on July 4th, 1776. By raising armies, directing strategy, appointing diplomats, and making formal treaties, the Congress acted as the de facto national government of what became the United States.
Decision	A decision, defined in Article 288 of the Treaty on the Functioning of the European Union (formerly Article 249 TEC), is one of the three binding instruments provided by secondary EU legislation. A decision is binding on the person or entity to which it is addressed. Decisions may be addressed to member states or individuals.

Chapter 2. Constructing a Government: The Founding and the Constitution

Canada	Canada was the name of the French colony that once stretched along the St. Lawrence River; the other colonies of New France were Acadia, Louisiana and Newfoundland. Canada, the most developed colony of New France, was divided into three districts, each with its own government: Québec, Trois-Rivières, and Montréal. The governor of the district of Québec was also the governor-general of all of New France.
Constitutional convention	A constitutional convention is an informal and uncodified procedural agreement that is followed by the institutions of a state. In some states, notably those Commonwealth of Nations states which follow the Westminster system and whose political systems are derived from British constitutional law, most of the functions of government are guided by constitutional convention rather than by a formal written constitution. In these states, the actual distribution of power may be markedly different from those which are described in the formal constitutional documents.
National Convention	During the French Revolution, the National Convention, in France, comprised the constitutional and legislative assembly which sat from 20 September 1792 to 26 October 1795 . It held executive power in France during the first years of the French First Republic. It was succeeded by the Directory, commencing 2 November 1795. Prominent members of the original Convention included Maximilien Robespierre of the Jacobin Club, Jean-Paul Marat (affiliated with the Jacobins, though never a formal member), and Georges Danton of the Cordeliers.
Hamilton	Hamilton is a former New Zealand Parliamentary electorate, which was replaced by Hamilton East and Hamilton West electorates. Population centres The electorate was mainly urban, covering the city of Hamilton. History The Hamilton electorate dates from 1922. In 1969 it was renamed Hamilton West.
Alexander Hamilton	Alexander Hamilton was a Scottish sea captain, privateer and merchant.

Chapter 2. Constructing a Government: The Founding and the Constitution

George Washington	George Washington is a public artwork that is a copy of an original bust created by French artist and neoclassical sculptor Jean Antoine Houdon, displayed inside of the Indiana Statehouse, which is located in Indianapolis, Indiana, USA. The bust is made of white plaster and its dimensions are 25x18x18 inches. Description This piece is a bust of the first President of the United States, George Washington. It is made of white plaster, and its dimensions are 25x18x18 inches.
Radicals	The Radicals were a parliamentary political grouping in the United Kingdom in the early to mid 19th century, who drew on earlier ideas of radicalism and helped to transform the Whigs into the Liberal Party. The Radical movement arose in the late 18th century to support parliamentary reform with additional aims including Catholic Emancipation and free trade. Working class and middle class "Popular radicals" agitated to demand the right to vote and assert other rights including freedom of the press and relief from economic distress, while middle class "Philosophic radicals" strongly supported parliamentary reform, but were generally hostile to the arguments and tactics of the "popular radicals".
Seat	Seats were territorial-administrative units in the medieval Kingdom of Hungary. The seats were autonomous regions within the Kingdom, and were independent from the feudal county system. Their autonomy was granted in return for the military services they provided to the Hungarian Kings.
Rebellion	Rebellion is a refusal of obedience or order. It may, therefore, be seen as encompassing a range of behaviors from civil disobedience and mass nonviolent resistance, to violent and organized attempts to destroy an established authority such as a government. Those who participate in rebellions are known as "rebels".

Chapter 2. Constructing a Government: The Founding and the Constitution

Daniel Shays	Daniel Shays was an American soldier, revolutionary, and farmer famous for leading the Shays' Rebellion. Reportedly born in Hopkinton, MA, in Middlesex County, Shays was the son of an Irish immigrant who had worked as an indentured servant. During his life, Shays never allowed a portrait of himself to be made, so his true appearance remains unknown.
Interest	Interest is a fee paid on borrowed assets. It is the price paid for the use of borrowed money, or, money earned by deposited funds. Assets that are sometimes lent with interest include money, shares, consumer goods through hire purchase, major assets such as aircraft, and even entire factories in finance lease arrangements.
New Jersey Plan	The New Jersey Plan was a proposal for the structure of the United States Government proposed by William Paterson at the Constitutional Convention on June 15, 1787. The plan was created in response to the Virginia Plan's call for two houses of Congress, both elected with apportionment according to population or direct taxes paid. The less populous states were adamantly opposed to giving most of the control of the national government to the larger states, and so proposed an alternate plan that would have given one vote per state for equal representation under one legislative body (i.e., a Unicameral Legislature). This was a compromise for the issue of the houses.
Virginia	The Commonwealth of Virginia is a U.S. state on the Atlantic Coast of the Southern United States. Virginia is nicknamed the "Old Dominion" and sometimes the "Mother of Presidents" because it is the birthplace of eight U.S. presidents. The geography and climate of the state are shaped by the Blue Ridge Mountains and the Chesapeake Bay, which provide habitat for much of its flora and fauna.
Opposition	In politics, the opposition comprises one or more political parties or other organized groups that are opposed to the government, party or group in political control of a city, region, state or country. The degree of opposition varies according to political conditions - for example, across authoritarian and liberal systems where opposition may be repressed or welcomed.
Connecticut Compromise	The Connecticut Compromise was an agreement between large and small states reached during the Constitutional Convention of 1787 that in part defined the legislative structure and representation that each state would have under the United States Constitution. It proposed a bicameral legislature, resulting in the current United States Senate and House of Representatives. Context

Chapter 2. Constructing a Government: The Founding and the Constitution

	On May 29, 1787, Edmund Randolph of the Virginia delegation proposed the creation of a bicameral legislature.
Senate	A senate is a deliberative assembly, often the upper house or chamber of a legislature or parliament. There have been many such bodies in history, since senate means the assembly of the eldest and wiser members of the society and ruling class. Two of the first official senates were the Spartan Gerousia (Γερουσ?α) and the Roman Senate.
Three-fifths compromise	The Three-Fifths compromise was a compromise between Southern and Northern states reached during the Philadelphia Convention of 1787 in which three-fifths of the population of slaves would be counted for enumeration purposes regarding both the distribution of taxes and the apportionment of the members of the United States House of Representatives. It was proposed by delegates James Wilson and Roger Sherman. Delegates opposed to slavery generally wished to count only the free inhabitants of each state.
Bank tax	A bank tax is a proposed tax on banks. One of the earliest modern uses of the term "bank tax" occurred in the context of the Financial crisis of 2007-2010. On April 16, 2010, the International Monetary Fund (IMF) proposed the idea of a "financial stability contribution" (FSC), which many media have referred to as a "bank tax." It was proposed as one of three possible options to deal with the crisis.
Gerrymandering	In the process of setting electoral boundaries, rather than using uniform geographic standards, Gerrymandering is a practice of political corruption that attempts to establish a political advantage for a particular party or group by manipulating geographic boundaries to create partisan, incumbent-protected, and neutral districts. The resulting district is known as a gerrymander; however, that word can also refer to the process.

Chapter 2. Constructing a Government: The Founding and the Constitution

	Gerrymandering may be used to achieve desired electoral results for a particular party, or may be used to help or hinder a particular group of constituents, such as a political, racial, linguistic, religious or class group.
Impeachment	Impeachment is a formal process in which an official is accused of unlawful activity and the outcome of which, depending on the country, can lead to the removal of that official from office or other punishment. Medieval popular etymology also associated it (wrongly) with derivations from the Latin impetere (to attack). (In its more frequent and more technical usage, impeachment of a person in the role of a witness is the act of challenging the honesty or credibility of that person).
Bicameralism	In government, bicameralism is the practice of having two legislative or parliamentary chambers. Thus, a bicameral parliament or bicameral legislature is a legislature which consists of two chambers or houses. Bicameralism is an essential and defining feature of the classical notion of mixed government.
Electoral college	An electoral college is a set of electors who are selected to elect a candidate to a particular office. Often these represent different organizations or entities, with each organization or entity represented by a particular number of electors or with votes weighted in a particular way. Many times, though, the electors are simply important people whose wisdom, ideally, would provide a better choice than a larger body.
Rights	Rights are legal, social, or ethical principles of freedom or entitlement; that is, rights are the fundamental normative rules about what is allowed of people or owed to people, according to some legal system, social convention, or ethical theory. Rights are of essential importance in such disciplines as law and ethics, especially theories of justice and deontology.
	Rights are often considered fundamental to civilization, being regarded as established pillars of society and culture, and the history of social conflicts can be found in the history of each right and its development.

Chapter 2. Constructing a Government: The Founding and the Constitution

Voting	Voting is a method for a group such as a meeting or an electorate to make a decision or express an opinion--often following discussions, debates, or election campaigns. It is often found in democracies and republics. Reasons for voting In a representative government, voting commonly implies election: a way for an electorate to select among candidates for office.
Social security	Social security is primarily a social insurance program providing social protection, or protection against socially recognized conditions, including poverty, old age, disability, unemployment and others. Social security may refer to: - social insurance, where people receive benefits or services in recognition of contributions to an insurance scheme. These services typically include provision for retirement pensions, disability insurance, survivor benefits and unemployment insurance. - income maintenance--mainly the distribution of cash in the event of interruption of employment, including retirement, disability and unemployment - services provided by administrations responsible for social security.

Chapter 2. Constructing a Government: The Founding and the Constitution

Appointee	An appointee may be one of the following: • A member who is appointed to a position or office is called an appointee. In law, such a term is applied to one who is granted power of appointment of property. • An appointee was also a foot soldier in the French army, who, for long service and bravery, received more pay than other privates. • An appointee is the third most lower rank of the Italian Corps of Carabineers • An appointee is the third most lower rank of the Swiss Armed Forces • An appointee is also a person or organisation entrusted with managing the daily finances of vulnerable individuals in the UK.
Executive	Executive branch of government is the part of government that has sole authority and responsibility for the daily administration of the state bureaucracy. The division of power into separate branches of government is central to the democratic idea of the separation of powers. In many countries, the term "government" connotes only the executive branch.
Executive order	An executive order in the United States is an order issued by the President, the head of the executive branch of the federal government.
Necessary and Proper Clause	The Necessary and Proper Clause is the provision in Article One of the United States Constitution, section 8, clause 18: Early controversy

Chapter 2. Constructing a Government: The Founding and the Constitution

The clause provoked controversy during discussions of the proposed constitution, and its inclusion became a focal point of criticism for those opposed to the Constitution's ratification. While Anti-Federalists expressed concern that the clause would grant the federal government boundless power, Federalists argued that the clause would only permit execution of power already granted by the Constitution. Alexander Hamilton spoke vigorously for this second interpretation in the Federalist Papers as part of his argument for why the federal government required the powers of taxation.

Government	In the social sciences, the term government refers to the particular group of people, the administrative bureaucracy, who control a state at a given time, and the manner in which their governing organizations are structured. That is, governments are the means through which state power is employed. States are served by a continuous succession of different governments.
Central government	A central government, union government and in federal states, the federal government, is the government at the level of the nation-state. The structure of central governments varies from institution to institution. Many countries have created autonomous regions by delegating powers from the central government to governments at a subnational level, such as a regional, local, or state level.
Power	Power is a measure of an entity's ability to control its environment, including the behavior of other entities. The term authority is often used for power, perceived as legitimate by the social structure. Power can be seen as evil or unjust, but the exercise of power is accepted as endemic to humans as social beings.
Allegiance	An allegiance is a duty of fidelity said to be owed by a subject or a citizen to his/her state or sovereign. Etymology From Middle English ligeaunce . The al- prefix was probably added through confusion with another legal term, allegeance, an "allegation" .

Chapter 2. Constructing a Government: The Founding and the Constitution

Pledge	A pledge is a bailment or deposit of personal property to a creditor to secure repayment for some debt or engagement, The term is also used to denote the property which constitutes the security. Pledge is the ravi of Roman law, from which most of the modern law on the subject is derived. It differs from hypothecation and from the more usual mortgage in that the pledge is in the possession of the pledgee; it also differs from mortgage in being confined to personal property (rather than real property).
Constitutional amendment	A constitutional amendment is a change to the constitution of a nation or a state. In jurisdictions with "rigid" or "entrenched" constitutions, amendments do not require a special procedure different from that used for enacting ordinary laws. Some constitutions do not have to be amended with the direct consent of the electorate in a referendum.
Discretion	Discretion is a noun in the English language. Meanings - "The Art of suiting action to particular circumstances" (Lord Scarman) - 'the quality of being discreet' (Concise Oxford Dictionary) Those in a position of power are most often able to exercise discretion as to how they will apply or exercise that power. In the criminal justice system

Chapter 2. Constructing a Government: The Founding and the Constitution

	In the criminal justice system, police, prosecutors, judges, and the jury are often able to exercise a degree of discretion in deciding who will be subject to criminal penalties and how they will be punished.
Federalism	In Europe, "federalist" is sometimes used to describe those who favor a common federal government, with distributed power at regional, national and supranational levels. Most European Federalists want this development to continue within the European Union. European federalism originated in post-war Europe; one of the more important initiatives was Winston Churchill's speech in Zurich in 1946.
Judicial discretion	Judicial discretion is the power of the judiciary to make some legal decisions according to their discretion. Under the doctrine of the separation of powers, the ability of judges to exercise discretion is an aspect of judicial independence. Where appropriate, judicial discretion allows a judge to decide a legal case or matter within a range of possible decisions.
Judicial review	Judicial review is the doctrine under which legislative and executive actions are subject to review, and possible invalidation, by the judiciary. Specific courts with judicial review power must annul the acts of the state when it finds them incompatible with a higher authority, such as the terms of a written constitution. Judicial review is an example of the functioning of separation of powers in a modern governmental system (where the judiciary is one of three branches of government).
Supremacy	The supremacy of EU law is a principle of by which the laws of European Union member states that conflict with laws of the European Union must be ignored by national courts so that the European Union law can take effect. The legal doctrine emerged from the European Court of Justice through a number of decisions. Development In Costa v. ENEL. Mr Costa was an Italian citizen opposed to nationalising energy.

Chapter 2. Constructing a Government: The Founding and the Constitution

Supremacy Clause	The Supremacy Clause is a clause in the United States Constitution, article VI, paragraph 2. The clause establishes the U.S. Constitution, Federal Statutes, and U.S. treaties as "the supreme law of the land." The text decrees these to be the highest form of law in the U.S. legal system, mandating that all state judges must follow federal law in the face of conflicting state law or when a conflict arises between federal law and a state constitution. (Note that the word "shall" is used here and in the language of the law, which makes it a necessity, a compulsion).
Administration	Administration, as a legal concept, is a procedure under the insolvency laws of a number of common law jurisdictions. It functions as a rescue mechanism for insolvent companies and allows them to carry on running their business. The process - an alternative to liquidation - is often known as going into administration.
Baron	Baron is a title of nobility. The word baron comes from Old French baron, itself from Old High German and Latin (liber) baro meaning "(free) man, (free) warrior"; it merged with cognate Old English beorn meaning "nobleman". Barons in the United Kingdom and the Commonwealth In the British peer system, barons rank below viscounts, and form the lowest rank in the peerage.
Bill of rights	A bill of rights is a list of the most important rights of the citizens of a country. The purpose of these bills is to protect those rights against infringement by the government. The term "bill of rights" originates from England, where it referred to the Bill of Rights 1689. Bills of rights may be entrenched or unentrenched.
Montesquieu	Charles-Louis de Secondat, baron de La Brède et de Montesquieu, generally referred to as simply Montesquieu, was a French social commentator and political thinker who lived during the Enlightenment. He is famous for his articulation of the theory of separation of powers, taken for granted in modern discussions of government and implemented in many constitutions throughout the world. He was largely responsible for the popularization of the terms feudalism and Byzantine Empire.

Chapter 2. Constructing a Government: The Founding and the Constitution

Ratification	Ratification is the approval by the principal of an act of its agent where the agent lacked authority to legally bind the principal. The term applies to private contract law, international treaties, and constitutionals in federations such as the United States and Canada. Private law In contract law, the need for ratification can arise in two ways: Where the agent attempts to bind the principal despite lacking the authority to do so, and where the principal authorizes the agent to make an agreement, but reserves the right to approve it.
Separation of powers	The separation of powers is a model for the governance of a state. The model was first developed in ancient Greece and came into widespread use by the Roman Republic as part of the unmodified Constitution of the Roman Republic. Under this model, the state is divided into branches, each with separate and independent powers and areas of responsibility so that no one branch has more power than the other branches.
Trusts	In Conflict of Laws, the Hague Convention on the Law Applicable to Trusts and on Their Recognition was concluded on 1 July 1985 and entered into force 1 January 1992. The Convention aims to harmonise not only the municipal law definitions of a trust both within the USA and outside the USA, but also the Conflict rules for resolving problems in the choice of the lex causae. Explanation Many states do not have a developed law of trusts, or the principles differ significantly between states. It was therefore necessary for the Hague Convention to define a trust to indicate the range of legal transactions regulated by the Convention and, perhaps more significantly, the range of applications not regulated.
State	Many sovereign independent state are made up of a number of country subdivisions also called states. In some cases, such as the United States, the national government arose from a union of sovereign entities, which transferred some of their powers to the national government, while retaining the remainder of their sovereignty. These are sometimes called federal states.

Chapter 2. Constructing a Government: The Founding and the Constitution

Rescue	Rescue refers to operations that usually involve the saving of life, or prevention of injury. Tools used might include search dogs, search and rescue horses, helicopters, the "Jaws of Life", and other hydraulic cutting and spreading tools used to extricate individuals from wrecked vehicles. Rescue operations are sometimes supported by special vehicles such as fire department's or EMS Heavy rescue vehicle.
Property	Property is any physical or intangible entity that is owned by a person or jointly by a group of people. Depending on the nature of the property, an owner of property has the right to consume, sell, rent, mortgage, transfer, exchange or destroy their property, and/or to exclude others from doing these things. Important widely recognized types of property include real property personal property private property public property and intellectual property., although the latter is not always as widely recognized or enforced.
Henry	Saint Henry was a medieval Swedish clergyman. According to legends, he conquered Finland together with King Eric the Saint of Sweden and died as a martyr, becoming a central figure in the local Roman Catholic Church. However, the authenticity of the accounts of his life, ministry, and death are widely disputed.
Publics	Publics are small groups of people who follow one or more particular issue very closely. They are well informed about the issue(s) and also have a very strong opinion on it/them. They tend to know more about politics than the average person, and, therefore, exert more influence, because these people care so deeply about their cause(s) that they donate much time and money.
Public works	Public works are the construction or engineering projects carried out by the state on behalf of the community. Overview "Public works" is a concept in economics and politics. The term public infrastructure refers only to the infrastructural capital involved in these activities.

Chapter 2. Constructing a Government: The Founding and the Constitution

Party system	A party system is a concept in comparative political science concerning the system of government by political parties in a democratic country. The idea is that political parties have basic similarities: they control the government, have a stable base of mass popular support, and create internal mechanisms for controlling funding, information and nominations. The concept was originated by European scholars studying the United States, especially James Bryce and Moisey Ostrogorsky, and has been expanded to cover other democracies.
Political Parties	Political Parties: A Sociological Study of the Oligarchical Tendencies of Modern Democracy is a book by sociologist Robert Michels, published in 1911, and first introducing the concept of iron law of oligarchy. It is considered one of the classics of sociology and political science. This work analyzes the power structures of organizations such as political parties and trade unions.
Soviet	Soviet was a name used for several Russian political organizations. Examples include the Czar's Council of Ministers, which was called the "Soviet of Ministers"; a workers' local council in late Imperial Russia; and the Supreme Soviet of the Soviet Union. Etymology "Soviet" is derived from a Russian word signifying council, advice, harmony, concord.[trans 1] The word "sovietnik" means councillor.
Soviet Union	The Union of Soviet Socialist Republics, informally known as the Soviet Union, was a constitutionally socialist state that existed on the territory of most of the former Russian Empire in Eurasia between 1922 and 1991.

Chapter 2. Constructing a Government: The Founding and the Constitution

The Soviet Union had a single-party political system dominated by the Communist Party until 1990. Although the USSR was nominally a union of Soviet republics (of which there were 15 after 1956) with the capital in Moscow, it was in actuality a highly centralized state with a planned economy.

The Soviet Union was founded in December 1922 when the Russian SFSR, which formed during the Russian Revolution of 1917 and emerged victorious in the ensuing Russian Civil War, unified with the Transcaucasian, Ukrainian and Belorussian SSRs.

Prohibition

Prohibition of alcohol, often referred to simply as prohibition, is the practice of prohibiting the manufacture, transportation, import, export, and sale of alcohol and alcoholic beverages. The term can also apply to the periods in the histories of the countries during which the prohibition of alcohol was enforced. Use of the term as applicable to a historical period is typically applied to countries of European culture.

Election

An election is a formal decision-making process by which a population chooses an individual to hold public office. Elections have been the usual mechanism by which modern representative democracy operates since the 17th century. Elections may fill offices in the legislature, sometimes in the executive and judiciary, and for regional and local government.

Industrial policy

The Industrial Policy plan of a nation, sometimes shortened Industrial policy, "denotes a nation's declared, official, total strategic effort to influence sectoral development and, thus, national industry portfolio." These interventionist measures comprise "policies that stimulate specific activities and promote structural change".

Industrial policies are sector specific, unlike broader macroeconomic policies. Examples of horizontal, economywide policies are tightening credit or taxing capital gain, while examples of vertical, sector-specific policies comprise protecting textiles from foreign imports or subsidizing export industries.

Policy

A policy is typically described as a principle or rule to guide decisions and achieve rational outcome(s). The term is not normally used to denote what is actually done, this is normally referred to as either procedure or protocol. Whereas a policy will contain the 'what' and the 'why', procedures or protocols contain the 'what', the 'how', the 'where', and the 'when'.

Chapter 2. Constructing a Government: The Founding and the Constitution

Rights of Englishmen	The rights of Englishmen are the perceived traditional rights of English subjects. The notion refers to various constitutional documents that were created throughout various stages of English history, such as the Magna Carta, the Declaration of Right (the text of which was recognised by Parliament in the Bill of Rights 1689), and others. Many Patriots in the Thirteen colonies argued that their rights as Englishmen were being violated, which subsequently became one of the original primary justifications for the American Revolution and the resulting separation from the British Empire.
Ensign	Ensign is a junior rank of commissioned officer in the armed forces of some countries, normally in the infantry or navy. As the junior officer in an infantry regiment was traditionally the carrier of the ensign flag, the rank itself acquired the name. The Spanish alférez and Portuguese alferes is a junior officer rank below lieutenant associated with carrying the flag, and so is often translated as "ensign".
Civil liberties	Civil liberties are rights and freedoms that provide an individual specific rights such as the right to life, freedom from torture, freedom from slavery and forced labour, the right to liberty and security, right to a fair trial, the right to defend one's self, the right to privacy, freedom of conscience, freedom of expression, freedom of assembly and association, and the right to marry and have a family. Within the distinctions between civil liberties and other types of liberty, it is important to note the distinctions between positive rights and negative rights. Common civil liberties include the rights of people, freedom of religion, and freedom of speech, and additionally, the right to due process, to a trial, to own property, and to privacy.

Chapter 2. Constructing a Government: The Founding and the Constitution

Chapter 2. Constructing a Government: The Founding and the Constitution

Chapter 3. Federalism and the Separation of Powers

Administration	Administration, as a legal concept, is a procedure under the insolvency laws of a number of common law jurisdictions. It functions as a rescue mechanism for insolvent companies and allows them to carry on running their business. The process - an alternative to liquidation - is often known as going into administration.
Court	A court is a form of tribunal, often a governmental institution, with the authority to adjudicate legal disputes between parties and carry out the administration of justice in civil, criminal, and administrative matters in accordance with the rule of law. In both common law and civil law legal systems, courts are the central means for dispute resolution, and it is generally understood that all persons have an ability to bring their claims before a court. Similarly, the rights of those accused of a crime include the right to present a defense before a court.
Appointee	An appointee may be one of the following: - A member who is appointed to a position or office is called an appointee. In law, such a term is applied to one who is granted power of appointment of property. - An appointee was also a foot soldier in the French army, who, for long service and bravery, received more pay than other privates. - An appointee is the third most lower rank of the Italian Corps of Carabineers - An appointee is the third most lower rank of the Swiss Armed Forces - An appointee is also a person or organisation entrusted with managing the daily finances of vulnerable individuals in the UK.
Federalism	In Europe, "federalist" is sometimes used to describe those who favor a common federal government, with distributed power at regional, national and supranational levels. Most European Federalists want this development to continue within the European Union. European federalism originated in post-war Europe; one of the more important initiatives was Winston Churchill's speech in Zurich in 1946.

Chapter 3. Federalism and the Separation of Powers

Power	Power is a measure of an entity's ability to control its environment, including the behavior of other entities. The term authority is often used for power, perceived as legitimate by the social structure. Power can be seen as evil or unjust, but the exercise of power is accepted as endemic to humans as social beings.
Separation of powers	The separation of powers is a model for the governance of a state. The model was first developed in ancient Greece and came into widespread use by the Roman Republic as part of the unmodified Constitution of the Roman Republic. Under this model, the state is divided into branches, each with separate and independent powers and areas of responsibility so that no one branch has more power than the other branches.
Rights	Rights are legal, social, or ethical principles of freedom or entitlement; that is, rights are the fundamental normative rules about what is allowed of people or owed to people, according to some legal system, social convention, or ethical theory. Rights are of essential importance in such disciplines as law and ethics, especially theories of justice and deontology. Rights are often considered fundamental to civilization, being regarded as established pillars of society and culture, and the history of social conflicts can be found in the history of each right and its development.
Voting	Voting is a method for a group such as a meeting or an electorate to make a decision or express an opinion--often following discussions, debates, or election campaigns. It is often found in democracies and republics. Reasons for voting In a representative government, voting commonly implies election: a way for an electorate to select among candidates for office.
Agenda	An agenda is a list of meeting activities in the order in which they are to be taken up, beginning with the call to order and ending with adjournment. It usually includes one or more specific items of business to be considered. It may, but is not required to, include specific times for one OR more activities.

Chapter 3. Federalism and the Separation of Powers

Decision	A decision, defined in Article 288 of the Treaty on the Functioning of the European Union (formerly Article 249 TEC), is one of the three binding instruments provided by secondary EU legislation. A decision is binding on the person or entity to which it is addressed. Decisions may be addressed to member states or individuals.
Congress	A congress is a formal meeting of the representatives of different nations, constituent states, independent organizations (such as trade unions), or groups. The term was chosen for the United States Congress to emphasize the status of each state represented there as a self-governing unit. Subsequent to the use of congress by the U.S. legislature, the term has been incorrectly adopted by many states within unions, and by unitary nation-states in the Americas, to refer to their legislatures.
Social security	Social security is primarily a social insurance program providing social protection, or protection against socially recognized conditions, including poverty, old age, disability, unemployment and others. Social security may refer to: - social insurance, where people receive benefits or services in recognition of contributions to an insurance scheme. These services typically include provision for retirement pensions, disability insurance, survivor benefits and unemployment insurance. - income maintenance--mainly the distribution of cash in the event of interruption of employment, including retirement, disability and unemployment - services provided by administrations responsible for social security.
State	Many sovereign independent state are made up of a number of country subdivisions also called states. In some cases, such as the United States, the national government arose from a union of sovereign entities, which transferred some of their powers to the national government, while retaining the remainder of their sovereignty. These are sometimes called federal states.
Vietnam	Vietnam, officially the Socialist Republic of Vietnam is the easternmost country on the Indochina Peninsula in Southeast Asia. It is bordered by People's Republic of China (PRC) to the north, Laos to the northwest, Cambodia to the southwest, and the South China Sea, referred to as East Sea (Vietnamese: Bi?n Đông), to the east. With a population of over 86 million, Vietnam is the 13th most populous country in the world.

Chapter 3. Federalism and the Separation of Powers

Legislation	Legislation is law which has been promulgated (or "enacted") by a legislature or other governing body, or the process of making it. (Another source of law is judge-made law or case law). Before an item of legislation becomes law it may be known as a bill, and may be broadly referred to as "legislation" while it remains under consideration to distinguish it from other business.
Sovereignty	Sovereignty is the quality of having supreme, independent authority over a geographic area, such as a territory. It can be found in a power to rule and make law that rests on a political fact for which no purely legal explanation can be provided. The concept has been discussed, debated and questioned throughout history, from the time of the Romans through to the present day, although it has changed in its definition, concept, and application throughout, especially during the Age of Enlightenment.
Articles of Confederation	The Articles of Confederation was the first constitution of the United States and specified how the Federal government was to operate, including adoption of an official name for the new nation, United States of America. The Second Continental Congress appointed a committee to draft the Articles in June 1776 and sent the draft to the states for ratification in November 1777. In practice, the Articles were in use beginning in 1777. The ratification process was completed in March 1781. Under the Articles, the states retained sovereignty over all governmental functions not specifically relinquished to the national government.
	On June 12, 1776, a day after appointing a committee to prepare a draft of the Declaration of Independence, the Second Continental Congress resolved to appoint a committee of thirteen to prepare a draft of a constitution for a confederate type of union. The last draft of the Articles was written in the summer of 1777 and the Second Continental Congress approved them for ratification by the States on November 15, 1777, after a year of debate.
Balkan Federation	The Balkan Federation was a project about the creation of a Balkan federation, based mainly on left political ideas.
	The concept of a Balkan federation emerged at the late 19th century from among left political forces in the region. The central aim was to establish a new political unity: a common federal republic unifying the Balkan Peninsula on the basis of internationalism, social solidarity, and economic equality.

Chapter 3. Federalism and the Separation of Powers

Constitutional convention	A constitutional convention is an informal and uncodified procedural agreement that is followed by the institutions of a state. In some states, notably those Commonwealth of Nations states which follow the Westminster system and whose political systems are derived from British constitutional law, most of the functions of government are guided by constitutional convention rather than by a formal written constitution. In these states, the actual distribution of power may be markedly different from those which are described in the formal constitutional documents.
National Convention	During the French Revolution, the National Convention, in France, comprised the constitutional and legislative assembly which sat from 20 September 1792 to 26 October 1795. It held executive power in France during the first years of the French First Republic. It was succeeded by the Directory, commencing 2 November 1795. Prominent members of the original Convention included Maximilien Robespierre of the Jacobin Club, Jean-Paul Marat (affiliated with the Jacobins, though never a formal member), and Georges Danton of the Cordeliers.
Rebellion	Rebellion is a refusal of obedience or order. It may, therefore, be seen as encompassing a range of behaviors from civil disobedience and mass nonviolent resistance, to violent and organized attempts to destroy an established authority such as a government. Those who participate in rebellions are known as "rebels".
Federal government	A federal government is the common government of a federation. The structure of federal governments varies from institution to institution. Based on a broad definition of a basic federal political system, there are two or more levels of government that exist within an established territory and govern through common institutions with overlapping or shared powers as prescribed by a constitution.
Government	In the social sciences, the term government refers to the particular group of people, the administrative bureaucracy, who control a state at a given time, and the manner in which their governing organizations are structured. That is, governments are the means through which state power is employed. States are served by a continuous succession of different governments.
Executive	Executive branch of government is the part of government that has sole authority and responsibility for the daily administration of the state bureaucracy. The division of power into separate branches of government is central to the democratic idea of the separation of powers. In many countries, the term "government" connotes only the executive branch.

Chapter 3. Federalism and the Separation of Powers

Executive order	An executive order in the United States is an order issued by the President, the head of the executive branch of the federal government.
Federalist	The term federalist describes several political beliefs around the world. Also, it may refer to the concept of federalism or the type of government called a federation. In early United States history, the Federalist Party was one of the first political parties; its members or supporters called themselves Federalists.
Coercion	Coercion is the practice of forcing another party to behave in an involuntary manner (whether through action or inaction) by use of threats, intimidation or some other form of pressure or force. Such actions are used as leverage, to force the victim to act in the desired way. Coercion may involve the actual infliction of physical pain/injury or psychological harm in order to enhance the credibility of a threat.
Declaration	In law, a declaration is a binding adjudication of the rights or other legal relations of the parties which does not provide for or order enforcement. Where the declaration is made by a court, it is usually referred to as a declaratory judgment. Less commonly, where declaratory relief is awarded by an arbitrator, it is normally called a declaratory award.
Impeachment	Impeachment is a formal process in which an official is accused of unlawful activity and the outcome of which, depending on the country, can lead to the removal of that official from office or other punishment. Medieval popular etymology also associated it (wrongly) with derivations from the Latin impetere (to attack). (In its more frequent and more technical usage, impeachment of a person in the role of a witness is the act of challenging the honesty or credibility of that person).
Implementation	Implementation is the realization of an application, or execution of a plan, idea, model, design, specification, standard, algorithm, or policy. Computer Science In computer science, an implementation is a realization of a technical specification or algorithm as a program, software component, or other computer system through programming and deployment. Many implementations may exist for a given specification or standard.

Chapter 3. Federalism and the Separation of Powers

Implied powers	Implied powers, in the United States, are those powers authorized by a legal document (from the Constitution) which, while not stated, are seemed to be implied by powers expressly stated. When George Washington asked Alexander Hamilton to defend the constitutionality of the First Bank of the United States against the protests of Thomas Jefferson, James Madison, and Attorney General Edmund Randolph, Hamilton produced what has now become the classic statement for implied powers. Hamilton argued that the sovereign duties of a government implied the right to use means adequate to its ends.
Central government	A central government, union government and in federal states, the federal government, is the government at the level of the nation-state. The structure of central governments varies from institution to institution. Many countries have created autonomous regions by delegating powers from the central government to governments at a subnational level, such as a regional, local, or state level.
Necessary and Proper Clause	The Necessary and Proper Clause is the provision in Article One of the United States Constitution, section 8, clause 18: Early controversy The clause provoked controversy during discussions of the proposed constitution, and its inclusion became a focal point of criticism for those opposed to the Constitution's ratification. While Anti-Federalists expressed concern that the clause would grant the federal government boundless power, Federalists argued that the clause would only permit execution of power already granted by the Constitution. Alexander Hamilton spoke vigorously for this second interpretation in the Federalist Papers as part of his argument for why the federal government required the powers of taxation.
Redistricting	Redistricting, a form of redistribution, is the process of drawing United States district lines. This often means changing electoral district and constituency boundaries in response to periodic census results. In 36 states, the state legislature has primary responsibility for creating a redistricting plan, in many cases subject to approval by the state governor.
Henry	Saint Henry was a medieval Swedish clergyman. According to legends, he conquered Finland together with King Eric the Saint of Sweden and died as a martyr, becoming a central figure in the local Roman Catholic Church. However, the authenticity of the accounts of his life, ministry, and death are widely disputed.

Chapter 3. Federalism and the Separation of Powers

Poland	Poland officially the Republic of Poland - is a country in Central Europe bordered by Germany to the west; the Czech Republic and Slovakia to the south; Ukraine, Belarus and Lithuania to the east; and the Baltic Sea and Kaliningrad Oblast, a Russian exclave, to the north. The total area of Poland is 312,679 square kilometres (120,726 sq mi), making it the 69th largest country in the world and the 9th largest in Europe. Poland has a population of over 38 million people, which makes it the 34th most populous country in the world and the sixth most populous member of the European Union, being its most populous post-communist member.
Concurrent powers	Concurrent powers are powers that are shared by the state and the federal government and may be exercised simultaneously within the same territory and in relation to the same body of citizens. These powers are commonly found in the United States of America and many other Federalist Nations. They are contrasted with delegated powers and reserved powers.
Credit	Credit is the trust which allows one party to provide resources to another party where that second party does not reimburse the first party immediately (thereby generating a debt), but instead arranges either to repay or return those resources (or other materials of equal value) at a later date. The resources provided may be financial (e.g. granting a loan), or they may consist of goods or services (e.g. consumer credit). Credit encompasses any form of deferred payment.
Full Faith and Credit Clause	The Full Faith and Credit Clause is the familiar name used to refer to Article IV, Section 1 of the United States Constitution, which addresses the duties that states within the United States have to respect the "public acts, records, and judicial proceedings of every other state." According to the Supreme Court, there is a difference between the credit owed to laws (i.e. legislative measures and common law) as compared to the credit owed to judgments. Judgments are generally entitled to greater respect than laws, in other states. At present, it is widely agreed that this Clause of the Constitution has little impact on a court's choice of law decision, although this Clause of the Constitution was once interpreted differently.
Police	The police are persons empowered to enforce the law, protect property and reduce civil disorder. Their powers include the legitimized use of force. The term is most commonly associated with police services of a state that are authorized to exercise the police power of that state within a defined legal or territorial area of responsibility.
Police power	In United States constitutional law, police power is the capacity of the federal government and the states to regulate behavior and enforce order within their territory for the betterment of the general welfare, morals, health, and safety of their inhabitants. Under the 10th Amendment to the United States Constitution, the powers prohibited from or not delegated to the Federal Government are reserved to the states respectively, or to the people. This implies that the states do not possess all possible powers, since some of these are reserved to the people.

Chapter 3. Federalism and the Separation of Powers

Trusts	In Conflict of Laws, the Hague Convention on the Law Applicable to Trusts and on Their Recognition was concluded on 1 July 1985 and entered into force 1 January 1992. The Convention aims to harmonise not only the municipal law definitions of a trust both within the USA and outside the USA, but also the Conflict rules for resolving problems in the choice of the lex causae. Explanation Many states do not have a developed law of trusts, or the principles differ significantly between states. It was therefore necessary for the Hague Convention to define a trust to indicate the range of legal transactions regulated by the Convention and, perhaps more significantly, the range of applications not regulated.
Cold War	The Cold War was the continuing state of political conflict, military tension, proxy wars, and economic competition existing after World War II (1939-1945) between the Communist World - primarily the Soviet Union and its satellite states and allies - and the powers of the Western world, primarily the United States and its allies. Although the primary participants' military force never officially clashed directly, they expressed the conflict through military coalitions, strategic conventional force deployments, extensive aid to states deemed vulnerable, proxy wars, espionage, propaganda, conventional and nuclear arms races, appeals to neutral nations, rivalry at sports events, and technological competitions such as the Space Race. Despite being allies against the Axis powers, the USSR and the US disagreed about political philosophy and the configuration of the post-war world while occupying most of Europe.
Conscience	Conscience is an aptitude, faculty, intuition, or judgment of the intellect that distinguishes right from wrong. Moral evaluations of this type may reference values or norms (principles and rules). In psychological terms conscience is often described as leading to feelings of remorse when a human does things that go against his/her moral values, and to feelings of rectitude or integrity when actions conform to such norms.

Chapter 3. Federalism and the Separation of Powers

Union State	The Union State, semi-officially known as Union State of Russia and Belarus, is a supranational entity consisting of the Russian Federation and the Republic of Belarus. Creation Originally, the Commonwealth of Russia and Belarus was formed on April 2, 1996. The basis of the union was strengthened on April 2, 1997, with the signing of the "Treaty on the Union between Belarus and Russia" at which time its name was changed to the Union of Belarus and Russia. Several further agreements were signed on December 25, 1998, with the intention of providing greater political, economic, and social integration.
Consent	In criminal law, consent may be used as an excuse and prevent the defendant from incurring liability for what was done. Baker, "The Moral Limits of Consent as a Defense in the Criminal Law," 12(1) New Criminal Law Review (2009), see also consensual crime. Generally A defense against criminal liability may arise when a defendant can argue that, because of consent, there was no crime (e.g., arguing that permission was given to use an automobile, so it was not theft or taken with out consent).
Privilege	Privilege is a way of framing issues surrounding social inequality, focusing as much on the advantages that one group accrues from society as on the disadvantages that another group experiences. Group role

Chapter 3. Federalism and the Separation of Powers

	Privilege differs from conditions of overt prejudice, in which a dominant group actively seeks to oppress or suppress another group for its own advantage. Instead, theories of privilege suggest that the privileged group views its social, cultural, and economic experiences as a norm that everyone should experience, rather than as an advantaged position that must be maintained at the expense of others.
Authority	Authority means invention, advice, opinion, influence, or command. Essentially authority is imposed by superiors upon inferiors either by force of arms (structural authority) or by force of argument (sapiential authority). Usually authority has components of both compulsion and persuasion.
Homeland	A homeland is the concept of the place (cultural geography) to which an ethnic group holds a long history and a deep cultural association with --the country in which a particular national identity began. As a common noun, it simply connotes the country of one's origin.
Homeland security	Homeland security is an umbrella term for security efforts to protect the United States against terrorist activity. The term arose following a reorganization of many U.S. government agencies in 2003 to form the United States Department of Homeland Security after the September 11 attacks, and may be used to refer to the actions of that department, the United States Senate Committee on Homeland Security and Governmental Affairs, or the United States House of Representatives Committee on Homeland Security. In the United States In the United States, the concept of "homeland security" extends and recombines responsibilities of government agencies and entities.
Port authority	In Canada and the United States a port authority is a governmental or quasi-governmental public authority for a special-purpose district usually formed by a legislative body (or bodies) to operate ports and other transportation infrastructure.

Chapter 3. Federalism and the Separation of Powers

	Port authorities are usually governed by boards or commissions, which are commonly appointed by governmental chief executives, often from different jurisdictions. For example, in Canada the federal Minister of Transport selects one board member, the local chief executive one, and the rest of the board are at the recommendation of port users to the federal Minister.
Dual federalism	Dual federalism, a legal theory which has prevailed in the United States since 1787, is the belief that the United States consists of two separate and co-sovereign branches of government. This form of government works on the principle that the national and state governments are split into their own spheres, and each is supreme within its respective sphere. Specifically, dual federalism discusses the relationship between the national government and the states' governments.
Home rule	Home rule is the power of a constituent part (administrative division) of a state to exercise such of the state's powers of governance within its own administrative area that have been devolved to it by the central government. In the United Kingdom, it has traditionally referred to self-government, or devolution or independence, of constituent nations (namely Scotland, Wales, and Northern Ireland), and at one point Ireland. In the United States and other countries organized as federations of states, the term usually refers to the process and mechanisms of self-government as exercised by municipalities, counties, or other units of local government at the level below that of a federal state.
Commerce Clause	The Commerce Clause is an enumerated power listed in the United States Constitution (Article I, Section 8, Clause 3). The clause states that the United States Congress shall have power "To regulate Commerce with foreign Nations, and among the several States, and with the Indian Tribes". Courts and commentators have tended to discuss each of these three areas of commerce as a separate power granted to Congress.
Senate	A senate is a deliberative assembly, often the upper house or chamber of a legislature or parliament. There have been many such bodies in history, since senate means the assembly of the eldest and wiser members of the society and ruling class. Two of the first official senates were the Spartan Gerousia (Γερουσ?α) and the Roman Senate.

Chapter 3. Federalism and the Separation of Powers

United States	The United States of America (also referred to as the United States, the U.S., the USA, or America) is a federal constitutional republic comprising fifty states and a federal district. The country is situated mostly in central North America, where its forty-eight contiguous states and Washington, D.C., the capital district, lie between the Pacific and Atlantic Oceans, bordered by Canada to the north and Mexico to the south. The state of Alaska is in the northwest of the continent, with Canada to the east and Russia to the west across the Bering Strait.
Bank tax	A bank tax is a proposed tax on banks. One of the earliest modern uses of the term "bank tax" occurred in the context of the Financial crisis of 2007-2010. On April 16, 2010, the International Monetary Fund (IMF) proposed the idea of a "financial stability contribution" (FSC), which many media have referred to as a "bank tax." It was proposed as one of three possible options to deal with the crisis.
Necessary and Proper Clause	The Necessary and Proper Clause is the provision in Article One of the United States Constitution, section 8, clause 18: Early controversy The clause provoked controversy during discussions of the proposed constitution, and its inclusion became a focal point of criticism for those opposed to the Constitution's ratification. While Anti-Federalists expressed concern that the clause would grant the federal government boundless power, Federalists argued that the clause would only permit execution of power already granted by the Constitution. Alexander Hamilton spoke vigorously for this second interpretation in the Federalist Papers as part of his argument for why the federal government required the powers of taxation.
Interest	Interest is a fee paid on borrowed assets. It is the price paid for the use of borrowed money, or, money earned by deposited funds. Assets that are sometimes lent with interest include money, shares, consumer goods through hire purchase, major assets such as aircraft, and even entire factories in finance lease arrangements.

Chapter 3. Federalism and the Separation of Powers

Gibbons v. Ogden	Gibbons v. Ogden, 22 U.S. 1 (1824), was a landmark decision in which the Supreme Court of the United States held that the power to regulate interstate commerce was granted to Congress by the Commerce Clause of the United States Constitution. The case was argued by some of America's most admired and capable attorneys at the time. Exiled Irish patriot Thomas Addis Emmet and Thomas J. Oakley argued for Ogden, while William Wirt and Daniel Webster argued for Gibbons.
Candidate	A candidate is the prospective recipient of an award or honor or a person seeking or being considered for some kind of position; for example: ● to be elected to an office -- in this case a candidate selection procedure occurs. ● to receive membership in a group "Nomination" is part of the process of selecting a candidate for either election to an office, or the bestowing of an honor or award. "Presumptive nominee" is a term used when a person or organization believes that the nomination is inevitable. The act of being a candidate in a race is called a "candidacy." "Candidate" is a derivative of the Latin "candida" (white).
Commission	A commission is a physical document issued to certify the appointment of a commissioned officer by a sovereign power. The more specific terms commissioning parchment or commissioning scroll are often used to avoid ambiguity, due to "commission" being a homonym which directs the individual in carrying out their duty regardless of what authority or responsibility they may have at any time. However the document is not usually in the form of a scroll and is more often printed on paper instead of parchment.

Chapter 3. Federalism and the Separation of Powers

Discrimination	Discrimination is the cognitive and sensory capacity or ability to see fine distinctions and perceive differences between objects, subjects, concepts and patterns, or possess exceptional development of the senses. Used in this way to identify exceptional discernment since the 17th century, the term begun to be used as an expression of derogatory racial prejudice from the 1830s Thomas D. Rice's performances as "Jim Crow".
	Since the American Civil War the term 'discrimination' generally evolved in American English usage as an understanding of prejudicial treatment of an individual based solely on their race, later generalized as membership in a certain socially undesirable group or social category.
Left Behind	Left Behind is a series of 16 best-selling novels by Tim LaHaye and Jerry Jenkins, dealing with Christian dispensationalist End Times: pretribulation, premillennial, Christian eschatological viewpoint of the end of the world. The primary conflict of the series is the members of the Tribulation Force against the Global Community and its leader Nicolae Carpathia--the Antichrist. Left Behind is also the title of the first book in the series.
No Child Left Behind Act	The No Child Left Behind Act of 2001 is a United States Act of Congress concerning the education of children in public schools.
	NCLB was originally proposed by the administration of George W. Bush immediately after taking office. The bill, shepherded through the Senate by Senator Ted Kennedy, one of the bill's co-authors, received overwhelming bipartisan support in Congress.
Cooperative federalism	Cooperative federalism is a concept of federalism in which national, state, and local governments interact cooperatively and collectively to solve common problems, rather than making policies separately but more or less equally (such as the nineteenth century's dual federalism) or clashing over a policy in a system dominated by the national government.
	The European Union and Germany
	Comparisons Between the European Union and the United States

Chapter 3. Federalism and the Separation of Powers

In the upcoming Lisbon Treaty the distribution of competences in various policy areas between Member States and the European union is redistributed in 3 categories. In the United States soon after its creation (1789), it had exclusive competences only(changed somewhat since then, but the basic design remain to this day).

Ensign	Ensign is a junior rank of commissioned officer in the armed forces of some countries, normally in the infantry or navy. As the junior officer in an infantry regiment was traditionally the carrier of the ensign flag, the rank itself acquired the name. The Spanish alférez and Portuguese alferes is a junior officer rank below lieutenant associated with carrying the flag, and so is often translated as "ensign".
Prohibition	Prohibition of alcohol, often referred to simply as prohibition, is the practice of prohibiting the manufacture, transportation, import, export, and sale of alcohol and alcoholic beverages. The term can also apply to the periods in the histories of the countries during which the prohibition of alcohol was enforced. Use of the term as applicable to a historical period is typically applied to countries of European culture.
Regent	A regent is a person selected to act as head of state (ruling or not) because the ruler is a minor, not present, or debilitated. In a monarchy, a regent usually governs due to one of these reasons, but may also be elected to rule during the interregnum when the royal line has died out. This was the case in Finland and Hungary, where the royal line was considered extinct in the aftermath of World War I. In Iceland, the regent represented the King of Denmark as sovereign of Iceland until the country became a republic in 1944.
Formula Grant	A formula grant is a US federal grant specifying a precise formula in the legislation creating the program. Formula Grants include quantifiable elements, such as population, amount of tax effort, proportion of population unemployed or below poverty level, density of housing, or rate of infant mortality. The specified formula is a rule that tells potential recipient governments precisely how they can calculate the quantity of aid to which they are entitled under the provisions of law, as long as the recipient qualifies for such assistance under the stipulations of the program.

Chapter 3. Federalism and the Separation of Powers

Disabilities	Disabilities were legal restrictions and limitations placed on Jews in the Middle Ages. They included provisions requiring Jews to wear specific and identifying clothing such as the Jewish hat and the yellow badge, restricting Jews to certain cities and towns or in certain parts of towns (ghettos), and forbidding Jews to enter certain trades. Disabilities also included special taxes levied on Jews, exclusion from public life, and restraints on the performance of religious ceremonies.
Americas	The Americas, are the lands of the western hemisphere, composed of numerous entities and regions variably defined by geography, politics, and culture. The Americas are frequently recognised to comprise two separate continents (North America and South America), particularly in English-speaking nations. The Americas may also be recognised to comprise a single continent , in Latin America and in some European nations.
Contract	In the Conflict of Laws, the validity of a contract with one or more foreign law elements will be decided by reference to the so-called "proper law" of the contract. History Until the middle of the 19th century, the courts applied the lex loci contractus or the law of the place where the contract was made to decide whether the given contract was valid. The apparent advantage of this approach was that the rule was easy to apply with certain and predictable outcomes.
Contract with America	The Contract with America was a document released by the United States Republican Party during the 1994 Congressional election campaign. Written by Larry Huuinter, who was aided by Newt Gingrich, Robert Walker, Richard Armey, Bill Paxon, Tom DeLay, John Boehner and Jim Nussle, and in part using text from former President Ronald Reagan's 1985 State of the Union Address, the Contract detailed the actions the Republicans promised to take if they became the majority party in the United States House of Representatives for the first time in 40 years. Many of the Contract's policy ideas originated at The Heritage Foundation, a conservative think tank.
Mandate	In politics, a mandate is the authority granted by a constituency to act as its representative.

Chapter 3. Federalism and the Separation of Powers

	The concept of a government having a legitimate mandate to govern via the fair winning of a democratic election is a central idea of democracy. New governments who attempt to introduce policies that they did not make public during an election campaign are said to not have a legitimate mandate to implement such policies.
Monitor	Monitor, is a non-departmental public body in the United Kingdom. Its purpose is to regulate NHS Foundation Trusts or Foundation Hospitals - hospitals that have opted out of direct governmental control. The body was established under the Health and Social Care (Community Health and Standards) Act 2003.
Reform Act	In the United Kingdom, Reform Act is a generic term used for legislation concerning electoral matters. It is most commonly used for laws passed to enfranchise new groups of voters and to redistribute seats in the British House of Commons. The periodic redrawing of constituency boundaries is now dealt with by a permanent Boundary Commission in each part of the United Kingdom, rather than by a Reform Act.
Unfunded mandate	In United States law and politics, unfunded mandates are regulations or conditions for receiving grants that impose costs on state or local governments or private entities for which they are not reimbursed by the federal government. • Any one of many federal legislations such as the Clean Air Act, and the Clean Water Act that require programs to be sponsored by the governments of the states, without providing any funds for those programs. • The provisions in the Americans with Disabilities Act that require nearly all American business owners to make their business premises available to disabled customers without providing any funds for the cost of reconstruction or additional interior space. • The provisions in the Emergency Medical Treatment and Active Labor Act that require nearly all American emergency rooms to accept and stabilize any patient regardless of the patient's ability to pay, but do not provide adequate reimbursement for indigent patients.
Congressional Budget Office	The Congressional Budget Office is a federal agency within the legislative branch of the United States government. It is a government agency that provides economic data to Congress. The Congressional Budget Office was created as a nonpartisan agency by the Congressional Budget and Impoundment Control Act of 1974.

Chapter 3. Federalism and the Separation of Powers

Health administration	Health administration is the field relating to leadership, management, and administration of hospitals, hospital networks, and health care systems. Health care administrators are considered health care professionals.
	The discipline is known by many names, including health management, healthcare management, health systems management, health care systems management, and medical and health services management.
Environmental protection	Environmental protection is a practice of protecting the environment, on individual, organizational or governmental level, for the benefit of the natural environment and (or) humans. Due to the pressures of population and our technology the biophysical environment is being degraded, sometimes permanently. This has been recognized and governments began placing restraints on activities that caused environmental degradation.
Reconciliation	Reconciliation is a legislative process of the United States Senate intended to allow consideration of a budget bill with debate limited to twenty hours under Senate Rules. Reconciliation also exists in the United States House of Representatives, but because the House regularly passes rules that constrain debate and amendment, the process has had a less significant impact on that body.
	A reconciliation instruction (Budget Reconciliation) is a provision in a budget resolution directing one or more committees to submit legislation changing existing law in order to bring spending, revenues, or the debt-limit into conformity with the budget resolution.
Devolution	Devolution is the statutory granting of powers from the central government of a sovereign state to government at a subnational level, such as a regional, local, or state level. It differs from federalism in that the powers devolved may be temporary and ultimately reside in central government, thus the state remains, de jure, unitary.
	Legislation creating devolved parliaments or assemblies can be repealed by central government in the same way as any statute.

Chapter 3. Federalism and the Separation of Powers

New Federalism	New Federalism is a political philosophy of devolution, or the transfer of certain powers from the United States federal government to the states. The primary objective of New Federalism, unlike that of the eighteenth-century political philosophy of Federalism, is the restoration to the states of some of the autonomy and power which they lost to the federal government as a consequence of President Franklin Roosevelt's New Deal. It relies upon a Federalist tradition dating back to the founding of the country, as well as the Tenth Amendment.
Medicare	Medicare is a social insurance program administered by the United States government, providing health insurance coverage to people who are aged 65 and over, or who meet other special criteria. Medicare operates similar to a single-payer health care system, but the key difference is that its coverage only extends to 80% of any given medical cost; the remaining 20% of cost must be paid by other means, such as privately-held supplemental insurance, or paid by the patient. The program also funds residency training programs for the vast majority of physicians in the United States.
Attack	In computer and computer networks an attack is any attempt to destroy, expose, alter, disable, steal or gain unauthorized access to or make unauthorized use of an asset. Definitions IETF Internet Engineering Task Force defines attack in RFC 2828 as: US Government

Chapter 3. Federalism and the Separation of Powers

CNSS Instruction No. 4009 dated 26 April 2010 by Committee on National Security Systems of United States of America defines an attack as:

The increasing dependencies of modern society on information and computers networks (both in private and public sectors, including military) has led to new terms like cyber attack and Cyberwarfare.

CNSS Instruction No. 4009 define a cyber attack as:

Phenomenology

An attack can be active or passive.

An attack can be perpetrated by an insider or from outside the organization;

>   An "inside attack" is an attack initiated by an entity inside the security perimeter (an "insider"), i.e., an entity that is authorized to access system resources but uses them in a way not approved by those who granted the authorization.
>   An "outside attack" is initiated from outside the perimeter, by an unauthorized or illegitimate user of the system (an "outsider").

Compassionate conservatism	Compassionate Conservatism is a political philosophy that stresses using traditionally conservative techniques and concepts in order to improve the general welfare of society.

Origins of the term

Historian and presidential advisor Doug Wead may have been the first person to use the phrase "compassionate conservative". In 1977, Wead wrote a book about Kolkata, India, entitled The Compassionate Touch.

Chapter 3. Federalism and the Separation of Powers

Conservatism	Conservatism is a political and social philosophy that promotes the maintenance of traditional institutions and supports, at the most, minimal and gradual change in society. Some conservatives seek to preserve things as they are, emphasizing stability and continuity, while others oppose modernism and seek a return to the way things were. The first established use of the term in a political context was by François-René de Chateaubriand in 1819, following the French Revolution.
Terrorism	Terrorism is the systematic use of terror especially as a means of coercion. No universally agreed, legally binding, criminal law definition of terrorism currently exists. Common definitions of terrorism refer only to those violent acts which are intended to create fear (terror), are perpetrated for a religious, political or ideological goal, deliberately target or disregard the safety of non-combatants (civilians), and are committed by non-government agencies.
Florida	Florida is a state located in the Southeastern United States. It borders Alabama to the northwest and Georgia to the north. Much of the state's land mass is a large peninsula with the Gulf of Mexico to the west, the Atlantic Ocean to the east, and the Florida Straits and Carribean to the south.
Sovereign immunity	Sovereign immunity, is a type of immunity that in common law jurisdictions traces its origins from early English law. Generally speaking it is the doctrine that the sovereign or state cannot commit a legal wrong and is immune from civil suit or criminal prosecution; hence the saying, "the king (or queen) can do no wrong". In many cases, states have waived this immunity to allow for suits; in some cases, an individual may technically appear as defendant on the state's behalf.
Brady Handgun Violence Prevention Act	The Brady Handgun Violence Prevention Act was an Act of the United States Congress that, for the first time, instituted federal background checks on firearm purchasers in the United States. It was signed into law by President Bill Clinton on November 30, 1993, and went into effect on February 28, 1994. The Act was named after James Brady, who was shot by John Hinckley, Jr. during an attempted assassination of President Ronald Reagan on March 30, 1981.

Chapter 3. Federalism and the Separation of Powers

Handgun	A handgun is a firearm designed to be held and operated by one hand, with the other hand optionally supporting the shooting hand. This characteristic differentiates handguns as a general class of firearms from their larger counterparts: long guns such as rifles and shotguns (which are held in both hands and usually braced against the shoulder), mounted weapons such as machine guns and autocannons, and larger weapons such as artillery.
	Some handgun subtypes include derringers, single-shot pistols, revolvers, semi-automatic pistols, pepperboxes, and machine pistols.
Printz v. United States	Printz v. United States, 521 U.S. 898 (1997), was a United States Supreme Court ruling that established the unconstitutionality of certain interim provisions of the Brady Handgun Violence Prevention Act.
	The Gun Control Act of 1968
	The Gun Control Act of 1968 established a detailed Federal scheme governing the distribution of firearms. The GCA prohibited firearms ownership by certain broad categories of individuals thought to pose a threat to public safety, such as convicted felons, fugitives from justice, unlawful aliens, and many others.
Sudan	Sudan officially the Republic of Sudan, Arabic: ??????? ???????? Jumhuriyat al Sudan, is a country in northeastern Africa. It is the largest country in Africa and the Arab world, and tenth largest in the world by area. It is bordered by Egypt to the north, the Red Sea to the northeast, Eritrea and Ethiopia to the east, Kenya and Uganda to the southeast, the Democratic Republic of the Congo and the Central African Republic to the southwest, Chad to the west and Libya to the northwest. The world's longest river, the Nile, divides the country between east and west sides.
United States v. Morrison	United States v. Morrison, 529 U.S. 598 (2000) is a United States Supreme Court decision which held that parts of the Violence Against Women Act of 1994 were unconstitutional because they exceeded congressional power under the Commerce Clause and under section 5 of the Fourteenth Amendment to the Constitution.

Chapter 3. Federalism and the Separation of Powers

	In 1994, the United States Congress passed the Violence Against Women Act, which contained a provision at 42 U.S.C. § 13981 for a federal civil remedy to victims of gender-based violence, even when no criminal charges were filed.
	That fall, at Virginia Tech, freshman student Christy Brzonkala was allegedly assaulted and raped repeatedly by Antonio Morrison and James Crawford, members of the school's football team.
Violence Against Women Act	The Violence Against Women Act of 1994 is a United States federal law. It was passed as Title IV, sec. 40001-40703 of the Violent Crime Control and Law Enforcement Act of 1994 HR 3355 and signed as Public Law 103-322 by President Bill Clinton on September 13, 1994. It provided $1.6 billion to enhance investigation and prosecution of the violent crime perpetrated against women, increased pre-trial detention of the accused, imposed automatic and mandatory restitution on those convicted, and allowed civil redress in cases prosecutors chose to leave unprosecuted.
	Violence Against Women Act was drafted by then-U.S. Senator Joseph R. Biden's office with support from a number of advocacy organizations including National Coalition Against Sexual Assault, National Coalition Against Domestic Violence, Legal Momentum and The National Organization for Women, which described the bill as "the greatest breakthrough in civil rights for women in nearly two decades."
	Violence Against Women Act was reauthorized by Congress in 2000, and again in December 2005. The bill was signed into law by President George W. Bush on January 5, 2006.
Assisted suicide	Assisted suicide is the common term for controversial actions by which an individual helps another person die upon their wanting to do so--a concept almost always reserved for people who are terminally ill. "Assistance" may mean providing one with the means (drugs or equipment) to end their own lives, but may extend to other actions. The current waves of global public debate have been ongoing for decades, centering on legal, religious, and moral conceptions of "suicide" and a personal "right to death".

Chapter 3. Federalism and the Separation of Powers

Suicide	Suicide is the act of a human being intentionally causing his or her own death. Suicide is often committed out of despair, or attributed to some underlying mental disorder which includes depression, bipolar disorder, schizophrenia, alcoholism and drug abuse. Financial difficulties, troubles with interpersonal relationships and other undesirable situations play a significant role.
Baron	Baron is a title of nobility. The word baron comes from Old French baron, itself from Old High German and Latin (liber) baro meaning "(free) man, (free) warrior"; it merged with cognate Old English beorn meaning "nobleman". Barons in the United Kingdom and the Commonwealth In the British peer system, barons rank below viscounts, and form the lowest rank in the peerage.
Montesquieu	Charles-Louis de Secondat, baron de La Brède et de Montesquieu, generally referred to as simply Montesquieu, was a French social commentator and political thinker who lived during the Enlightenment. He is famous for his articulation of the theory of separation of powers, taken for granted in modern discussions of government and implemented in many constitutions throughout the world. He was largely responsible for the popularization of the terms feudalism and Byzantine Empire.
New Deal	The New Deal is a programme of active labour market policies introduced in the United Kingdom by the Labour government in 1998, initially funded by a one off £5bn windfall tax on privatised utility companies. The stated purpose is to reduce unemployment by providing training, subsidised employment and voluntary work to the unemployed. Spending on the New Deal was £1.3 billion in 2001.
Leviathan	Leviathan, Forme and Power of a Common Wealth Ecclesiasticall and Civil, commonly called Leviathan, is a book written by Thomas Hobbes which was published in 1651. It is titled after the biblical Leviathan. The book concerns the structure of society and legitimate government, and is regarded as one of the earliest and most influential examples of social contract theory. The publisher was Andrew Crooke, partner in Andrew Crooke and William Cooke.

Chapter 3. Federalism and the Separation of Powers

Corporate action	A corporate action is an event initiated by a public company that affects the securities (equity or debt) issued by the company. Some corporate actions such as a dividend (for equity securities) or coupon payment (for debt securities (bonds)) may have a direct financial impact on the shareholders or bondholders; another example is a call (early redemption) of a debt security. Other corporate actions such as stock split may have an indirect impact, as the increased liquidity of shares may cause the price of the stock to rise.
Supremacy	The supremacy of EU law is a principle of by which the laws of European Union member states that conflict with laws of the European Union must be ignored by national courts so that the European Union law can take effect. The legal doctrine emerged from the European Court of Justice through a number of decisions. Development In Costa v. ENEL. Mr Costa was an Italian citizen opposed to nationalising energy.
Afghanistan	Afghanistan officially the Islamic Republic of Afghanistan, is a landlocked and mountainous country in south-central Asia. It is bordered by Pakistan in the south and east, Iran in the west, Turkmenistan, Uzbekistan and Tajikistan in the north, and China in the far northeast. The territories now comprising Afghanistan have been an ancient focal point of the Silk Road and human migration.
Allegiance	An allegiance is a duty of fidelity said to be owed by a subject or a citizen to his/her state or sovereign. Etymology From Middle English ligeaunce . The al- prefix was probably added through confusion with another legal term, allegeance, an "allegation" .
Pledge	A pledge is a bailment or deposit of personal property to a creditor to secure repayment for some debt or engagement, The term is also used to denote the property which constitutes the security.

Chapter 3. Federalism and the Separation of Powers

	Pledge is the ravi of Roman law, from which most of the modern law on the subject is derived. It differs from hypothecation and from the more usual mortgage in that the pledge is in the possession of the pledgee; it also differs from mortgage in being confined to personal property (rather than real property).
Divided government	In the United States, divided government describes a situation in which one party controls the White House and another party controls one or both houses of the United States Congress. Divided government is suggested by some to be an undesirable product of the separation of powers in the United States' political system. Earlier in the 20th century, divided government was rare.
Eminent domain	Eminent domain compulsory purchase (United Kingdom, New Zealand, Ireland), resumption/compulsory acquisition (Australia) or expropriation (South Africa and Canada) is an action of the state to seize a citizen's private property, expropriate property, or seize a citizen's rights in property with due monetary compensation, but without the owner's consent. The property is taken either for government use or by delegation to third parties who will devote it to public or civic use or, in some cases, economic development. The most common uses of property taken by eminent domain are for public utilities, highways, and railroads, however it may also be taken for reasons of public safety, such as in the case of Centralia, Pennsylvania.
Executive privilege	In the United States government, executive privilege is the power claimed by the President of the United States and other members of the executive branch to resist certain subpoenas and other interventions by the legislative and judicial branches of government. The concept of executive privilege is not mentioned explicitly in the United States Constitution, but the Supreme Court of the United States ruled it to be an element of the separation of powers doctrine, and/or derived from the supremacy of executive branch in its own area of Constitutional activity. The Supreme Court confirmed the legitimacy of this doctrine in United States v. Nixon, but only to the extent of confirming that there is a qualified privilege.
Marbury v. Madison	Marbury v. Madison, 5 U.S. (1 Cranch) 137 (1803) is a landmark case in United States law

Chapter 3. Federalism and the Separation of Powers

	This case resulted from a petition to the Supreme Court by William Marbury, who had been appointed by President John Adams as Justice of the Peace in the District of Columbia but whose commission was not subsequently delivered.
Ireland	Ireland is the third-largest island in Europe and the twentieth-largest island in the world. It lies to the northwest of continental Europe and is surrounded by hundreds of islands and islets. To the east of Ireland is Great Britain, separated from it by the Irish Sea.
LINCOLN	Lincoln was a parliamentary electorate in the Canterbury region of New Zealand from 1881 to 1890. The electorate was represented by two Members of Parliament: - Arthur Pyne O'Callaghan (1881-89), and - Alfred Saunders (1889-90)
Northern Ireland	Northern Ireland is one of the four countries of the United Kingdom. Situated in the north-east of the island of Ireland, it shares a border with the Republic of Ireland to the south and west. At the time of the 2001 UK Census, its population was 1,685,000, constituting about 30% of the island's total population and about 3% of the population of the United Kingdom.
Rasul v. Bush	Rasul v. Bush, 542 U.S. 466 (2004), is a landmark United States Supreme Court decision establishing that the U.S. court system has the authority to decide whether foreign nationals (non-U.S. citizens) held in Guantanamo Bay were wrongfully imprisoned. The 6-3 ruling on June 28, 2004, reversed a District Court decision, which held that the Judiciary had no jurisdiction to handle wrongful imprisonment cases involving foreign nationals who are held in Guantanamo Bay. Justice John Paul Stevens wrote the majority opinion and was joined by Sandra Day O'Connor, David Souter, Ruth Bader Ginsburg, and Stephen Breyer, with Anthony Kennedy concurring.

Chapter 3. Federalism and the Separation of Powers

United States v. Nixon	United States v. Nixon, 418 U.S. 683 (1974), was a landmark United States Supreme Court decision. It was a unanimous 8-0 ruling involving President Richard Nixon and was important to the late stages of the Watergate scandal. It is considered a crucial precedent limiting the power of any U.S. president.
Discretion	Discretion is a noun in the English language. Meanings - "The Art of suiting action to particular circumstances" (Lord Scarman) - 'the quality of being discreet' (Concise Oxford Dictionary) Those in a position of power are most often able to exercise discretion as to how they will apply or exercise that power. In the criminal justice system In the criminal justice system, police, prosecutors, judges, and the jury are often able to exercise a degree of discretion in deciding who will be subject to criminal penalties and how they will be punished.
Habeas corpus	Habeas corpus is a writ, or legal action, through which a prisoner can be released from unlawful detention. The remedy can be sought by the prisoner or by another person coming to his aid. Habeas corpus originated in the English legal system, but it is now available in many nations.
Judicial discretion	Judicial discretion is the power of the judiciary to make some legal decisions according to their discretion. Under the doctrine of the separation of powers, the ability of judges to exercise discretion is an aspect of judicial independence. Where appropriate, judicial discretion allows a judge to decide a legal case or matter within a range of possible decisions.

Chapter 3. Federalism and the Separation of Powers

Judicial review	Judicial review is the doctrine under which legislative and executive actions are subject to review, and possible invalidation, by the judiciary. Specific courts with judicial review power must annul the acts of the state when it finds them incompatible with a higher authority, such as the terms of a written constitution. Judicial review is an example of the functioning of separation of powers in a modern governmental system (where the judiciary is one of three branches of government).
Line-item veto	In government, the line-item veto, is the power of an executive authority to nullify or cancel specific provisions of a bill, usually a budget appropriations bill, without vetoing the entire legislative package. The line-item vetoes are usually subject to the possibility of legislative override as are traditional vetoes.
Prison	A prison is a place in which people are physically confined and, usually, deprived of a range of personal freedoms. Imprisonment or incarceration is a legal penalty that may be imposed by the state for the commission of a crime. Other terms are penitentiary, correctional facility, and gaol (or jail).
Resolution	In policy debate, a resolution is a normative statement which the affirmative team affirms and the negative team negates. Resolutions are selected annually by affiliated schools. At the college level, a number of topics are proposed and interested parties write 'topic papers' discussing the pros and cons of that individual topic.
Deference	Deference is the acknowledgement of the legitimacy of the power of one's superior or superiors. Deference implies a yielding or submitting to the judgment of a recognized superior out of respect or reverence. Deference has been studied extensively by political scientists, sociologists, and psychologists.
Party system	A party system is a concept in comparative political science concerning the system of government by political parties in a democratic country. The idea is that political parties have basic similarities: they control the government, have a stable base of mass popular support, and create internal mechanisms for controlling funding, information and nominations.

Chapter 3. Federalism and the Separation of Powers

The concept was originated by European scholars studying the United States, especially James Bryce and Moisey Ostrogorsky, and has been expanded to cover other democracies.

Political Parties

Political Parties: A Sociological Study of the Oligarchical Tendencies of Modern Democracy is a book by sociologist Robert Michels, published in 1911, and first introducing the concept of iron law of oligarchy. It is considered one of the classics of sociology and political science.

This work analyzes the power structures of organizations such as political parties and trade unions.

Chapter 3. Federalism and the Separation of Powers

Chapter 3. Federalism and the Separation of Powers

Chapter 4. Civil Liberties and Civil Rights

Poland	Poland officially the Republic of Poland - is a country in Central Europe bordered by Germany to the west; the Czech Republic and Slovakia to the south; Ukraine, Belarus and Lithuania to the east; and the Baltic Sea and Kaliningrad Oblast, a Russian exclave, to the north. The total area of Poland is 312,679 square kilometres (120,726 sq mi), making it the 69th largest country in the world and the 9th largest in Europe. Poland has a population of over 38 million people, which makes it the 34th most populous country in the world and the sixth most populous member of the European Union, being its most populous post-communist member.
Rights	Rights are legal, social, or ethical principles of freedom or entitlement; that is, rights are the fundamental normative rules about what is allowed of people or owed to people, according to some legal system, social convention, or ethical theory. Rights are of essential importance in such disciplines as law and ethics, especially theories of justice and deontology. Rights are often considered fundamental to civilization, being regarded as established pillars of society and culture, and the history of social conflicts can be found in the history of each right and its development.
Police	The police are persons empowered to enforce the law, protect property and reduce civil disorder. Their powers include the legitimized use of force. The term is most commonly associated with police services of a state that are authorized to exercise the police power of that state within a defined legal or territorial area of responsibility.
Police power	In United States constitutional law, police power is the capacity of the federal government and the states to regulate behavior and enforce order within their territory for the betterment of the general welfare, morals, health, and safety of their inhabitants. Under the 10th Amendment to the United States Constitution, the powers prohibited from or not delegated to the Federal Government are reserved to the states respectively, or to the people. This implies that the states do not possess all possible powers, since some of these are reserved to the people.
Power	Power is a measure of an entity's ability to control its environment, including the behavior of other entities. The term authority is often used for power, perceived as legitimate by the social structure. Power can be seen as evil or unjust, but the exercise of power is accepted as endemic to humans as social beings.

Chapter 4. Civil Liberties and Civil Rights

Terrorism	Terrorism is the systematic use of terror especially as a means of coercion. No universally agreed, legally binding, criminal law definition of terrorism currently exists. Common definitions of terrorism refer only to those violent acts which are intended to create fear (terror), are perpetrated for a religious, political or ideological goal, deliberately target or disregard the safety of non-combatants (civilians), and are committed by non-government agencies.
Bill of rights	A bill of rights is a list of the most important rights of the citizens of a country. The purpose of these bills is to protect those rights against infringement by the government. The term "bill of rights" originates from England, where it referred to the Bill of Rights 1689. Bills of rights may be entrenched or unentrenched.
Constitutional convention	A constitutional convention is an informal and uncodified procedural agreement that is followed by the institutions of a state. In some states, notably those Commonwealth of Nations states which follow the Westminster system and whose political systems are derived from British constitutional law, most of the functions of government are guided by constitutional convention rather than by a formal written constitution. In these states, the actual distribution of power may be markedly different from those which are described in the formal constitutional documents.
National Convention	During the French Revolution, the National Convention, in France, comprised the constitutional and legislative assembly which sat from 20 September 1792 to 26 October 1795. It held executive power in France during the first years of the French First Republic. It was succeeded by the Directory, commencing 2 November 1795. Prominent members of the original Convention included Maximilien Robespierre of the Jacobin Club, Jean-Paul Marat (affiliated with the Jacobins, though never a formal member), and Georges Danton of the Cordeliers.
Federalist	The term federalist describes several political beliefs around the world. Also, it may refer to the concept of federalism or the type of government called a federation. In early United States history, the Federalist Party was one of the first political parties; its members or supporters called themselves Federalists.
Hamilton	Hamilton is a former New Zealand Parliamentary electorate, which was replaced by Hamilton East and Hamilton West electorates. Population centres The electorate was mainly urban, covering the city of Hamilton. History

Chapter 4. Civil Liberties and Civil Rights

	The Hamilton electorate dates from 1922. In 1969 it was renamed Hamilton West.
Alexander Hamilton	Alexander Hamilton was a Scottish sea captain, privateer and merchant.
James Madison	James Madison, Jr. (March 16, 1751 - June 28, 1836) was an American politician and political philosopher who served as the fourth President of the United States (1809-1817) and is considered one of the Founding Fathers of the United States.
	He was the principal author of the United States Constitution, and is often called the "Father of the Constitution".
Senate	A senate is a deliberative assembly, often the upper house or chamber of a legislature or parliament. There have been many such bodies in history, since senate means the assembly of the eldest and wiser members of the society and ruling class. Two of the first official senates were the Spartan Gerousia (Γερουσ?α) and the Roman Senate.
George Washington	George Washington is a public artwork that is a copy of an original bust created by French artist and neoclassical sculptor Jean Antoine Houdon, displayed inside of the Indiana Statehouse, which is located in Indianapolis, Indiana, USA. The bust is made of white plaster and its dimensions are 25x18x18 inches.
	Description
	This piece is a bust of the first President of the United States, George Washington. It is made of white plaster, and its dimensions are 25x18x18 inches.
Federal government	A federal government is the common government of a federation. The structure of federal governments varies from institution to institution. Based on a broad definition of a basic federal political system, there are two or more levels of government that exist within an established territory and govern through common institutions with overlapping or shared powers as prescribed by a constitution.

Chapter 4. Civil Liberties and Civil Rights

Government	In the social sciences, the term government refers to the particular group of people, the administrative bureaucracy, who control a state at a given time, and the manner in which their governing organizations are structured. That is, governments are the means through which state power is employed. States are served by a continuous succession of different governments.
Corporation	In feudal Europe, corporations were aggregations of business interests in compact, usually with an explicit license from city, church, or national leaders. These functioned as effective monopolies for a particular good or labor.
	The term "corporation" was used as late as the 18th century in England to refer to such ventures as the East India Company or the Hudson's Bay Company: commercial organizations that operated under royal patent to have exclusive rights to a particular area of trade.
Citizenship	Citizenship is the state of being a citizen of a particular social, political, or national community.
	Citizenship status, under social contract theory, carries with it both rights and responsibilities. "Active citizenship" is the philosophy that citizens should work towards the betterment of their community through economic participation, public, volunteer work, and other such efforts to improve life for all citizens.
Central government	A central government, union government and in federal states, the federal government, is the government at the level of the nation-state. The structure of central governments varies from institution to institution. Many countries have created autonomous regions by delegating powers from the central government to governments at a subnational level, such as a regional, local, or state level.
Nationalization	Nationalization, also spelled nationalisation, is the process of taking an industry or assets into the public ownership of a national government or state. Nationalization usually refers to private assets, but may also mean assets owned by lower levels of government, such as municipalities, being transferred to the public sector to be operated by or owned by the state. The opposite of nationalization is usually privatization or de-nationalisation, but may also be municipalization.

Chapter 4. Civil Liberties and Civil Rights

State	Many sovereign independent state are made up of a number of country subdivisions also called states. In some cases, such as the United States, the national government arose from a union of sovereign entities, which transferred some of their powers to the national government, while retaining the remainder of their sovereignty. These are sometimes called federal states.
Civil War	"Civil War" is a song by the hard rock band Guns N' Roses, which originally appeared on the 1990 album Nobody's Child: Romanian Angel Appeal. It is a protest song on war, referring to all war as 'civil war' and that it only "feeds the rich while it buries the poor." In the song, singer Axl Rose asks, "What's so civil about war, anyway?"
	"Civil War" was the brainchild of the Guns N' Roses artists Slash, Axl Rose, and Duff McKagan. Slash stated that the song was an instrumental he had written right before the band left for the Japanese leg of its Appetite for Destruction world tour.
Commission	A commission is a physical document issued to certify the appointment of a commissioned officer by a sovereign power.
	The more specific terms commissioning parchment or commissioning scroll are often used to avoid ambiguity, due to "commission" being a homonym which directs the individual in carrying out their duty regardless of what authority or responsibility they may have at any time. However the document is not usually in the form of a scroll and is more often printed on paper instead of parchment.
Democrats	The Democrats is a centre-right political party in Brazil, considered the main in the right-wing spectrum. Despite its former name (Liberal Front Party), the party affiliates itself to the Centrist Democrat International, and the International Democrat Union. The name comes from its support to free market policies.
Prison	A prison is a place in which people are physically confined and, usually, deprived of a range of personal freedoms. Imprisonment or incarceration is a legal penalty that may be imposed by the state for the commission of a crime. Other terms are penitentiary, correctional facility, and gaol (or jail).

Chapter 4. Civil Liberties and Civil Rights

Secession	Secession is the act of withdrawing from an organization, union, or especially a political entity. Threats of secession also can be a strategy for achieving more limited goals. Secession theory Mainstream political theory largely ignored theories of secession until the dissolution of the Soviet Union, Yugoslavia and Czechoslovakia in the early 1990s through secession.
Court	A court is a form of tribunal, often a governmental institution, with the authority to adjudicate legal disputes between parties and carry out the administration of justice in civil, criminal, and administrative matters in accordance with the rule of law. In both common law and civil law legal systems, courts are the central means for dispute resolution, and it is generally understood that all persons have an ability to bring their claims before a court. Similarly, the rights of those accused of a crime include the right to present a defense before a court.
Due process	Due process is the principle that the government must respect all of the legal rights that are owed to a person according to the law. Due process holds the government subservient to the law of the land protecting individual persons from the state. When a government harms a person, without following the exact course of the law, then that is a due process violation which offends the rule of law.
Eminent domain	Eminent domain compulsory purchase (United Kingdom, New Zealand, Ireland), resumption/compulsory acquisition (Australia) or expropriation (South Africa and Canada) is an action of the state to seize a citizen's private property, expropriate property, or seize a citizen's rights in property with due monetary compensation, but without the owner's consent. The property is taken either for government use or by delegation to third parties who will devote it to public or civic use or, in some cases, economic development. The most common uses of property taken by eminent domain are for public utilities, highways, and railroads, however it may also be taken for reasons of public safety, such as in the case of Centralia, Pennsylvania.
Double jeopardy	Double jeopardy is a procedural defense that forbids a defendant from being tried again on the same, or similar charges following a legitimate acquittal or conviction. At common law a defendant may plead autrefois acquit or autrefois convict (a peremptory plea), meaning the defendant has been acquitted or convicted of the same offense. If this issue is raised, evidence will be placed before the court, which will normally rule as a preliminary matter whether the plea is substantiated, and if it so finds, the projected trial will be prevented from proceeding.

Chapter 4. Civil Liberties and Civil Rights

Policy	A policy is typically described as a principle or rule to guide decisions and achieve rational outcome(s). The term is not normally used to denote what is actually done, this is normally referred to as either procedure or protocol. Whereas a policy will contain the 'what' and the 'why', procedures or protocols contain the 'what', the 'how', the 'where', and the 'when'.
Brown v. Board of Education	Brown v. Board of Education of Topeka, 347 U.S. 483 (1954), was a landmark decision of the United States Supreme Court that declared state laws establishing separate public schools for black and white students unconstitutional. The decision overturned the Plessy v. Ferguson decision of 1896 which allowed state-sponsored segregation. Handed down on May 17, 1954, the Warren Court's unanimous (9-0) decision stated that "separate educational facilities are inherently unequal." As a result, de jure racial segregation was ruled a violation of the Equal Protection Clause of the Fourteenth Amendment of the United States Constitution.
Plessy v. Ferguson	Plessy v. Ferguson, 163 U.S. 537 (1896), is a landmark United States Supreme Court decision in the jurisprudence of the United States, upholding the constitutionality of state laws requiring racial segregation in private businesses (particularly railroads), under the doctrine of "separate but equal". The decision was handed down by a vote of 7 to 1 with the majority opinion written by Justice Henry Billings Brown and the dissent written by Justice John Marshall Harlan. Associate Justice David Josiah Brewer was absent at the ruling because of his daughter's sudden death the day before.
Duncan v. Louisiana	Duncan v. Louisiana, 391 U.S. 145 (1968), was a significant United States Supreme Court decision which incorporated the Sixth Amendment right to a jury trial and applied it to the states. Background of the case In October, 1966, Gary Duncan, a 19-year old African-American, was driving down a Louisiana highway when he noticed his two cousins with a group of white youths on the side of the road. He became concerned because his cousins had reported occurrences of "racial incidents" at the recently de-segregated school.

Chapter 4. Civil Liberties and Civil Rights

Gideon v. Wainwright	Gideon v. Wainwright, 372 U.S. 335 (1963), is a landmark case in United States Supreme Court history. In the case, the Supreme Court unanimously ruled that state courts are required under the Sixth Amendment of the Constitution to provide counsel in criminal cases for defendants who are unable to afford their own attorneys. Background of the case Between midnight and 8:00 am on June 3, 1961, a burglary occurred at the Bay Harbor Pool Room in Panama City, Florida.
Louisiana	Louisiana was the name of an administrative district of the Viceroyalty of New Spain from 1764 to 1803 that represented territory west of the Mississippi River basin, plus New Orleans. Spain acquired the territory from France: see Louisiana. History The area, comprising what is now known as the Louisiana Purchase, was turned over to the French for a few days in 1803 before it, in turn, was turned over to the United States.
Exclusionary rule	The exclusionary rule is a legal principle in the United States, under constitutional law, which holds that evidence collected or analyzed in violation of the defendant's constitutional rights is sometimes inadmissible for a criminal prosecution in a court of law. This may be considered an example of a prophylactic rule formulated by the judiciary in order to protect a constitutional right. However, in some circumstances at least, the exclusionary rule may also be considered to follow directly from the constitutional language, such as the Fifth Amendment's command that no person "shall be compelled in any criminal case to be a witness against himself" and that no person "shall be deprived of life, liberty or property without due process of law".

Chapter 4. Civil Liberties and Civil Rights

Strict scrutiny	Strict scrutiny is the most stringent standard of judicial review used by United States courts reviewing federal law. Along with the lower standards of rational basis review and exacting or intermediate scrutiny, strict scrutiny is part of a hierarchy of standards employed by courts to weigh an asserted government interest against a constitutional right or principle that conflicts with the manner in which the interest is being pursued. Strict scrutiny is applied based on the constitutional conflict at issue regardless of whether a law or action of the U.S. federal government, a state government, or a local municipality is at issue.
Advancement	Advancement is a common law doctrine of intestate succession that presumes that gifts given to a person's heir during that person's life are intended as an advance on what that heir would inherit upon the death of the parent. For example, suppose person P had two children, A and B. Suppose also that P had $100,000, and gave $20,000 to child A before P's death, leaving $80,000 in P's estate. If P died without a will, and A and B were P's only heirs, A and B would be entitled to split P's estate evenly.
Colored	Colored in the U.S.A (also coloured in Canadian, British and Commonwealth spelling) is a term once widely regarded as a description of black people (i.e., persons of sub-Saharan African ancestry; members of the "Black race") and Native Americans. It should not be confused with the more recent term people of color, which attempts to describe all "non-white peoples", not just black people. Today it is generally no longer regarded as a politically correct term, however even that is debatable, due to its continued occasional appearance, most notably its use in the acronym NAACP. Carla Sims, communications director for the NAACP in Washington, D.C., said "The term 'colored' is not derogatory, [the NAACP] chose the word 'colored' because it was the most positive description commonly used at that time.
Civil liberties	Civil liberties are rights and freedoms that provide an individual specific rights such as the right to life, freedom from torture, freedom from slavery and forced labour, the right to liberty and security, right to a fair trial, the right to defend one's self, the right to privacy, freedom of conscience, freedom of expression, freedom of assembly and association, and the right to marry and have a family. Within the distinctions between civil liberties and other types of liberty, it is important to note the distinctions between positive rights and negative rights.

Chapter 4. Civil Liberties and Civil Rights

	Common civil liberties include the rights of people, freedom of religion, and freedom of speech, and additionally, the right to due process, to a trial, to own property, and to privacy.
Election	An election is a formal decision-making process by which a population chooses an individual to hold public office. Elections have been the usual mechanism by which modern representative democracy operates since the 17th century. Elections may fill offices in the legislature, sometimes in the executive and judiciary, and for regional and local government.
Idea	In the most narrow sense, an idea is just whatever is before the mind when one thinks. Very often, ideas are construed as representational images; i.e. images of some object. In other contexts, ideas are taken to be concepts, although abstract concepts do not necessarily appear as images.
Interest	Interest is a fee paid on borrowed assets. It is the price paid for the use of borrowed money, or, money earned by deposited funds. Assets that are sometimes lent with interest include money, shares, consumer goods through hire purchase, major assets such as aircraft, and even entire factories in finance lease arrangements.
Henry	Saint Henry was a medieval Swedish clergyman. According to legends, he conquered Finland together with King Eric the Saint of Sweden and died as a martyr, becoming a central figure in the local Roman Catholic Church. However, the authenticity of the accounts of his life, ministry, and death are widely disputed.
United States	The United States of America (also referred to as the United States, the U.S., the USA, or America) is a federal constitutional republic comprising fifty states and a federal district. The country is situated mostly in central North America, where its forty-eight contiguous states and Washington, D.C., the capital district, lie between the Pacific and Atlantic Oceans, bordered by Canada to the north and Mexico to the south. The state of Alaska is in the northwest of the continent, with Canada to the east and Russia to the west across the Bering Strait.
Allegiance	An allegiance is a duty of fidelity said to be owed by a subject or a citizen to his/her state or sovereign.
	Etymology

Chapter 4. Civil Liberties and Civil Rights

	From Middle English ligeaunce . The al- prefix was probably added through confusion with another legal term, allegeance, an "allegation" .
Cold War	The Cold War was the continuing state of political conflict, military tension, proxy wars, and economic competition existing after World War II (1939-1945) between the Communist World - primarily the Soviet Union and its satellite states and allies - and the powers of the Western world, primarily the United States and its allies. Although the primary participants' military force never officially clashed directly, they expressed the conflict through military coalitions, strategic conventional force deployments, extensive aid to states deemed vulnerable, proxy wars, espionage, propaganda, conventional and nuclear arms races, appeals to neutral nations, rivalry at sports events, and technological competitions such as the Space Race.
	Despite being allies against the Axis powers, the USSR and the US disagreed about political philosophy and the configuration of the post-war world while occupying most of Europe.
Pledge	A pledge is a bailment or deposit of personal property to a creditor to secure repayment for some debt or engagement, The term is also used to denote the property which constitutes the security.
	Pledge is the ravi of Roman law, from which most of the modern law on the subject is derived. It differs from hypothecation and from the more usual mortgage in that the pledge is in the possession of the pledgee; it also differs from mortgage in being confined to personal property (rather than real property).

Chapter 4. Civil Liberties and Civil Rights

Pledge of Allegiance	The Pledge of Allegiance of the United States is an oath of loyalty to the national flag and the republic of the United States of America, originally composed by Francis Bellamy in 1892. The Pledge has been modified four times since then, with the most recent change adding the words "under God" in 1954. Congressional sessions open with the swearing of the Pledge, as do government meetings at local levels, meetings held by the Knights of Columbus, Royal Rangers, Boy Scouts of America, Girl Scouts of the USA, Fraternal Order of Eagles, Freemasons, Toastmasters International and their concordant bodies, as well as other organizations. The current version of the Pledge of Allegiance reads: The pledge was supposed to be quick and to the point. Bellamy designed it to be recited in 15 seconds.
Voting	Voting is a method for a group such as a meeting or an electorate to make a decision or express an opinion--often following discussions, debates, or election campaigns. It is often found in democracies and republics. Reasons for voting In a representative government, voting commonly implies election: a way for an electorate to select among candidates for office.
Charter	A charter is the grant of authority or rights, stating that the granter formally recognizes the prerogative of the recipient to exercise the rights specified. It is implicit that the granter retains superiority (or sovereignty), and that the recipient admits a limited (or inferior) status within the relationship, and it is within that sense that charters were historically granted, and that sense is retained in modern usage of the term. Also, charter can simply be a document giving royal permission to start a colony.

Chapter 4. Civil Liberties and Civil Rights

Charter school	Charter schools in the United States are primary or secondary schools that receive public money (and like other schools, may also receive private donations) but are not subject to some of the rules, regulations, and statutes that apply to other public schools in exchange for some type of accountability for producing certain results, which are set forth in each school's charter. Charter schools are opened and attended by choice. While charter schools provide an alternative to other public schools, they are part of the public education system and are not allowed to charge tuition.
School voucher	A school voucher, is a certificate issued by the government, which parents can apply toward tuition at a private school (or, by extension, to reimburse home schooling expenses), rather than at the state school to which their child is assigned. An alternative to the education voucher is the education tax credit, which allows individuals to use their own money to pay for the education of their children or to donate money towards the education other children. Under non-voucher education systems citizens who currently pay for private schooling are still taxed for public schools, therefore they fund both public and private schools simultaneously.
Freedom	Freedom is a London-based anarchist newspaper published fortnightly by Freedom Press. The paper was started in 1886 by volunteers including Peter Kropotkin and Charlotte Wilson and continues to this day as an unpaid project. Originally, the subtitle was "A Journal of Anarchist Socialism." The title was changed to "A Journal of Anarchist Communism" in June 1889. Today it is unlabelled.
Religious Freedom Restoration Act	The Religious Freedom Restoration Act of 1993, Pub. L. No. 103-141, 107 Stat. 1488 (Nov. 16, 1993), codified at 42 U.S.C. § 2000bb through 42 U.S.C. § 2000bb-4 (also known as Religious Freedom Restoration Act), is a 1993 United States federal law aimed at preventing laws that substantially burden a person's free exercise of their religion. The bill was introduced by Howard McKeon of California and Dean Gallo of New Jersey on March 11, 1993. The bill is sometimes unofficially referred to as one of the American Indian Religious Freedom Act Amendments.

Chapter 4. Civil Liberties and Civil Rights

Restoration	The Restoration of the monarchy began in 1660 when the English, Scottish and Irish monarchies were all restored under Charles II after the republic that followed the Wars of the Three Kingdoms. The term Restoration may apply both to the actual event by which the monarchy was restored, and to the period immediately following the event. Caribbean Barbados, as a haven for refugees fleeting the English republic, had held for Charles II under Lord Willoughby until defeated by George Ayscue.
Virginia	The Commonwealth of Virginia is a U.S. state on the Atlantic Coast of the Southern United States. Virginia is nicknamed the "Old Dominion" and sometimes the "Mother of Presidents" because it is the birthplace of eight U.S. presidents. The geography and climate of the state are shaped by the Blue Ridge Mountains and the Chesapeake Bay, which provide habitat for much of its flora and fauna.
Discretion	Discretion is a noun in the English language. Meanings - "The Art of suiting action to particular circumstances" (Lord Scarman) - 'the quality of being discreet' (Concise Oxford Dictionary) Those in a position of power are most often able to exercise discretion as to how they will apply or exercise that power. In the criminal justice system In the criminal justice system, police, prosecutors, judges, and the jury are often able to exercise a degree of discretion in deciding who will be subject to criminal penalties and how they will be punished.

Chapter 4. Civil Liberties and Civil Rights

Freedom of speech	Freedom of speech is the freedom to speak freely without censorship or limitation, or both. The synonymous term freedom of expression is sometimes used to indicate not only freedom of verbal speech but any act of seeking, receiving and imparting information or ideas, regardless of the medium used. In practice, the right to freedom of speech is not absolute in any country and the right is commonly subject to limitations, such as on "hate speech".
Judicial discretion	Judicial discretion is the power of the judiciary to make some legal decisions according to their discretion. Under the doctrine of the separation of powers, the ability of judges to exercise discretion is an aspect of judicial independence. Where appropriate, judicial discretion allows a judge to decide a legal case or matter within a range of possible decisions.
Judicial review	Judicial review is the doctrine under which legislative and executive actions are subject to review, and possible invalidation, by the judiciary. Specific courts with judicial review power must annul the acts of the state when it finds them incompatible with a higher authority, such as the terms of a written constitution. Judicial review is an example of the functioning of separation of powers in a modern governmental system (where the judiciary is one of three branches of government).
Congress	A congress is a formal meeting of the representatives of different nations, constituent states, independent organizations (such as trade unions), or groups. The term was chosen for the United States Congress to emphasize the status of each state represented there as a self-governing unit. Subsequent to the use of congress by the U.S. legislature, the term has been incorrectly adopted by many states within unions, and by unitary nation-states in the Americas, to refer to their legislatures.
Espionage	Espionage is considered secret or confidential without the permission of the holder of the information. Espionage is inherently clandestine, lest the legitimate holder of the information change plans or take other countermeasures once it is known that the information is in unauthorized hands. Espionage is usually part of an institutional effort by a government or corporation, and the term is most readily associated with state spying on potential or actual enemies, primarily for military purposes.

Chapter 4. Civil Liberties and Civil Rights

Exploitation	The term exploitation may carry two distinct meanings: • The act of using something for any purpose. In this case, exploit is a synonym for use. • The act of using something in an unjust or cruel manner. It is this meaning of exploitation which is discussed below. As unjust benefit In political economy, economics, and sociology, exploitation involves a persistent social relationship in which certain persons are being mistreated or unfairly used for the benefit of others.
Buckley v. Valeo	Buckley v. Valeo, 424 U.S. 1 (1976), was a case in which the Supreme Court of the United States upheld a federal law which set limits on campaign contributions, but ruled that spending money to influence elections is a form of constitutionally protected free speech, and struck down portions of the law. The court also stated candidates can give unlimited amounts of money to their own campaigns. Facts In 1974, over the veto of President Gerald R. Ford, the Congress passed significant amendments to the Federal Election Campaign Act of 1971, creating the first comprehensive effort by the federal government to regulate campaign contributions and spending.

Chapter 4. Civil Liberties and Civil Rights

Electoral Commission	An Electoral Commission is an election management body, in charge of overseeing the implementation of election procedures:
	
	- Australia: Australian Electoral Commission
	- Bangladesh: Bangladesh Election Commission
	- Belize: Belize Elections and Boundaries Commission
	- Brazil: Supreme Electoral Court (Brazil)
	- Colombia: National Electoral Council (Colombia)
	- Ghana: Electoral Commission of Ghana
	- Guyana:Guyana Elections Commission
	- Hong Kong: Electoral Affairs Commission
	- India: Election Commission of India
	- Iran: Guardian Council
	- Iraq: Independent High Electoral Commission
	- Kenya:
	    - Electoral Commission of Kenya (defunct)
	    - Interim Independent Electoral Commission
	- Liberia: National Election Commission (Liberia)
	- Malaysia: Election Commission of Malaysia
	- Mexico: Federal Electoral Institute
	- Nepal: Election Commission of Nepal
	- New Zealand: Electoral Commission
	- Pakistan: Election Commission of Pakistan
	- Poland: Panstwowa Komisja Wyborcza (National Electoral Commission)
	- Philippines: Commission on Elections (Philippines)
	- Thailand: Election Commission (Thailand)
	- Ukraine: Central Election Commission of Ukraine
	- United Kingdom: Electoral Commission
	- United States:
	    - Election Assistance Commission, administers Federal elections and establishing standards for State and local governments
	    - Electoral Commission created solely to resolve the disputed 1876 presidential election
	    - Federal Election Commission, regulates campaign finance legislation
	- Uruguay: Electoral Court
	- Zimbabwe: Zimbabwe Electoral Commission

Chapter 4. Civil Liberties and Civil Rights

Reform Act	In the United Kingdom, Reform Act is a generic term used for legislation concerning electoral matters. It is most commonly used for laws passed to enfranchise new groups of voters and to redistribute seats in the British House of Commons. The periodic redrawing of constituency boundaries is now dealt with by a permanent Boundary Commission in each part of the United Kingdom, rather than by a Reform Act.
Watergate scandal	The Watergate scandal was a 1970s United States political scandal resulting from the break-in to the Democratic National Committee headquarters at the Watergate office complex in Washington, D.C. Effects of the scandal ultimately led to the resignation of the President of the United States, Richard Nixon, on August 9, 1974, the first and only resignation of any U.S. President. It also resulted in the indictment, trial, conviction and incarceration of several Nixon administration officials. The affair began with the arrest of five men for breaking and entering into the Democratic National Committee headquarters at the Watergate complex on June 17, 1972. The FBI connected the payments to the burglars to a slush fund used by the 1972 Committee to Re-elect the President.
Bill	A bill is a proposed law under consideration by a legislature. A bill does not become law until it is passed by the legislature and, in most cases, approved by the executive. Once a bill has been enacted into law, it is called an act or a statute.
Flag Desecration Amendment	The Flag Desecration Amendment, often referred to as the flag burning amendment, is a controversial proposed constitutional amendment to the United States Constitution that would allow the United States Congress to statutorily prohibit expression of political views through the physical desecration of the flag of the United States. The concept of flag desecration continues to provoke a heated debate over protecting a national symbol, protecting free speech, and protecting the liberty represented by a national symbol. While the proposed amendment is most frequently referred to colloquially in terms of "flag burning," the language would permit the prohibition of all forms of flag desecration, which may take forms other than burning, such as using the flag for clothing or napkins.

Chapter 4. Civil Liberties and Civil Rights

Symbolic speech	Symbolic speech is a legal term in United States law used to describe actions that purposefully and discernibly convey a particular message or statement to those viewing it. Symbolic speech is recognized as being protected under the First Amendment as a form of speech, but this is not expressly written as such in the document. One possible explanation as to why the Framers did not address this issue in the Bill of rights is because the primary forms for both political debate and protest in their time were verbal expression and published word, and they may have been unaware of the possibility of future people using non-verbal expression.
Speaker	The term speaker is a title often given to the presiding officer (chair) of a deliberative assembly, especially a legislative body. The speaker's official role is to moderate debate, make rulings on procedure, announce the results of votes, and the like. The speaker decides who may speak and has the powers to discipline members who break the procedures of the house.
Assembly	Assembly is a bugle call used to call in a group of soldiers or scouts. It is also sometimes referred to as "Fall in".
Pentagon Papers	The Pentagon Papers, officially titled United States-Vietnam Relations, 1945-1967: A Study Prepared by the Department of Defense, was a top-secret United States Department of Defense history of the United States' political-military involvement in Vietnam from 1945 to 1967. The papers were first brought to the attention of the public on the front page of the New York Times in 1971

Contents

Secretary of Defense Robert McNamara created the Vietnam Study Task Force on June 17, 1967, for the purpose of writing an "encyclopedic history of the Vietnam War". The secretary's motivation for commissioning the study is unclear. |
| Attack | In computer and computer networks an attack is any attempt to destroy, expose, alter, disable, steal or gain unauthorized access to or make unauthorized use of an asset.

Definitions

IETF |

Chapter 4. Civil Liberties and Civil Rights

Internet Engineering Task Force defines attack in RFC 2828 as:

US Government

CNSS Instruction No. 4009 dated 26 April 2010 by Committee on National Security Systems of United States of America defines an attack as:

The increasing dependencies of modern society on information and computers networks (both in private and public sectors, including military) has led to new terms like cyber attack and Cyberwarfare.

CNSS Instruction No. 4009 define a cyber attack as:

Phenomenology

An attack can be active or passive.

An attack can be perpetrated by an insider or from outside the organization;

> An "inside attack" is an attack initiated by an entity inside the security perimeter (an "insider"), i.e., an entity that is authorized to access system resources but uses them in a way not approved by those who granted the authorization.
> An "outside attack" is initiated from outside the perimeter, by an unauthorized or illegitimate user of the system (an "outsider").

Prior restraint	In U.S. law, prior restraint is a form of censorship in which one is prevented, in advance, from communicating certain material, rather than made answerable afterwards. Prior restraint is particularly restrictive because it prevents the forbidden material from being heard or distributed at all. Other restrictions on expression provide sanctions only after the offending material has been communicated, such as suits for slander or libel.

Chapter 4. Civil Liberties and Civil Rights

Vietnam	Vietnam, officially the Socialist Republic of Vietnam is the easternmost country on the Indochina Peninsula in Southeast Asia. It is bordered by People's Republic of China (PRC) to the north, Laos to the northwest, Cambodia to the southwest, and the South China Sea, referred to as East Sea (Vietnamese: Bi?n Đông), to the east. With a population of over 86 million, Vietnam is the 13th most populous country in the world.
Obscenity	An obscenity is any statement or act which strongly offends the prevalent morality of the time, is a profanity, or is otherwise taboo, indecent, abhorrent, or disgusting, or is especially inauspicious. The term is also applied to an object that incorporates such a statement or displays such an act. In a legal context, the term obscenity is most often used to describe expressions (words, images, actions) of an explicitly sexual nature.
Communications Decency Act	The Communications Decency Act of 1996 was the first notable attempt by the United States Congress to regulate pornographic material on the Internet. In 1997, in the landmark cyberlaw case of Reno v. ACLU, the U.S. district court judge Stewart Dalzell partially overturned the law. The Act was Title V of the Telecommunications Act of 1996. It was introduced to the Senate Committee of Commerce, Science, and Transportation by Senators James Exon (D-NE) and Slade Gorton (R-WA) in 1995. The amendment that became the Communications Decency Act was added to the Telecommunications Act in the Senate by an 84-16 vote on June 14, 1995.
Internets	"Internets" is a Bushism-turned-catchphrase used humorously to portray the speaker as ignorant about the Internet or about technology in general, or as having a provincial or folksy attitude toward technology. Former United States President George W. Bush first used the word publicly during the 2000 election campaign. The term gained cachet as an Internet humor meme following Bush's use of the term in the second 2004 presidential election debate on October 8, 2004.

Chapter 4. Civil Liberties and Civil Rights

Caucus	A caucus is a meeting of supporters or members of a political party or movement, especially in the United States. As the use of the term has been expanded the exact definition has come to vary among political cultures.
	Origin of the term
	The origin of the word caucus is debated, but it is generally agreed that it first came into use in the English colonies of North America.
	A February 1763 entry in the diary of John Adams of Braintree, Massachusetts, is one of the earliest appearances of Caucas, already with its modern connotations of a "smoke-filled room" where candidates for public election are pre-selected in private
	This day learned that the Caucas Clubb meets at certain Times in the Garret of Tom Daws, the Adjutant of the Boston Regiment.
Political correctness	Political correctness is a term which denotes language, ideas, policies, and behavior seen as seeking to minimize social and institutional offense in occupational, gender, racial, cultural, sexual orientation, religious belief, disability, and age-related contexts. In current usage, the term is primarily pejorative, while the term politically incorrect has been used as an implicitly positive self-description. Examples of the latter include the conservative Politically Incorrect Guides published by the Regnery editorial house and the television talk show Politically Incorrect.
Morse v. Frederick	Morse v. Frederick, 551 U.S. 393 (2007) was a school speech case in which the United States Supreme Court held that the First Amendment does not prevent educators from suppressing student speech, at a school-supervised event, that is reasonably viewed as promoting illegal drug use.

Chapter 4. Civil Liberties and Civil Rights

	Background. In 2002, high school principal Deborah Morse suspended 18-year-old Joseph Frederick after he displayed a banner reading "BONG HiTS 4 JESUS" across the street from the school during the 2002 Olympic Torch Relay. Frederick sued, claiming his constitutional rights to free speech were violated.
Hate speech	Hate speech is, outside the law, any communication which disparages a person or a group on the basis of some characteristic such as race or sexual orientation. In law, hate speech is any speech, gesture or conduct, writing, or display which is forbidden because it may incite violence or prejudicial action against or by a protected individual or group, or because it disparages or intimidates a protected individual or group. The law may identify a protected individual or a protected group by race, gender, ethnicity, nationality, religion, sexual orientation, or other characteristic.
Sexual harassment	Sexual harassment, is intimidation, bullying or coercion of a sexual nature, or the unwelcome or inappropriate promise of rewards in exchange for sexual favors. In some contexts or circumstances, sexual harassment may be illegal. It includes a range of behavior from seemingly mild transgressions and annoyances to actual sexual abuse or sexual assault.
Medicaid	Medicaid is the United States health program for eligible individuals and families with low incomes and resources. It is a means tested program that is jointly funded by the state and federal governments, and is managed by the states. Among the groups of people served by Medicaid are certain eligible U.S. citizens and resident aliens, including low-income adults and their children, and people with certain disabilities.
Commercial speech	Commercial Speech is speech done on behalf of a company or individual for the intent of making a profit. It is economic in nature and usually has the intent of convincing the audience to partake in a particular action, often purchasing a specific product. Generally, the Supreme Court defines commercial speech as speech that "proposes a commercial transaction." Additionally, the Court developed a three factor inquiry in determining whether speech is commercial in Bolger v. Youngs Drug Products; however, those factors have yet to be utilized in any other Supreme Court case dealing with commercial speech.
Insurance	In law and economics, insurance is a form of risk management primarily used to hedge against the risk of a contingent, uncertain loss. Insurance is defined as the equitable transfer of the risk of a loss, from one entity to another, in exchange for payment. An insurer is a company selling the insurance; an insured, or policyholder, is the person or entity buying the insurance policy.

Chapter 4. Civil Liberties and Civil Rights

Justice	Justice was the weekly newspaper of the Social Democratic Federation (SDF) in the United Kingdom.
	The SDF had been known until January 1884 as the Democratic Federation. With the change of name, the organisation launched the paper.
Sale	Sale was an ancient Greek city located in Thrace, located in the region between the river Nestos to the river Hebros.
Social security	Social security is primarily a social insurance program providing social protection, or protection against socially recognized conditions, including poverty, old age, disability, unemployment and others. Social security may refer to:
	<ul><li>social insurance, where people receive benefits or services in recognition of contributions to an insurance scheme. These services typically include provision for retirement pensions, disability insurance, survivor benefits and unemployment insurance.</li><li>income maintenance--mainly the distribution of cash in the event of interruption of employment, including retirement, disability and unemployment</li><li>services provided by administrations responsible for social security.</li></ul>
Self-incrimination	Self-incrimination is the act of accusing oneself of a crime for which a person can then be prosecuted. Self-incrimination can occur either directly or indirectly: directly, by means of interrogation where information of a self-incriminatory nature is disclosed; indirectly, when information of a self-incriminatory nature is disclosed voluntarily without pressure from another person.
	United States law
	The Fifth Amendment to the United States Constitution protects witnesses from being forced to incriminate themselves.

Chapter 4. Civil Liberties and Civil Rights

Sovereignty	Sovereignty is the quality of having supreme, independent authority over a geographic area, such as a territory. It can be found in a power to rule and make law that rests on a political fact for which no purely legal explanation can be provided. The concept has been discussed, debated and questioned throughout history, from the time of the Romans through to the present day, although it has changed in its definition, concept, and application throughout, especially during the Age of Enlightenment.
Capital punishment	Capital punishment, the death penalty, or execution is the killing of a person by judicial process as a punishment for an offense. Crimes that can result in a death penalty are known as capital crimes or capital offences. The term capital originates from Latin capitalis, literally "regarding the head".
Cruel and unusual punishment	Cruel and unusual punishment is a phrase describing criminal punishment which is considered unacceptable due to the suffering or humiliation it inflicts on the condemned person.
Penalty	In the Mormonism, a penalty was an oath made by participants of the original Nauvoo Endowment instituted by Joseph Smith, Jr. in 1843 and further developed by Brigham Young after Smith's death. Mormon critics refer to the penalty as a blood oath, because it required the participant to swear never to reveal certain key symbols of the Endowment ceremony, including the penalty itself, while symbolically enacting ways in which a person may be executed.
Punishment	Punishment is the authoritative imposition of something negative or unpleasant on a person or animal in response to behavior deemed wrong by an individual or group. The authority may be either a group or a single person, and punishment may be carried out formally under a system of law or informally in other kinds of social settings such as within a family. Negative consequences that are not authorized or that are administered without a breach of rules are not considered to be punishment as defined here.
Escobedo v. Illinois	Escobedo v. Illinois, 378 U.S. 478 (1964), was a United States Supreme Court case holding that criminal suspects have a right to counsel during police interrogations under the Sixth Amendment. The case was decided a year after the court held in Gideon v. Wainwright, 372 U.S. 335 (1963) that indigent criminal defendants had a right to be provided counsel at trial. Danny Escobedo's Sister-in-law, Isabella Wyrosdic, a convict from Chicago, was shot and killed on the night of January 19, 1960. Danny Escobedo was arrested without warrant early the next morning and interrogated.

Chapter 4. Civil Liberties and Civil Rights

ARTHUR	ARTHUR is an abbreviation for mobile "Artillery Hunting Radar" system developed in Sweden. This field artillery acquisition radar was developed for the primary role as the core element of a brigade or division level counter battery sensor system. It can also be used for peace support operations.
Griswold v. Connecticut	Griswold v. Connecticut, 381 U.S. 479 (1965), was a landmark case in which the Supreme Court of the United States ruled that the Constitution protected a right to privacy. The case involved a Connecticut law that prohibited the use of contraceptives. By a vote of 7-2, the Supreme Court invalidated the law on the grounds that it violated the "right to marital privacy".
Prince	Prince is a general term for a ruler, monarch or member of a monarch's or former monarch's family, and is a hereditary title in the nobility of some European states. The feminine equivalent is a princess. The English word derives, via the French word prince, from the Latin noun princeps, from primus(first) + capio(to seize), meaning "the chief, most distinguished, ruler, prince".
Birth control	Birth control is an umbrella term for several techniques and methods use to prevent fertilization or to interrupt pregnancy at various stages. Birth control techniques and methods include contraception (the prevention of fertilization), contragestion (preventing the implantation of the blastocyst) and abortion (the removal or expulsion of a fetus or embryo from the uterus). The techniques and methods frequently overlap and many birth control techniques and methods are not strictly contraceptive as fertilization or conception may occure.
Homeland	A homeland is the concept of the place (cultural geography) to which an ethnic group holds a long history and a deep cultural association with --the country in which a particular national identity began. As a common noun, it simply connotes the country of one's origin.
Homeland security	Homeland security is an umbrella term for security efforts to protect the United States against terrorist activity. The term arose following a reorganization of many U.S. government agencies in 2003 to form the United States Department of Homeland Security after the September 11 attacks, and may be used to refer to the actions of that department, the United States Senate Committee on Homeland Security and Governmental Affairs, or the United States House of Representatives Committee on Homeland Security. In the United States

Chapter 4. Civil Liberties and Civil Rights

	In the United States, the concept of "homeland security" extends and recombines responsibilities of government agencies and entities.
International court	International courts are formed by treaties between nations, or under the authority of an international organization such as the United Nations -- this includes ad hoc tribunals and permanent institutions, but excludes any courts arising purely under national authority.
	Early examples of international courts include the Nuremberg and Tokyo tribunals established in the aftermath of World War II. Three such courts are presently located at The Hague in the Netherlands: The International Criminal Tribunal for the former Yugoslavia (ICTY), the International Court of Justice (ICJ), and the International Criminal Court (ICC). Further international courts exist elsewhere, usually with their jurisdiction restricted to a particular country or issue, such as the one dealing with the genocide in Rwanda.
Treaty	A treaty is an express agreement under international law entered into by actors in international law, namely sovereign states and international organizations. A treaty may also be known as: (international) agreement, protocol, covenant, convention, exchange of letters, etc. Regardless of the terminology, all of these international agreements under international law are equally treaties and the rules are the same.
Abortion	Abortion is the termination of a pregnancy by the removal or expulsion of a fetus or embryo from the uterus, resulting in or caused by its death. An abortion can occur spontaneously due to complications during pregnancy or can be induced, in humans and other species. In the context of human pregnancies, an abortion induced to preserve the health of the gravida (pregnant female) is termed a therapeutic abortion, while an abortion induced for any other reason is termed an elective abortion.
Homosexuality	Homosexuality is romantic and/or sexual attraction or behavior among members of the same sex or gender. As a sexual orientation, homosexuality refers to "an enduring pattern of or disposition to experience sexual, affectional, or romantic attractions" primarily or exclusively to people of the same sex; "it also refers to an individual's sense of personal and social identity based on those attractions, behaviors expressing them, and membership in a community of others who share them."

Chapter 4. Civil Liberties and Civil Rights

	Homosexuality is one of the three main categories of sexual orientation, along with bisexuality and heterosexuality, within the heterosexual-homosexual continuum. The consensus of the behavioral and social sciences and the health and mental health professions is that homosexuality is a normal and positive variation in human sexual orientation, though many religious societies, including Catholicism, Mormonism, and Islam, and some psychological associations, such as NARTH, teach that homosexual activity is sinful or dysfunctional.
Opposition	In politics, the opposition comprises one or more political parties or other organized groups that are opposed to the government, party or group in political control of a city, region, state or country. The degree of opposition varies according to political conditions - for example, across authoritarian and liberal systems where opposition may be repressed or welcomed.
Bowers v. Hardwick	Bowers v. Hardwick, 478 U.S. 186 (1986), is a United States Supreme Court decision that upheld the constitutionality of a Georgia sodomy law criminalizing oral and anal sex in private between consenting adults when applied to homosexuals. Seventeen years after Bowers v. Hardwick, the Supreme Court directly overruled the decision in Lawrence v. Texas, 539 U.S. 558 (2003), and held that such laws are unconstitutional. In overruling Bowers v. Hardwick, the 2003 Court stated that "Bowers was not correct when it was decided, and it is not correct today." In August 1982, an Atlanta Police Department officer entered the bedroom of Michael Hardwick to serve a summons for throwing out a beer bottle which Hardwick had thrown in a trash can located directly outside of the gay bar in which he worked; the specific citation was for public drinking.
Sudan	Sudan officially the Republic of Sudan, Arabic: ??????? ???????? Jumhuriyat al Sudan, is a country in northeastern Africa. It is the largest country in Africa and the Arab world, and tenth largest in the world by area. It is bordered by Egypt to the north, the Red Sea to the northeast, Eritrea and Ethiopia to the east, Kenya and Uganda to the southeast, the Democratic Republic of the Congo and the Central African Republic to the southwest, Chad to the west and Libya to the northwest. The world's longest river, the Nile, divides the country between east and west sides.

Chapter 4. Civil Liberties and Civil Rights

Right to die	The right to die is sometimes associated with the idea that one's body and one's life are one's own, to dispose of as one sees fit. However, there is sometimes deemed to be a legitimate state interest in preventing irrational suicides. Pilpel and Amsel write, "Contemporary proponents of 'rational suicide' or the 'right to die' usually demand by 'rationality' that the decision to kill oneself be both the autonomous choice of the agent (i.e., not due to the physician or the family pressuring them to 'do the right thing' and suicide) and a 'best option under the circumstances' choice desired by the stoics or utilitarians, as well as other natural conditions such as the choice being stable, not an impulsive decision, not due to mental illness, achieved after due deliberation, etc." Hinduism accepts the right to die for those who have no desire, ambition or no responsibilities remaining; and allows death through the non-violent practice of fasting to death (Prayopavesa).
Seat	Seats were territorial-administrative units in the medieval Kingdom of Hungary. The seats were autonomous regions within the Kingdom, and were independent from the feudal county system. Their autonomy was granted in return for the military services they provided to the Hungarian Kings.
Sodomy law	A sodomy law is a law that defines certain sexual acts as crimes. The precise sexual acts meant by the term sodomy are rarely spelled out in the law, but are typically understood by courts to include any sexual act deemed unnatural. It also has a range of similar euphemisms.
Suicide	Suicide is the act of a human being intentionally causing his or her own death. Suicide is often committed out of despair, or attributed to some underlying mental disorder which includes depression, bipolar disorder, schizophrenia, alcoholism and drug abuse. Financial difficulties, troubles with interpersonal relationships and other undesirable situations play a significant role.
Afghanistan	Afghanistan officially the Islamic Republic of Afghanistan, is a landlocked and mountainous country in south-central Asia. It is bordered by Pakistan in the south and east, Iran in the west, Turkmenistan, Uzbekistan and Tajikistan in the north, and China in the far northeast. The territories now comprising Afghanistan have been an ancient focal point of the Silk Road and human migration.

Chapter 4. Civil Liberties and Civil Rights

Hamdan v. Rumsfeld	Hamdan v. Rumsfeld, 548 U.S. 557 (2006), is a case in which the Supreme Court of the United States held that military commissions set up by the Bush administration to try detainees at Guantanamo Bay lack "the power to proceed because its structures and procedures violate both the Uniform Code of Military Justice and the four Geneva Conventions signed in 1949
	The case considered whether the United States Congress may pass legislation preventing the Supreme Court from hearing the case of an accused combatant before his military commission takes place, whether the special military commissions that had been set up violated federal law (including the Uniform Code of Military Justice and treaty obligations), and whether courts can enforce the articles of the 1949 Geneva Convention.
	An unusual aspect of the case was an amicus brief filed by Senators Jon Kyl and Lindsey Graham, which presented an "extensive colloquy" added to the Congressional record as evidence that "Congress was aware" that the Detainee Treatment Act would strip the Supreme Court of jurisdiction to hear cases brought by the Guantanamo detainees.
Patriot	Patriots was the name the peoples of the Spanish America, who rebelled against Spanish control during the Spanish American wars of independence, called themselves. They supported the principles of the Age of Enlightenment and sought to replace the existing governing structures with Juntas. At first they declared themselves loyal to Ferdinand VII, who was captive of Napoleon Bonaparte and who was seem as a supporter of the new ideals because of his conflict with his father, the absolutist Charles IV. However, when Ferdinand VII was restored to power and began the Absolutist Restauration, most patriots in South America decided to support independentism instead.
Nomination	Nomination is part of the process of selecting a candidate for either election to an office, or the bestowing of an honor or award.
	In the context of elections for public office, a candidate who has been selected by a political party is normally said to be the nominee of that party. The party's selection (that is, the nomination) is typically accomplished either based on one or more primary elections or by means of a political party convention or caucus, according to the rules of the party and any applicable election laws.

Chapter 4. Civil Liberties and Civil Rights

National Convention	During the French Revolution, the National Convention, in France, comprised the constitutional and legislative assembly which sat from 20 September 1792 to 26 October 1795 . It held executive power in France during the first years of the French First Republic. It was succeeded by the Directory, commencing 2 November 1795. Prominent members of the original Convention included Maximilien Robespierre of the Jacobin Club, Jean-Paul Marat (affiliated with the Jacobins, though never a formal member), and Georges Danton of the Cordeliers.
Geneva	Geneva is the second-most-populous city in Switzerland (after Zürich) and is the most populous city of Romandie . Situated where the Rhône River exits Lake Geneva, it is the capital of the Republic and Canton of Geneva. While the municipality itself (ville de Genève) has a population (as of December 2009) of 189,313, the canton of Geneva has 457,628 residents (as of December 2009).
Geneva Conventions	The Geneva Conventions comprise four treaties and three additional protocols that set the standards in international law for humanitarian treatment of the victims of war. The singular term Geneva Convention refers to the agreements of 1949, negotiated in the aftermath of World War II, updating the terms of the first three treaties and adding a fourth treaty. The language is extensive, with articles defining the basic rights of those captured during a military conflict, establishing protections for the wounded, and addressing protections for civilians in and around a war zone.
Medicare	Medicare is a social insurance program administered by the United States government, providing health insurance coverage to people who are aged 65 and over, or who meet other special criteria. Medicare operates similar to a single-payer health care system, but the key difference is that its coverage only extends to 80% of any given medical cost; the remaining 20% of cost must be paid by other means, such as privately-held supplemental insurance, or paid by the patient. The program also funds residency training programs for the vast majority of physicians in the United States.
Military justice	Military justice is the body of laws and procedures governing members of the armed forces. Many states have separate and distinct bodies of law that govern the conduct of members of their armed forces. Some states use special judicial and other arrangements to enforce those laws, while others use civilian judicial systems.

Chapter 4. Civil Liberties and Civil Rights

Rasul v. Bush	Rasul v. Bush, 542 U.S. 466 (2004), is a landmark United States Supreme Court decision establishing that the U.S. court system has the authority to decide whether foreign nationals (non-U.S. citizens) held in Guantanamo Bay were wrongfully imprisoned. The 6-3 ruling on June 28, 2004, reversed a District Court decision, which held that the Judiciary had no jurisdiction to handle wrongful imprisonment cases involving foreign nationals who are held in Guantanamo Bay. Justice John Paul Stevens wrote the majority opinion and was joined by Sandra Day O'Connor, David Souter, Ruth Bader Ginsburg, and Stephen Breyer, with Anthony Kennedy concurring.
Uniform Code of Military Justice	The Uniform Code of Military Justice (UCMJ, 64 Stat. 109, 10 U.S.C.
Habeas corpus	Habeas corpus is a writ, or legal action, through which a prisoner can be released from unlawful detention. The remedy can be sought by the prisoner or by another person coming to his aid. Habeas corpus originated in the English legal system, but it is now available in many nations.
Disabilities	Disabilities were legal restrictions and limitations placed on Jews in the Middle Ages. They included provisions requiring Jews to wear specific and identifying clothing such as the Jewish hat and the yellow badge, restricting Jews to certain cities and towns or in certain parts of towns (ghettos), and forbidding Jews to enter certain trades. Disabilities also included special taxes levied on Jews, exclusion from public life, and restraints on the performance of religious ceremonies.
Iraq	Iraq; officially the Republic of Iraq is a country in Western Asia spanning most of the northwestern end of the Zagros mountain range, the eastern part of the Syrian Desert and the northern part of the Arabian Desert.
	Iraq is bordered by Jordan to the west, Syria to the northwest, Turkey to the north, Iran to the east, and Kuwait and Saudi Arabia to the south. Iraq has a narrow section of coastline measuring 58 km (35 miles) on the northern Persian Gulf.

Chapter 4. Civil Liberties and Civil Rights

Discrimination	Discrimination is the cognitive and sensory capacity or ability to see fine distinctions and perceive differences between objects, subjects, concepts and patterns, or possess exceptional development of the senses. Used in this way to identify exceptional discernment since the 17th century, the term begun to be used as an expression of derogatory racial prejudice from the 1830s Thomas D. Rice's performances as "Jim Crow". Since the American Civil War the term 'discrimination' generally evolved in American English usage as an understanding of prejudicial treatment of an individual based solely on their race, later generalized as membership in a certain socially undesirable group or social category.
Shelley v. Kraemer	Shelley v. Kraemer, 334 U.S. 1 (1948), is a United States Supreme Court case which held that courts could not enforce racial covenants on real estate. Facts of the case In 1945, a black family by the name of Shelley purchased a house in St. Louis, Missouri. At the time of purchase, they were unaware that a restrictive covenant had been in place on the property since 1911. The restrictive covenant barred "people of the Negro or Mongolian Race" from owning the property.

Chapter 4. Civil Liberties and Civil Rights

Appointee	An appointee may be one of the following: - A member who is appointed to a position or office is called an appointee. In law, such a term is applied to one who is granted power of appointment of property. - An appointee was also a foot soldier in the French army, who, for long service and bravery, received more pay than other privates. - An appointee is the third most lower rank of the Italian Corps of Carabineers - An appointee is the third most lower rank of the Swiss Armed Forces - An appointee is also a person or organisation entrusted with managing the daily finances of vulnerable individuals in the UK.
Covenant	A covenant, in its most general sense, is a solemn promise to engage in or refrain from a specified action. A covenant is a type of contract in which the covenantor makes a promise to a covenantee to do or not do some action. In real property law, the term real covenants is used for conditions tied to the use of land.
Redistricting	Redistricting, a form of redistribution, is the process of drawing United States district lines. This often means changing electoral district and constituency boundaries in response to periodic census results. In 36 states, the state legislature has primary responsibility for creating a redistricting plan, in many cases subject to approval by the state governor.
Leadership	Leadership has been described as the "process of social influence in which one person can enlist the aid and support of others in the accomplishment of a common task". Definitions more inclusive of followers have also emerged. Alan Keith of Genentech states that, "Leadership is ultimately about creating a way for people to contribute to making something extraordinary happen." According to Ken "SKC" Ogbonnia, "effective leadership is the ability to successfully integrate and maximize available resources within the internal and external environment for the attainment of organizational or societal goals."

Chapter 4. Civil Liberties and Civil Rights

	The following sections discuss several important aspects of leadership including a description of what leadership is and a description of several popular theories and styles of leadership.
Student Nonviolent Coordinating Committee	The Student Nonviolent Coordinating Committee was one of the principal organizations of the American Civil Rights Movement in the 1960s. It emerged from a series of student meetings led by Ella Baker held at Shaw University in Raleigh, North Carolina in April 1960. Student Nonviolent Coordinating Committee grew into a large organization with many supporters in the North who helped raise funds to support Student Nonviolent Coordinating Committee's work in the South, allowing full-time Student Nonviolent Coordinating Committee workers to have a $10 a week salary. Many unpaid volunteers also worked with Student Nonviolent Coordinating Committee on projects in Mississippi, Alabama, Georgia, Arkansas, and Maryland.
Martin Luther King, Jr.	Martin Luther King, Jr. was an American clergyman, activist, and prominent leader in the African American civil rights movement. He is best known for being an iconic figure in the advancement of civil rights in the United States and around the world, using nonviolent methods following the teachings of Mahatma Gandhi.
Martin Luther	Martin Luther is a public artwork by German artist Ernst Rietschel, located at Luther Place Memorial Church in Washington, D.C., United States. Martin Luther was originally surveyed as part of the Smithsonian's Save Outdoor Sculpture! survey in 1993. The monument is a bronze full length portrait dedicated to theologian Martin Luther. Description Martin Luther stands dressed in long robes with his proper right leg moving slightly forward.
Civil rights movement	The civil rights movement was a worldwide political movement for equality before the law occurring between approximately 1950 and 1980. It was accompanied by much civil unrest and popular rebellion. The process was long and tenuous in many countries, and most of these movements did not fully achieve their goals although, the efforts of these movements did lead to improvements in the legal rights of previously oppressed groups of peoples. Civil rights movement in Northern Ireland

Chapter 4. Civil Liberties and Civil Rights

	Northern Ireland is a province of the United Kingdom which has witnessed violence over many decades, mainly because of sectarian tensions between the Catholic and Protestant community, known as the Troubles.
Little Rock	Little Rock (ca. 1805-1868) was a council chief of the Wutapiu band of Southern Cheyennes. He was the only council chief who remained with Black Kettle following the Sand Creek massacre of 1864.
	Little Rock was a signatory of the Medicine Lodge Treaty of 1867. In August 1868, Little Rock was interviewed at Fort Lyon by Indian agent Edward W. Wynkoop about raids by a large Cheyenne war party on white settlements along the Saline and Solomon in Kansas.
Desegregation	Desegregation is the process of ending the separation of two groups usually referring to races. This is most commonly used in reference to the United States. Desegregation was long a focus of the American Civil Rights Movement, both before and after the United States Supreme Court's decision in Brown v. Board of Education, particularly desegregation of the school systems and the military .
Regulation	Regulation is "controlling human or societal behavior by rules or restrictions." Regulation can take many forms: legal restrictions promulgated by a government authority, self-regulation by an industry such as through a trade association, social regulation co-regulation and market regulation. One can consider regulation as actions of conduct imposing sanctions (such as a fine). This action of administrative law, or implementing regulatory law, may be contrasted with statutory or case law.
Threat	In Computer security a threat is a potential for violation of security, which exists when there is a circumstance, capability, action, or event that could breach security and cause harm.
	That is, a threat is a possible danger that might exploit a vulnerability. A threat can be either "intentional" (i.e., intelligent; e.g., an individual cracker or a criminal organization) or "accidental" (e.g., the possibility of a computer malfunctioning, or the possibility of an "act of God" such as an earthquake, a fire, or a tornado). The definition is as IETF RFC 2828
	Definitions

Chapter 4. Civil Liberties and Civil Rights

ISO 27005 defines threat as:

A more comprehensive definition, tied to an Information assurance point of view, can be found in "Federal Information Processing Standards (FIPS) 200, Minimum Security Requirements for Federal Information and Information Systems" by NIST of United States of America

ENISA gives a similar definition:

The Open Group defines threat in as:

National Information Assurance Training and Education Center gives a more articulated definition of threat:

Phenomenology

The term "threat" relates to some other basic security terms as shown in the following diagram:

```
+ - - - - - - - - - - - - + + - - - - + + - - - - - - - - - - -+ An Attack: Counter- A System Resource: i.e., A
Threat Action measure Target of the Attack +---------+ +----------------+ Attacker
<====================<========= i.e., Passive Vulnerability A Threat
<==================><========> Agent or Active +--------------+ +----------+ Attack VVV
Threat Consequences + - - - - - - - - - - - - + + - - - - + + - - - - - - - - - - -+
```

A resource (both physical or logical) can have one or more vulnerabilities that can be exploited by a threat agent in a threat action.

| Employment discrimination | Employment discrimination is discrimination in hiring, promotion, job assignment, termination, and compensation. It includes various types of harassment. |

Chapter 4. Civil Liberties and Civil Rights

	Many jurisdictions prohibit some types of employment discrimination, often by forbidding discrimination based on certain traits ("protected categories").
Equal Employment Opportunity Commission	The U.S. Equal Employment Opportunity Commission is an independent federal law enforcement agency that enforces laws against workplace discrimination. The Equal Employment Opportunity Commission investigates discrimination complaints based on an individual's race, color, national origin, religion, sex, age, perceived intelligence, disability and retaliation for reporting and/or opposing a discriminatory practice. It is empowered to file discrimination suits against employers on behalf of alleged victims and to adjudicate claims of discrimination brought against federal agencies.
Equity	Equity is the concept or idea of fairness in economics, particularly as to taxation or welfare economics. Overview Equity may be distinguished from economic efficiency in overall evaluation of social welfare. Although 'equity' has broader uses, it may be posed as a counterpart to economic inequality in yielding a "good" distribution of welfare.
Lawsuit	A lawsuit is a civil action brought in a court of law in which a plaintiff, a party who claims to have incurred damages as a result of a defendant's actions, demands a legal or equitable remedy. The defendant is required to respond to the plaintiff's complaint. If the plaintiff is successful, judgment will be given in the plaintiff's favor, and a variety of court orders may be issued to enforce a right, award damages, or impose an injunction to prevent an act or compel an act.
County	A county is a land area of local government within a country. A county may have cities and towns within its area. Originally, in continental Europe, a county was the land under the jurisdiction of a count (conte, comte, conde, Graf).
Left Behind	Left Behind is a series of 16 best-selling novels by Tim LaHaye and Jerry Jenkins, dealing with Christian dispensationalist End Times: pretribulation, premillennial, Christian eschatological viewpoint of the end of the world. The primary conflict of the series is the members of the Tribulation Force against the Global Community and its leader Nicolae Carpathia--the Antichrist. Left Behind is also the title of the first book in the series.

Chapter 4. Civil Liberties and Civil Rights

Publics	Publics are small groups of people who follow one or more particular issue very closely. They are well informed about the issue(s) and also have a very strong opinion on it/them. They tend to know more about politics than the average person, and, therefore, exert more influence, because these people care so deeply about their cause(s) that they donate much time and money.
Intermediate scrutiny	Intermediate scrutiny, in U.S. constitutional law, is the middle level of scrutiny applied by courts deciding constitutional issues through judicial review. The other levels are typically referred to as rational basis review (least rigorous) and strict scrutiny (most rigorous).
	In order to overcome the intermediate scrutiny test, it must be shown that the law or policy being challenged furthers an important government interest in a way that is substantially related to that interest.
Lobbying	Lobbying is the intention of influencing decisions made by legislators and officials in the government by individuals, other legislators, constituents, or advocacy groups. A lobbyist is a person who tries to influence legislation on behalf of a special interest or a member of a lobby. Governments often define and regulate organized group lobbying that has become influential.
Violence Against Women Act	The Violence Against Women Act of 1994 is a United States federal law. It was passed as Title IV, sec. 40001-40703 of the Violent Crime Control and Law Enforcement Act of 1994 HR 3355 and signed as Public Law 103-322 by President Bill Clinton on September 13, 1994. It provided $1.6 billion to enhance investigation and prosecution of the violent crime perpetrated against women, increased pre-trial detention of the accused, imposed automatic and mandatory restitution on those convicted, and allowed civil redress in cases prosecutors chose to leave unprosecuted.
	Violence Against Women Act was drafted by then-U.S. Senator Joseph R. Biden's office with support from a number of advocacy organizations including National Coalition Against Sexual Assault, National Coalition Against Domestic Violence, Legal Momentum and The National Organization for Women, which described the bill as "the greatest breakthrough in civil rights for women in nearly two decades."

Chapter 4. Civil Liberties and Civil Rights

	Violence Against Women Act was reauthorized by Congress in 2000, and again in December 2005. The bill was signed into law by President George W. Bush on January 5, 2006.
La Raza	In the Spanish language the term La Raza literally means "the race" or generally and symbolically "the people." Its meaning varies amongst various Spanish-speaking peoples. For instance, in Spain, "Raza" may denote specifically Spanish and often of a something or someone of an European Christian heritage. The Francoist film Raza, from 1944, which celebrates ideally Spanish qualities, is an example of this usage.
Lau v. Nichols	Lau v. Nichols, 414 U.S. 563 (1974), was a civil rights case that was brought by Chinese American students living in San Francisco, California who had limited English proficiency. The students claimed that they were not receiving special help in school due to their inability to speak English, help which they argued they were entitled to under Title VI of the Civil Rights Act of 1964 because of its ban on educational discrimination on the basis of national origin. Finding that the lack of linguistically-appropriate accommodations effectively denied the Chinese students equal educational opportunities on the basis of their ethnicity, the U.S. Supreme Court in 1974 ruled in favor of the students, thus expanding rights of students nationwide with limited English proficiency.
Nationality	Nationality is membership of a nation or sovereign state. Citizenship is determined by jus soli, jus sanguinis, or naturalization. In some areas of the world, one's nationality is determined by their ethnicity, rather than citizenship.
United States v. Wong Kim Ark	United States v. Wong Kim Ark, 169 U.S. 649 (1898), was a United States Supreme Court decision that set an important legal precedent about the role of jus soli (birth in the United States) as a factor in determining a person's claim to United States citizenship. The citizenship status of a man born in the United States to Chinese parents was challenged because of a law restricting Chinese immigration and prohibiting immigrants from China from becoming naturalized U.S. citizens, but the Supreme Court ruled that the citizenship language in the Fourteenth Amendment to the Constitution could not be limited in its effect by an act of Congress.

Chapter 4. Civil Liberties and Civil Rights

	Wong Kim Ark (???; Toisanese: wong11 gim33 'ak3; Cantonese: wong4 gam1 dak1; Mandarin: huáng jīn dé) was born in San Francisco, California, sometime between 1868 and 1873. His father, Wong Si Ping and his mother, Wee Lee were immigrants from Taishan, China and were not United States citizens.
Bilingual education	Bilingual education involves teaching academic content in two languages, in a native and secondary language with varying amounts of each language used in accordance with the program model. The following are several different types of bilingual education program models: • Transitional Bilingual Education. This involves education in a child's native language, typically for no more than three years, to ensure that students do not fall behind in content areas like math, science, and social studies while they are learning English.
Balkanization	Balkanization, is a pejorative geopolitical term originally used to describe the process of fragmentation or division of a region or state into smaller regions or states that are often hostile or non-cooperative with each other. The term has arisen from the conflicts in the 20th century Balkans. While what is now termed Balkanization has occurred throughout history, the term originally described the creation of smaller, ethnically diverse states following the breakup of the Ottoman Empire after World War I. The term is also used to describe other forms of disintegration, including, for instance, the subdivision of the Internet into separate enclaves, the division of subfields and the creation of new fields from sociology, and the breakdown of cooperative arrangements due to the rise of independent competitive entities engaged in "beggar thy neighbour" bidding wars.

Chapter 4. Civil Liberties and Civil Rights

Immigration reform	Immigration reform is a term used in political discussion regarding changes to current immigration policy of a country. In its strict definition, "reform " means to change into an improved form or condition, by amending or removing faults or abuses. In the political sense, immigration reform may include promoted, expanded, or open immigration, as well as reduced or eliminated immigration.
Affair	Affair may refer to professional, personal, or public business matters or to a particular business or private activity of a temporary duration, as in family affair, a private affair, or a romantic affair. Political affair Political affair may refer to the illicit or scandalous activities of public, such as the Watergate affair, or to a legally constituted government department, for example, the United Nations Department of Political Affairs. Romantic affair A romantic affair, also called an affair of the heart, may refer to sexual liaisons among unwed parties, or to various forms of nonmonogamy.
Dennis Banks	Dennis Banks a Native American leader, teacher, lecturer, activist and author, is an Anishinaabe born on Leech Lake Indian Reservation in northern Minnesota. Banks is also known as Nowa Cumig (Naawakamig in the Double Vowel System). His name in the Ojibwe language means "In the Center of the Ground." Work with AIM In 1968 he co-founded the American Indian Movement (AIM), and established it to protect the traditional ways of Indian people and to engage in legal cases protecting treaty rights of Natives, such as hunting and fishing, trapping, and wild rice farming.

Chapter 4. Civil Liberties and Civil Rights

Self-determination	The right of nations to self-determination is the principle in international law, that nations have the right to freely choose their sovereignty and international political status with no external compulsion or external interference. The principle does not state how the decision is to be made, or what the outcome should be, be it independence, federation, protection, some form of autonomy or even full assimilation. Neither does it state what the delimitation between nations should be -- or even what constitutes a nation.
Human rights	Human rights are "rights and freedoms to which all humans are entitled." Proponents of the concept usually assert that everyone is endowed with certain entitlements merely by reason of being human. Human rights are thus conceived in a universalist and egalitarian fashion. Such entitlements can exist as shared norms of actual human moralities, as justified moral norms or natural rights supported by strong reasons, or as legal rights either at a national level or within international law.
Political action committee	In the United States, a political action committee, is the name commonly given to a private group, regardless of size, organized to elect political candidates or to advance the outcome of a political issue or legislation. Legally, what constitutes a "Political action committee" for purposes of regulation is a matter of state and federal law. Under the Federal Election Campaign Act, an organization becomes a "political committee" by receiving contributions or making expenditures in excess of $1,000 for the purpose of influencing a federal election.
Rebellion	Rebellion is a refusal of obedience or order. It may, therefore, be seen as encompassing a range of behaviors from civil disobedience and mass nonviolent resistance, to violent and organized attempts to destroy an established authority such as a government. Those who participate in rebellions are known as "rebels".
Romer v. Evans	Romer v. Evans, 517 U.S. 620 (1996), is a United States Supreme Court case dealing with civil rights and state laws. The Court gave its ruling on May 20, 1996 against an amendment to the Colorado state constitution that would have prevented any city, town or county in the state from taking any legislative, executive, or judicial action to recognize gay and lesbian citizens as a Protected class. Supreme Court ruling The case was argued on October 10, 1995. On May 20, 1996, the court ruled 6-3 that Colorado's Amendment 2 was unconstitutional, though on different reasoning than the Colorado courts.

Chapter 4. Civil Liberties and Civil Rights

Trusts	In Conflict of Laws, the Hague Convention on the Law Applicable to Trusts and on Their Recognition was concluded on 1 July 1985 and entered into force 1 January 1992. The Convention aims to harmonise not only the municipal law definitions of a trust both within the USA and outside the USA, but also the Conflict rules for resolving problems in the choice of the lex causae. Explanation Many states do not have a developed law of trusts, or the principles differ significantly between states. It was therefore necessary for the Hague Convention to define a trust to indicate the range of legal transactions regulated by the Convention and, perhaps more significantly, the range of applications not regulated.
Regent	A regent is a person selected to act as head of state (ruling or not) because the ruler is a minor, not present, or debilitated. In a monarchy, a regent usually governs due to one of these reasons, but may also be elected to rule during the interregnum when the royal line has died out. This was the case in Finland and Hungary, where the royal line was considered extinct in the aftermath of World War I. In Iceland, the regent represented the King of Denmark as sovereign of Iceland until the country became a republic in 1944.
Regents of the University of California v. Bakke	Regents of the University of California v. Bakke, 438 U.S. 265 (1978) was a landmark decision of the Supreme Court of the United States on the permissible scopefactors in an admissions program, but only for the purpose of improving the learning environment through diversity in accordance with the university's constitutionally protected First Amendment right to Academic Freedom (at page 311-315 of the opinion).

Chapter 4. Civil Liberties and Civil Rights

The "diversity in the classroom" justification for considering race as "one" of the factors in admissions policies was different from the original purpose stated by UC Davis Medical School, whose special admissions program under review was designed to ensure admissions of traditionally discriminated-against minorities. UC Davis Medical School originally developed the program to (i) reduce the historic deficit of traditionally disfavored minorities in medical schools and the medical profession, (ii) counter the effects of societal discrimination, (iii) increase the number of physicians who will practice in communities currently underserved, and (iv) obtain the educational benefits that flow from an ethnically diverse student body.

Abortion law	Abortion law is legislation which pertains to the provision of abortion. Abortion has been a controversial subject in several societies around the world because of the moral and ethical issues that surround it, though other considerations, such as a state's pro- or antinatalist policies or questions of inheritance and patriarchy, also dictate abortion law and regulation. It has been regularly banned and otherwise limited.
Affirmative action	Affirmative action refers to policies that take factors including "race, color, religion, sex or national origin" into consideration in order to benefit an underrepresented group at the expense of a majority group, usually as a means to counter the effects of a history of discrimination. The focus of such policies ranges from employment and education to public contracting and health programs. "Affirmative action" is action taken to increase the representation of women and minorities in areas of employment, education, and business from which they have been historically excluded.
Ward	In Australia, Canada, Monaco, New Zealand, South Africa, the United Kingdom, and the United States, a ward is an electoral district within a municipality used in local politics. Wards are usually named after neighbourhoods, thoroughfares, parishes, landmarks, geographical features and in some cases historical figures connected to the area. It is common in the United States for wards to simply be numbered.
Mississippi	Mississippi is a U.S. state located in the Southern United States. Jackson is the state capital and largest city. The state is heavily forested outside of the Mississippi Delta area, and its catfish aquaculture farms produce the majority of farm-raised catfish consumed in the United States.

Chapter 4. Civil Liberties and Civil Rights

Gratz v. Bollinger	Gratz v. Bollinger, 539 U.S. 244 (2003), was a United States Supreme Court case regarding the University of Michigan undergraduate affirmative action admissions policy. In a 6-3 decision announced on June 23, 2003, the Supreme Court ruled the university's point system (which automatically awarded points to underrepresented ethnic groups) was too mechanistic in its use of race as a factor in admissions, and was therefore unconstitutional. Case The University of Michigan used a 150-point scale to rank applicant, with 100 points needed to guarantee admission.
Grutter v. Bollinger	Grutter v. Bollinger, 539 U.S. 306 (2003), is a case in which the United States Supreme Court upheld the affirmative action admissions policy of the University of Michigan Law School. The 5-4 decision was announced on June 23, 2003. Case When the Law School denied admission to petitioner Grutter, a white Michigan resident with a 3.8 GPA and 161 LSAT score, she filed this suit, alleging that respondents had discriminated against her on the basis of race in violation of the Fourteenth Amendment, Title VI of the Civil Rights Act of 1964, and 42 U.S.C. § 1981; that she was rejected because the Law School uses race as a "predominant" factor, giving applicants belonging to certain minority groups a significantly greater chance of admission than students with similar credentials from disfavored racial groups; and that respondents had no compelling interest to justify that use of race.
Korematsu v. United States	Korematsu v. United States, 323 U.S. 214 (1944), was a landmark United States Supreme Court case concerning the constitutionality of Executive Order 9066, which ordered Japanese Americans into internment camps during World War II.

Chapter 4. Civil Liberties and Civil Rights

In a 6-3 decision, the Court sided with the government, ruling that the exclusion order was constitutional. The opinion, written by Supreme Court justice Hugo Black, held that the need to protect against espionage outweighed Fred Korematsu's individual rights, and the rights of Americans of Japanese descent.

The decision in Korematsu v. United States has been very controversial.

Initiative

In political science, the initiative provides a means by which a petition signed by a certain minimum number of registered voters can force a public vote (plebiscite) on a proposed statute, constitutional amendment, charter amendment or ordinance, or, in its minimal form, to simply oblige the executive or legislative bodies to consider the subject by submitting it to the order of the day. It is a form of direct democracy.

The initiative may take the form of either the direct initiative or indirect initiative.

Chapter 4. Civil Liberties and Civil Rights

Chapter 4. Civil Liberties and Civil Rights

Chapter 5. Congress: The First Branch

Congress	A congress is a formal meeting of the representatives of different nations, constituent states, independent organizations (such as trade unions), or groups.
	The term was chosen for the United States Congress to emphasize the status of each state represented there as a self-governing unit. Subsequent to the use of congress by the U.S. legislature, the term has been incorrectly adopted by many states within unions, and by unitary nation-states in the Americas, to refer to their legislatures.
Allegiance	An allegiance is a duty of fidelity said to be owed by a subject or a citizen to his/her state or sovereign.
	Etymology
	From Middle English ligeaunce . The al- prefix was probably added through confusion with another legal term, allegeance, an "allegation" .
Court	A court is a form of tribunal, often a governmental institution, with the authority to adjudicate legal disputes between parties and carry out the administration of justice in civil, criminal, and administrative matters in accordance with the rule of law. In both common law and civil law legal systems, courts are the central means for dispute resolution, and it is generally understood that all persons have an ability to bring their claims before a court. Similarly, the rights of those accused of a crime include the right to present a defense before a court.
Louisiana	Louisiana was the name of an administrative district of the Viceroyalty of New Spain from 1764 to 1803 that represented territory west of the Mississippi River basin, plus New Orleans. Spain acquired the territory from France: see Louisiana.
	History

Chapter 5. Congress: The First Branch

	The area, comprising what is now known as the Louisiana Purchase, was turned over to the French for a few days in 1803 before it, in turn, was turned over to the United States.
Pledge	A pledge is a bailment or deposit of personal property to a creditor to secure repayment for some debt or engagement, The term is also used to denote the property which constitutes the security.
	Pledge is the ravi of Roman law, from which most of the modern law on the subject is derived. It differs from hypothecation and from the more usual mortgage in that the pledge is in the possession of the pledgee; it also differs from mortgage in being confined to personal property (rather than real property).
Appointee	An appointee may be one of the following: • A member who is appointed to a position or office is called an appointee. In law, such a term is applied to one who is granted power of appointment of property. • An appointee was also a foot soldier in the French army, who, for long service and bravery, received more pay than other privates. • An appointee is the third most lower rank of the Italian Corps of Carabineers • An appointee is the third most lower rank of the Swiss Armed Forces • An appointee is also a person or organisation entrusted with managing the daily finances of vulnerable individuals in the UK.
Declaration	In law, a declaration is a binding adjudication of the rights or other legal relations of the parties which does not provide for or order enforcement. Where the declaration is made by a court, it is usually referred to as a declaratory judgment. Less commonly, where declaratory relief is awarded by an arbitrator, it is normally called a declaratory award.

Chapter 5. Congress: The First Branch

Executive	Executive branch of government is the part of government that has sole authority and responsibility for the daily administration of the state bureaucracy. The division of power into separate branches of government is central to the democratic idea of the separation of powers. In many countries, the term "government" connotes only the executive branch.
Foreign policy	A country's foreign policy, called the foreign relations policy, consists of self-interest strategies chosen by the state to safeguard its national interests and to achieve its goals within international relations milieu. The approaches are strategically employed to interact with other countries. In recent times, due to the deepening level of globalization and transnational activities, the states will also have to interact with non-state actors.
Policy	A policy is typically described as a principle or rule to guide decisions and achieve rational outcome(s). The term is not normally used to denote what is actually done, this is normally referred to as either procedure or protocol. Whereas a policy will contain the 'what' and the 'why', procedures or protocols contain the 'what', the 'how', the 'where', and the 'when'.
Power	Power is a measure of an entity's ability to control its environment, including the behavior of other entities. The term authority is often used for power, perceived as legitimate by the social structure. Power can be seen as evil or unjust, but the exercise of power is accepted as endemic to humans as social beings.
Constituency	A constituency is any cohesive body of people bound by shared identity, goals, or loyalty. Constituency can be used to describe a business's customer base and shareholders, or a charity's donors or those it serves. In politics, a constituency can mean either the people from whom an individual or organization hopes to attract support, or geographical area that a particular elected official represents.
Trustee	Trustee is a legal term for a holder of property on behalf of a beneficiary. A trust can be set up either to benefit particular persons, or for any charitable purposes (but not generally for non-charitable purposes): typical examples are a will trust for the testator's children and family, a pension trust (to confer benefits on employees and their families), and a charitable trust. In all cases, the trustee may be a person or company, whether or not they are a prospective beneficiary.

Chapter 5. Congress: The First Branch

Rights	Rights are legal, social, or ethical principles of freedom or entitlement; that is, rights are the fundamental normative rules about what is allowed of people or owed to people, according to some legal system, social convention, or ethical theory. Rights are of essential importance in such disciplines as law and ethics, especially theories of justice and deontology. Rights are often considered fundamental to civilization, being regarded as established pillars of society and culture, and the history of social conflicts can be found in the history of each right and its development.
Voting	Voting is a method for a group such as a meeting or an electorate to make a decision or express an opinion--often following discussions, debates, or election campaigns. It is often found in democracies and republics. Reasons for voting In a representative government, voting commonly implies election: a way for an electorate to select among candidates for office.
Affair	Affair may refer to professional, personal, or public business matters or to a particular business or private activity of a temporary duration, as in family affair, a private affair, or a romantic affair. Political affair Political affair may refer to the illicit or scandalous activities of public, such as the Watergate affair, or to a legally constituted government department, for example, the United Nations Department of Political Affairs. Romantic affair

Chapter 5. Congress: The First Branch

	A romantic affair, also called an affair of the heart, may refer to sexual liaisons among unwed parties, or to various forms of nonmonogamy.
Armed Services	Armed Services is a collective term that refers to the major organisational entities of national armed forces, so named because they service a combat need in a specific combat environment. In most states Armed Services include the Army also known as Land Force or Ground Force, Navy also know a Marine Defence Force, and Air Force. Some countries have a separate service for the Space Forces or Military Space Forces, and the Russian Federation also has the Strategic Missile Troops and the Airborne Troops as independent Armed Services.
Homeland	A homeland is the concept of the place (cultural geography) to which an ethnic group holds a long history and a deep cultural association with --the country in which a particular national identity began. As a common noun, it simply connotes the country of one's origin.
Homeland security	Homeland security is an umbrella term for security efforts to protect the United States against terrorist activity. The term arose following a reorganization of many U.S. government agencies in 2003 to form the United States Department of Homeland Security after the September 11 attacks, and may be used to refer to the actions of that department, the United States Senate Committee on Homeland Security and Governmental Affairs, or the United States House of Representatives Committee on Homeland Security. In the United States In the United States, the concept of "homeland security" extends and recombines responsibilities of government agencies and entities.
Judiciary	The judiciary is the system of courts that interprets and applies the law in the name of the state. The judiciary also provides a mechanism for the resolution of disputes. Under the doctrine of the separation of powers, the judiciary generally does not make law (that is, in a plenary fashion, which is the responsibility of the legislature) or enforce law (which is the responsibility of the executive), but rather interprets law and applies it to the facts of each case.

Chapter 5. Congress: The First Branch

Bicameralism — In government, bicameralism is the practice of having two legislative or parliamentary chambers. Thus, a bicameral parliament or bicameral legislature is a legislature which consists of two chambers or houses. Bicameralism is an essential and defining feature of the classical notion of mixed government.

Leadership — Leadership has been described as the "process of social influence in which one person can enlist the aid and support of others in the accomplishment of a common task". Definitions more inclusive of followers have also emerged. Alan Keith of Genentech states that, "Leadership is ultimately about creating a way for people to contribute to making something extraordinary happen." According to Ken "SKC" Ogbonnia, "effective leadership is the ability to successfully integrate and maximize available resources within the internal and external environment for the attainment of organizational or societal goals."

The following sections discuss several important aspects of leadership including a description of what leadership is and a description of several popular theories and styles of leadership.

Adjustment — In law, the term adjustment may appear in varied contexts, as a synonym for terms with unrelated definitions:

General Definition

Chapter 5. Congress: The First Branch

Adjust:

1. To settle or to bring to a satisfactory state, so that the parties are agreed in the result; as, to adjust accounts.
2. When applied to a liquidated demand, the verb "adjust" has the same meaning as the word "settle" in the same connection, and means to pay the demand. When applied to an unliquidated demand, it means to ascertain the amount due or to settle. In the latter connection, to settle means to effect a mutual adjustment between the parties and to agree upon the balance.

Common Uses

General Debt

- Debtor and creditor adjustment: As the term appears in an assignment for the benefit of creditors, "Creditor" means one who has a definite demand against the assignor, or a cause of action capable of adjustment and liquidation at trial. 6 Am J2d Assign for Crs § 109.
- Adjustable Rate Loan: Loan arrangement which permits the lender to change the interest rate based on a specific factor such as the prime lending rate charged by banks.
- Adjusting agency: In one sense, a collection agency; in another sense, an agency representing a debtor in making an arrangement with his creditors for the settlement of his obligations by modification of the indebtedness.

House of Representatives	House of Representatives is the name of a legislative bodies in many countries and sub-national states. In some countries, the House of Representatives is the lower house of a bicameral legislature, with the corresponding upper house often called a "senate". In other countries, the House of Representatives is the sole chamber of a unicameral legislature.
Senate	A senate is a deliberative assembly, often the upper house or chamber of a legislature or parliament. There have been many such bodies in history, since senate means the assembly of the eldest and wiser members of the society and ruling class. Two of the first official senates were the Spartan Gerousia (Γερουσ?α) and the Roman Senate.

Chapter 5. Congress: The First Branch

Impeachment	Impeachment is a formal process in which an official is accused of unlawful activity and the outcome of which, depending on the country, can lead to the removal of that official from office or other punishment. Medieval popular etymology also associated it (wrongly) with derivations from the Latin impetere (to attack). (In its more frequent and more technical usage, impeachment of a person in the role of a witness is the act of challenging the honesty or credibility of that person).
Trade union	A trade union is an organization of workers that have banded together to achieve common goals such as better working conditions. The trade union, through its leadership, bargains with the employer on behalf of union members (rank and file members) and negotiates labour contracts (collective bargaining) with employers. This may include the negotiation of wages, work rules, complaint procedures, rules governing hiring, firing and promotion of workers, benefits, workplace safety and policies.
Constitutional amendment	A constitutional amendment is a change to the constitution of a nation or a state. In jurisdictions with "rigid" or "entrenched" constitutions, amendments do not require a special procedure different from that used for enacting ordinary laws. Some constitutions do not have to be amended with the direct consent of the electorate in a referendum.
Voting system	A voting system is a method by which voters make a choice between options, often in an election or on a policy referendum. A voting system contains rules for valid voting, and how votes are counted and aggregated to yield a final result. Since voting involves counting, it is algorithmic in nature, and, since it involves polling the sentiments of a person, this represents affective data.
Implementation	Implementation is the realization of an application, or execution of a plan, idea, model, design, specification, standard, algorithm, or policy. Computer Science

Chapter 5. Congress: The First Branch

	In computer science, an implementation is a realization of a technical specification or algorithm as a program, software component, or other computer system through programming and deployment. Many implementations may exist for a given specification or standard.
Stimulus	In economics, stimulus refers to attempts to use monetary or fiscal policy (or stabilization policy in general) to stimulate the economy. Recently "stimulus" has become particularly associated with Keynesian economics and the theory that government spending projects can generate economic growth in a recession. Stimulus can also refer to monetary policies like lowering interest rates and quantitative easing.
Gerrymandering	In the process of setting electoral boundaries, rather than using uniform geographic standards, Gerrymandering is a practice of political corruption that attempts to establish a political advantage for a particular party or group by manipulating geographic boundaries to create partisan, incumbent-protected, and neutral districts. The resulting district is known as a gerrymander; however, that word can also refer to the process. Gerrymandering may be used to achieve desired electoral results for a particular party, or may be used to help or hinder a particular group of constituents, such as a political, racial, linguistic, religious or class group.
Highway Trust Fund	The United States Highway Trust Fund is a transportation fund with three accounts - the bulk composed of the 'Highway Account', a smaller Mass Transit Account and a comparatively small Leaking Underground Storage Tank Trust Fund. Lawmakers established it in 1956 to ensure dependable financing for maintenance of the United States Interstate Highway System and certain other roads. Money in the fund is raised indirectly via a federal fuel tax of 18.4 cents per gallon on gasoline and 24.4 cents per gallon of diesel fuel and related excise taxes.
Patriot	Patriots was the name the peoples of the Spanish America, who rebelled against Spanish control during the Spanish American wars of independence, called themselves. They supported the principles of the Age of Enlightenment and sought to replace the existing governing structures with Juntas. At first they declared themselves loyal to Ferdinand VII, who was captive of Napoleon Bonaparte and who was seem as a supporter of the new ideals because of his conflict with his father, the absolutist Charles IV. However, when Ferdinand VII was restored to power and began the Absolutist Restauration, most patriots in South America decided to support independentism instead.

Chapter 5. Congress: The First Branch

Trusts	In Conflict of Laws, the Hague Convention on the Law Applicable to Trusts and on Their Recognition was concluded on 1 July 1985 and entered into force 1 January 1992. The Convention aims to harmonise not only the municipal law definitions of a trust both within the USA and outside the USA, but also the Conflict rules for resolving problems in the choice of the lex causae. Explanation Many states do not have a developed law of trusts, or the principles differ significantly between states. It was therefore necessary for the Hague Convention to define a trust to indicate the range of legal transactions regulated by the Convention and, perhaps more significantly, the range of applications not regulated.
Earmark	In United States politics, an earmark is a legislative (especially congressional) provision that directs approved funds to be spent on specific projects, or that directs specific exemptions from taxes or mandated fees. The term "earmark" is used in this sense in several countries, such as the US and South Africa. Earmarks can be found both in legislation (also called "Hard earmarks" or "Hardmarks") and in the text of Congressional committee reports (also called "Soft earmarks" or "Softmarks"). Hard earmarks are binding and have the effect of law, while soft earmarks do not have the effect of law but by custom are acted on as if they were binding.
Election	An election is a formal decision-making process by which a population chooses an individual to hold public office. Elections have been the usual mechanism by which modern representative democracy operates since the 17th century. Elections may fill offices in the legislature, sometimes in the executive and judiciary, and for regional and local government.
Legislation	Legislation is law which has been promulgated (or "enacted") by a legislature or other governing body, or the process of making it. (Another source of law is judge-made law or case law). Before an item of legislation becomes law it may be known as a bill, and may be broadly referred to as "legislation" while it remains under consideration to distinguish it from other business.

Chapter 5. Congress: The First Branch

LINCOLN	Lincoln was a parliamentary electorate in the Canterbury region of New Zealand from 1881 to 1890. The electorate was represented by two Members of Parliament: • Arthur Pyne O'Callaghan (1881-89), and • Alfred Saunders (1889-90)
Social security	Social security is primarily a social insurance program providing social protection, or protection against socially recognized conditions, including poverty, old age, disability, unemployment and others. Social security may refer to: • social insurance, where people receive benefits or services in recognition of contributions to an insurance scheme. These services typically include provision for retirement pensions, disability insurance, survivor benefits and unemployment insurance. • income maintenance--mainly the distribution of cash in the event of interruption of employment, including retirement, disability and unemployment • services provided by administrations responsible for social security.
Sophomore surge	A sophomore surge is a term used in the political science of the United States Congress that refers to an increase in votes that congressional candidates (candidates for the House of Representatives) usually receive when running for their first re-election. The phrase has been adopted in Australia by psephologist Malcolm Mackerras who is well-known for his electoral pendulums. History This phenomenon first started in the 1960s.

Chapter 5. Congress: The First Branch

North American Free Trade Agreement	The North American Free Trade Agreement is an agreement signed by the governments of Canada, Mexico, and the United States, creating a trilateral trade bloc in North America. The agreement came into force on January 1, 1994. It superseded the Canada-United States Free Trade Agreement between the U.S. and Canada. In terms of combined purchasing power parity GDP of its members, as of 2007 the trade bloc is the largest in the world and second largest by nominal GDP comparison.
	The North American Free Trade Agreement has two supplements, the North American Agreement on Environmental Cooperation (NAAEC) and the North American Agreement on Labor Cooperation (NAALC).
Redistricting	Redistricting, a form of redistribution, is the process of drawing United States district lines. This often means changing electoral district and constituency boundaries in response to periodic census results. In 36 states, the state legislature has primary responsibility for creating a redistricting plan, in many cases subject to approval by the state governor.
Seat	Seats were territorial-administrative units in the medieval Kingdom of Hungary. The seats were autonomous regions within the Kingdom, and were independent from the feudal county system. Their autonomy was granted in return for the military services they provided to the Hungarian Kings.
State	Many sovereign independent state are made up of a number of country subdivisions also called states. In some cases, such as the United States, the national government arose from a union of sovereign entities, which transferred some of their powers to the national government, while retaining the remainder of their sovereignty. These are sometimes called federal states.
Ensign	Ensign is a junior rank of commissioned officer in the armed forces of some countries, normally in the infantry or navy. As the junior officer in an infantry regiment was traditionally the carrier of the ensign flag, the rank itself acquired the name. The Spanish alférez and Portuguese alferes is a junior officer rank below lieutenant associated with carrying the flag, and so is often translated as "ensign".

Chapter 5. Congress: The First Branch

Political action committee	In the United States, a political action committee, is the name commonly given to a private group, regardless of size, organized to elect political candidates or to advance the outcome of a political issue or legislation. Legally, what constitutes a "Political action committee" for purposes of regulation is a matter of state and federal law. Under the Federal Election Campaign Act, an organization becomes a "political committee" by receiving contributions or making expenditures in excess of $1,000 for the purpose of influencing a federal election.
Volunteer	Volunteer, often abbreviated Vol., is a term used by a number of Irish republican paramilitary organisations to describe their members. Among these have been the various forms of the Irish Republican Army (IRA) and the Irish National Liberation Army (INLA). Óglach is the equivalent title used in the Irish language.
Abortion	Abortion is the termination of a pregnancy by the removal or expulsion of a fetus or embryo from the uterus, resulting in or caused by its death. An abortion can occur spontaneously due to complications during pregnancy or can be induced, in humans and other species. In the context of human pregnancies, an abortion induced to preserve the health of the gravida (pregnant female) is termed a therapeutic abortion, while an abortion induced for any other reason is termed an elective abortion.
Democratic Party	The Democratic Party is a social democratic political party in Italy, that is the largest party of Italian centre-left and the second largest of the country. It was founded on 14 October 2007 as a merger of various left-wing and centrist parties which were part of The Union in the 2006 general election. Several parties merged into the Democratic Party, however its bulk was formed by the Democrats of the Left and Democracy is Freedom - The Daisy.
Speaker	The term speaker is a title often given to the presiding officer (chair) of a deliberative assembly, especially a legislative body. The speaker's official role is to moderate debate, make rulings on procedure, announce the results of votes, and the like. The speaker decides who may speak and has the powers to discipline members who break the procedures of the house.

Chapter 5. Congress: The First Branch

Tribune	Tribune is a democratic socialist weekly, currently a magazine though in the past more often a newspaper, published in London. It considers itself "A thorn in the side of all governments, constructively to Labour, unforgiving to Conservatives."
	Origins
	Tribune was set up in early 1937 by two left-wing Labour Party Members of Parliament (MPs), Stafford Cripps and George Strauss, to back the Unity Campaign, an attempt to secure an anti-fascist and anti-appeasement United Front between the Labour Party and socialist parties to its left which involved Cripps's (Labour-affiliated) Socialist League, the Independent Labour Party and the Communist Party of Great Britain (CP).
	The paper's first editor was William Mellor, and its journalists included Michael Foot and Barbara Betts (later Barbara Castle).
Whig Party	The Whig Party was a political party of the United States during the era of Jacksonian democracy. Considered integral to the Second Party System and operating from the early 1830s to the mid-1850s, the party was formed in opposition to the policies of President Andrew Jackson and his Democratic Party. In particular, the Whigs supported the supremacy of Congress over the presidency and favored a program of modernization and economic protectionism.
Caucus	A caucus is a meeting of supporters or members of a political party or movement, especially in the United States. As the use of the term has been expanded the exact definition has come to vary among political cultures.
	Origin of the term
	The origin of the word caucus is debated, but it is generally agreed that it first came into use in the English colonies of North America.

Chapter 5. Congress: The First Branch

A February 1763 entry in the diary of John Adams of Braintree, Massachusetts, is one of the earliest appearances of Caucas, already with its modern connotations of a "smoke-filled room" where candidates for public election are pre-selected in private

This day learned that the Caucas Clubb meets at certain Times in the Garret of Tom Daws, the Adjutant of the Boston Regiment.

Majority	A majority, is a subset of a group consisting of more than half of the group. This should not be confused with a plurality, which is a subset having the largest number of parts. A plurality is not necessarily a majority, as the largest subset may be less than half of the entire group.
Minority	Minority, and the related concept of "becoming-minor," is a philosophical concept developed by Gilles Deleuze and Félix Guattari in their books Kafka: Towards a Minor Literature (1975), A Thousand Plateaus (1980), and elsewhere. In these texts, they criticize the concept of "majority". For Deleuze and Guattari, "becoming-minoritarian" is primarily an ethical action, one of the becomings one is affected by when avoiding "becoming-fascist".
Minority leader	In U.S. politics, the minority leader is the floor leader of the second largest caucus in a legislative body. Given the two-party nature of the U.S. system, the minority leader is almost inevitably either a Republican or a Democrat, with their counterpart being of the opposite party. The position is essentially that of the Leader of the Opposition.
Party conference	The terms party conference, political convention, and party congress usually refer to a general meeting of a political party. The conference is attended by certain delegates who represent the party membership. In most political parties, the party conference is the highest decision-making body of the organization, tasked with electing or nominating the party's leaders or leadership bodies, deciding party policy, and setting the party's platform and agendas.
Political Parties	Political Parties: A Sociological Study of the Oligarchical Tendencies of Modern Democracy is a book by sociologist Robert Michels, published in 1911, and first introducing the concept of iron law of oligarchy. It is considered one of the classics of sociology and political science. This work analyzes the power structures of organizations such as political parties and trade unions.

Chapter 5. Congress: The First Branch

Appropriation	In law and government, appropriation is the act of setting apart something for its application to a particular usage, to the exclusion of all other uses.
	It typically refers to the legislative designation of money for particular uses, in the context of a budget or spending bill.
	Ecclesiastical law
	In ecclesiastical law, appropriation is the perpetual annexation of an ecclesiastical benefice to the use of some spiritual corporation, either aggregate or sole.
Government	In the social sciences, the term government refers to the particular group of people, the administrative bureaucracy, who control a state at a given time, and the manner in which their governing organizations are structured. That is, governments are the means through which state power is employed. States are served by a continuous succession of different governments.
Stamp Act	A stamp act is a law enacted by government that requires a tax to be paid on the transfer of certain documents. The stamp act was considered unfair by many people. Those that pay the tax receive an official stamp on their documents.
ARTHUR	ARTHUR is an abbreviation for mobile "Artillery Hunting Radar" system developed in Sweden. This field artillery acquisition radar was developed for the primary role as the core element of a brigade or division level counter battery sensor system. It can also be used for peace support operations.
Rescue	Rescue refers to operations that usually involve the saving of life, or prevention of injury.
	Tools used might include search dogs, search and rescue horses, helicopters, the "Jaws of Life", and other hydraulic cutting and spreading tools used to extricate individuals from wrecked vehicles. Rescue operations are sometimes supported by special vehicles such as fire department's or EMS Heavy rescue vehicle.

Chapter 5. Congress: The First Branch

Affirmative action	Affirmative action refers to policies that take factors including "race, color, religion, sex or national origin" into consideration in order to benefit an underrepresented group at the expense of a majority group, usually as a means to counter the effects of a history of discrimination. The focus of such policies ranges from employment and education to public contracting and health programs. "Affirmative action" is action taken to increase the representation of women and minorities in areas of employment, education, and business from which they have been historically excluded.
Authority	Authority means invention, advice, opinion, influence, or command. Essentially authority is imposed by superiors upon inferiors either by force of arms (structural authority) or by force of argument (sapiential authority). Usually authority has components of both compulsion and persuasion.
Bill	A bill is a proposed law under consideration by a legislature. A bill does not become law until it is passed by the legislature and, in most cases, approved by the executive. Once a bill has been enacted into law, it is called an act or a statute.
Conference committee	A conference committee is a joint committee of a bicameral legislature, which is appointed by, and consists of, members of both chambers to resolve disagreements on a particular bill. While such committees are common in the United States Congress and other U.S. no longer in use in the Parliament of the United Kingdom or most other bicameral Westminster system parliaments. conference committee is usually composed of the senior members of the standing committees of each House that originally considered the legislation.
Gatekeeping	Gatekeeping is the process through which information is filtered for dissemination, be it publication, broadcasting, the Internet, or some other type of communication. As an academic theory, it is found in several fields, including communication studies, journalism, political science, and sociology. Originally focused on the mass media with its few-to-masses dynamic, theories of gatekeeping also now include the workings of face-to-face communication and the many-to-many dynamic now easily available via the Internet.
Session	In parliamentary procedure, a session is a meeting or series of connected meetings devoted to a single order of business, program, agenda, or announced purpose. Explanation Robert's Rules of Order Newly Revised (RONR)

Chapter 5. Congress: The First Branch

	An organization's bylaws may define a specific meaning and/or length of the term "session." The main significance of a session is that one session generally cannot tie the hands of a majority at a future session, except by adopting a special rule of order or an amendment to the bylaws, each of which require more than a majority vote. A session has implications for the renewability of motions.
Seniority	In finance, seniority refers to the order of repayment in the event of bankruptcy. Senior debt must be repaid before subordinated debt is repaid. Bonds that have the same seniority in a company's capital structure are described as being pari passu.
Virginia	The Commonwealth of Virginia is a U.S. state on the Atlantic Coast of the Southern United States. Virginia is nicknamed the "Old Dominion" and sometimes the "Mother of Presidents" because it is the birthplace of eight U.S. presidents. The geography and climate of the state are shaped by the Blue Ridge Mountains and the Chesapeake Bay, which provide habitat for much of its flora and fauna.
Lobbying	Lobbying is the intention of influencing decisions made by legislators and officials in the government by individuals, other legislators, constituents, or advocacy groups. A lobbyist is a person who tries to influence legislation on behalf of a special interest or a member of a lobby. Governments often define and regulate organized group lobbying that has become influential.
Accountability	Accountability is a concept in ethics and governance with several meanings. It is often used synonymously with such concepts as responsibility, answerability, blameworthiness, liability, and other terms associated with the expectation of account-giving. As an aspect of governance, it has been central to discussions related to problems in the public sector, nonprofit and private (corporate) worlds.
Administration	Administration, as a legal concept, is a procedure under the insolvency laws of a number of common law jurisdictions. It functions as a rescue mechanism for insolvent companies and allows them to carry on running their business. The process - an alternative to liquidation - is often known as going into administration.
Congressional Budget Office	The Congressional Budget Office is a federal agency within the legislative branch of the United States government. It is a government agency that provides economic data to Congress. The Congressional Budget Office was created as a nonpartisan agency by the Congressional Budget and Impoundment Control Act of 1974.

Chapter 5. Congress: The First Branch

Congressional Research Service	The Congressional Research Service known as "Congress's think tank", is the public policy research arm of the United States Congress. As a legislative branch agency within the Library of Congress, Congressional Research Service works exclusively and directly for Members of Congress, their Committees and staff on a confidential, nonpartisan basis.
	Its staff of approximately 900 employees includes lawyers, economists, reference librarians, and social, natural, and physical scientists.
Forum	A forum was the public space in the middle of a Roman city.
	In addition to its standard function as a marketplace, a forum was a gathering place of great social significance, and often the scene of diverse activities, including political discussions and debates, rendezvous, meetings, et cetera.
	Modelled on the Roman Forum in Rome itself, several smaller or more specialised forums appeared throughout Rome's archaic history.
General	General, Finnish: kenraali is the highest officer's rank in Sweden and Finland. In Sweden, it is held by the supreme commander of the Swedish Armed Forces and the monarch. In Finland, it is held by the Chief of Defence.

Chapter 5. Congress: The First Branch

Issue	In law, issue can mean several things: • In wills and trusts, a person's issue are his or her lineal descendants or offspring. These are distinguished from heirs, which can include other kin such as a brother, sister, mother, father, grandfather, uncle, aunt, nephew, niece, or cousin. • In corporations and business associations law, issue can refer to areas involving stocks. • In evidence as well as civil and criminal procedure, there are issues of fact. Issues of fact are rhetorically presented by statements of fact which are each put to a test: Is the statement true or false? Often, different parties have conflicting statements of fact.
Debate	Debate is a formal method of interactive and representational argument. Debate is a broader form of argument than logical argument, which only examines consistency from axiom, and factual argument, which only examines what is or isn't the case or rhetoric which is a technique of persuasion. Though logical consistency, factual accuracy and some degree of emotional appeal to the audience are important elements of the art of persuasion, in debating, one side often prevails over the other side by presenting a superior "context" and/or framework of the issue, which is far more subtle and strategic.
Deliberation	Deliberation is a process of thoughtfully weighing options, usually prior to voting. In legal settings a jury famously uses deliberation because it is given specific options, like guilty or not guilty, along with information and arguments to evaluate. Deliberation emphasizes the use of logic and reason as opposed to power-struggle, creativity, or dialog.
Publics	Publics are small groups of people who follow one or more particular issue very closely. They are well informed about the issue(s) and also have a very strong opinion on it/them. They tend to know more about politics than the average person, and, therefore, exert more influence, because these people care so deeply about their cause(s) that they donate much time and money.

Chapter 5. Congress: The First Branch

Public relations	Public relations is a field concerned with maintaining a public image for businesses, non-profit organizations or high-profile people, such as celebrities and politicians. An earlier definition of public relations, by The first World Assembly of Public Relations Associations held in Mexico City in August 1978, was "the art and social science of analyzing trends, predicting their consequences, counseling organizational leaders, and implementing planned programs of action, which will serve both the organization and the public interest." Others define it as the practice of managing communication between an organization and its publics. Public relations provides an organization or individual exposure to their audiences using topics of public interest and news items that provide a third-party endorsement and do not direct payment.
Filibuster	A filibuster is a type of parliamentary procedure. Specifically, it is a form of obstruction in a legislature or other decision-making body whereby a lone member can elect to delay or entirely prevent a vote on a proposal. The term "filibuster" was first used in 1851. It was derived from the Spanish filibustero, which translates as "pirate" or "freebooter." This term had evolved from the French word flibustier, which itself evolved from the Dutch vrijbuiter (free outsider).
Hold	Hold is a title of nobility, used in viking times used both in Scandinavia and in England. History Recognized as title for "noblemen of exalted rank" by Sir Francis Stenton in his renowned standard work Anglo-Saxon England, and described as a title just below the earl in Oxford Dictionary of Surnames, the title nevertheless has become somewhat obsolete even in historical treatises.

Chapter 5. Congress: The First Branch

	But in the main work on the topic the definition of hold as a noble title, both in Norway and old Northumbria, is crystal clear: Die norwegischen Höldar.
George Washington	George Washington is a public artwork that is a copy of an original bust created by French artist and neoclassical sculptor Jean Antoine Houdon, displayed inside of the Indiana Statehouse, which is located in Indianapolis, Indiana, USA. The bust is made of white plaster and its dimensions are 25x18x18 inches. Description This piece is a bust of the first President of the United States, George Washington. It is made of white plaster, and its dimensions are 25x18x18 inches.
Federalist	The term federalist describes several political beliefs around the world. Also, it may refer to the concept of federalism or the type of government called a federation. In early United States history, the Federalist Party was one of the first political parties; its members or supporters called themselves Federalists.
Advice	Advice, in constitutional law, is formal, usually binding, instruction given by one constitutional officer of state to another. Especially in parliamentary systems of government, Heads of state often act on the basis of advice issued by prime ministers or other government ministers. For example, Queen Elizabeth II formally appoints her British ministers on the advice of the British Prime Minister.
Consent	In criminal law, consent may be used as an excuse and prevent the defendant from incurring liability for what was done. Baker, "The Moral Limits of Consent as a Defense in the Criminal Law," 12(1) New Criminal Law Review (2009), see also consensual crime. Generally

Chapter 5. Congress: The First Branch

	A defense against criminal liability may arise when a defendant can argue that, because of consent, there was no crime (e.g., arguing that permission was given to use an automobile, so it was not theft or taken with out consent).
Nomination	Nomination is part of the process of selecting a candidate for either election to an office, or the bestowing of an honor or award.
	In the context of elections for public office, a candidate who has been selected by a political party is normally said to be the nominee of that party. The party's selection (that is, the nomination) is typically accomplished either based on one or more primary elections or by means of a political party convention or caucus, according to the rules of the party and any applicable election laws.
Nuclear option	In U.S. politics, the "nuclear option" (or "constitutional option") allows the United States Senate to reinterpret a procedural rule by invoking the argument that the constitution requires that the will of the majority be effective on specific Senate duties and procedures. This option allows a simple majority to override the rules of the Senate and end a filibuster or other delaying tactic. In contrast, the cloture rule requires a supermajority of 60 votes (out of 100) to end a filibuster.
Option	In finance, an option is a derivative financial instrument that establishes a contract between two parties concerning the buying or selling of an asset at a reference price. The buyer of the option gains the right, but not the obligation, to engage in some specific transaction on the asset, while the seller incurs the obligation to fulfill the transaction if so requested by the buyer. Other types of options exist, and options can in principle be created for any type of valuable asset.
Health care	Health or healthcare is the treatment and prevention of illness. Health care is delivered by professionals in medicine, dentistry, nursing, pharmacy and allied health.
	The social and political issues surrounding access to healthcare in the US have led to vigorous public debate and the almost colloquial use of terms such as health care health insurance (reimbursement of health care costs), and public health (the collective state and range of health in a population).

Chapter 5. Congress: The First Branch

Initiative	In political science, the initiative provides a means by which a petition signed by a certain minimum number of registered voters can force a public vote (plebiscite) on a proposed statute, constitutional amendment, charter amendment or ordinance, or, in its minimal form, to simply oblige the executive or legislative bodies to consider the subject by submitting it to the order of the day. It is a form of direct democracy.
	The initiative may take the form of either the direct initiative or indirect initiative.
Interest	Interest is a fee paid on borrowed assets. It is the price paid for the use of borrowed money, or, money earned by deposited funds. Assets that are sometimes lent with interest include money, shares, consumer goods through hire purchase, major assets such as aircraft, and even entire factories in finance lease arrangements.
Medicare	Medicare is a social insurance program administered by the United States government, providing health insurance coverage to people who are aged 65 and over, or who meet other special criteria. Medicare operates similar to a single-payer health care system, but the key difference is that its coverage only extends to 80% of any given medical cost; the remaining 20% of cost must be paid by other means, such as privately-held supplemental insurance, or paid by the patient.
	The program also funds residency training programs for the vast majority of physicians in the United States.
Left Behind	Left Behind is a series of 16 best-selling novels by Tim LaHaye and Jerry Jenkins, dealing with Christian dispensationalist End Times: pretribulation, premillennial, Christian eschatological viewpoint of the end of the world. The primary conflict of the series is the members of the Tribulation Force against the Global Community and its leader Nicolae Carpathia--the Antichrist. Left Behind is also the title of the first book in the series.

Chapter 5. Congress: The First Branch

Attack	In computer and computer networks an attack is any attempt to destroy, expose, alter, disable, steal or gain unauthorized access to or make unauthorized use of an asset. Definitions IETF Internet Engineering Task Force defines attack in RFC 2828 as: US Government CNSS Instruction No. 4009 dated 26 April 2010 by Committee on National Security Systems of United States of America defines an attack as: The increasing dependencies of modern society on information and computers networks (both in private and public sectors, including military) has led to new terms like cyber attack and Cyberwarfare. CNSS Instruction No. 4009 define a cyber attack as: Phenomenology An attack can be active or passive. An attack can be perpetrated by an insider or from outside the organization; <ul><li>An "inside attack" is an attack initiated by an entity inside the security perimeter (an "insider"), i.e., an entity that is authorized to access system resources but uses them in a way not approved by those who granted the authorization.</li><li>An "outside attack" is initiated from outside the perimeter, by an unauthorized or illegitimate user of the system (an "outsider").</li></ul>

Chapter 5. Congress: The First Branch

Invasion	An invasion is a military offensive consisting of all, or large parts of the armed forces of one geopolitical entity aggressively entering territory controlled by another such entity, generally with the objective of either conquering, liberating or re-establishing control or authority over a territory, forcing the partition of a country, altering the established government or gaining concessions from said government, or a combination thereof. An invasion can be the cause of a war, be a part of a larger strategy to end a war, or it can constitute an entire war in itself. Due to the large scale of the operations associated with invasions, they are usually strategic in planning and execution.
Mixed member proportional representation	Mixed member proportional representation, also termed mixed-member proportional voting and commonly abbreviated to MMP, is an 'additional member' voting system used to elect representatives to numerous legislatures around the world. MMP is similar to other forms of proportional representation (PR) in that the overall total of party members in the elected body is intended to mirror the overall proportion of votes received; it differs by including a set of members elected by geographic constituency who are deducted from the party totals so as to maintain overall proportionality. Therefore, the additional party seats are compensatory: they top up the local results.
Vietnam	Vietnam, officially the Socialist Republic of Vietnam is the easternmost country on the Indochina Peninsula in Southeast Asia. It is bordered by People's Republic of China (PRC) to the north, Laos to the northwest, Cambodia to the southwest, and the South China Sea, referred to as East Sea (Vietnamese: Bi?n Đông), to the east. With a population of over 86 million, Vietnam is the 13th most populous country in the world.
Logrolling	Logrolling is the trading of favors, or quid pro quo, such as vote trading by legislative members to obtain passage of actions of interest to each legislative member. It is also the "cross quoting" of papers by academics in order to drive up reference counts. The Nuttall Encyclopedia describes log-rolling as "mutual praise by authors of each other's work." American frontiersman Davy Crockett was one of the first to apply the term to legislation: The first known use of the term was by Congressman Davy Crockett, who said on the floor (of the U.S. House of Representatives) in 1835, "my people don't like me to log-roll in their business, and vote away pre-emption rights to fellows in other states that never kindle a fire on their own land."

Chapter 5. Congress: The First Branch

	The widest accepted origin is the old custom of neighbors assisting each other with the moving of logs.
Prison	A prison is a place in which people are physically confined and, usually, deprived of a range of personal freedoms. Imprisonment or incarceration is a legal penalty that may be imposed by the state for the commission of a crime. Other terms are penitentiary, correctional facility, and gaol (or jail).
Retirement	Retirement is the point where a person stops employment completely. A person may also semi-retire by reducing work hours.
	Many people choose to retire when they are eligible for private or public pension benefits, although some are forced to retire when physical conditions don't allow the person to work any more (by illness or accident) or as a result of legislation concerning their position.
Immigration reform	Immigration reform is a term used in political discussion regarding changes to current immigration policy of a country. In its strict definition, "reform " means to change into an improved form or condition, by amending or removing faults or abuses. In the political sense, immigration reform may include promoted, expanded, or open immigration, as well as reduced or eliminated immigration.
Watergate scandal	The Watergate scandal was a 1970s United States political scandal resulting from the break-in to the Democratic National Committee headquarters at the Watergate office complex in Washington, D.C. Effects of the scandal ultimately led to the resignation of the President of the United States, Richard Nixon, on August 9, 1974, the first and only resignation of any U.S. President. It also resulted in the indictment, trial, conviction and incarceration of several Nixon administration officials.
	The affair began with the arrest of five men for breaking and entering into the Democratic National Committee headquarters at the Watergate complex on June 17, 1972. The FBI connected the payments to the burglars to a slush fund used by the 1972 Committee to Re-elect the President.

Chapter 5. Congress: The First Branch

Amnesty	Amnesty is a legislative or executive act by which a state restores those who may have been guilty of an offense against it to the positions of innocent people. It includes more than pardon, in as much as it obliterates all legal remembrance of the offense. The word has the same root as amnesia.
Homosexuality	Homosexuality is romantic and/or sexual attraction or behavior among members of the same sex or gender. As a sexual orientation, homosexuality refers to "an enduring pattern of or disposition to experience sexual, affectional, or romantic attractions" primarily or exclusively to people of the same sex; "it also refers to an individual's sense of personal and social identity based on those attractions, behaviors expressing them, and membership in a community of others who share them."
	Homosexuality is one of the three main categories of sexual orientation, along with bisexuality and heterosexuality, within the heterosexual-homosexual continuum. The consensus of the behavioral and social sciences and the health and mental health professions is that homosexuality is a normal and positive variation in human sexual orientation, though many religious societies, including Catholicism, Mormonism, and Islam, and some psychological associations, such as NARTH, teach that homosexual activity is sinful or dysfunctional.
Civil War	"Civil War" is a song by the hard rock band Guns N' Roses, which originally appeared on the 1990 album Nobody's Child: Romanian Angel Appeal. It is a protest song on war, referring to all war as 'civil war' and that it only "feeds the rich while it buries the poor." In the song, singer Axl Rose asks, "What's so civil about war, anyway?"
	"Civil War" was the brainchild of the Guns N' Roses artists Slash, Axl Rose, and Duff McKagan. Slash stated that the song was an instrumental he had written right before the band left for the Japanese leg of its Appetite for Destruction world tour.
Commission	A commission is a physical document issued to certify the appointment of a commissioned officer by a sovereign power.

Chapter 5. Congress: The First Branch

	The more specific terms commissioning parchment or commissioning scroll are often used to avoid ambiguity, due to "commission" being a homonym which directs the individual in carrying out their duty regardless of what authority or responsibility they may have at any time. However the document is not usually in the form of a scroll and is more often printed on paper instead of parchment.
Frontier	A frontier is a political and geographical term referring to areas near or beyond a boundary. 'Frontier' was borrowed into English from French in the 15th century, with the meaning "borderland"--the region of a country that fronts on another country .
	The use of "frontier" to mean "a region at the edge of a settled area" is a special North American development.
Great Society	The Great Society was a set of domestic programs proposed or enacted in the United States on the initiative of President Lyndon B. Johnson. Two main goals of the Great Society social reforms were the elimination of poverty and racial injustice. New major spending programs that addressed education, medical care, urban problems, and transportation were launched during this period.
New Deal	The New Deal is a programme of active labour market policies introduced in the United Kingdom by the Labour government in 1998, initially funded by a one off £5bn windfall tax on privatised utility companies. The stated purpose is to reduce unemployment by providing training, subsidised employment and voluntary work to the unemployed. Spending on the New Deal was £1.3 billion in 2001.
New Frontier	The term New Frontier was used by John F. Kennedy in his acceptance speech in the 1960 United States presidential election to the Democratic National Convention at the Los Angeles Memorial Coliseum as the Democratic slogan to inspire America to support him. The phrase developed into a label for his administration's domestic and foreign programs.
	In the words of Robert D. Marcus: "Kennedy entered office with ambitions to eradicate poverty and to raise America's eyes to the stars through the space program".

Chapter 5. Congress: The First Branch

Society	A society is (1) a group of people related to each other through persistent relations such as social status, roles and social networks. (2) A large social grouping that shares the same geographical territory and is subject to the same political authority and dominant cultural expectations. Human societies are characterized by patterns of relationships between individuals sharing a distinctive culture and institutions.

Chapter 5. Congress: The First Branch

Chapter 5. Congress: The First Branch

CLAM 101

Chapter 6. The Presidency as an Institution

Congress	A congress is a formal meeting of the representatives of different nations, constituent states, independent organizations (such as trade unions), or groups.
	The term was chosen for the United States Congress to emphasize the status of each state represented there as a self-governing unit. Subsequent to the use of congress by the U.S. legislature, the term has been incorrectly adopted by many states within unions, and by unitary nation-states in the Americas, to refer to their legislatures.
Vietnam	Vietnam, officially the Socialist Republic of Vietnam is the easternmost country on the Indochina Peninsula in Southeast Asia. It is bordered by People's Republic of China (PRC) to the north, Laos to the northwest, Cambodia to the southwest, and the South China Sea, referred to as East Sea (Vietnamese: Bi?n Đông), to the east. With a population of over 86 million, Vietnam is the 13th most populous country in the world.
Watergate scandal	The Watergate scandal was a 1970s United States political scandal resulting from the break-in to the Democratic National Committee headquarters at the Watergate office complex in Washington, D.C. Effects of the scandal ultimately led to the resignation of the President of the United States, Richard Nixon, on August 9, 1974, the first and only resignation of any U.S. President. It also resulted in the indictment, trial, conviction and incarceration of several Nixon administration officials.
	The affair began with the arrest of five men for breaking and entering into the Democratic National Committee headquarters at the Watergate complex on June 17, 1972. The FBI connected the payments to the burglars to a slush fund used by the 1972 Committee to Re-elect the President.
Presidency	The word presidency is often used to describe the administration or the executive, the collective administrative and governmental entity that exists around an office of president of a state or nation. It is also the governing authority of some churches.

Chapter 6. The Presidency as an Institution

For example, in a republic with a presidential system of government, the presidency is the executive branch of government, and is personified by a single elected man or woman who holds the office of "president".

Attack

In computer and computer networks an attack is any attempt to destroy, expose, alter, disable, steal or gain unauthorized access to or make unauthorized use of an asset.

Definitions

IETF

Internet Engineering Task Force defines attack in RFC 2828 as:

US Government

CNSS Instruction No. 4009 dated 26 April 2010 by Committee on National Security Systems of United States of America defines an attack as:

The increasing dependencies of modern society on information and computers networks (both in private and public sectors, including military) has led to new terms like cyber attack and Cyberwarfare.

CNSS Instruction No. 4009 define a cyber attack as:

Phenomenology

An attack can be active or passive.

Chapter 6. The Presidency as an Institution

	An attack can be perpetrated by an insider or from outside the organization;
	An "inside attack" is an attack initiated by an entity inside the security perimeter (an "insider"), i.e., an entity that is authorized to access system resources but uses them in a way not approved by those who granted the authorization.
	An "outside attack" is initiated from outside the perimeter, by an unauthorized or illegitimate user of the system (an "outsider").
Affair	Affair may refer to professional, personal, or public business matters or to a particular business or private activity of a temporary duration, as in family affair, a private affair, or a romantic affair.
	Political affair
	Political affair may refer to the illicit or scandalous activities of public, such as the Watergate affair, or to a legally constituted government department, for example, the United Nations Department of Political Affairs.
	Romantic affair
	A romantic affair, also called an affair of the heart, may refer to sexual liaisons among unwed parties, or to various forms of nonmonogamy.
Allegiance	An allegiance is a duty of fidelity said to be owed by a subject or a citizen to his/her state or sovereign.
	Etymology
	From Middle English ligeaunce . The al- prefix was probably added through confusion with another legal term, allegeance, an "allegation" .

Chapter 6. The Presidency as an Institution

Homeland	A homeland is the concept of the place (cultural geography) to which an ethnic group holds a long history and a deep cultural association with --the country in which a particular national identity began. As a common noun, it simply connotes the country of one's origin.
Homeland security	Homeland security is an umbrella term for security efforts to protect the United States against terrorist activity. The term arose following a reorganization of many U.S. government agencies in 2003 to form the United States Department of Homeland Security after the September 11 attacks, and may be used to refer to the actions of that department, the United States Senate Committee on Homeland Security and Governmental Affairs, or the United States House of Representatives Committee on Homeland Security. In the United States In the United States, the concept of "homeland security" extends and recombines responsibilities of government agencies and entities.
Pledge	A pledge is a bailment or deposit of personal property to a creditor to secure repayment for some debt or engagement, The term is also used to denote the property which constitutes the security. Pledge is the ravi of Roman law, from which most of the modern law on the subject is derived. It differs from hypothecation and from the more usual mortgage in that the pledge is in the possession of the pledgee; it also differs from mortgage in being confined to personal property (rather than real property).
Election	An election is a formal decision-making process by which a population chooses an individual to hold public office. Elections have been the usual mechanism by which modern representative democracy operates since the 17th century. Elections may fill offices in the legislature, sometimes in the executive and judiciary, and for regional and local government.

Chapter 6. The Presidency as an Institution

Electoral college	An electoral college is a set of electors who are selected to elect a candidate to a particular office. Often these represent different organizations or entities, with each organization or entity represented by a particular number of electors or with votes weighted in a particular way. Many times, though, the electors are simply important people whose wisdom, ideally, would provide a better choice than a larger body.
Executive	Executive branch of government is the part of government that has sole authority and responsibility for the daily administration of the state bureaucracy. The division of power into separate branches of government is central to the democratic idea of the separation of powers. In many countries, the term "government" connotes only the executive branch.
Nomination	Nomination is part of the process of selecting a candidate for either election to an office, or the bestowing of an honor or award. In the context of elections for public office, a candidate who has been selected by a political party is normally said to be the nominee of that party. The party's selection (that is, the nomination) is typically accomplished either based on one or more primary elections or by means of a political party convention or caucus, according to the rules of the party and any applicable election laws.
Presidential election	A presidential election is the election of any head of state whose official title is president. List of presidential elections • Presidential elections of Mexico • United States presidential election

Chapter 6. The Presidency as an Institution

Caucus	A caucus is a meeting of supporters or members of a political party or movement, especially in the United States. As the use of the term has been expanded the exact definition has come to vary among political cultures.
	Origin of the term
	The origin of the word caucus is debated, but it is generally agreed that it first came into use in the English colonies of North America.
	A February 1763 entry in the diary of John Adams of Braintree, Massachusetts, is one of the earliest appearances of Caucas, already with its modern connotations of a "smoke-filled room" where candidates for public election are pre-selected in private
	This day learned that the Caucas Clubb meets at certain Times in the Garret of Tom Daws, the Adjutant of the Boston Regiment.
Executive order	An executive order in the United States is an order issued by the President, the head of the executive branch of the federal government.
New Deal	The New Deal is a programme of active labour market policies introduced in the United Kingdom by the Labour government in 1998, initially funded by a one off £5bn windfall tax on privatised utility companies. The stated purpose is to reduce unemployment by providing training, subsidised employment and voluntary work to the unemployed. Spending on the New Deal was £1.3 billion in 2001.
Power	Power is a measure of an entity's ability to control its environment, including the behavior of other entities. The term authority is often used for power, perceived as legitimate by the social structure. Power can be seen as evil or unjust, but the exercise of power is accepted as endemic to humans as social beings.
Civil War	"Civil War" is a song by the hard rock band Guns N' Roses, which originally appeared on the 1990 album Nobody's Child: Romanian Angel Appeal. It is a protest song on war, referring to all war as 'civil war' and that it only "feeds the rich while it buries the poor." In the song, singer Axl Rose asks, "What's so civil about war, anyway?"

Chapter 6. The Presidency as an Institution

"Civil War" was the brainchild of the Guns N' Roses artists Slash, Axl Rose, and Duff McKagan. Slash stated that the song was an instrumental he had written right before the band left for the Japanese leg of its Appetite for Destruction world tour.

Commission

A commission is a physical document issued to certify the appointment of a commissioned officer by a sovereign power.

The more specific terms commissioning parchment or commissioning scroll are often used to avoid ambiguity, due to "commission" being a homonym which directs the individual in carrying out their duty regardless of what authority or responsibility they may have at any time. However the document is not usually in the form of a scroll and is more often printed on paper instead of parchment.

Medicare

Medicare is a social insurance program administered by the United States government, providing health insurance coverage to people who are aged 65 and over, or who meet other special criteria. Medicare operates similar to a single-payer health care system, but the key difference is that its coverage only extends to 80% of any given medical cost; the remaining 20% of cost must be paid by other means, such as privately-held supplemental insurance, or paid by the patient.

The program also funds residency training programs for the vast majority of physicians in the United States.

Rights

Rights are legal, social, or ethical principles of freedom or entitlement; that is, rights are the fundamental normative rules about what is allowed of people or owed to people, according to some legal system, social convention, or ethical theory. Rights are of essential importance in such disciplines as law and ethics, especially theories of justice and deontology.

Chapter 6. The Presidency as an Institution

	Rights are often considered fundamental to civilization, being regarded as established pillars of society and culture, and the history of social conflicts can be found in the history of each right and its development.
Debate	Debate is a formal method of interactive and representational argument. Debate is a broader form of argument than logical argument, which only examines consistency from axiom, and factual argument, which only examines what is or isn't the case or rhetoric which is a technique of persuasion. Though logical consistency, factual accuracy and some degree of emotional appeal to the audience are important elements of the art of persuasion, in debating, one side often prevails over the other side by presenting a superior "context" and/or framework of the issue, which is far more subtle and strategic.
Habeas corpus	Habeas corpus is a writ, or legal action, through which a prisoner can be released from unlawful detention. The remedy can be sought by the prisoner or by another person coming to his aid. Habeas corpus originated in the English legal system, but it is now available in many nations.
Inherent Powers	Inherent powers are those powers that a sovereign state holds. The President derives these powers from the loosely worded statements in the Constitution that "the executive Power shall be vested in a President" and that the President should "take Care that the Laws be faithfully executed"; defined through practice rather than through constitutional or statutory law
	In re-re's, 158 U.S. 564 (1895), was a United States Supreme Court decision handed down concerning Eugene V. Debs and labor unions.
Afghanistan	Afghanistan officially the Islamic Republic of Afghanistan, is a landlocked and mountainous country in south-central Asia. It is bordered by Pakistan in the south and east, Iran in the west, Turkmenistan, Uzbekistan and Tajikistan in the north, and China in the far northeast. The territories now comprising Afghanistan have been an ancient focal point of the Silk Road and human migration.

Chapter 6. The Presidency as an Institution

National security	National security is the requirement to maintain the survival of the nation-state through the use of economic, military and political power and the exercise of diplomacy. The concept developed mostly in the United States of America after World War II. Initially focusing on military might, it now encompasses a broad range of facets, all of which impinge on the military or economic security of the nation and the values espoused by the national society. Accordingly, in order to possess national security, a nation needs to possess economic security, energy security, environmental security, etc.
National Security Council	A National Security Council is usually an executive branch governmental body responsible for coordinating policy on national security issues and advising chief executives on matters related to national security. An National Security Council is often headed by a national security advisor and staffed with senior-level officials from military, diplomatic, intelligence, law enforcement and other governmental bodies. The functions and responsibilities of an National Security Council at the strategic state level are different from those of the United Nations Security Council, which is more of a diplomatic forum.
North Korea	North Korea officially the Democratic People's Republic of Korea (DPRK; Chosongul: ??????????), is a country in East Asia, occupying the northern half of the Korean Peninsula. Its capital and largest city is Pyongyang. The Korean Demilitarized Zone serves as the buffer zone between North Korea and South Korea.
Security Council	The Security Council (?????? Anzen-Hosho-Kaigi?) of Japan is the nine-person national security council which advises the prime minister on national security and the military and deals with a wide spectrum of issues which indirectly affect Japan's broader interests, including basic national defense policy, the National Defense Program Outline, the outline on coordinating industrial production and other matters related to the National Defense Program Outline, including decisions on diplomatic initiatives and defense operations.
Senate	A senate is a deliberative assembly, often the upper house or chamber of a legislature or parliament. There have been many such bodies in history, since senate means the assembly of the eldest and wiser members of the society and ruling class. Two of the first official senates were the Spartan Gerousia (Γερουσ?α) and the Roman Senate.
Commander	Commander is a naval rank which is also sometimes used as a military title depending on the individual customs of a given military service. Commander is also used as a rank or title in some organizations outside of the armed forces, particularly in police and law enforcement. Commander as a naval rank

Chapter 6. The Presidency as an Institution

	Commander is a rank used in many navies and some air forces but is very rarely used as a rank in armies (except in special forces where it designates the team leader).
Surveillance	Surveillance is the monitoring of the behavior, activities, or other changing information, usually of people and often in a surreptitious manner. It most usually refers to observation of individuals or groups by government organizations, but disease surveillance, for example, is monitoring the progress of a disease in a community. The word surveillance is the French word for "watching over".
Resolution	In policy debate, a resolution is a normative statement which the affirmative team affirms and the negative team negates. Resolutions are selected annually by affiliated schools. At the college level, a number of topics are proposed and interested parties write 'topic papers' discussing the pros and cons of that individual topic.
Taliban	The Taliban, alternative spelling Taleban, is an Islamist militia group that ruled large parts of Afghanistan from September 1996 onwards. Although in control of Afghanistan's capital (Kabul) and most of the country for five years, the Taliban's Islamic Emirate of Afghanistan gained diplomatic recognition from only three states: Pakistan, Saudi Arabia, and the United Arab Emirates. After the attacks of September 11 2001 the Taliban regime was overthrown by Operation Enduring Freedom.

Chapter 6. The Presidency as an Institution

War Powers Resolution	The War Powers Resolution of 1973 (50 U.S.C. 1541-1548) was a United States Congress joint resolution providing that the President can send U.S. armed forces into action abroad only by authorization of Congress or if the United States is already under attack or serious threat. The War Powers Resolution requires the president to notify Congress within 48 hours of committing armed forces to military action and forbids armed forces from remaining for more than 60 days, with a further 30 day withdrawal period, without an authorization of the use of military force or a declaration of war. The resolution was passed by two-thirds of Congress, overriding a presidential veto.
George Washington	George Washington is a public artwork that is a copy of an original bust created by French artist and neoclassical sculptor Jean Antoine Houdon, displayed inside of the Indiana Statehouse, which is located in Indianapolis, Indiana, USA. The bust is made of white plaster and its dimensions are 25x18x18 inches. Description This piece is a bust of the first President of the United States, George Washington. It is made of white plaster, and its dimensions are 25x18x18 inches.
Invasion	An invasion is a military offensive consisting of all, or large parts of the armed forces of one geopolitical entity aggressively entering territory controlled by another such entity, generally with the objective of either conquering, liberating or re-establishing control or authority over a territory, forcing the partition of a country, altering the established government or gaining concessions from said government, or a combination thereof. An invasion can be the cause of a war, be a part of a larger strategy to end a war, or it can constitute an entire war in itself. Due to the large scale of the operations associated with invasions, they are usually strategic in planning and execution.
Terrorism	Terrorism is the systematic use of terror especially as a means of coercion. No universally agreed, legally binding, criminal law definition of terrorism currently exists. Common definitions of terrorism refer only to those violent acts which are intended to create fear (terror), are perpetrated for a religious, political or ideological goal, deliberately target or disregard the safety of non-combatants (civilians), and are committed by non-government agencies.

Chapter 6. The Presidency as an Institution

Little Rock	Little Rock (ca. 1805-1868) was a council chief of the Wutapiu band of Southern Cheyennes. He was the only council chief who remained with Black Kettle following the Sand Creek massacre of 1864. Little Rock was a signatory of the Medicine Lodge Treaty of 1867. In August 1868, Little Rock was interviewed at Fort Lyon by Indian agent Edward W. Wynkoop about raids by a large Cheyenne war party on white settlements along the Saline and Solomon in Kansas.
National Guard	The National Guard was the name given at the time of the French Revolution to the militias formed in each city, in imitation of the National Guard created in Paris. It was a military force separate from the regular army. Initially under the command of the Marquis de Lafayette, then briefly under the Marquis de Mandat, it was strongly identified until the summer of 1792 with the middle class and its support for constitutional monarchy.
Patriot	Patriots was the name the peoples of the Spanish America, who rebelled against Spanish control during the Spanish American wars of independence, called themselves. They supported the principles of the Age of Enlightenment and sought to replace the existing governing structures with Juntas. At first they declared themselves loyal to Ferdinand VII, who was captive of Napoleon Bonaparte and who was seem as a supporter of the new ideals because of his conflict with his father, the absolutist Charles IV. However, when Ferdinand VII was restored to power and began the Absolutist Restauration, most patriots in South America decided to support independentism instead.
Pardon	A pardon is the forgiveness of a crime and the penalty associated with it. It is granted by a head of state, such as a monarch or president, or by a competent church authority. Commutation is an associated term, meaning the lessening of the penalty of the crime without forgiving the crime itself.
Amnesty	Amnesty is a legislative or executive act by which a state restores those who may have been guilty of an offense against it to the positions of innocent people. It includes more than pardon, in as much as it obliterates all legal remembrance of the offense. The word has the same root as amnesia.
Constitutional amendment	A constitutional amendment is a change to the constitution of a nation or a state. In jurisdictions with "rigid" or "entrenched" constitutions, amendments do not require a special procedure different from that used for enacting ordinary laws.

Chapter 6. The Presidency as an Institution

	Some constitutions do not have to be amended with the direct consent of the electorate in a referendum.
Diplomacy	Diplomacy is the art and practice of conducting negotiations between representatives of groups or states. It usually refers to international diplomacy, the conduct of international relations through the intercession of professional diplomats with regard to issues of peace-making, trade, war, economics, culture, environment and human rights. International treaties are usually negotiated by diplomats prior to endorsement by national politicians.
Draft	In elections in the United States, political drafts are used to encourage or compel a certain person to enter a political race, by demonstrating a significant groundswell of support for the candidate. A write-in campaign may also be considered a draft campaign. Political history of draft movements The movement to draft Dwight D. Eisenhower Movements to draft five-star general Dwight D. Eisenhower to run as a candidate for President of the United States appeared in both the Democratic and Republican parties in 1948 and again during 1951. Eisenhower did his best to ignore them, but Henry Cabot Lodge entered Eisenhower in the 1952 New Hampshire Republican primary without the general's authorization.
State	Many sovereign independent state are made up of a number of country subdivisions also called states. In some cases, such as the United States, the national government arose from a union of sovereign entities, which transferred some of their powers to the national government, while retaining the remainder of their sovereignty. These are sometimes called federal states.
United States	The United States of America (also referred to as the United States, the U.S., the USA, or America) is a federal constitutional republic comprising fifty states and a federal district. The country is situated mostly in central North America, where its forty-eight contiguous states and Washington, D.C., the capital district, lie between the Pacific and Atlantic Oceans, bordered by Canada to the north and Mexico to the south. The state of Alaska is in the northwest of the continent, with Canada to the east and Russia to the west across the Bering Strait.

Chapter 6. The Presidency as an Institution

United States v. Nixon	United States v. Nixon, 418 U.S. 683 (1974), was a landmark United States Supreme Court decision. It was a unanimous 8-0 ruling involving President Richard Nixon and was important to the late stages of the Watergate scandal. It is considered a crucial precedent limiting the power of any U.S. president.
Divided government	In the United States, divided government describes a situation in which one party controls the White House and another party controls one or both houses of the United States Congress. Divided government is suggested by some to be an undesirable product of the separation of powers in the United States' political system. Earlier in the 20th century, divided government was rare.
Executive privilege	In the United States government, executive privilege is the power claimed by the President of the United States and other members of the executive branch to resist certain subpoenas and other interventions by the legislative and judicial branches of government. The concept of executive privilege is not mentioned explicitly in the United States Constitution, but the Supreme Court of the United States ruled it to be an element of the separation of powers doctrine, and/or derived from the supremacy of executive branch in its own area of Constitutional activity.
	The Supreme Court confirmed the legitimacy of this doctrine in United States v. Nixon, but only to the extent of confirming that there is a qualified privilege.
Government	In the social sciences, the term government refers to the particular group of people, the administrative bureaucracy, who control a state at a given time, and the manner in which their governing organizations are structured. That is, governments are the means through which state power is employed. States are served by a continuous succession of different governments.
Privilege	Privilege is a way of framing issues surrounding social inequality, focusing as much on the advantages that one group accrues from society as on the disadvantages that another group experiences.
	Group role

Chapter 6. The Presidency as an Institution

Privilege differs from conditions of overt prejudice, in which a dominant group actively seeks to oppress or suppress another group for its own advantage. Instead, theories of privilege suggest that the privileged group views its social, cultural, and economic experiences as a norm that everyone should experience, rather than as an advantaged position that must be maintained at the expense of others.

Court

A court is a form of tribunal, often a governmental institution, with the authority to adjudicate legal disputes between parties and carry out the administration of justice in civil, criminal, and administrative matters in accordance with the rule of law. In both common law and civil law legal systems, courts are the central means for dispute resolution, and it is generally understood that all persons have an ability to bring their claims before a court. Similarly, the rights of those accused of a crime include the right to present a defense before a court.

LINCOLN

Lincoln was a parliamentary electorate in the Canterbury region of New Zealand from 1881 to 1890.

The electorate was represented by two Members of Parliament:

- Arthur Pyne O'Callaghan (1881-89), and
- Alfred Saunders (1889-90)

Chapter 6. The Presidency as an Institution

Appointee	An appointee may be one of the following: • A member who is appointed to a position or office is called an appointee. In law, such a term is applied to one who is granted power of appointment of property. • An appointee was also a foot soldier in the French army, who, for long service and bravery, received more pay than other privates. • An appointee is the third most lower rank of the Italian Corps of Carabineers • An appointee is the third most lower rank of the Swiss Armed Forces • An appointee is also a person or organisation entrusted with managing the daily finances of vulnerable individuals in the UK.
Gerrymandering	In the process of setting electoral boundaries, rather than using uniform geographic standards, Gerrymandering is a practice of political corruption that attempts to establish a political advantage for a particular party or group by manipulating geographic boundaries to create partisan, incumbent-protected, and neutral districts. The resulting district is known as a gerrymander; however, that word can also refer to the process. Gerrymandering may be used to achieve desired electoral results for a particular party, or may be used to help or hinder a particular group of constituents, such as a political, racial, linguistic, religious or class group.
Line-item veto	In government, the line-item veto, is the power of an executive authority to nullify or cancel specific provisions of a bill, usually a budget appropriations bill, without vetoing the entire legislative package. The line-item vetoes are usually subject to the possibility of legislative override as are traditional vetoes.
Prison	A prison is a place in which people are physically confined and, usually, deprived of a range of personal freedoms. Imprisonment or incarceration is a legal penalty that may be imposed by the state for the commission of a crime. Other terms are penitentiary, correctional facility, and gaol (or jail).

Chapter 6. The Presidency as an Institution

Federalist	The term federalist describes several political beliefs around the world. Also, it may refer to the concept of federalism or the type of government called a federation. In early United States history, the Federalist Party was one of the first political parties; its members or supporters called themselves Federalists.
Social security	Social security is primarily a social insurance program providing social protection, or protection against socially recognized conditions, including poverty, old age, disability, unemployment and others. Social security may refer to: - social insurance, where people receive benefits or services in recognition of contributions to an insurance scheme. These services typically include provision for retirement pensions, disability insurance, survivor benefits and unemployment insurance. - income maintenance--mainly the distribution of cash in the event of interruption of employment, including retirement, disability and unemployment - services provided by administrations responsible for social security.
Bailout	In economics, a bailout is an act of loaning or giving capital to an entity (a company, a country, or an individual) that is in danger of failing, in an attempt to save it from bankruptcy, insolvency, or total liquidation and ruin; or to allow a failing entity to fail gracefully without spreading contagion. Overview A bailout could be done for mere profit, as when a predatory investor resurrects a floundering company by buying its shares at fire-sale prices; for social improvement, as when, hypothetically speaking, a wealthy philanthropist reinvents an unprofitable fast food company into a non-profit food distribution network; or the bailout of a company might be seen as a necessity in order to prevent greater, socioeconomic failures: For example, the US government assumes transportation to be the backbone of America's general economic fluency, which maintains the nation's geopolitical power. As such, it is the policy of the US government to protect the biggest American companies responsible for transportation--airliners, petrol companies, etc.--from failure through subsidies and low-interest loans.

Chapter 6. The Presidency as an Institution

Initiative	In political science, the initiative provides a means by which a petition signed by a certain minimum number of registered voters can force a public vote (plebiscite) on a proposed statute, constitutional amendment, charter amendment or ordinance, or, in its minimal form, to simply oblige the executive or legislative bodies to consider the subject by submitting it to the order of the day. It is a form of direct democracy.
	The initiative may take the form of either the direct initiative or indirect initiative.
Institution	An institution is any structure or mechanism of social order and cooperation governing the behavior of a set of individuals within a given human community. Institutions are identified with a social purpose and permanence, transcending individual human lives and intentions, and with the making and enforcing of rules governing cooperative human behavior.
	The term "institution" is commonly applied to customs and behavior patterns important to a society, as well as to particular formal organizations of government and public service.
National Convention	During the French Revolution, the National Convention, in France, comprised the constitutional and legislative assembly which sat from 20 September 1792 to 26 October 1795. It held executive power in France during the first years of the French First Republic. It was succeeded by the Directory, commencing 2 November 1795. Prominent members of the original Convention included Maximilien Robespierre of the Jacobin Club, Jean-Paul Marat (affiliated with the Jacobins, though never a formal member), and Georges Danton of the Cordeliers.
Environmental protection	Environmental protection is a practice of protecting the environment, on individual, organizational or governmental level, for the benefit of the natural environment and (or) humans. Due to the pressures of population and our technology the biophysical environment is being degraded, sometimes permanently. This has been recognized and governments began placing restraints on activities that caused environmental degradation.
Environmental Protection Agency	The Environmental Protection Agency (Irish: An Ghníomhaireacht um Chaomhnú Comhshaoil) has responsibilities for a wide range of licensing, enforcement, monitoring and assessment activities associated with environmental protection.

Chapter 6. The Presidency as an Institution

Geneva	Geneva is the second-most-populous city in Switzerland (after Zürich) and is the most populous city of Romandie. Situated where the Rhône River exits Lake Geneva, it is the capital of the Republic and Canton of Geneva. While the municipality itself (ville de Genève) has a population (as of December 2009) of 189,313, the canton of Geneva has 457,628 residents (as of December 2009).
Geneva Conventions	The Geneva Conventions comprise four treaties and three additional protocols that set the standards in international law for humanitarian treatment of the victims of war. The singular term Geneva Convention refers to the agreements of 1949, negotiated in the aftermath of World War II, updating the terms of the first three treaties and adding a fourth treaty. The language is extensive, with articles defining the basic rights of those captured during a military conflict, establishing protections for the wounded, and addressing protections for civilians in and around a war zone.
Deregulation	Deregulation is the removal or simplification of government rules and regulations that constrain the operation of market forces. Deregulation does not mean elimination of laws against fraud, but eliminating or reducing government control of how business is done, thereby moving toward a more laissez-faire, free market. It is different from liberalization, where more players enter in the market, but continues the regulation and guarantee of consumer rights and maximum and minimum prices.
Detention	Detention is the process when a state, government or citizen lawfully holds a person by removing their freedom of liberty at that time. This can be due to (pending) criminal charges being raised against the individual as part of a prosecution or to protect a person or property. Being detained does not always result in being taken to a particular area (generally called a detention centre), either for interrogation, or as punishment for a crime.
Rendition	Rendition is a 2007 work of interactive fiction by "nespresso", written using Inform 7 and published in z-code format, in which the player performs an interrogation of a suspected terrorist. The game describes itself as a "political art experiment in text adventure form". It was submitted to the 2007 Interactive Fiction Art Show in the "Portrait" category.
Torture	Torture, according to the United Nations Convention Against Torture is:

Chapter 6. The Presidency as an Institution

Throughout history, torture has often been used as a method of political re-education, interrogation, punishment, and coercion. In addition to state-sponsored torture, individuals or groups may be motivated to inflict torture on others for similar reasons to those of a state; however, the motive for torture can also be for the sadistic gratification of the torturer, as in the Moors murders.

Torture is prohibited under international law and the domestic laws of most countries in the 21st century.

Administration	Administration, as a legal concept, is a procedure under the insolvency laws of a number of common law jurisdictions. It functions as a rescue mechanism for insolvent companies and allows them to carry on running their business. The process - an alternative to liquidation - is often known as going into administration.
Health administration	Health administration is the field relating to leadership, management, and administration of hospitals, hospital networks, and health care systems. Health care administrators are considered health care professionals.
	The discipline is known by many names, including health management, healthcare management, health systems management, health care systems management, and medical and health services management.
Tariff	A tariff is a tax levied on imports or exports.
	History
	Tariffs are usually associated with protectionism, a government's policy of controlling trade between nations to support the interests of its own citizens. For economic reasons, tariffs are usually imposed on imported goods.

Chapter 6. The Presidency as an Institution

Adjustment	In law, the term adjustment may appear in varied contexts, as a synonym for terms with unrelated definitions: General Definition Adjust: 1. To settle or to bring to a satisfactory state, so that the parties are agreed in the result; as, to adjust accounts. 2. When applied to a liquidated demand, the verb "adjust" has the same meaning as the word "settle" in the same connection, and means to pay the demand. When applied to an unliquidated demand, it means to ascertain the amount due or to settle. In the latter connection, to settle means to effect a mutual adjustment between the parties and to agree upon the balance. Common Uses General Debt - Debtor and creditor adjustment: As the term appears in an assignment for the benefit of creditors, "Creditor" means one who has a definite demand against the assignor, or a cause of action capable of adjustment and liquidation at trial. 6 Am J2d Assign for Crs § 109. - Adjustable Rate Loan: Loan arrangement which permits the lender to change the interest rate based on a specific factor such as the prime lending rate charged by banks. - Adjusting agency: In one sense, a collection agency; in another sense, an agency representing a debtor in making an arrangement with his creditors for the settlement of his obligations by modification of the indebtedness.
Consumer product	A consumer product is generally any tangible personal property for sale and that is used for personal, family, or household for non-business purposes. The determination whether a good is a consumer product requires a factual finding, on a case-by-case basis. This basis will vary from one jurisdiction to another.

Chapter 6. The Presidency as an Institution

Democratic Party	The Democratic Party is a social democratic political party in Italy, that is the largest party of Italian centre-left and the second largest of the country.
	It was founded on 14 October 2007 as a merger of various left-wing and centrist parties which were part of The Union in the 2006 general election. Several parties merged into the Democratic Party, however its bulk was formed by the Democrats of the Left and Democracy is Freedom - The Daisy.
Leviathan	Leviathan, Forme and Power of a Common Wealth Ecclesiasticall and Civil, commonly called Leviathan, is a book written by Thomas Hobbes which was published in 1651. It is titled after the biblical Leviathan. The book concerns the structure of society and legitimate government, and is regarded as one of the earliest and most influential examples of social contract theory. The publisher was Andrew Crooke, partner in Andrew Crooke and William Cooke.
Corporate action	A corporate action is an event initiated by a public company that affects the securities (equity or debt) issued by the company. Some corporate actions such as a dividend (for equity securities) or coupon payment (for debt securities (bonds)) may have a direct financial impact on the shareholders or bondholders; another example is a call (early redemption) of a debt security. Other corporate actions such as stock split may have an indirect impact, as the increased liquidity of shares may cause the price of the stock to rise.
Woodrow Wilson	Thomas Woodrow Wilson was the 28th President of the United States from 1913 to 1921. A leader of the Progressive Movement, he served as President of Princeton University from 1902 to 1910, and then as the Governor of New Jersey from 1911 to 1913. With Theodore Roosevelt and William Howard Taft dividing the Republican Party vote, Wilson was elected President as a Democrat in 1912. He is the only U.S. President to hold a Ph.D. degree, which he obtained from Johns Hopkins University.
	In his first term, Wilson persuaded a Democratic Congress to pass the Federal Reserve Act, Federal Trade Commission Act, the Clayton Antitrust Act, the Federal Farm Loan Act and America's first-ever federal progressive income tax in the Revenue Act of 1913. Wilson brought many white Southerners into his administration, and tolerated their expansion of segregation in many federal agencies.

Chapter 6. The Presidency as an Institution

	Narrowly re-elected in 1916, Wilson's second term centered on World War I. He based his re-election campaign around the slogan "he kept us out of war", but U.S. neutrality was challenged in early 1917 when the German government sent the Zimmermann Telegram to Mexico and proposed a military alliance in a war against the U.S., and began unrestricted submarine warfare, sinking, without warning, every American merchant ship its submarines could find.
Supremacy	The supremacy of EU law is a principle of by which the laws of European Union member states that conflict with laws of the European Union must be ignored by national courts so that the European Union law can take effect. The legal doctrine emerged from the European Court of Justice through a number of decisions. Development In Costa v. ENEL. Mr Costa was an Italian citizen opposed to nationalising energy.
Hundred Days	The Hundred Days, marked the period between Emperor Napoleon I of France's return from exile on Elba to Paris on 20 March 1815 and the second restoration of King Louis XVIII on 8 July 1815 (a period of 111 days). This period saw the War of the Seventh Coalition, and includes the Waterloo Campaign and the Neapolitan War. The phrase les Cent Jours was first used by the prefect of Paris, Gaspard, comte de Chabrol, in his speech welcoming the King.
Corporation	In feudal Europe, corporations were aggregations of business interests in compact, usually with an explicit license from city, church, or national leaders. These functioned as effective monopolies for a particular good or labor. The term "corporation" was used as late as the 18th century in England to refer to such ventures as the East India Company or the Hudson's Bay Company: commercial organizations that operated under royal patent to have exclusive rights to a particular area of trade.

Chapter 6. The Presidency as an Institution

Poland	Poland officially the Republic of Poland - is a country in Central Europe bordered by Germany to the west; the Czech Republic and Slovakia to the south; Ukraine, Belarus and Lithuania to the east; and the Baltic Sea and Kaliningrad Oblast, a Russian exclave, to the north. The total area of Poland is 312,679 square kilometres (120,726 sq mi), making it the 69th largest country in the world and the 9th largest in Europe. Poland has a population of over 38 million people, which makes it the 34th most populous country in the world and the sixth most populous member of the European Union, being its most populous post-communist member.
Economic policy	Economic policy refers to the actions that governments take in the economic field. It covers the systems for setting interest rates and government budget as well as the labour market, national ownership, and many other areas of government interventions into the economy. Such policies are often influenced by international institutions like the International Monetary Fund or World Bank as well as political beliefs and the consequent policies of parties.
Policy	A policy is typically described as a principle or rule to guide decisions and achieve rational outcome(s). The term is not normally used to denote what is actually done, this is normally referred to as either procedure or protocol. Whereas a policy will contain the 'what' and the 'why', procedures or protocols contain the 'what', the 'how', the 'where', and the 'when'.
Cabinet	In the European Commission, a cabinet is the personal office of a European Commissioner. The role of a cabinet is to give political guidance to its Commissioner, while technical preparation is handled by the DGs (the European Civil Service). Composition The Commissioner's cabinets are seen as the real concentration of power within the Commission and consists of six members, but the exact membership faces restrictions.

Chapter 6. The Presidency as an Institution

Impeachment	Impeachment is a formal process in which an official is accused of unlawful activity and the outcome of which, depending on the country, can lead to the removal of that official from office or other punishment. Medieval popular etymology also associated it (wrongly) with derivations from the Latin impetere (to attack). (In its more frequent and more technical usage, impeachment of a person in the role of a witness is the act of challenging the honesty or credibility of that person).
Equity	Equity is the concept or idea of fairness in economics, particularly as to taxation or welfare economics.
	Overview
	Equity may be distinguished from economic efficiency in overall evaluation of social welfare. Although 'equity' has broader uses, it may be posed as a counterpart to economic inequality in yielding a "good" distribution of welfare.
Office of Management and Budget	The Office of Management and Budget is a Cabinet-level office, and is the largest office within the Executive Office of the President of the United States (EOP).
	The current OMB Director is Jacob Lew.
	History
	The Bureau of the Budget, OMB's predecessor, was established as a part of the Department of the Treasury by the Budget and Accounting Act of 1921, which was signed into law by President Warren G. Harding.
Decision	A decision, defined in Article 288 of the Treaty on the Functioning of the European Union (formerly Article 249 TEC), is one of the three binding instruments provided by secondary EU legislation. A decision is binding on the person or entity to which it is addressed. Decisions may be addressed to member states or individuals.

Chapter 6. The Presidency as an Institution

Military base	A military base is a facility directly owned and operated by and/or for the military or one of its branches that shelters military equipment and personnel, and facilitates training and operations. In general, a military base provides accommodations for one or more units, but it may also be used as a command center, a training ground, or a proving ground. In most cases, a military base relies on some outside help in order to operate.
Weapon	A weapon is an instrument used with the aim of causing harm or death to human being -- and for inflicting damage upon civil or military infrastructure and life-sustaining natural resources. In essence, it is a tool made with the purpose of increasing the efficacy and efficiency of such activities as hunting, fighting, the committing of criminal acts, the preserving of law and order, and the waging of war in an offensive or defensive fashion.
	Weapons are employed individually or collectively and can be improvised or purpose-built, sometimes with great skill and ingenuity.
Election Day	Election Day refers to the day when general elections are held. In many countries, general elections are always held on a Sunday, to enable as many voters as possible to participate, while in other countries elections are always held on a weekday. However, some countries, or regions within a country, always make a weekday election day a public holiday, thus satisfying both demands.
Environmental quality	Environmental quality is a set of properties and characteristics of the environment, either generalized or local, as they impinge on human beings and other organisms. It is a measure of the condition of an environment relative to the requirements of one or more species and or to any human need or purpose.
	Environmental quality is a general term which can refer to varied characteristics that relate to the natural environment as well as the built environment, such as air and water purity or pollution, noise and the potential effects which such characteristics may have on physical and mental health caused by human activities.

Chapter 6. The Presidency as an Institution

Great Society	The Great Society was a set of domestic programs proposed or enacted in the United States on the initiative of President Lyndon B. Johnson. Two main goals of the Great Society social reforms were the elimination of poverty and racial injustice. New major spending programs that addressed education, medical care, urban problems, and transportation were launched during this period.
Henry	Saint Henry was a medieval Swedish clergyman. According to legends, he conquered Finland together with King Eric the Saint of Sweden and died as a martyr, becoming a central figure in the local Roman Catholic Church. However, the authenticity of the accounts of his life, ministry, and death are widely disputed.
Society	A society is (1) a group of people related to each other through persistent relations such as social status, roles and social networks. (2) A large social grouping that shares the same geographical territory and is subject to the same political authority and dominant cultural expectations. Human societies are characterized by patterns of relationships between individuals sharing a distinctive culture and institutions.
Interest	Interest is a fee paid on borrowed assets. It is the price paid for the use of borrowed money, or, money earned by deposited funds. Assets that are sometimes lent with interest include money, shares, consumer goods through hire purchase, major assets such as aircraft, and even entire factories in finance lease arrangements.
Baker	Baker is the code-name for a series of training exercises conducted by the United States Army and several Asian countries which hosted the exercises. The purpose of the exercises is to practice and develop counter-narcotics operations.

Some of the operations in this series include:

- Baker Blade: Classified exercise.
- Baker Mint: Conducted by the US Army and Malaysia in 1997.
- Baker Mint 99-1: Conducted by the US Army and Malaysia in 1999. Trained on military intelligence and photo-surveillance.
- Baker Mint Lens 99: Conducted by the US Army and Malaysia in 1999.
- Baker Mondial V: Conducted by the US Army and Mongolia in 1997. Trained on medical procedures.
- Baker Mongoose II: Conducted by the US Army and Mongolia in 1995.
- Baker Piston Lens 2000: Conducted by the US Army and the Philippines in 2000.
- Baker Tepid: A series of eight exercises conducted by the US Army and Thailand.
- Baker Torch: A series of three exercises conducted by the US Army and Thailand from 1999 to 2001. Trained on border control.
- Baker Torch Lens: Conducted by the US Army and Thailand.

Energy policy

Energy policy is the manner in which a given entity (often governmental) has decided to address issues of energy development including energy production, distribution and consumption. The attributes of energy policy may include legislation, international treaties, incentives to investment, guidelines for energy conservation, taxation and other public policy techniques.

National energy policy

Measures used to produce an energy policy

A national energy policy comprises a set of measures involving that country's laws, treaties and agency directives.

Mandate

In politics, a mandate is the authority granted by a constituency to act as its representative.

Chapter 6. The Presidency as an Institution

	The concept of a government having a legitimate mandate to govern via the fair winning of a democratic election is a central idea of democracy. New governments who attempt to introduce policies that they did not make public during an election campaign are said to not have a legitimate mandate to implement such policies.
Monitor	Monitor, is a non-departmental public body in the United Kingdom. Its purpose is to regulate NHS Foundation Trusts or Foundation Hospitals - hospitals that have opted out of direct governmental control. The body was established under the Health and Social Care (Community Health and Standards) Act 2003.
Base	In politics, the term base refers to a group of voters who almost always support a single party's candidates for elected office. Base voters are very unlikely to vote for the candidate of an opposing party, regardless of the specific views each candidate holds. In the United States, this is typically because high-level candidates must hold the same stances on key issues as a party's base in order to gain the party's nomination and thus be guaranteed ballot access.
Voting	Voting is a method for a group such as a meeting or an electorate to make a decision or express an opinion--often following discussions, debates, or election campaigns. It is often found in democracies and republics. Reasons for voting In a representative government, voting commonly implies election: a way for an electorate to select among candidates for office.
Judiciary	The judiciary is the system of courts that interprets and applies the law in the name of the state. The judiciary also provides a mechanism for the resolution of disputes. Under the doctrine of the separation of powers, the judiciary generally does not make law (that is, in a plenary fashion, which is the responsibility of the legislature) or enforce law (which is the responsibility of the executive), but rather interprets law and applies it to the facts of each case.
Filibuster	A filibuster is a type of parliamentary procedure. Specifically, it is a form of obstruction in a legislature or other decision-making body whereby a lone member can elect to delay or entirely prevent a vote on a proposal.

Chapter 6. The Presidency as an Institution

	The term "filibuster" was first used in 1851. It was derived from the Spanish filibustero, which translates as "pirate" or "freebooter." This term had evolved from the French word flibustier, which itself evolved from the Dutch vrijbuiter (free outsider).
Threat	In Computer security a threat is a potential for violation of security, which exists when there is a circumstance, capability, action, or event that could breach security and cause harm.
	That is, a threat is a possible danger that might exploit a vulnerability. A threat can be either "intentional" (i.e., intelligent; e.g., an individual cracker or a criminal organization) or "accidental" (e.g., the possibility of a computer malfunctioning, or the possibility of an "act of God" such as an earthquake, a fire, or a tornado). The definition is as IETF RFC 2828
	Definitions
	ISO 27005 defines threat as:
	A more comprehensive definition, tied to an Information assurance point of view, can be found in "Federal Information Processing Standards (FIPS) 200, Minimum Security Requirements for Federal Information and Information Systems" by NIST of United States of America
	ENISA gives a similar definition:
	The Open Group defines threat in as:
	National Information Assurance Training and Education Center gives a more articulated definition of threat:
	Phenomenology
	The term "threat" relates to some other basic security terms as shown in the following diagram:

Chapter 6. The Presidency as an Institution

```
+-------------++----++-----------+  An Attack:    Counter-   A System Resource: i.e., A
Threat Action measure Target of the Attack  +--------+  +---------------+ Attacker
<====================<=========  i.e., Passive Vulnerability  A Threat
<===================><========>  Agent or Active  +-------------+  +---------+ Attack VVV
Threat Consequences  +------------++----++----------+
```

A resource (both physical or logical) can have one or more vulnerabilities that can be exploited by a threat agent in a threat action.

New Politics | New Politics is an independent socialist journal founded in 1961 and still published in the United States today. While it is inclusive of articles from a variety of left-of-center positions, the publication leans strongly toward a Third Camp, democratic Marxist perspective, placing it typically to the left of the liberal or social democratic views in the journal Dissent, although over the years a number of authors have published in both periodicals.

Julius and Phyllis Jacobson were the founders and longtime co-editors of the journal, which had a political center of gravity reflective of their youthful formative experience in the Independent Socialist League of the 1940s and 1950s.

Publics | Publics are small groups of people who follow one or more particular issue very closely. They are well informed about the issue(s) and also have a very strong opinion on it/them. They tend to know more about politics than the average person, and, therefore, exert more influence, because these people care so deeply about their cause(s) that they donate much time and money.

Public health | Public health is "the science and art of preventing disease, prolonging life and promoting health through the organized efforts and informed choices of society, organizations, public and private, communities and individuals" (1920, C.E.A. Winslow). It is concerned with threats to the overall health of a community based on population health analysis. The population in question can be as small as a handful of people or as large as all the inhabitants of several continents (for instance, in the case of a pandemic).

Chapter 6. The Presidency as an Institution

News conference	A news conference is a media event in which newsmakers invite journalists to hear them speak and, most often, ask questions. A joint press conference instead is held between two or more talking sides. Practice In a news conference, one or more speakers may make a statement, which may be followed by questions from reporters.
News conference	A news conference is a media event in which newsmakers invite journalists to hear them speak and, most often, ask questions. A joint press conference instead is held between two or more talking sides. Practice In a news conference, one or more speakers may make a statement, which may be followed by questions from reporters.
Public opinion	Public opinion is the aggregate of individual attitudes or beliefs held by the adult population. Public opinion can also be defined as the complex collection of opinions of many different people and the sum of all their views.

Chapter 6. The Presidency as an Institution

The principle approaches to the study of public opinion may be divided into 4 categories:

1. quantitative measurement of opinion distributions;
2. investigation of the internal relationships among the individual opinions that make up public opinion on an issue;
3. description or analysis of the public role of public opinion;
4. study both of the communication media that disseminate the ideas on which opinions are based and of the uses that propagandists and other manipulators make of these media.

Concepts of "public opinion"

Public opinion as a concept gained credence with the rise of "public" in the eighteenth century.

Public relations	Public relations is a field concerned with maintaining a public image for businesses, non-profit organizations or high-profile people, such as celebrities and politicians.
	An earlier definition of public relations, by The first World Assembly of Public Relations Associations held in Mexico City in August 1978, was "the art and social science of analyzing trends, predicting their consequences, counseling organizational leaders, and implementing planned programs of action, which will serve both the organization and the public interest."
	Others define it as the practice of managing communication between an organization and its publics. Public relations provides an organization or individual exposure to their audiences using topics of public interest and news items that provide a third-party endorsement and do not direct payment.
Community	A community is an administrative division found in Belgium, Canada, Greece, Iceland, Wales, and the League of Nations Class A mandates
Regent	A regent is a person selected to act as head of state (ruling or not) because the ruler is a minor, not present, or debilitated.

Chapter 6. The Presidency as an Institution

In a monarchy, a regent usually governs due to one of these reasons, but may also be elected to rule during the interregnum when the royal line has died out. This was the case in Finland and Hungary, where the royal line was considered extinct in the aftermath of World War I. In Iceland, the regent represented the King of Denmark as sovereign of Iceland until the country became a republic in 1944.

Democrats | The Democrats is a centre-right political party in Brazil, considered the main in the right-wing spectrum. Despite its former name (Liberal Front Party), the party affiliates itself to the Centrist Democrat International, and the International Democrat Union. The name comes from its support to free market policies.

Louisiana

Louisiana was the name of an administrative district of the Viceroyalty of New Spain from 1764 to 1803 that represented territory west of the Mississippi River basin, plus New Orleans. Spain acquired the territory from France: see Louisiana.

History

The area, comprising what is now known as the Louisiana Purchase, was turned over to the French for a few days in 1803 before it, in turn, was turned over to the United States.

Louisiana Purchase | The Louisiana Purchase was the acquisition by the United States of America of 828,800 square miles (2,147,000 km^2) of France's claim to the territory of Louisiana in 1803. The U.S. paid 60 million francs ($11,250,000) plus cancellation of debts worth 18 million francs ($3,750,000), for a total sum of 15 million dollars for the Louisiana territory ($219 million in 2010 dollars).

Chapter 6. The Presidency as an Institution

	The Louisiana Purchase encompassed all or part of 14 current U.S. states and two Canadian provinces. The land purchased contained all of present-day Arkansas, Missouri, Iowa, Oklahoma, Kansas, Nebraska, parts of Minnesota that were west of the Mississippi River, most of North Dakota, nearly all of South Dakota, northeastern New Mexico, the portions of Montana, Wyoming, and Colorado east of the Continental Divide, and Louisiana west of the Mississippi River, including the city of New Orleans.
Peace	Peace describes a society or a relationship that is operating harmoniously and without violent conflict. Peace is commonly understood as the absence of hostility, or the existence of healthy or newly healed interpersonal or international relationships, safety in matters of social or economic welfare, the acknowledgment of equality and fairness in political relationships. In international relations, peacetime is the absence of any war or conflict.
Peace Corps	The Peace Corps is an American volunteer program run by the United States Government, as well as a government agency of the same name. The mission of the Peace Corps includes three goals: providing technical assistance, helping people outside the United States to understand U.S. culture, and helping Americans understand the cultures of other countries. Generally, the work is related to social and economic development.
Annexation	Annexation is the de jure incorporation of some territory into another geo-political entity (either adjacent or non-contiguous). Usually, it is implied that the territory and population being annexed is the smaller, more peripheral, and weaker of the two merging entities, barring physical size. It can also imply a certain measure of coercion, expansionism or unilateralism on the part of the stronger of the merging entities.
Emancipation	Emancipation is a broad term used to describe various efforts to obtain political rights or equality, often for a specifically disenfranchised group, or more generally in discussion of such matters. Emancipation stems from "ex manus capere": Take out the hand. Among others, Karl Marx discussed political emancipation in his 1844 essay "On the Jewish Question", although often in addition to (or in contrast with) the term human emancipation.
Internment	Internment is the imprisonment or confinement of people, commonly in large groups, without trial. The Oxford English Dictionary (1989) gives the meaning as: "The action of 'interning'; confinement within the limits of a country or place." Most modern usage is about individuals, and there is a distinction between internment, which is being confined usually for preventive or political reasons, and imprisonment, which is being closely confined as a punishment for crime.

Chapter 6. The Presidency as an Institution

	Internment also refers to the practice of neutral countries in time of war in detaining belligerent armed forces and equipment in their territories under the Second Hague Convention.
Central government	A central government, union government and in federal states, the federal government, is the government at the level of the nation-state. The structure of central governments varies from institution to institution. Many countries have created autonomous regions by delegating powers from the central government to governments at a subnational level, such as a regional, local, or state level.
Hamdan v. Rumsfeld	Hamdan v. Rumsfeld, 548 U.S. 557 (2006), is a case in which the Supreme Court of the United States held that military commissions set up by the Bush administration to try detainees at Guantanamo Bay lack "the power to proceed because its structures and procedures violate both the Uniform Code of Military Justice and the four Geneva Conventions signed in 1949
	The case considered whether the United States Congress may pass legislation preventing the Supreme Court from hearing the case of an accused combatant before his military commission takes place, whether the special military commissions that had been set up violated federal law (including the Uniform Code of Military Justice and treaty obligations), and whether courts can enforce the articles of the 1949 Geneva Convention.
	An unusual aspect of the case was an amicus brief filed by Senators Jon Kyl and Lindsey Graham, which presented an "extensive colloquy" added to the Congressional record as evidence that "Congress was aware" that the Detainee Treatment Act would strip the Supreme Court of jurisdiction to hear cases brought by the Guantanamo detainees.
Justice	Justice was the weekly newspaper of the Social Democratic Federation (SDF) in the United Kingdom.
	The SDF had been known until January 1884 as the Democratic Federation. With the change of name, the organisation launched the paper.

Chapter 6. The Presidency as an Institution

Military justice	Military justice is the body of laws and procedures governing members of the armed forces. Many states have separate and distinct bodies of law that govern the conduct of members of their armed forces. Some states use special judicial and other arrangements to enforce those laws, while others use civilian judicial systems.
Uniform Code of Military Justice	The Uniform Code of Military Justice (UCMJ, 64 Stat. 109, 10 U.S.C.
Veteran	A veteran is a person who has had long service or experience in a particular occupation or field; " A veteran of ..." . This page refers to military veterans, i.e., a person who has served or is serving in the armed forces, and has direct exposure to acts of military conflict, commonly known as war veterans (although not all military conflicts, or areas in which armed combat takes place, are necessarily referred to as "wars"). Public attitude towards veterans Military veterans often receive special treatment in their respective countries due to the sacrifices they made during wars.
Tax cut	A tax cut is a reduction in taxes. The immediate effects of a tax cut are a decrease in the real income of the government and an increase in the real income of those whose tax rate has been lowered. In the longer term, however, the loss of government income may be mitigated, depending on the response that tax-payers make.
Hamilton	Hamilton is a former New Zealand Parliamentary electorate, which was replaced by Hamilton East and Hamilton West electorates. Population centres The electorate was mainly urban, covering the city of Hamilton. History

Chapter 6. The Presidency as an Institution

	The Hamilton electorate dates from 1922. In 1969 it was renamed Hamilton West.
Alexander Hamilton	Alexander Hamilton was a Scottish sea captain, privateer and merchant.
James Madison	James Madison, Jr. (March 16, 1751 - June 28, 1836) was an American politician and political philosopher who served as the fourth President of the United States (1809-1817) and is considered one of the Founding Fathers of the United States. He was the principal author of the United States Constitution, and is often called the "Father of the Constitution".
Continental Congress	The Continental Congress was a convention of delegates called together from the Thirteen Colonies that became the governing body of the United States during the American Revolution. The Congress met from 1774 to 1789 in three incarnations. The first call for a convention was made over issues of mounting taxation without representation in Parliament and because of the British blockade.
Foundation	A foundation in the United States is a type of charitable organization. However, the Internal Revenue Code distinguishes between private foundations (usually funded by an individual, family, or corporation) and public charities (community foundations and other nonprofit groups that raise money from the general public). Private foundations have more restrictions and fewer tax benefits than public charities like community foundations.

Chapter 6. The Presidency as an Institution

Chapter 6. The Presidency as an Institution

Chapter 7. The Executive Branch: Bureaucracy in a Democracy

Homeland	A homeland is the concept of the place (cultural geography) to which an ethnic group holds a long history and a deep cultural association with --the country in which a particular national identity began. As a common noun, it simply connotes the country of one's origin.
Homeland security	Homeland security is an umbrella term for security efforts to protect the United States against terrorist activity. The term arose following a reorganization of many U.S. government agencies in 2003 to form the United States Department of Homeland Security after the September 11 attacks, and may be used to refer to the actions of that department, the United States Senate Committee on Homeland Security and Governmental Affairs, or the United States House of Representatives Committee on Homeland Security.
	In the United States
	In the United States, the concept of "homeland security" extends and recombines responsibilities of government agencies and entities.
Attack	In computer and computer networks an attack is any attempt to destroy, expose, alter, disable, steal or gain unauthorized access to or make unauthorized use of an asset.
	Definitions
	IETF
	Internet Engineering Task Force defines attack in RFC 2828 as:
	US Government
	CNSS Instruction No. 4009 dated 26 April 2010 by Committee on National Security Systems of United States of America defines an attack as:
	The increasing dependencies of modern society on information and computers networks (both in private and public sectors, including military) has led to new terms like cyber attack and Cyberwarfare.

Chapter 7. The Executive Branch: Bureaucracy in a Democracy

CNSS Instruction No. 4009 define a cyber attack as:

Phenomenology

An attack can be active or passive.

An attack can be perpetrated by an insider or from outside the organization;

> An "inside attack" is an attack initiated by an entity inside the security perimeter (an "insider"), i.e., an entity that is authorized to access system resources but uses them in a way not approved by those who granted the authorization.
> An "outside attack" is initiated from outside the perimeter, by an unauthorized or illegitimate user of the system (an "outsider").

Bureaucracy

In the social sciences, a bureaucracy is a large organization characterized by hierarchy, fixed rules, impersonal relationships, rigid adherence to procedures, and a highly specialized division of labor.

Development

Modern bureaucracies arose as the government of states grew larger during the modern period, and especially following the Industrial Revolution. As the authors David Osborne and Ted Gaebler point out

"It is hard to imagine today, but a hundred years ago bureaucracy meant something positive.

Executive

Executive branch of government is the part of government that has sole authority and responsibility for the daily administration of the state bureaucracy. The division of power into separate branches of government is central to the democratic idea of the separation of powers.

Chapter 7. The Executive Branch: Bureaucracy in a Democracy

	In many countries, the term "government" connotes only the executive branch.
Mandate	In politics, a mandate is the authority granted by a constituency to act as its representative.
	The concept of a government having a legitimate mandate to govern via the fair winning of a democratic election is a central idea of democracy. New governments who attempt to introduce policies that they did not make public during an election campaign are said to not have a legitimate mandate to implement such policies.
Monitor	Monitor, is a non-departmental public body in the United Kingdom. Its purpose is to regulate NHS Foundation Trusts or Foundation Hospitals - hospitals that have opted out of direct governmental control. The body was established under the Health and Social Care (Community Health and Standards) Act 2003.
Social security	Social security is primarily a social insurance program providing social protection, or protection against socially recognized conditions, including poverty, old age, disability, unemployment and others. Social security may refer to: • social insurance, where people receive benefits or services in recognition of contributions to an insurance scheme. These services typically include provision for retirement pensions, disability insurance, survivor benefits and unemployment insurance. • income maintenance--mainly the distribution of cash in the event of interruption of employment, including retirement, disability and unemployment • services provided by administrations responsible for social security.
Congress	A congress is a formal meeting of the representatives of different nations, constituent states, independent organizations (such as trade unions), or groups.

Chapter 7. The Executive Branch: Bureaucracy in a Democracy

	The term was chosen for the United States Congress to emphasize the status of each state represented there as a self-governing unit. Subsequent to the use of congress by the U.S. legislature, the term has been incorrectly adopted by many states within unions, and by unitary nation-states in the Americas, to refer to their legislatures.
Emergency management	Emergency Management is the generic name of an interdisciplinary field dealing with the strategic organizational management processes used to protect critical assets of an organization from hazard risks that can cause disasters or catastrophes, and to ensure their continuance within their planned lifetime. Assets are categorized as either living things, non-living things, cultural or economic. Hazards are categorized by their cause, either natural or human-made.
Fire Equipment Manufacturers' Association	History Founded in 1930, The Fire Equipment Manufacturers' Association is an international, non-profit trade association dedicated to manufacturing commercial fire protection equipment to serve as the first line of defense against fire in its early stages. The association centers its efforts around the key premise that safety to life is best achieved through the implementation of a "balanced fire protection design" - a concept in which a proactive safety plan does not rely on any single safeguard. The Fire Equipment Manufacturers' Association works in conjunction with the NFPA, International Code Council, local, state, national officials to advance positive fire and building codes, laws and Underwriters Laboratories, Inc.
Federal Emergency Management Agency	The Federal Emergency Management Agency is an agency of the United States Department of Homeland Security, initially created by Presidential Order on 1 April 1979. The primary purpose of Federal Emergency Management Agency is to coordinate the response to a disaster that has occurred in the United States and that overwhelms the resources of local and state authorities. The governor of the state in which the disaster occurs must declare a state of emergency and formally request from the president that Federal Emergency Management Agency and the federal government respond to the disaster. Federal Emergency Management Agency also provides these services for territories of the United States, such as Puerto Rico.

Chapter 7. The Executive Branch: Bureaucracy in a Democracy

Division of labour	Division of labour is the specialisation of cooperative labour in specific, circumscribed tasks and like roles. Historically an increasingly complex division of labour is closely associated with the growth of total output and trade, the rise of capitalism, and of the complexity of industrialisation processes. Division of labour was also a method used by the Sumerians to categorise different jobs, and divide them to skilled members of a society.
Poland	Poland officially the Republic of Poland - is a country in Central Europe bordered by Germany to the west; the Czech Republic and Slovakia to the south; Ukraine, Belarus and Lithuania to the east; and the Baltic Sea and Kaliningrad Oblast, a Russian exclave, to the north. The total area of Poland is 312,679 square kilometres (120,726 sq mi), making it the 69th largest country in the world and the 9th largest in Europe. Poland has a population of over 38 million people, which makes it the 34th most populous country in the world and the sixth most populous member of the European Union, being its most populous post-communist member.
Impeachment	Impeachment is a formal process in which an official is accused of unlawful activity and the outcome of which, depending on the country, can lead to the removal of that official from office or other punishment. Medieval popular etymology also associated it (wrongly) with derivations from the Latin impetere (to attack). (In its more frequent and more technical usage, impeachment of a person in the role of a witness is the act of challenging the honesty or credibility of that person).
Implementation	Implementation is the realization of an application, or execution of a plan, idea, model, design, specification, standard, algorithm, or policy. Computer Science In computer science, an implementation is a realization of a technical specification or algorithm as a program, software component, or other computer system through programming and deployment. Many implementations may exist for a given specification or standard.
Military base	A military base is a facility directly owned and operated by and/or for the military or one of its branches that shelters military equipment and personnel, and facilitates training and operations. In general, a military base provides accommodations for one or more units, but it may also be used as a command center, a training ground, or a proving ground. In most cases, a military base relies on some outside help in order to operate.

Chapter 7. The Executive Branch: Bureaucracy in a Democracy

Rulemaking	In administrative law, rulemaking refers to the process that executive and independent agencies use to create, or promulgate, regulations. In general, legislatures first set broad policy mandates by passing statutes, then agencies create more detailed regulations through rulemaking.
	By bringing detailed scientific and other types of expertise to bear on policy, the rulemaking process has been the means by which some of the most far-reaching government regulations of the 20th century have been created.
Abortion	Abortion is the termination of a pregnancy by the removal or expulsion of a fetus or embryo from the uterus, resulting in or caused by its death. An abortion can occur spontaneously due to complications during pregnancy or can be induced, in humans and other species. In the context of human pregnancies, an abortion induced to preserve the health of the gravida (pregnant female) is termed a therapeutic abortion, while an abortion induced for any other reason is termed an elective abortion.
Discrimination	Discrimination is the cognitive and sensory capacity or ability to see fine distinctions and perceive differences between objects, subjects, concepts and patterns, or possess exceptional development of the senses. Used in this way to identify exceptional discernment since the 17th century, the term begun to be used as an expression of derogatory racial prejudice from the 1830s Thomas D. Rice's performances as "Jim Crow".
	Since the American Civil War the term 'discrimination' generally evolved in American English usage as an understanding of prejudicial treatment of an individual based solely on their race, later generalized as membership in a certain socially undesirable group or social category.
Freedom	Freedom is a London-based anarchist newspaper published fortnightly by Freedom Press.

Chapter 7. The Executive Branch: Bureaucracy in a Democracy

The paper was started in 1886 by volunteers including Peter Kropotkin and Charlotte Wilson and continues to this day as an unpaid project. Originally, the subtitle was "A Journal of Anarchist Socialism." The title was changed to "A Journal of Anarchist Communism" in June 1889. Today it is unlabelled.

Adjudication

Adjudication is the legal process by which an arbiter or judge reviews evidence and argumentation including legal reasoning set forth by opposing parties or litigants to come to a decision which determines rights and obligations between the parties involved. Three types of disputes are resolved through adjudication:

1. Disputes between private parties, such as individuals or corporations.
2. Disputes between private parties and public officials.
3. Disputes between public officials or public bodies.

Other meanings

Adjudication can also be the process (at dance competitions, in television game shows and at other competitive forums) by which competitors are evaluated and ranked and a winner is found.

In construction

The relevant legislation in the UK is the Housing Grants, Construction and Regeneration Act 1996, (1996 Chapter 53).

Identity

Identity is an umbrella term used throughout the social sciences to describe a person's conception and expression of their individuality or group affiliations (such as national identity and cultural identity). The term is used more specifically in psychology and sociology, including the two forms of social psychology. The term is also used with respect to place identity.

Service club

A service club is a voluntary non-profit organization where members meet regularly to perform charitable works either by direct hands-on efforts or by raising money for other organizations. A service club is defined first by its service mission. Secondary membership benefits, such as social occasions, networking, and personal growth opportunities encourage involvement.

Chapter 7. The Executive Branch: Bureaucracy in a Democracy

Cabinet	In the European Commission, a cabinet is the personal office of a European Commissioner. The role of a cabinet is to give political guidance to its Commissioner, while technical preparation is handled by the DGs (the European Civil Service). Composition The Commissioner's cabinets are seen as the real concentration of power within the Commission and consists of six members, but the exact membership faces restrictions.
Administration	Administration, as a legal concept, is a procedure under the insolvency laws of a number of common law jurisdictions. It functions as a rescue mechanism for insolvent companies and allows them to carry on running their business. The process - an alternative to liquidation - is often known as going into administration.
Commission	A commission is a physical document issued to certify the appointment of a commissioned officer by a sovereign power. The more specific terms commissioning parchment or commissioning scroll are often used to avoid ambiguity, due to "commission" being a homonym which directs the individual in carrying out their duty regardless of what authority or responsibility they may have at any time. However the document is not usually in the form of a scroll and is more often printed on paper instead of parchment.
Election	An election is a formal decision-making process by which a population chooses an individual to hold public office. Elections have been the usual mechanism by which modern representative democracy operates since the 17th century. Elections may fill offices in the legislature, sometimes in the executive and judiciary, and for regional and local government.

Chapter 7. The Executive Branch: Bureaucracy in a Democracy

Electoral Commission	An Electoral Commission is an election management body, in charge of overseeing the implementation of election procedures:
	
	 - Australia: Australian Electoral Commission
	 - Bangladesh: Bangladesh Election Commission
	 - Belize: Belize Elections and Boundaries Commission
	 - Brazil: Supreme Electoral Court (Brazil)
	 - Colombia: National Electoral Council (Colombia)
	 - Ghana: Electoral Commission of Ghana
	 - Guyana: Guyana Elections Commission
	 - Hong Kong: Electoral Affairs Commission
	 - India: Election Commission of India
	 - Iran: Guardian Council
	 - Iraq: Independent High Electoral Commission
	 - Kenya:
	      - Electoral Commission of Kenya (defunct)
	      - Interim Independent Electoral Commission
	 - Liberia: National Election Commission (Liberia)
	 - Malaysia: Election Commission of Malaysia
	 - Mexico: Federal Electoral Institute
	 - Nepal: Election Commission of Nepal
	 - New Zealand: Electoral Commission
	 - Pakistan: Election Commission of Pakistan
	 - Poland: Panstwowa Komisja Wyborcza (National Electoral Commission)
	 - Philippines: Commission on Elections (Philippines)
	 - Thailand: Election Commission (Thailand)
	 - Ukraine: Central Election Commission of Ukraine
	 - United Kingdom: Electoral Commission
	 - United States:
	      - Election Assistance Commission, administers Federal elections and establishing standards for State and local governments
	      - Electoral Commission created solely to resolve the disputed 1876 presidential election
	      - Federal Election Commission, regulates campaign finance legislation
	 - Uruguay: Electoral Court
	 - Zimbabwe: Zimbabwe Electoral Commission

Chapter 7. The Executive Branch: Bureaucracy in a Democracy

Environmental protection	Environmental protection is a practice of protecting the environment, on individual, organizational or governmental level, for the benefit of the natural environment and (or) humans. Due to the pressures of population and our technology the biophysical environment is being degraded, sometimes permanently. This has been recognized and governments began placing restraints on activities that caused environmental degradation.
Environmental Protection Agency	The Environmental Protection Agency (Irish: An Ghníomhaireacht um Chaomhnú Comhshaoil) has responsibilities for a wide range of licensing, enforcement, monitoring and assessment activities associated with environmental protection.
Federal Communications Commission	The Federal Communications Commission is an independent agency of the United States government, created, Congressional statute , and with the majority of its commissioners appointed by the current President. The Federal Communications Commission works towards six goals in the areas of broadband, competition, the spectrum, the media, public safety and homeland security, and modernizing the Federal Communications Commission. The Federal Communications Commission was established by the Communications Act of 1934 as the successor to the Federal Radio Commission and is charged with regulating all non-federal government use of the radio spectrum (including radio and television broadcasting), and all interstate telecommunications (wire, satellite and cable) as well as all international communications that originate or terminate in the United States. It is an important factor in U.S. telecommunication policy.
Federal Election Commission	The Federal Election Commission is an independent regulatory agency that was founded in 1975 by the United States Congress to regulate the campaign finance legislation in the United States. It was created in a provision of the 1975 amendment to the Federal Election Campaign Act. It describes its duties as "to disclose campaign finance information, to enforce the provisions of the law such as the limits and prohibitions on contributions, and to oversee the public funding of Presidential elections." Membership The Commission is made up of six members, who are appointed by the President of the United States and confirmed by the United States Senate.

Chapter 7. The Executive Branch: Bureaucracy in a Democracy

Justice	Justice was the weekly newspaper of the Social Democratic Federation (SDF) in the United Kingdom. The SDF had been known until January 1884 as the Democratic Federation. With the change of name, the organisation launched the paper.
Senate	A senate is a deliberative assembly, often the upper house or chamber of a legislature or parliament. There have been many such bodies in history, since senate means the assembly of the eldest and wiser members of the society and ruling class. Two of the first official senates were the Spartan Gerousia (Γερουσ?α) and the Roman Senate.
Speaker	The term speaker is a title often given to the presiding officer (chair) of a deliberative assembly, especially a legislative body. The speaker's official role is to moderate debate, make rulings on procedure, announce the results of votes, and the like. The speaker decides who may speak and has the powers to discipline members who break the procedures of the house.
State	Many sovereign independent state are made up of a number of country subdivisions also called states. In some cases, such as the United States, the national government arose from a union of sovereign entities, which transferred some of their powers to the national government, while retaining the remainder of their sovereignty. These are sometimes called federal states.
Lobbying	Lobbying is the intention of influencing decisions made by legislators and officials in the government by individuals, other legislators, constituents, or advocacy groups. A lobbyist is a person who tries to influence legislation on behalf of a special interest or a member of a lobby. Governments often define and regulate organized group lobbying that has become influential.
Force	In the field of law, the word force has two main meanings: unlawful violence and lawful compulsion. "Forced entry" is an expression falling under the category of unlawful violence; "in force" or "forced sale" would be examples of expressions in the category of lawful compulsion. When something is said to have been done "by force", it usually implies that it was done by actual or threatened violence ("might"), not necessarily by legal authority ("right").

Chapter 7. The Executive Branch: Bureaucracy in a Democracy

Foundation	A foundation in the United States is a type of charitable organization. However, the Internal Revenue Code distinguishes between private foundations (usually funded by an individual, family, or corporation) and public charities (community foundations and other nonprofit groups that raise money from the general public). Private foundations have more restrictions and fewer tax benefits than public charities like community foundations.
National security	National security is the requirement to maintain the survival of the nation-state through the use of economic, military and political power and the exercise of diplomacy. The concept developed mostly in the United States of America after World War II. Initially focusing on military might, it now encompasses a broad range of facets, all of which impinge on the military or economic security of the nation and the values espoused by the national society. Accordingly, in order to possess national security, a nation needs to possess economic security, energy security, environmental security, etc.
Health administration	Health administration is the field relating to leadership, management, and administration of hospitals, hospital networks, and health care systems. Health care administrators are considered health care professionals. The discipline is known by many names, including health management, healthcare management, health systems management, health care systems management, and medical and health services management.
Regent	A regent is a person selected to act as head of state (ruling or not) because the ruler is a minor, not present, or debilitated. In a monarchy, a regent usually governs due to one of these reasons, but may also be elected to rule during the interregnum when the royal line has died out. This was the case in Finland and Hungary, where the royal line was considered extinct in the aftermath of World War I. In Iceland, the regent represented the King of Denmark as sovereign of Iceland until the country became a republic in 1944.

Chapter 7. The Executive Branch: Bureaucracy in a Democracy

Legislation	Legislation is law which has been promulgated (or "enacted") by a legislature or other governing body, or the process of making it. (Another source of law is judge-made law or case law). Before an item of legislation becomes law it may be known as a bill, and may be broadly referred to as "legislation" while it remains under consideration to distinguish it from other business.
Federal Reserve System	The Federal Reserve System is the central banking system of the United States. It was created in 1913 with the enactment of the Federal Reserve Act, largely in response to a series of financial panics, particularly a severe panic in 1907. Over time, the roles and responsibilities of the Federal Reserve System have expanded and its structure has evolved. Events such as the Great Depression were major factors leading to changes in the system.
James Madison	James Madison, Jr. (March 16, 1751 - June 28, 1836) was an American politician and political philosopher who served as the fourth President of the United States (1809-1817) and is considered one of the Founding Fathers of the United States. He was the principal author of the United States Constitution, and is often called the "Father of the Constitution".
Rights	Rights are legal, social, or ethical principles of freedom or entitlement; that is, rights are the fundamental normative rules about what is allowed of people or owed to people, according to some legal system, social convention, or ethical theory. Rights are of essential importance in such disciplines as law and ethics, especially theories of justice and deontology. Rights are often considered fundamental to civilization, being regarded as established pillars of society and culture, and the history of social conflicts can be found in the history of each right and its development.
Consideration	Consideration is the concept of legal value in connection with contracts. It is anything of value promised to another when making a contract. It can take the form of money, physical objects, services, promised actions, abstinence from a future action and much more.

Chapter 7. The Executive Branch: Bureaucracy in a Democracy

Presidency	The word presidency is often used to describe the administration or the executive, the collective administrative and governmental entity that exists around an office of president of a state or nation. It is also the governing authority of some churches.
	For example, in a republic with a presidential system of government, the presidency is the executive branch of government, and is personified by a single elected man or woman who holds the office of "president".
Budget and Accounting Act	The Budget and Accounting Act of 1921 (Pub.L. 67-13, 42 Stat. 20, enacted June 10, 1921) was landmark legislation that established the framework for the modern federal budget. Link to 1921 Act For the first time, it required the President to submit to Congress an annual budget for the entire federal government. The Act also created the Bureau of the Budget, now called the Office of Management and Budget, to review funding requests from government departments and assist the president in formulating the budget.
Woodrow Wilson	Thomas Woodrow Wilson was the 28th President of the United States from 1913 to 1921. A leader of the Progressive Movement, he served as President of Princeton University from 1902 to 1910, and then as the Governor of New Jersey from 1911 to 1913. With Theodore Roosevelt and William Howard Taft dividing the Republican Party vote, Wilson was elected President as a Democrat in 1912. He is the only U.S. President to hold a Ph.D. degree, which he obtained from Johns Hopkins University.
	In his first term, Wilson persuaded a Democratic Congress to pass the Federal Reserve Act, Federal Trade Commission Act, the Clayton Antitrust Act, the Federal Farm Loan Act and America's first-ever federal progressive income tax in the Revenue Act of 1913. Wilson brought many white Southerners into his administration, and tolerated their expansion of segregation in many federal agencies.
	Narrowly re-elected in 1916, Wilson's second term centered on World War I. He based his re-election campaign around the slogan "he kept us out of war", but U.S. neutrality was challenged in early 1917 when the German government sent the Zimmermann Telegram to Mexico and proposed a military alliance in a war against the U.S., and began unrestricted submarine warfare, sinking, without warning, every American merchant ship its submarines could find.

Chapter 7. The Executive Branch: Bureaucracy in a Democracy

Affair	Affair may refer to professional, personal, or public business matters or to a particular business or private activity of a temporary duration, as in family affair, a private affair, or a romantic affair.
	Political affair
	Political affair may refer to the illicit or scandalous activities of public, such as the Watergate affair, or to a legally constituted government department, for example, the United Nations Department of Political Affairs.
	Romantic affair
	A romantic affair, also called an affair of the heart, may refer to sexual liaisons among unwed parties, or to various forms of nonmonogamy.
Judiciary	The judiciary is the system of courts that interprets and applies the law in the name of the state. The judiciary also provides a mechanism for the resolution of disputes. Under the doctrine of the separation of powers, the judiciary generally does not make law (that is, in a plenary fashion, which is the responsibility of the legislature) or enforce law (which is the responsibility of the executive), but rather interprets law and applies it to the facts of each case.
Gerrymandering	In the process of setting electoral boundaries, rather than using uniform geographic standards, Gerrymandering is a practice of political corruption that attempts to establish a political advantage for a particular party or group by manipulating geographic boundaries to create partisan, incumbent-protected, and neutral districts. The resulting district is known as a gerrymander; however, that word can also refer to the process.
	Gerrymandering may be used to achieve desired electoral results for a particular party, or may be used to help or hinder a particular group of constituents, such as a political, racial, linguistic, religious or class group.

Chapter 7. The Executive Branch: Bureaucracy in a Democracy

Accountability	Accountability is a concept in ethics and governance with several meanings. It is often used synonymously with such concepts as responsibility, answerability, blameworthiness, liability, and other terms associated with the expectation of account-giving. As an aspect of governance, it has been central to discussions related to problems in the public sector, nonprofit and private (corporate) worlds.
Congressional Budget Office	The Congressional Budget Office is a federal agency within the legislative branch of the United States government. It is a government agency that provides economic data to Congress. The Congressional Budget Office was created as a nonpartisan agency by the Congressional Budget and Impoundment Control Act of 1974.
Congressional Research Service	The Congressional Research Service known as "Congress's think tank", is the public policy research arm of the United States Congress. As a legislative branch agency within the Library of Congress, Congressional Research Service works exclusively and directly for Members of Congress, their Committees and staff on a confidential, nonpartisan basis. Its staff of approximately 900 employees includes lawyers, economists, reference librarians, and social, natural, and physical scientists.
Enron	Enron Corporation (former NYSE ticker symbol ENE) was an American energy, commodities, and services company based in Houston, Texas. Before its bankruptcy in late 2001, Enron employed approximately 22,000 staff and was one of the world's leading electricity, natural gas, communications, and pulp and paper companies, with claimed revenues of nearly $101 billion in 2000. Fortune named Enron "America's Most Innovative Company" for six consecutive years. At the end of 2001, it was revealed that its reported financial condition was sustained substantially by institutionalized, systematic, and creatively planned accounting fraud, known as the "Enron scandal".
Government	In the social sciences, the term government refers to the particular group of people, the administrative bureaucracy, who control a state at a given time, and the manner in which their governing organizations are structured. That is, governments are the means through which state power is employed. States are served by a continuous succession of different governments.

Chapter 7. The Executive Branch: Bureaucracy in a Democracy

Hungary	Hungary, officially the Republic of Hungary is a landlocked country in Central Europe. It is situated in the Pannonian Basin and it is bordered by Slovakia to the north, Ukraine and Romania to the east, Serbia and Croatia to the south, Slovenia to the southwest and Austria to the west. The capital and largest city is Budapest.
Leviathan	Leviathan, Forme and Power of a Common Wealth Ecclesiasticall and Civil, commonly called Leviathan, is a book written by Thomas Hobbes which was published in 1651. It is titled after the biblical Leviathan. The book concerns the structure of society and legitimate government, and is regarded as one of the earliest and most influential examples of social contract theory. The publisher was Andrew Crooke, partner in Andrew Crooke and William Cooke.
Corporate action	A corporate action is an event initiated by a public company that affects the securities (equity or debt) issued by the company. Some corporate actions such as a dividend (for equity securities) or coupon payment (for debt securities (bonds)) may have a direct financial impact on the shareholders or bondholders; another example is a call (early redemption) of a debt security. Other corporate actions such as stock split may have an indirect impact, as the increased liquidity of shares may cause the price of the stock to rise.
Federalism	In Europe, "federalist" is sometimes used to describe those who favor a common federal government, with distributed power at regional, national and supranational levels. Most European Federalists want this development to continue within the European Union. European federalism originated in post-war Europe; one of the more important initiatives was Winston Churchill's speech in Zurich in 1946.
Alarm	An alarm gives an audible or visual warning about a problem or condition.

Chapter 7. The Executive Branch: Bureaucracy in a Democracy

Alarms include:

- burglar alarms, designed to warn of burglaries; this is often a silent alarm: the police or guards are warned without indication to the burglar, which increases the chances of catching him or her.
- alarm clocks can produce an alarm at a given time
- distributed control manufacturing systems or DCSs, found in nuclear power plants, refineries and chemical facilities also generate alarms to direct the operator's attention to an important event that he or she needs to address.
- alarms in an operation and maintenance (O'M) monitoring system, which informs the bad working state of (a particular part of) the system under monitoring.
    - first-out alarm
- safety alarms, which go off if a dangerous condition occurs.

Police	The police are persons empowered to enforce the law, protect property and reduce civil disorder. Their powers include the legitimized use of force. The term is most commonly associated with police services of a state that are authorized to exercise the police power of that state within a defined legal or territorial area of responsibility.
Vietnam	Vietnam, officially the Socialist Republic of Vietnam is the easternmost country on the Indochina Peninsula in Southeast Asia. It is bordered by People's Republic of China (PRC) to the north, Laos to the northwest, Cambodia to the southwest, and the South China Sea, referred to as East Sea (Vietnamese: Bi?n Đông), to the east. With a population of over 86 million, Vietnam is the 13th most populous country in the world.
Court	A court is a form of tribunal, often a governmental institution, with the authority to adjudicate legal disputes between parties and carry out the administration of justice in civil, criminal, and administrative matters in accordance with the rule of law. In both common law and civil law legal systems, courts are the central means for dispute resolution, and it is generally understood that all persons have an ability to bring their claims before a court. Similarly, the rights of those accused of a crime include the right to present a defense before a court.

Chapter 7. The Executive Branch: Bureaucracy in a Democracy

Discretion	Discretion is a noun in the English language. Meanings - "The Art of suiting action to particular circumstances" (Lord Scarman) - 'the quality of being discreet' (Concise Oxford Dictionary) Those in a position of power are most often able to exercise discretion as to how they will apply or exercise that power. In the criminal justice system In the criminal justice system, police, prosecutors, judges, and the jury are often able to exercise a degree of discretion in deciding who will be subject to criminal penalties and how they will be punished.
Judicial discretion	Judicial discretion is the power of the judiciary to make some legal decisions according to their discretion. Under the doctrine of the separation of powers, the ability of judges to exercise discretion is an aspect of judicial independence. Where appropriate, judicial discretion allows a judge to decide a legal case or matter within a range of possible decisions.
Cold War	The Cold War was the continuing state of political conflict, military tension, proxy wars, and economic competition existing after World War II (1939-1945) between the Communist World - primarily the Soviet Union and its satellite states and allies - and the powers of the Western world, primarily the United States and its allies. Although the primary participants' military force never officially clashed directly, they expressed the conflict through military coalitions, strategic conventional force deployments, extensive aid to states deemed vulnerable, proxy wars, espionage, propaganda, conventional and nuclear arms races, appeals to neutral nations, rivalry at sports events, and technological competitions such as the Space Race. Despite being allies against the Axis powers, the USSR and the US disagreed about political philosophy and the configuration of the post-war world while occupying most of Europe.

Chapter 7. The Executive Branch: Bureaucracy in a Democracy

Deregulation	Deregulation is the removal or simplification of government rules and regulations that constrain the operation of market forces. Deregulation does not mean elimination of laws against fraud, but eliminating or reducing government control of how business is done, thereby moving toward a more laissez-faire, free market. It is different from liberalization, where more players enter in the market, but continues the regulation and guarantee of consumer rights and maximum and minimum prices.
Devolution	Devolution is the statutory granting of powers from the central government of a sovereign state to government at a subnational level, such as a regional, local, or state level. It differs from federalism in that the powers devolved may be temporary and ultimately reside in central government, thus the state remains, de jure, unitary.
	Legislation creating devolved parliaments or assemblies can be repealed by central government in the same way as any statute.
Reconciliation	Reconciliation is a legislative process of the United States Senate intended to allow consideration of a budget bill with debate limited to twenty hours under Senate Rules. Reconciliation also exists in the United States House of Representatives, but because the House regularly passes rules that constrain debate and amendment, the process has had a less significant impact on that body.
	A reconciliation instruction (Budget Reconciliation) is a provision in a budget resolution directing one or more committees to submit legislation changing existing law in order to bring spending, revenues, or the debt-limit into conformity with the budget resolution.
Privatization	Privatization is the incidence or process of transferring ownership of a business, enterprise, agency or public service from the public sector (the state or government) to the private sector (businesses that operate for a private profit) or to private non-profit organizations. In a broader sense, privatization refers to transfer of any government function to the private sector - including governmental functions like revenue collection and law enforcement.

Chapter 7. The Executive Branch: Bureaucracy in a Democracy

The term "privatization" also has been used to describe two unrelated transactions.

Terrorism | Terrorism is the systematic use of terror especially as a means of coercion. No universally agreed, legally binding, criminal law definition of terrorism currently exists. Common definitions of terrorism refer only to those violent acts which are intended to create fear (terror), are perpetrated for a religious, political or ideological goal, deliberately target or disregard the safety of non-combatants (civilians), and are committed by non-government agencies.

Chapter 7. The Executive Branch: Bureaucracy in a Democracy

Chapter 7. The Executive Branch: Bureaucracy in a Democracy

Chapter 8. The Federal Courts: Structure and Strategies

Congress	A congress is a formal meeting of the representatives of different nations, constituent states, independent organizations (such as trade unions), or groups.
	The term was chosen for the United States Congress to emphasize the status of each state represented there as a self-governing unit. Subsequent to the use of congress by the U.S. legislature, the term has been incorrectly adopted by many states within unions, and by unitary nation-states in the Americas, to refer to their legislatures.
Court	A court is a form of tribunal, often a governmental institution, with the authority to adjudicate legal disputes between parties and carry out the administration of justice in civil, criminal, and administrative matters in accordance with the rule of law. In both common law and civil law legal systems, courts are the central means for dispute resolution, and it is generally understood that all persons have an ability to bring their claims before a court. Similarly, the rights of those accused of a crime include the right to present a defense before a court.
Veteran	A veteran is a person who has had long service or experience in a particular occupation or field; " A veteran of ..." . This page refers to military veterans, i.e., a person who has served or is serving in the armed forces, and has direct exposure to acts of military conflict, commonly known as war veterans (although not all military conflicts, or areas in which armed combat takes place, are necessarily referred to as "wars").
	Public attitude towards veterans
	Military veterans often receive special treatment in their respective countries due to the sacrifices they made during wars.
Discretion	Discretion is a noun in the English language.
	Meanings
	<ul><li>"The Art of suiting action to particular circumstances" (Lord Scarman)</li><li>'the quality of being discreet' (Concise Oxford Dictionary)</li></ul>

Chapter 8. The Federal Courts: Structure and Strategies

	Those in a position of power are most often able to exercise discretion as to how they will apply or exercise that power.
	In the criminal justice system
	In the criminal justice system, police, prosecutors, judges, and the jury are often able to exercise a degree of discretion in deciding who will be subject to criminal penalties and how they will be punished.
Judicial discretion	Judicial discretion is the power of the judiciary to make some legal decisions according to their discretion. Under the doctrine of the separation of powers, the ability of judges to exercise discretion is an aspect of judicial independence. Where appropriate, judicial discretion allows a judge to decide a legal case or matter within a range of possible decisions.
Judicial review	Judicial review is the doctrine under which legislative and executive actions are subject to review, and possible invalidation, by the judiciary. Specific courts with judicial review power must annul the acts of the state when it finds them incompatible with a higher authority, such as the terms of a written constitution. Judicial review is an example of the functioning of separation of powers in a modern governmental system (where the judiciary is one of three branches of government).
Power	Power is a measure of an entity's ability to control its environment, including the behavior of other entities. The term authority is often used for power, perceived as legitimate by the social structure. Power can be seen as evil or unjust, but the exercise of power is accepted as endemic to humans as social beings.
Separation of powers	The separation of powers is a model for the governance of a state. The model was first developed in ancient Greece and came into widespread use by the Roman Republic as part of the unmodified Constitution of the Roman Republic. Under this model, the state is divided into branches, each with separate and independent powers and areas of responsibility so that no one branch has more power than the other branches.
Executive	Executive branch of government is the part of government that has sole authority and responsibility for the daily administration of the state bureaucracy. The division of power into separate branches of government is central to the democratic idea of the separation of powers.

Chapter 8. The Federal Courts: Structure and Strategies

	In many countries, the term "government" connotes only the executive branch.
Activism	Activism consists of intentional action to bring about social, political, economic, or environmental change. This action is in support of, or opposition to, one side of an often controversial argument.
	The word "activism" is used synonymously with protest or dissent, but activism can take a wide range of forms from writing letters to newspapers or politicians, political campaigning, economic activism such as boycotts or preferentially patronizing businesses, rallies, street marches, strikes, both sit-ins and hunger strikes, or even guerrilla tactics.
Judicial activism	Judicial activism describes judicial ruling suspected of being based on personal or political considerations rather than on existing law. It is sometimes used as an antonym of judicial restraint. The definition of judicial activism, and which specific decisions are activist, is a controversial political issue, particularly in the United States.
Great Society	The Great Society was a set of domestic programs proposed or enacted in the United States on the initiative of President Lyndon B. Johnson. Two main goals of the Great Society social reforms were the elimination of poverty and racial injustice. New major spending programs that addressed education, medical care, urban problems, and transportation were launched during this period.
Society	A society is (1) a group of people related to each other through persistent relations such as social status, roles and social networks. (2) A large social grouping that shares the same geographical territory and is subject to the same political authority and dominant cultural expectations. Human societies are characterized by patterns of relationships between individuals sharing a distinctive culture and institutions.
Continental Congress	The Continental Congress was a convention of delegates called together from the Thirteen Colonies that became the governing body of the United States during the American Revolution. The Congress met from 1774 to 1789 in three incarnations. The first call for a convention was made over issues of mounting taxation without representation in Parliament and because of the British blockade.

Chapter 8. The Federal Courts: Structure and Strategies

Justice	Justice was the weekly newspaper of the Social Democratic Federation (SDF) in the United Kingdom.
	The SDF had been known until January 1884 as the Democratic Federation. With the change of name, the organisation launched the paper.
Civil law	Civil law is a legal system inspired by Roman law, the primary feature of which is that laws are written into a collection, codified, and not (as in common law) determined by judges.
	Conceptually, it is the group of legal ideas and systems ultimately derived from the Code of Justinian, but heavily overlaid by Germanic, ecclesiastical, feudal, and local practices, as well as doctrinal strains such as natural law, codification, and legislative positivism.
	Materially, civil law proceeds from abstractions, formulates general principles, and distinguishes substantive rules from procedural rules.
Contract	In the Conflict of Laws, the validity of a contract with one or more foreign law elements will be decided by reference to the so-called "proper law" of the contract.
	History
	Until the middle of the 19th century, the courts applied the lex loci contractus or the law of the place where the contract was made to decide whether the given contract was valid. The apparent advantage of this approach was that the rule was easy to apply with certain and predictable outcomes.

Chapter 8. The Federal Courts: Structure and Strategies

Criminal law	Criminal law, is the body of rules that defines conduct which is prohibited by the state because it is held to threaten, harm or otherwise endanger the safety and welfare of the public, and that sets out the punishment to be imposed on those who breach these laws. Criminal law is enforced by the state, unlike the civil law which may be enforced by private parties. History The first civilizations generally did not distinguish between civil law and criminal law.
Defendant	A defendant is required to answer the complaint of a plaintiff or pursuer in a civil lawsuit before a court, or any party who has been formally charged or accused of violating a criminal statute. A respondent is the parallel term used in a proceeding which is commenced by petition. In criminal law, a defendant is anyone tried under the court of law as the ones who have committed the crime.
Judge	A judge is a person who presides over a court of law, either alone or as part of a panel of judges. The powers, functions, method of appointment, discipline, and training of judges vary widely across different jurisdictions. The judge conducts the trial impartially and in an open court.
Lawsuit	A lawsuit is a civil action brought in a court of law in which a plaintiff, a party who claims to have incurred damages as a result of a defendant's actions, demands a legal or equitable remedy. The defendant is required to respond to the plaintiff's complaint. If the plaintiff is successful, judgment will be given in the plaintiff's favor, and a variety of court orders may be issued to enforce a right, award damages, or impose an injunction to prevent an act or compel an act.
Publics	Publics are small groups of people who follow one or more particular issue very closely. They are well informed about the issue(s) and also have a very strong opinion on it/them. They tend to know more about politics than the average person, and, therefore, exert more influence, because these people care so deeply about their cause(s) that they donate much time and money.

Chapter 8. The Federal Courts: Structure and Strategies

Public health	Public health is "the science and art of preventing disease, prolonging life and promoting health through the organized efforts and informed choices of society, organizations, public and private, communities and individuals" (1920, C.E.A. Winslow). It is concerned with threats to the overall health of a community based on population health analysis. The population in question can be as small as a handful of people or as large as all the inhabitants of several continents (for instance, in the case of a pandemic).
Stamp Act	A stamp act is a law enacted by government that requires a tax to be paid on the transfer of certain documents. The stamp act was considered unfair by many people. Those that pay the tax receive an official stamp on their documents.
Precedent	In common law legal systems, a precedent is a legal case establishing a principle or rule that a court or other judicial body may utilize when deciding subsequent cases with similar issues or facts. Types of precedents Binding precedent Precedent that must be applied or followed is known as binding precedent.. Under the doctrine of stare decisis, a lower court must honor findings of law made by a higher court that is within the appeals path of cases the court hears.
Public law	Public law is a theory of law governing the relationship between individuals (citizens, companies) and the state. Under this theory, constitutional law, administrative law and criminal law are sub-divisions of public law. This theory is at odds with the concept of Constitutional law, which requires all laws to be specifically enabled, and thereby sub-divisions, of a Constitution.
Military justice	Military justice is the body of laws and procedures governing members of the armed forces. Many states have separate and distinct bodies of law that govern the conduct of members of their armed forces. Some states use special judicial and other arrangements to enforce those laws, while others use civilian judicial systems.
State	Many sovereign independent state are made up of a number of country subdivisions also called states. In some cases, such as the United States, the national government arose from a union of sovereign entities, which transferred some of their powers to the national government, while retaining the remainder of their sovereignty. These are sometimes called federal states.

Chapter 8. The Federal Courts: Structure and Strategies

Uniform Code of Military Justice	The Uniform Code of Military Justice (UCMJ, 64 Stat. 109, 10 U.S.C.
Appellate court	An appellate court is any court of law that is empowered to hear an appeal of a trial court or other lower tribunal. In most jurisdictions, the court system is divided into at least three levels: the trial court, which initially hears cases and reviews evidence and testimony to determine the facts of the case; at least one intermediate appellate court; and a supreme court (or court of last resort) which primarily reviews the decisions of the intermediate courts. A supreme court is therefore itself a kind of appellate court.
Federalist	The term federalist describes several political beliefs around the world. Also, it may refer to the concept of federalism or the type of government called a federation. In early United States history, the Federalist Party was one of the first political parties; its members or supporters called themselves Federalists.
Nomination	Nomination is part of the process of selecting a candidate for either election to an office, or the bestowing of an honor or award. In the context of elections for public office, a candidate who has been selected by a political party is normally said to be the nominee of that party. The party's selection (that is, the nomination) is typically accomplished either based on one or more primary elections or by means of a political party convention or caucus, according to the rules of the party and any applicable election laws.
Armed Services	Armed Services is a collective term that refers to the major organisational entities of national armed forces, so named because they service a combat need in a specific combat environment. In most states Armed Services include the Army also known as Land Force or Ground Force, Navy also know a Marine Defence Force, and Air Force. Some countries have a separate service for the Space Forces or Military Space Forces, and the Russian Federation also has the Strategic Missile Troops and the Airborne Troops as independent Armed Services.
Foundation	A foundation in the United States is a type of charitable organization. However, the Internal Revenue Code distinguishes between private foundations (usually funded by an individual, family, or corporation) and public charities (community foundations and other nonprofit groups that raise money from the general public). Private foundations have more restrictions and fewer tax benefits than public charities like community foundations.

Chapter 8. The Federal Courts: Structure and Strategies

International trade	International trade is exchange of capital, goods, and services across international borders or territories. In most countries, it represents a significant share of gross domestic product (GDP). While international trade has been present throughout much of history, its economic, social, and political importance has been on the rise in recent centuries.
Privatization	Privatization is the incidence or process of transferring ownership of a business, enterprise, agency or public service from the public sector (the state or government) to the private sector (businesses that operate for a private profit) or to private non-profit organizations. In a broader sense, privatization refers to transfer of any government function to the private sector - including governmental functions like revenue collection and law enforcement. The term "privatization" also has been used to describe two unrelated transactions.
Due process	Due process is the principle that the government must respect all of the legal rights that are owed to a person according to the law. Due process holds the government subservient to the law of the land protecting individual persons from the state. When a government harms a person, without following the exact course of the law, then that is a due process violation which offends the rule of law.
Habeas corpus	Habeas corpus is a writ, or legal action, through which a prisoner can be released from unlawful detention. The remedy can be sought by the prisoner or by another person coming to his aid. Habeas corpus originated in the English legal system, but it is now available in many nations.
Morse v. Frederick	Morse v. Frederick, 551 U.S. 393 (2007) was a school speech case in which the United States Supreme Court held that the First Amendment does not prevent educators from suppressing student speech, at a school-supervised event, that is reasonably viewed as promoting illegal drug use. Background.↓ In 2002, high school principal Deborah Morse suspended 18-year-old Joseph Frederick after he displayed a banner reading "BONG HiTS 4 JESUS" across the street from the school during the 2002 Olympic Torch Relay. Frederick sued, claiming his constitutional rights to free speech were violated.

Chapter 8. The Federal Courts: Structure and Strategies

Landmark	Originally, a landmark literally meant a geographic feature used by explorers and others to find their way back or through an area.
	In modern usage, a landmark includes anything that is easily recognizable, such as a monument, building, or other structure. In American English it is the main term used to designate places that might be of interest to tourists due to notable physical features or historical significance.
Prison	A prison is a place in which people are physically confined and, usually, deprived of a range of personal freedoms. Imprisonment or incarceration is a legal penalty that may be imposed by the state for the commission of a crime. Other terms are penitentiary, correctional facility, and gaol (or jail).
Rights	Rights are legal, social, or ethical principles of freedom or entitlement; that is, rights are the fundamental normative rules about what is allowed of people or owed to people, according to some legal system, social convention, or ethical theory. Rights are of essential importance in such disciplines as law and ethics, especially theories of justice and deontology.
	Rights are often considered fundamental to civilization, being regarded as established pillars of society and culture, and the history of social conflicts can be found in the history of each right and its development.
Constitutional amendment	A constitutional amendment is a change to the constitution of a nation or a state. In jurisdictions with "rigid" or "entrenched" constitutions, amendments do not require a special procedure different from that used for enacting ordinary laws.
	Some constitutions do not have to be amended with the direct consent of the electorate in a referendum.

Chapter 8. The Federal Courts: Structure and Strategies

Judiciary	The judiciary is the system of courts that interprets and applies the law in the name of the state. The judiciary also provides a mechanism for the resolution of disputes. Under the doctrine of the separation of powers, the judiciary generally does not make law (that is, in a plenary fashion, which is the responsibility of the legislature) or enforce law (which is the responsibility of the executive), but rather interprets law and applies it to the facts of each case.
Appointee	An appointee may be one of the following: • A member who is appointed to a position or office is called an appointee. In law, such a term is applied to one who is granted power of appointment of property. • An appointee was also a foot soldier in the French army, who, for long service and bravery, received more pay than other privates. • An appointee is the third most lower rank of the Italian Corps of Carabineers • An appointee is the third most lower rank of the Swiss Armed Forces • An appointee is also a person or organisation entrusted with managing the daily finances of vulnerable individuals in the UK.
Sandra Day O'Connor	Sandra Day O'Connor is an American jurist who was the first female member of the Supreme Court of the United States. She served as an Associate Justice from 1981 until her retirement from the Court in 2006. O'Connor was appointed by President Ronald Reagan in 1981. In the latter years of her tenure, she was regarded as having the swing opinion in many cases.
Treaty	A treaty is an express agreement under international law entered into by actors in international law, namely sovereign states and international organizations. A treaty may also be known as: (international) agreement, protocol, covenant, convention, exchange of letters, etc. Regardless of the terminology, all of these international agreements under international law are equally treaties and the rules are the same.
Abortion	Abortion is the termination of a pregnancy by the removal or expulsion of a fetus or embryo from the uterus, resulting in or caused by its death. An abortion can occur spontaneously due to complications during pregnancy or can be induced, in humans and other species. In the context of human pregnancies, an abortion induced to preserve the health of the gravida (pregnant female) is termed a therapeutic abortion, while an abortion induced for any other reason is termed an elective abortion.

Chapter 8. The Federal Courts: Structure and Strategies

Retirement	Retirement is the point where a person stops employment completely. A person may also semi-retire by reducing work hours. Many people choose to retire when they are eligible for private or public pension benefits, although some are forced to retire when physical conditions don't allow the person to work any more (by illness or accident) or as a result of legislation concerning their position.
Dispute resolution	Dispute resolution is the process of resolving disputes between parties. Methods Methods of dispute resolution include: - lawsuits (litigation) - arbitration - collaborative law - mediation - conciliation - many types of negotiation - facilitation One could theoretically include violence or even war as part of this spectrum, but dispute resolution practitioners do not usually do so; violence rarely ends disputes effectively, and indeed, often only escalates them. Some individuals, notably Joseph Stalin, have stated that all problems emanate from man, and absent man, no problems ensue.
Opposition	In politics, the opposition comprises one or more political parties or other organized groups that are opposed to the government, party or group in political control of a city, region, state or country. The degree of opposition varies according to political conditions - for example, across authoritarian and liberal systems where opposition may be repressed or welcomed.

Chapter 8. The Federal Courts: Structure and Strategies

Resolution	In policy debate, a resolution is a normative statement which the affirmative team affirms and the negative team negates. Resolutions are selected annually by affiliated schools. At the college level, a number of topics are proposed and interested parties write 'topic papers' discussing the pros and cons of that individual topic.
Constitutional convention	A constitutional convention is an informal and uncodified procedural agreement that is followed by the institutions of a state. In some states, notably those Commonwealth of Nations states which follow the Westminster system and whose political systems are derived from British constitutional law, most of the functions of government are guided by constitutional convention rather than by a formal written constitution. In these states, the actual distribution of power may be markedly different from those which are described in the formal constitutional documents.
National Convention	During the French Revolution, the National Convention, in France, comprised the constitutional and legislative assembly which sat from 20 September 1792 to 26 October 1795 . It held executive power in France during the first years of the French First Republic. It was succeeded by the Directory, commencing 2 November 1795. Prominent members of the original Convention included Maximilien Robespierre of the Jacobin Club, Jean-Paul Marat (affiliated with the Jacobins, though never a formal member), and Georges Danton of the Cordeliers.
Discrimination	Discrimination is the cognitive and sensory capacity or ability to see fine distinctions and perceive differences between objects, subjects, concepts and patterns, or possess exceptional development of the senses. Used in this way to identify exceptional discernment since the 17th century, the term begun to be used as an expression of derogatory racial prejudice from the 1830s Thomas D. Rice's performances as "Jim Crow". Since the American Civil War the term 'discrimination' generally evolved in American English usage as an understanding of prejudicial treatment of an individual based solely on their race, later generalized as membership in a certain socially undesirable group or social category.
Statutory interpretation	Statutory interpretation is the process of interpreting and applying legislation. Some amount of interpretation is always necessary when case involves a statute. Sometimes the words of a statute have a plain and straightforward meaning.

Chapter 8. The Federal Courts: Structure and Strategies

Session	In parliamentary procedure, a session is a meeting or series of connected meetings devoted to a single order of business, program, agenda, or announced purpose. Explanation Robert's Rules of Order Newly Revised (RONR) An organization's bylaws may define a specific meaning and/or length of the term "session." The main significance of a session is that one session generally cannot tie the hands of a majority at a future session, except by adopting a special rule of order or an amendment to the bylaws, each of which require more than a majority vote. A session has implications for the renewability of motions.
James Madison	James Madison, Jr. (March 16, 1751 - June 28, 1836) was an American politician and political philosopher who served as the fourth President of the United States (1809-1817) and is considered one of the Founding Fathers of the United States. He was the principal author of the United States Constitution, and is often called the "Father of the Constitution".
Marbury v. Madison	Marbury v. Madison, 5 U.S. (1 Cranch) 137 (1803) is a landmark case in United States law This case resulted from a petition to the Supreme Court by William Marbury, who had been appointed by President John Adams as Justice of the Peace in the District of Columbia but whose commission was not subsequently delivered.

Chapter 8. The Federal Courts: Structure and Strategies

John G. Adams	John G. Adams was the US Army's counsel in the Army-McCarthy Hearings. He was an Army veteran of World War II, and he worked in Washington, DC for the Defense Department before he became the US Army general counsel in 1953. From 1953 to 1955 he was the chief legal adviser to Army Secretary Robert Ten Broeck Stevens. Publications - Adams, John G. (1983).
Brown v. Board of Education	Brown v. Board of Education of Topeka, 347 U.S. 483 (1954), was a landmark decision of the United States Supreme Court that declared state laws establishing separate public schools for black and white students unconstitutional. The decision overturned the Plessy v. Ferguson decision of 1896 which allowed state-sponsored segregation. Handed down on May 17, 1954, the Warren Court's unanimous (9-0) decision stated that "separate educational facilities are inherently unequal." As a result, de jure racial segregation was ruled a violation of the Equal Protection Clause of the Fourteenth Amendment of the United States Constitution.
Commission	A commission is a physical document issued to certify the appointment of a commissioned officer by a sovereign power. The more specific terms commissioning parchment or commissioning scroll are often used to avoid ambiguity, due to "commission" being a homonym which directs the individual in carrying out their duty regardless of what authority or responsibility they may have at any time. However the document is not usually in the form of a scroll and is more often printed on paper instead of parchment.
Loving v. Virginia	Loving v. Virginia, 388 U.S. 1 (1967), was a landmark civil rights case in which the United States Supreme Court, by a 9-0 vote, declared Virginia's anti-miscegenation statute, the "Racial Integrity Act of 1924", unconstitutional, thereby overturning Pace v. Alabama (1883) and ending all race-based legal restrictions on marriage in the United States. Facts

Chapter 8. The Federal Courts: Structure and Strategies

	The plaintiffs, Mildred Loving (née Mildred Delores Jeter, a woman of African and Rappahannock Native American descent, July 22, 1939 - May 2, 2008) and Richard Perry Loving (a white man, October 29, 1933 - June 1975), were residents of the Commonwealth of Virginia who had been married in June 1958 in the District of Columbia, having left Virginia to evade the Racial Integrity Act, a state law banning marriages between any white person and any non-white person. Upon their return to Caroline County, Virginia, they were charged with violation of the ban.
Missouri Compromise	The Missouri Compromise was an agreement passed in 1820 between the pro-slavery and anti-slavery factions in the United States Congress, involving primarily the regulation of slavery in the western territories. It prohibited slavery in the former Louisiana Territory north of the parallel 36° 30' north except within the boundaries of the proposed state of Missouri. Prior to the agreement, the House of Representatives had refused to accept this compromise and a conference committee was appointed.
Senate	A senate is a deliberative assembly, often the upper house or chamber of a legislature or parliament. There have been many such bodies in history, since senate means the assembly of the eldest and wiser members of the society and ruling class. Two of the first official senates were the Spartan Gerousia (Γερουσ?α) and the Roman Senate.
Virginia	The Commonwealth of Virginia is a U.S. state on the Atlantic Coast of the Southern United States. Virginia is nicknamed the "Old Dominion" and sometimes the "Mother of Presidents" because it is the birthplace of eight U.S. presidents. The geography and climate of the state are shaped by the Blue Ridge Mountains and the Chesapeake Bay, which provide habitat for much of its flora and fauna.
Supremacy	The supremacy of EU law is a principle of by which the laws of European Union member states that conflict with laws of the European Union must be ignored by national courts so that the European Union law can take effect. The legal doctrine emerged from the European Court of Justice through a number of decisions. Development In Costa v. ENEL. Mr Costa was an Italian citizen opposed to nationalising energy.

Chapter 8. The Federal Courts: Structure and Strategies

Supremacy Clause	The Supremacy Clause is a clause in the United States Constitution, article VI, paragraph 2. The clause establishes the U.S. Constitution, Federal Statutes, and U.S. treaties as "the supreme law of the land." The text decrees these to be the highest form of law in the U.S. legal system, mandating that all state judges must follow federal law in the face of conflicting state law or when a conflict arises between federal law and a state constitution. (Note that the word "shall" is used here and in the language of the law, which makes it a necessity, a compulsion).
Democratic Party	The Democratic Party is a social democratic political party in Italy, that is the largest party of Italian centre-left and the second largest of the country.
	It was founded on 14 October 2007 as a merger of various left-wing and centrist parties which were part of The Union in the 2006 general election. Several parties merged into the Democratic Party, however its bulk was formed by the Democrats of the Left and Democracy is Freedom - The Daisy.
Griswold v. Connecticut	Griswold v. Connecticut, 381 U.S. 479 (1965), was a landmark case in which the Supreme Court of the United States ruled that the Constitution protected a right to privacy. The case involved a Connecticut law that prohibited the use of contraceptives. By a vote of 7-2, the Supreme Court invalidated the law on the grounds that it violated the "right to marital privacy".
Presidency	The word presidency is often used to describe the administration or the executive, the collective administrative and governmental entity that exists around an office of president of a state or nation. It is also the governing authority of some churches.
	For example, in a republic with a presidential system of government, the presidency is the executive branch of government, and is personified by a single elected man or woman who holds the office of "president".
Community	A community is an administrative division found in Belgium, Canada, Greece, Iceland, Wales, and the League of Nations Class A mandates

Chapter 8. The Federal Courts: Structure and Strategies

Environmental protection	Environmental protection is a practice of protecting the environment, on individual, organizational or governmental level, for the benefit of the natural environment and (or) humans. Due to the pressures of population and our technology the biophysical environment is being degraded, sometimes permanently. This has been recognized and governments began placing restraints on activities that caused environmental degradation.
Hamdi v. Rumsfeld	Hamdi v. Rumsfeld, 542 U.S. 507 (2004) was a U.S. Supreme Court decision reversing the dismissal of a habeas corpus petition brought on behalf of Yaser Esam Hamdi, a U.S. citizen being detained indefinitely as an "illegal enemy combatant." The Court recognized the power of the government to detain enemy combatants, but ruled that detainees who are U.S. citizens must have the ability to challenge their enemy combatant status before an impartial judge. Background of the case Hamdi was captured in Afghanistan by the Afghan Northern Alliance in 2001 and then turned over to U.S. military authorities during the U.S. invasion. The U.S. government alleged that Hamdi was there fighting for the Taliban, while Hamdi, through his father, has claimed that he was merely there as a relief worker and was mistakenly captured.
Social security	Social security is primarily a social insurance program providing social protection, or protection against socially recognized conditions, including poverty, old age, disability, unemployment and others. Social security may refer to: - social insurance, where people receive benefits or services in recognition of contributions to an insurance scheme. These services typically include provision for retirement pensions, disability insurance, survivor benefits and unemployment insurance. - income maintenance--mainly the distribution of cash in the event of interruption of employment, including retirement, disability and unemployment - services provided by administrations responsible for social security.
Taliban	

Chapter 8. The Federal Courts: Structure and Strategies

	The Taliban, alternative spelling Taleban, is an Islamist militia group that ruled large parts of Afghanistan from September 1996 onwards. Although in control of Afghanistan's capital (Kabul) and most of the country for five years, the Taliban's Islamic Emirate of Afghanistan gained diplomatic recognition from only three states: Pakistan, Saudi Arabia, and the United Arab Emirates. After the attacks of September 11 2001 the Taliban regime was overthrown by Operation Enduring Freedom.
United States	The United States of America (also referred to as the United States, the U.S., the USA, or America) is a federal constitutional republic comprising fifty states and a federal district. The country is situated mostly in central North America, where its forty-eight contiguous states and Washington, D.C., the capital district, lie between the Pacific and Atlantic Oceans, bordered by Canada to the north and Mexico to the south. The state of Alaska is in the northwest of the continent, with Canada to the east and Russia to the west across the Bering Strait.
United States v. Nixon	United States v. Nixon, 418 U.S. 683 (1974), was a landmark United States Supreme Court decision. It was a unanimous 8-0 ruling involving President Richard Nixon and was important to the late stages of the Watergate scandal. It is considered a crucial precedent limiting the power of any U.S. president.
Executive privilege	In the United States government, executive privilege is the power claimed by the President of the United States and other members of the executive branch to resist certain subpoenas and other interventions by the legislative and judicial branches of government. The concept of executive privilege is not mentioned explicitly in the United States Constitution, but the Supreme Court of the United States ruled it to be an element of the separation of powers doctrine, and/or derived from the supremacy of executive branch in its own area of Constitutional activity. The Supreme Court confirmed the legitimacy of this doctrine in United States v. Nixon, but only to the extent of confirming that there is a qualified privilege.
Privilege	Privilege is a way of framing issues surrounding social inequality, focusing as much on the advantages that one group accrues from society as on the disadvantages that another group experiences. Group role

Chapter 8. The Federal Courts: Structure and Strategies

	Privilege differs from conditions of overt prejudice, in which a dominant group actively seeks to oppress or suppress another group for its own advantage. Instead, theories of privilege suggest that the privileged group views its social, cultural, and economic experiences as a norm that everyone should experience, rather than as an advantaged position that must be maintained at the expense of others.
Terrorism	Terrorism is the systematic use of terror especially as a means of coercion. No universally agreed, legally binding, criminal law definition of terrorism currently exists. Common definitions of terrorism refer only to those violent acts which are intended to create fear (terror), are perpetrated for a religious, political or ideological goal, deliberately target or disregard the safety of non-combatants (civilians), and are committed by non-government agencies.
Circuit court	Circuit court is the name of court systems in several common law jurisdictions. History King Henry II instituted the custom of having judges ride around the countryside ("ride circuit") each year to hear appeals, rather than forcing everyone to bring their appeals to London . Thus, the term "circuit court" is derived from the practice of having judges ride around the countryside each year on pre-set paths to hear cases.
National Convention	During the French Revolution, the National Convention, in France, comprised the constitutional and legislative assembly which sat from 20 September 1792 to 26 October 1795 . It held executive power in France during the first years of the French First Republic. It was succeeded by the Directory, commencing 2 November 1795. Prominent members of the original Convention included Maximilien Robespierre of the Jacobin Club, Jean-Paul Marat (affiliated with the Jacobins, though never a formal member), and Georges Danton of the Cordeliers.
Geneva	Geneva is the second-most-populous city in Switzerland (after Zürich) and is the most populous city of Romandie . Situated where the Rhône River exits Lake Geneva, it is the capital of the Republic and Canton of Geneva. While the municipality itself (ville de Genève) has a population (as of December 2009) of 189,313, the canton of Geneva has 457,628 residents (as of December 2009).

Chapter 8. The Federal Courts: Structure and Strategies

Geneva Conventions	The Geneva Conventions comprise four treaties and three additional protocols that set the standards in international law for humanitarian treatment of the victims of war. The singular term Geneva Convention refers to the agreements of 1949, negotiated in the aftermath of World War II, updating the terms of the first three treaties and adding a fourth treaty. The language is extensive, with articles defining the basic rights of those captured during a military conflict, establishing protections for the wounded, and addressing protections for civilians in and around a war zone.
Gideon v. Wainwright	Gideon v. Wainwright, 372 U.S. 335 (1963), is a landmark case in United States Supreme Court history. In the case, the Supreme Court unanimously ruled that state courts are required under the Sixth Amendment of the Constitution to provide counsel in criminal cases for defendants who are unable to afford their own attorneys. Background of the case Between midnight and 8:00 am on June 3, 1961, a burglary occurred at the Bay Harbor Pool Room in Panama City, Florida.
Hamdan v. Rumsfeld	Hamdan v. Rumsfeld, 548 U.S. 557 (2006), is a case in which the Supreme Court of the United States held that military commissions set up by the Bush administration to try detainees at Guantanamo Bay lack "the power to proceed because its structures and procedures violate both the Uniform Code of Military Justice and the four Geneva Conventions signed in 1949 The case considered whether the United States Congress may pass legislation preventing the Supreme Court from hearing the case of an accused combatant before his military commission takes place, whether the special military commissions that had been set up violated federal law (including the Uniform Code of Military Justice and treaty obligations), and whether courts can enforce the articles of the 1949 Geneva Convention. An unusual aspect of the case was an amicus brief filed by Senators Jon Kyl and Lindsey Graham, which presented an "extensive colloquy" added to the Congressional record as evidence that "Congress was aware" that the Detainee Treatment Act would strip the Supreme Court of jurisdiction to hear cases brought by the Guantanamo detainees.

Chapter 8. The Federal Courts: Structure and Strategies

Common law	Common law, is law developed by judges through decisions of courts and similar tribunals rather than through legislative statutes or executive branch action. A "common law system" is a legal system that gives great precedential weight to common law, on the principle that it is unfair to treat similar facts differently on different occasions. The body of precedent is called "common law" and it binds future decisions.
Statutory law	Statutory law is written law (as opposed to oral or customary law) set down by a legislature (as opposed to regulatory law promulgated by the executive branch or common law of the judiciary in a typical democracy/republic) or legislator (in the case of an absolute monarchy).
	Statutes may originate with national, state legislatures or local municipalities. Statutes of lower jurisdictions are subordinate to the law of higher.
Baker	Baker is the code-name for a series of training exercises conducted by the United States Army and several Asian countries which hosted the exercises. The purpose of the exercises is to practice and develop counter-narcotics operations.
	Some of the operations in this series include:
	- Baker Blade: Classified exercise.
- Baker Mint: Conducted by the US Army and Malaysia in 1997.
- Baker Mint 99-1: Conducted by the US Army and Malaysia in 1999. Trained on military intelligence and photo-surveillance.
- Baker Mint Lens 99: Conducted by the US Army and Malaysia in 1999.
- Baker Mondial V: Conducted by the US Army and Mongolia in 1997. Trained on medical procedures.
- Baker Mongoose II: Conducted by the US Army and Mongolia in 1995.
- Baker Piston Lens 2000: Conducted by the US Army and the Philippines in 2000.
- Baker Tepid: A series of eight exercises conducted by the US Army and Thailand.
- Baker Torch: A series of three exercises conducted by the US Army and Thailand from 1999 to 2001. Trained on border control.
- Baker Torch Lens: Conducted by the US Army and Thailand.

Chapter 8. The Federal Courts: Structure and Strategies

Baker v. Carr	Baker v. Carr, 369 U.S. 186 (1962), was a landmark United States Supreme Court case that retreated from the Court's political question doctrine, deciding that reapportionment (attempts to change the way voting districts are delineated) issues present justiciable questions, thus enabling federal courts to intervene in and to decide reapportionment cases. The defendants unsuccessfully argued that reapportionment of legislative districts is a "political question," and hence not a question that may be resolved by federal courts. Plaintiff Charles Baker was a Republican who lived in Shelby County, Tennessee, the county in which Memphis is located.
Escobedo v. Illinois	Escobedo v. Illinois, 378 U.S. 478 (1964), was a United States Supreme Court case holding that criminal suspects have a right to counsel during police interrogations under the Sixth Amendment. The case was decided a year after the court held in Gideon v. Wainwright, 372 U.S. 335 (1963) that indigent criminal defendants had a right to be provided counsel at trial. Danny Escobedo's Sister-in-law, Isabella Wyrosdic, a convict from Chicago, was shot and killed on the night of January 19, 1960. Danny Escobedo was arrested without warrant early the next morning and interrogated.
Montreal Protocol	The Montreal Protocol on Substances That Deplete the Ozone Layer (a protocol to the Vienna Convention for the Protection of the Ozone Layer) is an international treaty designed to protect the ozone layer by phasing out the production of numerous substances believed to be responsible for ozone depletion. The treaty was opened for signature on September 16, 1987, and entered into force on January 1, 1989, followed by a first meeting in Helsinki, May 1989. Since then, it has undergone seven revisions, in 1990 (London), 1991 (Nairobi), 1992 (Copenhagen), 1993 (Bangkok), 1995 (Vienna), 1997 (Montreal), and 1999 (Beijing). It is believed that if the international agreement is adhered to, the ozone layer is expected to recover by 2050. Due to its widespread adoption and implementation it has been hailed as an example of exceptional international co-operation, with Kofi Annan quoted as saying that "perhaps the single most successful international agreement to date has been the Montreal Protocol".

Chapter 8. The Federal Courts: Structure and Strategies

Minutes	Minutes, are the instant written record of a meeting or hearing. They often give an overview of the structure of the meeting, starting with a list of those present, a statement of the various issues before the participants, and each of their responses thereto. They are often created at the moment of the hearing by a typist or court recorder at the meeting, who may record the meeting in shorthand, and then prepare the minutes and issue them to the participants afterwards.
United States v. Miller	United States v. Miller, 307 U.S. 174 (1939), was the first Supreme Court of the United States decision to involve the Second Amendment to the United States Constitution. Miller is a controversial decision in the ongoing American gun politics debate, as both sides claim that it supports their position. United States v. Miller involved a criminal prosecution under the National Firearms Act of 1934 (NFA).
Trusts	In Conflict of Laws, the Hague Convention on the Law Applicable to Trusts and on Their Recognition was concluded on 1 July 1985 and entered into force 1 January 1992. The Convention aims to harmonise not only the municipal law definitions of a trust both within the USA and outside the USA, but also the Conflict rules for resolving problems in the choice of the lex causae. Explanation Many states do not have a developed law of trusts, or the principles differ significantly between states. It was therefore necessary for the Hague Convention to define a trust to indicate the range of legal transactions regulated by the Convention and, perhaps more significantly, the range of applications not regulated.
General	General, Finnish: kenraali is the highest officer's rank in Sweden and Finland. In Sweden, it is held by the supreme commander of the Swedish Armed Forces and the monarch. In Finland, it is held by the Chief of Defence.

Chapter 8. The Federal Courts: Structure and Strategies

Solicitor	Solicitors are lawyers who traditionally deal with any legal matter including conducting proceedings in courts. In the United Kingdom, a few Australian states and the Republic of Ireland, the legal profession is split between solicitors and barristers, and a lawyer will usually only hold one title. However, in Canada, New Zealand and most Australian states, the legal profession is now for practical purposes "fused", allowing lawyers to hold the title of "barrister and solicitor" and practice as both.
Americas	The Americas, are the lands of the western hemisphere, composed of numerous entities and regions variably defined by geography, politics, and culture. The Americas are frequently recognised to comprise two separate continents (North America and South America), particularly in English-speaking nations. The Americas may also be recognised to comprise a single continent, in Latin America and in some European nations.
Amicus curiae	An amicus curiae is someone, not a party to a case, who volunteers to offer information to assist a court in deciding a matter before it. The information provided may be a legal opinion in the form of a brief (which is called an amicus brief when offered by an amicus curiae), a testimony that has not been solicited by any of the parties, or a learned treatise on a matter that bears on the case. The decision on whether to admit the information lies at the discretion of the court.
Thurgood Marshall	Thurgood Marshall was an American jurist and the first African American to serve on the Supreme Court of the United States. Before becoming a judge, he was a lawyer who was best remembered for his high success rate in arguing before the Supreme Court and for the victory in Brown v. Board of Education. He was nominated to the court by President Lyndon Johnson in 1967.
Law clerk	A law clerk is a person who provides assistance to a judge in researching issues before the court and in writing opinions. Law clerks are not court clerks or courtroom deputies, who are administrative staff for the court. Most law clerks are recent law school graduates who performed at or near the top of their class.

Chapter 8. The Federal Courts: Structure and Strategies

Civil liberties	Civil liberties are rights and freedoms that provide an individual specific rights such as the right to life, freedom from torture, freedom from slavery and forced labour, the right to liberty and security, right to a fair trial, the right to defend one's self, the right to privacy, freedom of conscience, freedom of expression, freedom of assembly and association, and the right to marry and have a family. Within the distinctions between civil liberties and other types of liberty, it is important to note the distinctions between positive rights and negative rights. Common civil liberties include the rights of people, freedom of religion, and freedom of speech, and additionally, the right to due process, to a trial, to own property, and to privacy.
The Jukes family	The Jukes family was a New York hill family studied in the late 19th and early 20th centuries. The studies are part of a series of other family studies, including the Kallikaks, the Zeros and the Nams, that were often quoted as arguments in support of eugenics, though the original Jukes study, by Richard L. Dugdale, placed considerable emphasis on the environment as a determining factor in criminality, disease and poverty. Dugdale's study In 1874, sociologist Richard L. Dugdale, a member of the executive committee of the Prison Association of New York, was delegated to visit jails in upstate New York.
Smith v. Allwright	Smith v. Allwright, 321 U.S. 649 (1944), was an important decision of the United States Supreme Court with regard to voting rights and, by extension, racial desegregation. It overturned the Democratic Party's use of all-white primaries in Texas, and other states where the party used the rule. Lonnie E. Smith, a black voter in Harris County, Texas, sued county election official S. S. Allwright for the right to vote in a primary election being conducted by the Democratic Party.

Chapter 8. The Federal Courts: Structure and Strategies

Voting	Voting is a method for a group such as a meeting or an electorate to make a decision or express an opinion--often following discussions, debates, or election campaigns. It is often found in democracies and republics. Reasons for voting In a representative government, voting commonly implies election: a way for an electorate to select among candidates for office.
Dissenting opinion	A dissenting opinion is an opinion in a legal case written by one or more judges expressing disagreement with the majority opinion of the court which gives rise to its judgment. A dissenting opinion does not create binding precedent or become part of case law. However, dissenting opinions are sometimes cited as persuasive authority when arguing that the court's holding should be limited or overturned.
Bush v. Gore	Bush v. Gore, 531 U.S. 98 (2000), is the landmark United States Supreme Court decision that effectively resolved the 2000 presidential election in favor of George W. Bush. Only eight days earlier, the United States Supreme Court had unanimously decided the closely related case of Bush v. Palm Beach County Canvassing Board, 531 U.S. 70 (2000), and only three days earlier, had preliminarily halted the recount that was occurring in Florida. In a per curiam decision, the Court ruled that the Florida Supreme Court's method for recounting ballots was a violation of the Equal Protection Clause of the Fourteenth Amendment.
Election	An election is a formal decision-making process by which a population chooses an individual to hold public office. Elections have been the usual mechanism by which modern representative democracy operates since the 17th century. Elections may fill offices in the legislature, sometimes in the executive and judiciary, and for regional and local government.

Chapter 8. The Federal Courts: Structure and Strategies

Electoral Commission	An Electoral Commission is an election management body, in charge of overseeing the implementation of election procedures:
	
	- Australia: Australian Electoral Commission
	- Bangladesh: Bangladesh Election Commission
	- Belize: Belize Elections and Boundaries Commission
	- Brazil: Supreme Electoral Court (Brazil)
	- Colombia: National Electoral Council (Colombia)
	- Ghana: Electoral Commission of Ghana
	- Guyana:Guyana Elections Commission
	- Hong Kong: Electoral Affairs Commission
	- India: Election Commission of India
	- Iran: Guardian Council
	- Iraq: Independent High Electoral Commission
	- Kenya:
	    - Electoral Commission of Kenya (defunct)
	    - Interim Independent Electoral Commission
	- Liberia: National Election Commission (Liberia)
	- Malaysia: Election Commission of Malaysia
	- Mexico: Federal Electoral Institute
	- Nepal: Election Commission of Nepal
	- New Zealand: Electoral Commission
	- Pakistan: Election Commission of Pakistan
	- Poland: Panstwowa Komisja Wyborcza (National Electoral Commission)
	- Philippines: Commission on Elections (Philippines)
	- Thailand: Election Commission (Thailand)
	- Ukraine: Central Election Commission of Ukraine
	- United Kingdom: Electoral Commission
	- United States:
	    - Election Assistance Commission, administers Federal elections and establishing standards for State and local governments
	    - Electoral Commission created solely to resolve the disputed 1876 presidential election
	    - Federal Election Commission, regulates campaign finance legislation
	- Uruguay: Electoral Court
	- Zimbabwe: Zimbabwe Electoral Commission

Chapter 8. The Federal Courts: Structure and Strategies

Reform Act	In the United Kingdom, Reform Act is a generic term used for legislation concerning electoral matters. It is most commonly used for laws passed to enfranchise new groups of voters and to redistribute seats in the British House of Commons. The periodic redrawing of constituency boundaries is now dealt with by a permanent Boundary Commission in each part of the United Kingdom, rather than by a Reform Act.
Bill	A bill is a proposed law under consideration by a legislature. A bill does not become law until it is passed by the legislature and, in most cases, approved by the executive. Once a bill has been enacted into law, it is called an act or a statute.
Swing	An electoral swing analysis (or swing) shows the extent of change in voter support from one election to another. It is an indicator of voter support for individual candidates or political parties, or voter preference between two or more candidates or parties. A swing can be calculated for the electorate as a whole, or for a given electoral district or demographic.
Swing vote	Swing vote is a term used to describe a vote that may go to any of a number of candidates in an election, or, in a two-party system, may go to either of the two dominant political parties. Such votes are usually sought after in elections, since they can play a big role in determining the outcome.

A swing voter or floating voter is a voter who may not be affiliated with a particular political party (Independent) or who will vote across party lines. |
| Federalism | In Europe, "federalist" is sometimes used to describe those who favor a common federal government, with distributed power at regional, national and supranational levels. Most European Federalists want this development to continue within the European Union. European federalism originated in post-war Europe; one of the more important initiatives was Winston Churchill's speech in Zurich in 1946. |
| Diversity | In the political arena, the term diversity is used to describe political entities (neighborhoods, student bodies, etc) with members who have identifiable differences in their backgrounds or lifestyles. |

Chapter 8. The Federal Courts: Structure and Strategies

	The term describes differences in racial or ethnic classifications, age, gender, religion, philosophy, physical abilities, socioeconomic background, sexual orientation, gender identity, intelligence, mental health, physical health, genetic attributes, behavior, attractiveness, or other identifying features.
	In measuring human diversity, a diversity index measures the probability that any two residents, chosen at random, would be of different ethnicities.
Filibuster	A filibuster is a type of parliamentary procedure. Specifically, it is a form of obstruction in a legislature or other decision-making body whereby a lone member can elect to delay or entirely prevent a vote on a proposal.
	The term "filibuster" was first used in 1851. It was derived from the Spanish filibustero, which translates as "pirate" or "freebooter." This term had evolved from the French word flibustier, which itself evolved from the Dutch vrijbuiter (free outsider).
Debate	Debate is a formal method of interactive and representational argument. Debate is a broader form of argument than logical argument, which only examines consistency from axiom, and factual argument, which only examines what is or isn't the case or rhetoric which is a technique of persuasion. Though logical consistency, factual accuracy and some degree of emotional appeal to the audience are important elements of the art of persuasion, in debating, one side often prevails over the other side by presenting a superior "context" and/or framework of the issue, which is far more subtle and strategic.
Decision	A decision, defined in Article 288 of the Treaty on the Functioning of the European Union (formerly Article 249 TEC), is one of the three binding instruments provided by secondary EU legislation. A decision is binding on the person or entity to which it is addressed. Decisions may be addressed to member states or individuals.
Implementation	Implementation is the realization of an application, or execution of a plan, idea, model, design, specification, standard, algorithm, or policy.
	Computer Science

Chapter 8. The Federal Courts: Structure and Strategies

	In computer science, an implementation is a realization of a technical specification or algorithm as a program, software component, or other computer system through programming and deployment. Many implementations may exist for a given specification or standard.
Nuclear option	In U.S. politics, the "nuclear option" (or "constitutional option") allows the United States Senate to reinterpret a procedural rule by invoking the argument that the constitution requires that the will of the majority be effective on specific Senate duties and procedures. This option allows a simple majority to override the rules of the Senate and end a filibuster or other delaying tactic. In contrast, the cloture rule requires a supermajority of 60 votes (out of 100) to end a filibuster.
Option	In finance, an option is a derivative financial instrument that establishes a contract between two parties concerning the buying or selling of an asset at a reference price. The buyer of the option gains the right, but not the obligation, to engage in some specific transaction on the asset, while the seller incurs the obligation to fulfill the transaction if so requested by the buyer. Other types of options exist, and options can in principle be created for any type of valuable asset.
Environmental policy	Environmental policy is any [course of] action deliberately taken [or not taken] to manage human activities with a view to prevent, reduce, or mitigate harmful effects on nature and natural resources, and ensuring that man-made changes to the environment do not have harmful effects on humans. It is useful to consider that environmental policy comprises two major terms: environment and policy. Environment primarily refers to the ecological dimension (ecosystems), but can also take account of social dimension (quality of life) and an economic dimension (resource management).
Policy	A policy is typically described as a principle or rule to guide decisions and achieve rational outcome(s). The term is not normally used to denote what is actually done, this is normally referred to as either procedure or protocol. Whereas a policy will contain the 'what' and the 'why', procedures or protocols contain the 'what', the 'how', the 'where', and the 'when'.
ARTHUR	ARTHUR is an abbreviation for mobile "Artillery Hunting Radar" system developed in Sweden. This field artillery acquisition radar was developed for the primary role as the core element of a brigade or division level counter battery sensor system. It can also be used for peace support operations.

Chapter 8. The Federal Courts: Structure and Strategies

Chapter 8. The Federal Courts: Structure and Strategies

Chapter 9. Public Opinion

Congress	A congress is a formal meeting of the representatives of different nations, constituent states, independent organizations (such as trade unions), or groups. The term was chosen for the United States Congress to emphasize the status of each state represented there as a self-governing unit. Subsequent to the use of congress by the U.S. legislature, the term has been incorrectly adopted by many states within unions, and by unitary nation-states in the Americas, to refer to their legislatures.
Publics	Publics are small groups of people who follow one or more particular issue very closely. They are well informed about the issue(s) and also have a very strong opinion on it/them. They tend to know more about politics than the average person, and, therefore, exert more influence, because these people care so deeply about their cause(s) that they donate much time and money.
Public health	Public health is "the science and art of preventing disease, prolonging life and promoting health through the organized efforts and informed choices of society, organizations, public and private, communities and individuals" (1920, C.E.A. Winslow). It is concerned with threats to the overall health of a community based on population health analysis. The population in question can be as small as a handful of people or as large as all the inhabitants of several continents (for instance, in the case of a pandemic).
Constituency	A constituency is any cohesive body of people bound by shared identity, goals, or loyalty. Constituency can be used to describe a business's customer base and shareholders, or a charity's donors or those it serves. In politics, a constituency can mean either the people from whom an individual or organization hopes to attract support, or geographical area that a particular elected official represents.
Political science	Political Science is a social science concerned with the theory and practice of politics and the analysis of political systems and political behavior. Political scientists "see themselves engaged in revealing the relationships underlying political events and conditions. And from these revelations they attempt to construct general principles about the way the world of politics work." Political science intersects with other fields; including public policy, national politics, economics, international relations, comparative politics, psychology, sociology, history, law, and political theory.

Chapter 9. Public Opinion

Public opinion	Public opinion is the aggregate of individual attitudes or beliefs held by the adult population. Public opinion can also be defined as the complex collection of opinions of many different people and the sum of all their views. The principle approaches to the study of public opinion may be divided into 4 categories: 1. quantitative measurement of opinion distributions; 2. investigation of the internal relationships among the individual opinions that make up public opinion on an issue; 3. description or analysis of the public role of public opinion; 4. study both of the communication media that disseminate the ideas on which opinions are based and of the uses that propagandists and other manipulators make of these media. Concepts of "public opinion" Public opinion as a concept gained credence with the rise of "public" in the eighteenth century.
Tax cut	A tax cut is a reduction in taxes. The immediate effects of a tax cut are a decrease in the real income of the government and an increase in the real income of those whose tax rate has been lowered. In the longer term, however, the loss of government income may be mitigated, depending on the response that tax-payers make.
Brown v. Board of Education	Brown v. Board of Education of Topeka, 347 U.S. 483 (1954), was a landmark decision of the United States Supreme Court that declared state laws establishing separate public schools for black and white students unconstitutional. The decision overturned the Plessy v. Ferguson decision of 1896 which allowed state-sponsored segregation. Handed down on May 17, 1954, the Warren Court's unanimous (9-0) decision stated that "separate educational facilities are inherently unequal." As a result, de jure racial segregation was ruled a violation of the Equal Protection Clause of the Fourteenth Amendment of the United States Constitution.
Desegregation	Desegregation is the process of ending the separation of two groups usually referring to races. This is most commonly used in reference to the United States. Desegregation was long a focus of the American Civil Rights Movement, both before and after the United States Supreme Court's decision in Brown v. Board of Education, particularly desegregation of the school systems and the military.

Chapter 9. Public Opinion

Regulation	Regulation is "controlling human or societal behavior by rules or restrictions." Regulation can take many forms: legal restrictions promulgated by a government authority, self-regulation by an industry such as through a trade association, social regulation co-regulation and market regulation. One can consider regulation as actions of conduct imposing sanctions (such as a fine). This action of administrative law, or implementing regulatory law, may be contrasted with statutory or case law.
Bill of rights	A bill of rights is a list of the most important rights of the citizens of a country. The purpose of these bills is to protect those rights against infringement by the government. The term "bill of rights" originates from England, where it referred to the Bill of Rights 1689. Bills of rights may be entrenched or unentrenched.
Rights	Rights are legal, social, or ethical principles of freedom or entitlement; that is, rights are the fundamental normative rules about what is allowed of people or owed to people, according to some legal system, social convention, or ethical theory. Rights are of essential importance in such disciplines as law and ethics, especially theories of justice and deontology. Rights are often considered fundamental to civilization, being regarded as established pillars of society and culture, and the history of social conflicts can be found in the history of each right and its development.
Social security	Social security is primarily a social insurance program providing social protection, or protection against socially recognized conditions, including poverty, old age, disability, unemployment and others. Social security may refer to: - social insurance, where people receive benefits or services in recognition of contributions to an insurance scheme. These services typically include provision for retirement pensions, disability insurance, survivor benefits and unemployment insurance. - income maintenance--mainly the distribution of cash in the event of interruption of employment, including retirement, disability and unemployment - services provided by administrations responsible for social security.

Chapter 9. Public Opinion

Lobbying	Lobbying is the intention of influencing decisions made by legislators and officials in the government by individuals, other legislators, constituents, or advocacy groups. A lobbyist is a person who tries to influence legislation on behalf of a special interest or a member of a lobby. Governments often define and regulate organized group lobbying that has become influential.
Marquess	A marquess is a nobleman of hereditary rank in various European monarchies and some of their colonies. The term is also used to render equivalent oriental styles as in imperial China, Japan, and Vietnam (Annam). In the British peerage it ranks below a duke and above an earl.
Election	An election is a formal decision-making process by which a population chooses an individual to hold public office. Elections have been the usual mechanism by which modern representative democracy operates since the 17th century. Elections may fill offices in the legislature, sometimes in the executive and judiciary, and for regional and local government.
Preventive war	A preventive war is a war initiated to prevent another party from attacking, when an attack by that party is not imminent or known to be planned. Preventive war aims to forestall a shift in the balance of power by strategically attacking before the balance of power has a chance to shift in the direction of the adversary. Preventive war is distinct from preemptive war, which is first strike when an attack is imminent.
Commission	A commission is a physical document issued to certify the appointment of a commissioned officer by a sovereign power.
	The more specific terms commissioning parchment or commissioning scroll are often used to avoid ambiguity, due to "commission" being a homonym which directs the individual in carrying out their duty regardless of what authority or responsibility they may have at any time. However the document is not usually in the form of a scroll and is more often printed on paper instead of parchment.
Government	In the social sciences, the term government refers to the particular group of people, the administrative bureaucracy, who control a state at a given time, and the manner in which their governing organizations are structured. That is, governments are the means through which state power is employed. States are served by a continuous succession of different governments.

Chapter 9. Public Opinion

Central government	A central government, union government and in federal states, the federal government, is the government at the level of the nation-state. The structure of central governments varies from institution to institution. Many countries have created autonomous regions by delegating powers from the central government to governments at a subnational level, such as a regional, local, or state level.
Identity	Identity is an umbrella term used throughout the social sciences to describe a person's conception and expression of their individuality or group affiliations (such as national identity and cultural identity). The term is used more specifically in psychology and sociology, including the two forms of social psychology. The term is also used with respect to place identity.
Party system	A party system is a concept in comparative political science concerning the system of government by political parties in a democratic country. The idea is that political parties have basic similarities: they control the government, have a stable base of mass popular support, and create internal mechanisms for controlling funding, information and nominations. The concept was originated by European scholars studying the United States, especially James Bryce and Moisey Ostrogorsky, and has been expanded to cover other democracies.
Election Day	Election Day refers to the day when general elections are held. In many countries, general elections are always held on a Sunday, to enable as many voters as possible to participate, while in other countries elections are always held on a weekday. However, some countries, or regions within a country, always make a weekday election day a public holiday, thus satisfying both demands.
Medicaid	Medicaid is the United States health program for eligible individuals and families with low incomes and resources. It is a means tested program that is jointly funded by the state and federal governments, and is managed by the states. Among the groups of people served by Medicaid are certain eligible U.S. citizens and resident aliens, including low-income adults and their children, and people with certain disabilities.
Treaty	A treaty is an express agreement under international law entered into by actors in international law, namely sovereign states and international organizations. A treaty may also be known as: (international) agreement, protocol, covenant, convention, exchange of letters, etc. Regardless of the terminology, all of these international agreements under international law are equally treaties and the rules are the same.

Chapter 9. Public Opinion

Abortion	Abortion is the termination of a pregnancy by the removal or expulsion of a fetus or embryo from the uterus, resulting in or caused by its death. An abortion can occur spontaneously due to complications during pregnancy or can be induced, in humans and other species. In the context of human pregnancies, an abortion induced to preserve the health of the gravida (pregnant female) is termed a therapeutic abortion, while an abortion induced for any other reason is termed an elective abortion.
Attack	In computer and computer networks an attack is any attempt to destroy, expose, alter, disable, steal or gain unauthorized access to or make unauthorized use of an asset. Definitions IETF Internet Engineering Task Force defines attack in RFC 2828 as: US Government CNSS Instruction No. 4009 dated 26 April 2010 by Committee on National Security Systems of United States of America defines an attack as: The increasing dependencies of modern society on information and computers networks (both in private and public sectors, including military) has led to new terms like cyber attack and Cyberwarfare. CNSS Instruction No. 4009 define a cyber attack as: Phenomenology An attack can be active or passive.

Chapter 9. Public Opinion

	An attack can be perpetrated by an insider or from outside the organization;
	An "inside attack" is an attack initiated by an entity inside the security perimeter (an "insider"), i.e., an entity that is authorized to access system resources but uses them in a way not approved by those who granted the authorization. An "outside attack" is initiated from outside the perimeter, by an unauthorized or illegitimate user of the system (an "outsider").
Terrorism	Terrorism is the systematic use of terror especially as a means of coercion. No universally agreed, legally binding, criminal law definition of terrorism currently exists. Common definitions of terrorism refer only to those violent acts which are intended to create fear (terror), are perpetrated for a religious, political or ideological goal, deliberately target or disregard the safety of non-combatants (civilians), and are committed by non-government agencies.
Voting	Voting is a method for a group such as a meeting or an electorate to make a decision or express an opinion--often following discussions, debates, or election campaigns. It is often found in democracies and republics. Reasons for voting In a representative government, voting commonly implies election: a way for an electorate to select among candidates for office.
Interest	Interest is a fee paid on borrowed assets. It is the price paid for the use of borrowed money, or, money earned by deposited funds. Assets that are sometimes lent with interest include money, shares, consumer goods through hire purchase, major assets such as aircraft, and even entire factories in finance lease arrangements.
Policy	A policy is typically described as a principle or rule to guide decisions and achieve rational outcome(s). The term is not normally used to denote what is actually done, this is normally referred to as either procedure or protocol. Whereas a policy will contain the 'what' and the 'why', procedures or protocols contain the 'what', the 'how', the 'where', and the 'when'.

Chapter 9. Public Opinion

Domestic policy	Domestic policy, presents decisions, laws, and programs made by the government which are directly related to issues in the country.
	Domestic policy is the set of laws and regulations that a government establishes within a nation's borders. It differs from foreign policy, which refers to the ways a government advances its interests in world politics.
Conservative Party	The Conservative Party was a Brazilian political party of the imperial period, which was formed circa 1836 and ended with the proclamation of the Republic in 1889. This party arose mostly from the Coimbra bloc and also from members of the Restorationist Party (Partido Restaurador), also called the Caramuru Party; it called itself the Party of Order (Portuguese: partido de ordem) to distinguish itself from the liberal opposition, which they accused of disorder and anarchy, and both the party and its leadership were known as "saquarema" after the village of Saquarema, where the leadership had plantations and support.
Liberals	Liberals is a free market liberal party in Finland. Founded in 1965 as a reunification of the People's Party of Finland and Liberal League. Originally named Liberal People's Party (Finnish: Liberaalinen Kansanpuolue), it restyled its name as Liberals in 2000.
Liberal Party	The Liberal Party was a Belgian political party that existed from 1846 until 1961, when it became the Party for Freedom and Progress, Partij voor Vrijheid en Vooruitgang/Parti de la Liberté et du Progrès or PVV-PLP, under the leadership of Omer Vanaudenhove.
	History
	The Liberal Party was founded in 1846 and as such was the first political party of Belgium. Walthère Frère-Orban wrote the first charter for the new party.
Conservatism	Conservatism is a political and social philosophy that promotes the maintenance of traditional institutions and supports, at the most, minimal and gradual change in society. Some conservatives seek to preserve things as they are, emphasizing stability and continuity, while others oppose modernism and seek a return to the way things were. The first established use of the term in a political context was by François-René de Chateaubriand in 1819, following the French Revolution.

Chapter 9. Public Opinion

Liberalism	Liberalism is the belief in the importance of liberty and equal rights. Liberals espouse a wide array of views depending on their understanding of these principles, but most liberals support such fundamental ideas as constitutions, liberal democracy, free and fair elections, human rights, capitalism, free trade, and the separation of church and state. These ideas are widely accepted, even by political groups that do not openly profess a liberal ideological orientation.
Census	A census is the procedure of systematically acquiring and recording information about the members of a given population. It is a regularly occurring and official count of a particular population. The term is used mostly in connection with national population and housing censuses; other common censuses include agriculture, business, and traffic censuses.
James Madison	James Madison, Jr. (March 16, 1751 - June 28, 1836) was an American politician and political philosopher who served as the fourth President of the United States (1809-1817) and is considered one of the Founding Fathers of the United States. He was the principal author of the United States Constitution, and is often called the "Father of the Constitution".
Demographics	Demographics are the characteristics of a human population. These types of data are used widely in sociology, public policy, and marketing. Commonly used demographics include gender, race, age, income, disabilities, mobility (in terms of travel time to work or number of vehicles available), educational attainment, home ownership, employment status, and even location.
Homosexuality	Homosexuality is romantic and/or sexual attraction or behavior among members of the same sex or gender. As a sexual orientation, homosexuality refers to "an enduring pattern of or disposition to experience sexual, affectional, or romantic attractions" primarily or exclusively to people of the same sex; "it also refers to an individual's sense of personal and social identity based on those attractions, behaviors expressing them, and membership in a community of others who share them."

Chapter 9. Public Opinion

	Homosexuality is one of the three main categories of sexual orientation, along with bisexuality and heterosexuality, within the heterosexual-homosexual continuum. The consensus of the behavioral and social sciences and the health and mental health professions is that homosexuality is a normal and positive variation in human sexual orientation, though many religious societies, including Catholicism, Mormonism, and Islam, and some psychological associations, such as NARTH, teach that homosexual activity is sinful or dysfunctional.
Political socialization	Political socialization is a concept concerning the "study of the developmental processes by which children and adolescents acquire political cognition, attitudes and behaviors". It refers to a learning process by which norms and behavior acceptable to a well running political system are transmitted from one generation to another. It is through the performance of this function individuals are inducted into the political culture and their orientations towards political objects are formed.
Socialization	In economic discourse, socialization refers to the process of transforming an activity into a social relationship. Socialization of production and labor is a phenomenon that takes place under capitalism due to centralization of capital and in industries where there are increasing returns to scale, eventually leading to a situation where socialization of output (or surplus value) and co-operative ownership of the means of production is necessitated. Socialization of surplus output (profit) and ownership is one aspect of transitioning from capitalism to socialism.
Reconciliation	Reconciliation is a legislative process of the United States Senate intended to allow consideration of a budget bill with debate limited to twenty hours under Senate Rules. Reconciliation also exists in the United States House of Representatives, but because the House regularly passes rules that constrain debate and amendment, the process has had a less significant impact on that body.
	A reconciliation instruction (Budget Reconciliation) is a provision in a budget resolution directing one or more committees to submit legislation changing existing law in order to bring spending, revenues, or the debt-limit into conformity with the budget resolution.
Cuba	The Republic of Cuba is an island country in the Caribbean. The nation of Cuba consists of the main island of Cuba, the Isla de la Juventud, and several archipelagos. Havana is the largest city in Cuba and the country's capital.

Chapter 9. Public Opinion

Rebellion	Rebellion is a refusal of obedience or order. It may, therefore, be seen as encompassing a range of behaviors from civil disobedience and mass nonviolent resistance, to violent and organized attempts to destroy an established authority such as a government. Those who participate in rebellions are known as "rebels".
Trusts	In Conflict of Laws, the Hague Convention on the Law Applicable to Trusts and on Their Recognition was concluded on 1 July 1985 and entered into force 1 January 1992. The Convention aims to harmonise not only the municipal law definitions of a trust both within the USA and outside the USA, but also the Conflict rules for resolving problems in the choice of the lex causae. Explanation Many states do not have a developed law of trusts, or the principles differ significantly between states. It was therefore necessary for the Hague Convention to define a trust to indicate the range of legal transactions regulated by the Convention and, perhaps more significantly, the range of applications not regulated.
Gerrymandering	In the process of setting electoral boundaries, rather than using uniform geographic standards, Gerrymandering is a practice of political corruption that attempts to establish a political advantage for a particular party or group by manipulating geographic boundaries to create partisan, incumbent-protected, and neutral districts. The resulting district is known as a gerrymander; however, that word can also refer to the process. Gerrymandering may be used to achieve desired electoral results for a particular party, or may be used to help or hinder a particular group of constituents, such as a political, racial, linguistic, religious or class group.
Trade union	A trade union is an organization of workers that have banded together to achieve common goals such as better working conditions. The trade union, through its leadership, bargains with the employer on behalf of union members (rank and file members) and negotiates labour contracts (collective bargaining) with employers. This may include the negotiation of wages, work rules, complaint procedures, rules governing hiring, firing and promotion of workers, benefits, workplace safety and policies.

Chapter 9. Public Opinion

Political Parties	Political Parties: A Sociological Study of the Oligarchical Tendencies of Modern Democracy is a book by sociologist Robert Michels, published in 1911, and first introducing the concept of iron law of oligarchy. It is considered one of the classics of sociology and political science.
	This work analyzes the power structures of organizations such as political parties and trade unions.
Caucus	A caucus is a meeting of supporters or members of a political party or movement, especially in the United States. As the use of the term has been expanded the exact definition has come to vary among political cultures.
	Origin of the term
	The origin of the word caucus is debated, but it is generally agreed that it first came into use in the English colonies of North America.
	A February 1763 entry in the diary of John Adams of Braintree, Massachusetts, is one of the earliest appearances of Caucas, already with its modern connotations of a "smoke-filled room" where candidates for public election are pre-selected in private
	This day learned that the Caucas Clubb meets at certain Times in the Garret of Tom Daws, the Adjutant of the Boston Regiment.
Civil War	"Civil War" is a song by the hard rock band Guns N' Roses, which originally appeared on the 1990 album Nobody's Child: Romanian Angel Appeal. It is a protest song on war, referring to all war as 'civil war' and that it only "feeds the rich while it buries the poor." In the song, singer Axl Rose asks, "What's so civil about war, anyway?"

Chapter 9. Public Opinion

	"Civil War" was the brainchild of the Guns N' Roses artists Slash, Axl Rose, and Duff McKagan. Slash stated that the song was an instrumental he had written right before the band left for the Japanese leg of its Appetite for Destruction world tour.
Class conflict	Class conflict refers to the concept of underlying tensions or antagonisms which exist in society due to conflicting interests that arise from different socioeconomic positions and dispositions. Class conflict is thought to play a pivotal role in history of class societies (such as capitalism and feudalism) by Marxists who refer to its overt manifestations as class war, a struggle whose resolution in favor of the working class is viewed by them as inevitable under capitalism. Class conflict can take many different shapes.
Objective	A military objective is a clearly defined desired result in a given campaign, major operation, battle, or engagement set by the senior command for their formations and units to achieve. Military objectives can be set within a three-tier scale of combat structure of tactical, operational and strategic management of the conflict, and the conduct of its combat operations process. The objective is usually defined in the orders within the operational plan's written specification.
Opposition	In politics, the opposition comprises one or more political parties or other organized groups that are opposed to the government, party or group in political control of a city, region, state or country. The degree of opposition varies according to political conditions - for example, across authoritarian and liberal systems where opposition may be repressed or welcomed.
Spiral of silence	The spiral of silence is a political science and mass communication theory propounded by the German political scientist Elisabeth Noelle-Neumann. The theory asserts that a person is less likely to voice an opinion on a topic if one feels that one is in the minority for fear of reprisal or isolation from the majority. Basic framework The spiral of silence begins with fear of reprisal or isolation, and escalates from there.

Chapter 9. Public Opinion

Independent	In politics, an independent is an individual not affiliated to any political party. Independents may hold a centrist viewpoint between those of major political parties, or they may have a viewpoint based on issues that they do not feel that any major party addresses. Other independent candidates are associated with a political party and may be former members of it, but choose not to stand under its label.
Independent Party	The Independent Party is a social democratic and christian humanist political party in Uruguay. The party is leadered by Pablo Mieres, who was presidential candidate in the 2004 national elections and in 2009. Aims Its goal is to build a third way away from the heterodox left-wing coalition Frente Amplio and the traditional parties Colorado Party and National Party.
Ideology	An ideology is a set of ideas that constitutes one's goals, expectations, and actions. An ideology can be thought of as a comprehensive vision, as a way of looking at things (compare worldview), as in common sense and several philosophical tendencies , or a set of ideas proposed by the dominant class of a society to all members of this society (a "received consciousness" or product of socialization). The main purpose behind an ideology is to offer either change in society, or adherence to a set of ideals where conformity already exists, through a normative thought process.
Redistricting	Redistricting, a form of redistribution, is the process of drawing United States district lines. This often means changing electoral district and constituency boundaries in response to periodic census results. In 36 states, the state legislature has primary responsibility for creating a redistricting plan, in many cases subject to approval by the state governor.
Nation	Nation has different meanings in different contexts. In worldwide diplomacy, nation can mean country or sovereign state. The United Nations, for instance, speaks of how it was founded after the Second World War with "51 countries" and currently has "192 member states".
United Nations	The United Nations are facilitating cooperation in international law, international security, economic development, social progress, human rights, and achievement of world peace. The United Nations was founded in 1945 after World War II to replace the League of Nations, to stop wars between countries, and to provide a platform for dialogue. It contains multiple subsidiary organizations to carry out its missions.

Chapter 9. Public Opinion

Communism	Communism is a sociopolitical movement that aims for a classless and stateless society structured upon common ownership of the means of production, free access to articles of consumption, and the end of wage labour and private property in the means of production and real estate.
	In Marxist theory, communism is a specific stage of historical development that inevitably emerges from the development of the productive forces that leads to a superabundance of material wealth, allowing for distribution based on need and social relations based on freely-associated individuals.
	The exact definition of communism varies, and it is often mistakenly used interchangeably with socialism; however, Marxist theory contends that socialism is just a transitional stage on the way to communism.
Fascism	Fascism is a radical, authoritarian nationalist political ideology. Fascists advocate the creation of a totalitarian single-party state that seeks the mass mobilization of a nation through indoctrination, physical education, and family policy including eugenics. Fascists seek to purge forces and ideas deemed to be the cause of decadence and degeneration and produce their nation's rebirth based on commitment to the national community based on organic unity where individuals are bound together by suprapersonal connections of ancestry, culture, and "blood".
Homeland	A homeland is the concept of the place (cultural geography) to which an ethnic group holds a long history and a deep cultural association with --the country in which a particular national identity began. As a common noun, it simply connotes the country of one's origin.
Homeland security	Homeland security is an umbrella term for security efforts to protect the United States against terrorist activity. The term arose following a reorganization of many U.S. government agencies in 2003 to form the United States Department of Homeland Security after the September 11 attacks, and may be used to refer to the actions of that department, the United States Senate Committee on Homeland Security and Governmental Affairs, or the United States House of Representatives Committee on Homeland Security.
	In the United States

Chapter 9. Public Opinion

	In the United States, the concept of "homeland security" extends and recombines responsibilities of government agencies and entities.
Court	A court is a form of tribunal, often a governmental institution, with the authority to adjudicate legal disputes between parties and carry out the administration of justice in civil, criminal, and administrative matters in accordance with the rule of law. In both common law and civil law legal systems, courts are the central means for dispute resolution, and it is generally understood that all persons have an ability to bring their claims before a court. Similarly, the rights of those accused of a crime include the right to present a defense before a court.
Administration	Administration, as a legal concept, is a procedure under the insolvency laws of a number of common law jurisdictions. It functions as a rescue mechanism for insolvent companies and allows them to carry on running their business. The process - an alternative to liquidation - is often known as going into administration.
Public relations	Public relations is a field concerned with maintaining a public image for businesses, non-profit organizations or high-profile people, such as celebrities and politicians.
	An earlier definition of public relations, by The first World Assembly of Public Relations Associations held in Mexico City in August 1978, was "the art and social science of analyzing trends, predicting their consequences, counseling organizational leaders, and implementing planned programs of action, which will serve both the organization and the public interest."
	Others define it as the practice of managing communication between an organization and its publics. Public relations provides an organization or individual exposure to their audiences using topics of public interest and news items that provide a third-party endorsement and do not direct payment.

Chapter 9. Public Opinion

Medicare	Medicare is a social insurance program administered by the United States government, providing health insurance coverage to people who are aged 65 and over, or who meet other special criteria. Medicare operates similar to a single-payer health care system, but the key difference is that its coverage only extends to 80% of any given medical cost; the remaining 20% of cost must be paid by other means, such as privately-held supplemental insurance, or paid by the patient. The program also funds residency training programs for the vast majority of physicians in the United States.
Common Cause	Common Cause is an alliance of four republican political organisations in the Commonwealth of Nations seeking to remove the Monarchy in each realm and replace it with a Republic, with an elected Head of State. As of May 2008, the four members are: - Republic in the United Kingdom - The Republican Movement of Aotearoa New Zealand - The Australian Republican Movement - Citizens for a Canadian Republic
Foundation	A foundation in the United States is a type of charitable organization. However, the Internal Revenue Code distinguishes between private foundations (usually funded by an individual, family, or corporation) and public charities (community foundations and other nonprofit groups that raise money from the general public). Private foundations have more restrictions and fewer tax benefits than public charities like community foundations.
Institution	An institution is any structure or mechanism of social order and cooperation governing the behavior of a set of individuals within a given human community. Institutions are identified with a social purpose and permanence, transcending individual human lives and intentions, and with the making and enforcing of rules governing cooperative human behavior.

Chapter 9. Public Opinion

	The term "institution" is commonly applied to customs and behavior patterns important to a society, as well as to particular formal organizations of government and public service.
Physicians for Social Responsibility	Physicians for Social Responsibility is the largest physician-led organization in the country working to protect the public from the threats of nuclear proliferation, climate change, and environmental toxins. Continuing its long and respected history of physician-led activism, PSR produces and disseminates its own publications, provides specialized training, offers written and oral testimony to congress, conducts media interviews, and delivers professional and public education. PSR's 50,000 members and e-activists, 30 state and local chapters, 39 student chapters, and 14 national staff form a nationwide network that effectively targets threats to global survival, specifically nuclear warfare, nuclear proliferation, global warming, and toxic degradation of the environment.
Affair	Affair may refer to professional, personal, or public business matters or to a particular business or private activity of a temporary duration, as in family affair, a private affair, or a romantic affair. Political affair Political affair may refer to the illicit or scandalous activities of public, such as the Watergate affair, or to a legally constituted government department, for example, the United Nations Department of Political Affairs. Romantic affair A romantic affair, also called an affair of the heart, may refer to sexual liaisons among unwed parties, or to various forms of nonmonogamy.
Germany	Germany officially the Federal Republic of Germany, is a country in Western Europe. It is bordered to the north by the North Sea, Denmark, and the Baltic Sea; to the east by Poland and the Czech Republic; to the south by Austria and Switzerland; and to the west by France, Luxembourg, Belgium, and the Netherlands. The territory of Germany covers an area of 357,021 km^2 and is influenced by a temperate seasonal climate.

Chapter 9. Public Opinion

Internets	"Internets" is a Bushism-turned-catchphrase used humorously to portray the speaker as ignorant about the Internet or about technology in general, or as having a provincial or folksy attitude toward technology. Former United States President George W. Bush first used the word publicly during the 2000 election campaign. The term gained cachet as an Internet humor meme following Bush's use of the term in the second 2004 presidential election debate on October 8, 2004.
Blog	A blog is a type of website or part of a website. Blogs are usually maintained by an individual with regular entries of commentary, descriptions of events, or other material such as graphics or video. Entries are commonly displayed in reverse-chronological order.
Impeachment	Impeachment is a formal process in which an official is accused of unlawful activity and the outcome of which, depending on the country, can lead to the removal of that official from office or other punishment. Medieval popular etymology also associated it (wrongly) with derivations from the Latin impetere (to attack). (In its more frequent and more technical usage, impeachment of a person in the role of a witness is the act of challenging the honesty or credibility of that person).
Implementation	Implementation is the realization of an application, or execution of a plan, idea, model, design, specification, standard, algorithm, or policy. Computer Science In computer science, an implementation is a realization of a technical specification or algorithm as a program, software component, or other computer system through programming and deployment. Many implementations may exist for a given specification or standard.
News conference	A news conference is a media event in which newsmakers invite journalists to hear them speak and, most often, ask questions. A joint press conference instead is held between two or more talking sides. Practice

In a news conference, one or more speakers may make a statement, which may be followed by questions from reporters.

Equity

Equity is the concept or idea of fairness in economics, particularly as to taxation or welfare economics.

Overview

Equity may be distinguished from economic efficiency in overall evaluation of social welfare. Although 'equity' has broader uses, it may be posed as a counterpart to economic inequality in yielding a "good" distribution of welfare.

Debate

Debate is a formal method of interactive and representational argument. Debate is a broader form of argument than logical argument, which only examines consistency from axiom, and factual argument, which only examines what is or isn't the case or rhetoric which is a technique of persuasion. Though logical consistency, factual accuracy and some degree of emotional appeal to the audience are important elements of the art of persuasion, in debating, one side often prevails over the other side by presenting a superior "context" and/or framework of the issue, which is far more subtle and strategic.

Weapon

A weapon is an instrument used with the aim of causing harm or death to human being -- and for inflicting damage upon civil or military infrastructure and life-sustaining natural resources. In essence, it is a tool made with the purpose of increasing the efficacy and efficiency of such activities as hunting, fighting, the committing of criminal acts, the preserving of law and order, and the waging of war in an offensive or defensive fashion.

Weapons are employed individually or collectively and can be improvised or purpose-built, sometimes with great skill and ingenuity.

Chapter 9. Public Opinion

Great Society	The Great Society was a set of domestic programs proposed or enacted in the United States on the initiative of President Lyndon B. Johnson. Two main goals of the Great Society social reforms were the elimination of poverty and racial injustice. New major spending programs that addressed education, medical care, urban problems, and transportation were launched during this period.
Society	A society is (1) a group of people related to each other through persistent relations such as social status, roles and social networks. (2) A large social grouping that shares the same geographical territory and is subject to the same political authority and dominant cultural expectations. Human societies are characterized by patterns of relationships between individuals sharing a distinctive culture and institutions.
Sampling	Sampling is that part of statistical practice concerned with the selection of a subset of individual observations within a population of individuals intended to yield some knowledge about the population of concern, especially for the purposes of making predictions based on statistical inference. Sampling is an important aspect of data collection. Researchers rarely survey the entire population for two reasons (Adèr, Mellenbergh, ' Hand, 2008): the cost is too high, and the population is dynamic in that the individuals making up the population may change over time.
New Deal	The New Deal is a programme of active labour market policies introduced in the United Kingdom by the Labour government in 1998, initially funded by a one off £5bn windfall tax on privatised utility companies. The stated purpose is to reduce unemployment by providing training, subsidised employment and voluntary work to the unemployed. Spending on the New Deal was £1.3 billion in 2001.
Tribune	Tribune is a democratic socialist weekly, currently a magazine though in the past more often a newspaper, published in London. It considers itself "A thorn in the side of all governments, constructively to Labour, unforgiving to Conservatives." Origins

Chapter 9. Public Opinion

Tribune was set up in early 1937 by two left-wing Labour Party Members of Parliament (MPs), Stafford Cripps and George Strauss, to back the Unity Campaign, an attempt to secure an anti-fascist and anti-appeasement United Front between the Labour Party and socialist parties to its left which involved Cripps's (Labour-affiliated) Socialist League, the Independent Labour Party and the Communist Party of Great Britain (CP).

The paper's first editor was William Mellor, and its journalists included Michael Foot and Barbara Betts (later Barbara Castle).

Sample size

The sample size of a statistical sample is the number of observations that constitute it. It is typically denoted n, a positive integer. The sample size is an important feature of any empirical study in which the goal is to make inferences about a population from a sample.

Bailout

In economics, a bailout is an act of loaning or giving capital to an entity (a company, a country, or an individual) that is in danger of failing, in an attempt to save it from bankruptcy, insolvency, or total liquidation and ruin; or to allow a failing entity to fail gracefully without spreading contagion.

Overview

A bailout could be done for mere profit, as when a predatory investor resurrects a floundering company by buying its shares at fire-sale prices; for social improvement, as when, hypothetically speaking, a wealthy philanthropist reinvents an unprofitable fast food company into a non-profit food distribution network; or the bailout of a company might be seen as a necessity in order to prevent greater, socioeconomic failures: For example, the US government assumes transportation to be the backbone of America's general economic fluency, which maintains the nation's geopolitical power. As such, it is the policy of the US government to protect the biggest American companies responsible for transportation--airliners, petrol companies, etc.--from failure through subsidies and low-interest loans.

Chapter 9. Public Opinion

Push poll	A push poll is a political campaign technique in which an individual or organization attempts to influence or alter the view of respondents under the guise of conducting a poll. In a push poll, large numbers of respondents are contacted, and little or no effort is made to collect and analyze response data. Instead, the push poll is a form of telemarketing-based propaganda and rumor mongering, masquerading as a poll.
Bandwagon effect	The bandwagon effect, closely related to opportunism, is a phenomenon--observed primarily within the fields of microeconomics, political science, and behaviorism--that people often do and believe things merely because many other people do and believe the same things. The effect is often called herd instinct, though strictly speaking, this effect is not a result of herd instinct. The bandwagon effect is the reason for the bandwagon fallacy's success.
Poland	Poland officially the Republic of Poland - is a country in Central Europe bordered by Germany to the west; the Czech Republic and Slovakia to the south; Ukraine, Belarus and Lithuania to the east; and the Baltic Sea and Kaliningrad Oblast, a Russian exclave, to the north. The total area of Poland is 312,679 square kilometres (120,726 sq mi), making it the 69th largest country in the world and the 9th largest in Europe. Poland has a population of over 38 million people, which makes it the 34th most populous country in the world and the sixth most populous member of the European Union, being its most populous post-communist member.
Brady Handgun Violence Prevention Act	The Brady Handgun Violence Prevention Act was an Act of the United States Congress that, for the first time, instituted federal background checks on firearm purchasers in the United States. It was signed into law by President Bill Clinton on November 30, 1993, and went into effect on February 28, 1994. The Act was named after James Brady, who was shot by John Hinckley, Jr. during an attempted assassination of President Ronald Reagan on March 30, 1981.
Crime	Crime is the breach of rules or laws for which some governing authority (via mechanisms such as legal systems) can ultimately prescribe a conviction. Individual human societies may each define crime and crimes differently. While every crime violates the law, not every violation of the law counts as a crime; for example: breaches of contract and of other civil law may rank as "offences" or as "infractions".

Chapter 9. Public Opinion

Handgun	A handgun is a firearm designed to be held and operated by one hand, with the other hand optionally supporting the shooting hand. This characteristic differentiates handguns as a general class of firearms from their larger counterparts: long guns such as rifles and shotguns (which are held in both hands and usually braced against the shoulder), mounted weapons such as machine guns and autocannons, and larger weapons such as artillery.
	Some handgun subtypes include derringers, single-shot pistols, revolvers, semi-automatic pistols, pepperboxes, and machine pistols.
Detention	Detention is the process when a state, government or citizen lawfully holds a person by removing their freedom of liberty at that time. This can be due to (pending) criminal charges being raised against the individual as part of a prosecution or to protect a person or property. Being detained does not always result in being taken to a particular area (generally called a detention centre), either for interrogation, or as punishment for a crime .
Health care	Health or healthcare is the treatment and prevention of illness. Health care is delivered by professionals in medicine, dentistry, nursing, pharmacy and allied health.
	The social and political issues surrounding access to healthcare in the US have led to vigorous public debate and the almost colloquial use of terms such as health care health insurance (reimbursement of health care costs), and public health (the collective state and range of health in a population).

Chapter 9. Public Opinion

Health care reform	Health care reform is a general rubric used for discussing major health policy creation or changes--for the most part, governmental policy that affects health care delivery in a given place. Health care reform typically attempts to: • Broaden the population that receives health care coverage through either public sector insurance programs or private sector insurance companies • Expand the array of health care providers consumers may choose among • Improve the access to health care specialists • Improve the quality of health care • Decrease the cost of health care United States The debate regarding healthcare reform in the United States includes questions of a right to health care, access, fairness, sustainability, quality and amounts spent by government. The mixed public-private health care system in the United States is the most expensive in the world, with health care costing more per person than in any other nation, and a greater portion of gross domestic product (GDP) is spent on it than in any other United Nations member state except for East Timor (Timor-Leste).
Initiative	In political science, the initiative provides a means by which a petition signed by a certain minimum number of registered voters can force a public vote (plebiscite) on a proposed statute, constitutional amendment, charter amendment or ordinance, or, in its minimal form, to simply oblige the executive or legislative bodies to consider the subject by submitting it to the order of the day. It is a form of direct democracy. The initiative may take the form of either the direct initiative or indirect initiative.

Chapter 9. Public Opinion

Prescription	In law, prescription is the method of sovereignty transfer of a territory through international law analogous to the common law doctrine of adverse possession for private real-estate. Prescription involves the open encroachment by the new sovereign upon the territory in question for a prolonged period of time, acting as the sovereign, without protest or other contest by the original sovereign. This doctrine legalizes de jure the de facto transfer of sovereignty caused in part by the original sovereign's extended negligence and/or neglect of the area in question.
State	Many sovereign independent state are made up of a number of country subdivisions also called states. In some cases, such as the United States, the national government arose from a union of sovereign entities, which transferred some of their powers to the national government, while retaining the remainder of their sovereignty. These are sometimes called federal states.

Chapter 9. Public Opinion

Chapter 9. Public Opinion

Chapter 10. Elections

Election	An election is a formal decision-making process by which a population chooses an individual to hold public office. Elections have been the usual mechanism by which modern representative democracy operates since the 17th century. Elections may fill offices in the legislature, sometimes in the executive and judiciary, and for regional and local government.
Election Day	Election Day refers to the day when general elections are held. In many countries, general elections are always held on a Sunday, to enable as many voters as possible to participate, while in other countries elections are always held on a weekday. However, some countries, or regions within a country, always make a weekday election day a public holiday, thus satisfying both demands.
Rights	Rights are legal, social, or ethical principles of freedom or entitlement; that is, rights are the fundamental normative rules about what is allowed of people or owed to people, according to some legal system, social convention, or ethical theory. Rights are of essential importance in such disciplines as law and ethics, especially theories of justice and deontology. Rights are often considered fundamental to civilization, being regarded as established pillars of society and culture, and the history of social conflicts can be found in the history of each right and its development.
Voting	Voting is a method for a group such as a meeting or an electorate to make a decision or express an opinion--often following discussions, debates, or election campaigns. It is often found in democracies and republics. Reasons for voting In a representative government, voting commonly implies election: a way for an electorate to select among candidates for office.
Government	In the social sciences, the term government refers to the particular group of people, the administrative bureaucracy, who control a state at a given time, and the manner in which their governing organizations are structured. That is, governments are the means through which state power is employed. States are served by a continuous succession of different governments.

Chapter 10. Elections

Canada	Canada was the name of the French colony that once stretched along the St. Lawrence River; the other colonies of New France were Acadia, Louisiana and Newfoundland. Canada, the most developed colony of New France, was divided into three districts, each with its own government: Québec, Trois-Rivières, and Montréal. The governor of the district of Québec was also the governor-general of all of New France.
Court	A court is a form of tribunal, often a governmental institution, with the authority to adjudicate legal disputes between parties and carry out the administration of justice in civil, criminal, and administrative matters in accordance with the rule of law. In both common law and civil law legal systems, courts are the central means for dispute resolution, and it is generally understood that all persons have an ability to bring their claims before a court. Similarly, the rights of those accused of a crime include the right to present a defense before a court.
Foundation	A foundation in the United States is a type of charitable organization. However, the Internal Revenue Code distinguishes between private foundations (usually funded by an individual, family, or corporation) and public charities (community foundations and other nonprofit groups that raise money from the general public). Private foundations have more restrictions and fewer tax benefits than public charities like community foundations.
Montreal Protocol	The Montreal Protocol on Substances That Deplete the Ozone Layer (a protocol to the Vienna Convention for the Protection of the Ozone Layer) is an international treaty designed to protect the ozone layer by phasing out the production of numerous substances believed to be responsible for ozone depletion. The treaty was opened for signature on September 16, 1987, and entered into force on January 1, 1989, followed by a first meeting in Helsinki, May 1989. Since then, it has undergone seven revisions, in 1990 (London), 1991 (Nairobi), 1992 (Copenhagen), 1993 (Bangkok), 1995 (Vienna), 1997 (Montreal), and 1999 (Beijing). It is believed that if the international agreement is adhered to, the ozone layer is expected to recover by 2050. Due to its widespread adoption and implementation it has been hailed as an example of exceptional international co-operation, with Kofi Annan quoted as saying that "perhaps the single most successful international agreement to date has been the Montreal Protocol".
Minutes	Minutes, are the instant written record of a meeting or hearing. They often give an overview of the structure of the meeting, starting with a list of those present, a statement of the various issues before the participants, and each of their responses thereto. They are often created at the moment of the hearing by a typist or court recorder at the meeting, who may record the meeting in shorthand, and then prepare the minutes and issue them to the participants afterwards.

Chapter 10. Elections

Treaty	A treaty is an express agreement under international law entered into by actors in international law, namely sovereign states and international organizations. A treaty may also be known as: (international) agreement, protocol, covenant, convention, exchange of letters, etc. Regardless of the terminology, all of these international agreements under international law are equally treaties and the rules are the same.
Abortion	Abortion is the termination of a pregnancy by the removal or expulsion of a fetus or embryo from the uterus, resulting in or caused by its death. An abortion can occur spontaneously due to complications during pregnancy or can be induced, in humans and other species. In the context of human pregnancies, an abortion induced to preserve the health of the gravida (pregnant female) is termed a therapeutic abortion, while an abortion induced for any other reason is termed an elective abortion.
Adverse	Adverse, in law, is anything that functions contrary to a party's interest. This word should not be confused with averse. Adverse possession In property law, adverse possession refers to an interest in real property which is contrary to the in-fact owner of the property.
Candidate	A candidate is the prospective recipient of an award or honor or a person seeking or being considered for some kind of position; for example: • to be elected to an office -- in this case a candidate selection procedure occurs. • to receive membership in a group "Nomination" is part of the process of selecting a candidate for either election to an office, or the bestowing of an honor or award. "Presumptive nominee" is a term used when a person or organization believes that the nomination is inevitable. The act of being a candidate in a race is called a "candidacy." "Candidate" is a derivative of the Latin "candida" (white).

Chapter 10. Elections

Impeachment	Impeachment is a formal process in which an official is accused of unlawful activity and the outcome of which, depending on the country, can lead to the removal of that official from office or other punishment. Medieval popular etymology also associated it (wrongly) with derivations from the Latin impetere (to attack). (In its more frequent and more technical usage, impeachment of a person in the role of a witness is the act of challenging the honesty or credibility of that person).
Implementation	Implementation is the realization of an application, or execution of a plan, idea, model, design, specification, standard, algorithm, or policy. Computer Science In computer science, an implementation is a realization of a technical specification or algorithm as a program, software component, or other computer system through programming and deployment. Many implementations may exist for a given specification or standard.
Minimum wage	A minimum wage is the lowest hourly, daily or monthly wage that employers may legally pay to employees or workers. Equivalently, it is the lowest wage at which workers may sell their labor. Although minimum wage laws are in effect in a great many jurisdictions, there are differences of opinion about the benefits and drawbacks of a minimum wage.
Moral hazard	Moral hazard occurs when a party insulated from risk behaves differently than it would behave if it were fully exposed to the risk. Moral hazard arises because an individual or institution does not take the full consequences and responsibilities of its actions, and therefore has a tendency to act less carefully than it otherwise would, leaving another party to hold some responsibility for the consequences of those actions. For example, a person with insurance against automobile theft may be less cautious about locking his or her car, because the negative consequences of vehicle theft are (partially) the responsibility of the insurance company.

Chapter 10. Elections

Political campaign	A political campaign is an organized effort which seeks to influence the decision making process within a specific group. In democracies, political campaigns often refer to electoral campaigns, wherein representatives are chosen or referendums are decided. Campaign message The message of the campaign contains the ideas that the candidate wants to share with the voters.
Campaign finance	Campaign finance refers to the fundraising and spending that political campaigns do in their election campaigns. As campaigns have many expenditures, ranging from the cost of travel for the candidate and others might include the purchasing of air time for TV advertisements, however in some countries, such as Britain TV advertising is free. Candidates often devote substantial time and effort raising money to finance campaigns.
Voter turnout	Voter turnout is the percentage of eligible voters who cast a ballot in an election. After increasing for many decades, there has been a trend of decreasing voter turnout in most established democracies since the 1960s. In general, low turnout may be due to disenchantment, indifference, or contentment.
Americas	The Americas, are the lands of the western hemisphere, composed of numerous entities and regions variably defined by geography, politics, and culture. The Americas are frequently recognised to comprise two separate continents (North America and South America), particularly in English-speaking nations. The Americas may also be recognised to comprise a single continent , in Latin America and in some European nations.
Contract	In the Conflict of Laws, the validity of a contract with one or more foreign law elements will be decided by reference to the so-called "proper law" of the contract. History

Chapter 10. Elections

	Until the middle of the 19th century, the courts applied the lex loci contractus or the law of the place where the contract was made to decide whether the given contract was valid. The apparent advantage of this approach was that the rule was easy to apply with certain and predictable outcomes.
Jim Crow laws	The Jim Crow laws were state and local laws in the United States enacted between 1876 and 1965. They mandated de jure racial segregation in all public facilities, with a supposedly "separate but equal" status for black Americans. In reality, this led to treatment and accommodations that were usually inferior to those provided for white Americans, systematizing a number of economic, educational and social disadvantages. Some examples of Jim Crow laws are the segregation of public schools, public places and public transportation, and the segregation of restrooms, restaurants and drinking fountains for whites and blacks.
Social security	Social security is primarily a social insurance program providing social protection, or protection against socially recognized conditions, including poverty, old age, disability, unemployment and others. Social security may refer to: - social insurance, where people receive benefits or services in recognition of contributions to an insurance scheme. These services typically include provision for retirement pensions, disability insurance, survivor benefits and unemployment insurance. - income maintenance--mainly the distribution of cash in the event of interruption of employment, including retirement, disability and unemployment - services provided by administrations responsible for social security.
Absentee ballot	An absentee ballot is a vote cast by someone who is unable or unwilling to attend the official polling station. Numerous methods have been devised to facilitate this. Increasing the ease of access to absentee ballots are seen by many as one way to improve voter turnout, though some countries require that a valid reason, such as infirmity or travel, be given before a voter can participate in an absentee ballot.

Mail	Mail, is a method for transmitting information and tangible objects, wherein written documents, typically enclosed in envelopes and also small packages are delivered to destinations around the world. Anything sent through the postal system is called mail or post. In principle, a postal service can be private or public.
Federalist	The term federalist describes several political beliefs around the world. Also, it may refer to the concept of federalism or the type of government called a federation. In early United States history, the Federalist Party was one of the first political parties; its members or supporters called themselves Federalists.
Constitutional amendment	A constitutional amendment is a change to the constitution of a nation or a state. In jurisdictions with "rigid" or "entrenched" constitutions, amendments do not require a special procedure different from that used for enacting ordinary laws. Some constitutions do not have to be amended with the direct consent of the electorate in a referendum.
Federalism	In Europe, "federalist" is sometimes used to describe those who favor a common federal government, with distributed power at regional, national and supranational levels. Most European Federalists want this development to continue within the European Union. European federalism originated in post-war Europe; one of the more important initiatives was Winston Churchill's speech in Zurich in 1946.
Power	Power is a measure of an entity's ability to control its environment, including the behavior of other entities. The term authority is often used for power, perceived as legitimate by the social structure. Power can be seen as evil or unjust, but the exercise of power is accepted as endemic to humans as social beings.

Chapter 10. Elections

Democracy	Democracy is a political form of government in which governing power is derived from the people, by consensus (consensus democracy), by direct referendum (direct democracy), or by means of elected representatives of the people (representative democracy). The term comes from the Greek: δημοκρατ?α - (demokratía) "rule of the people", which was coined from δ?μος (dêmos) "people" and κρ?τος (Kratos) "power", in the middle of the 5th-4th century BC to denote the political systems then existing in some Greek city-states, notably Athens following a popular uprising in 508 BC. Even though there is no specific, universally accepted definition of 'democracy', equality and freedom have been identified as important characteristics of democracy since ancient times. These principles are reflected in all citizens being equal before the law and having equal access to power.
Participatory democracy	Participatory democracy is a process emphasizing the broad participation of constituents in the direction and operation of political systems. Etymological roots of democracy imply that the people are in power and thus that all democracies are participatory. However, traditional representative democracy tends to limit citizen participation to voting, leaving actual governance to politicians.
Vietnam	Vietnam, officially the Socialist Republic of Vietnam is the easternmost country on the Indochina Peninsula in Southeast Asia. It is bordered by People's Republic of China (PRC) to the north, Laos to the northwest, Cambodia to the southwest, and the South China Sea, referred to as East Sea (Vietnamese: Bi?n Đông), to the east. With a population of over 86 million, Vietnam is the 13th most populous country in the world.
Nation	Nation has different meanings in different contexts. In worldwide diplomacy, nation can mean country or sovereign state. The United Nations, for instance, speaks of how it was founded after the Second World War with "51 countries" and currently has "192 member states".
Status	A person's status is a set of social conditions or relationships created and vested in an individual by an act of law rather than by the consensual acts of the parties, and it is in rem, i.e. these conditions must be recognised by the world. It is the qualities of universality and permanence that distinguish status from consensual relationships such as employment and agency. Hence, a person's status and its attributes are set by the law of the domicile if born in a common law state, or by the law of nationality if born in a civil law state and this status and its attendant capacities should be recognised wherever the person may later travel.

Chapter 10. Elections

Voter registration	Voter registration is the requirement in some democracies for citizens and residents to check in with some central registry specifically for the purpose of being allowed to vote in elections. An effort to get people to register is known as a voter registration drive. Centralized/compulsory vs. opt-in In some countries, including most developed countries, registration is the responsibility of the government, either local or national; and in over 30 countries some form of compulsory voting is required as part of each citizen's civic duty.
Regent	A regent is a person selected to act as head of state (ruling or not) because the ruler is a minor, not present, or debilitated. In a monarchy, a regent usually governs due to one of these reasons, but may also be elected to rule during the interregnum when the royal line has died out. This was the case in Finland and Hungary, where the royal line was considered extinct in the aftermath of World War I. In Iceland, the regent represented the King of Denmark as sovereign of Iceland until the country became a republic in 1944.
Congress	A congress is a formal meeting of the representatives of different nations, constituent states, independent organizations (such as trade unions), or groups. The term was chosen for the United States Congress to emphasize the status of each state represented there as a self-governing unit. Subsequent to the use of congress by the U.S. legislature, the term has been incorrectly adopted by many states within unions, and by unitary nation-states in the Americas, to refer to their legislatures.

Chapter 10. Elections

Continental Congress	The Continental Congress was a convention of delegates called together from the Thirteen Colonies that became the governing body of the United States during the American Revolution. The Congress met from 1774 to 1789 in three incarnations. The first call for a convention was made over issues of mounting taxation without representation in Parliament and because of the British blockade.
Caucus	A caucus is a meeting of supporters or members of a political party or movement, especially in the United States. As the use of the term has been expanded the exact definition has come to vary among political cultures.
	Origin of the term
	The origin of the word caucus is debated, but it is generally agreed that it first came into use in the English colonies of North America.
	A February 1763 entry in the diary of John Adams of Braintree, Massachusetts, is one of the earliest appearances of Caucas, already with its modern connotations of a "smoke-filled room" where candidates for public election are pre-selected in private
	This day learned that the Caucas Clubb meets at certain Times in the Garret of Tom Daws, the Adjutant of the Boston Regiment.
Publics	Publics are small groups of people who follow one or more particular issue very closely. They are well informed about the issue(s) and also have a very strong opinion on it/them. They tend to know more about politics than the average person, and, therefore, exert more influence, because these people care so deeply about their cause(s) that they donate much time and money.
Secret ballot	The secret ballot is a voting method in which a voter's choices in an election or a referendum are confidential. The key aim is to ensure the voter records a sincere choice by forestalling attempts to influence the voter by intimidation or bribery. The system is one means of achieving the goal of political privacy.

Chapter 10. Elections

Speaker	The term speaker is a title often given to the presiding officer (chair) of a deliberative assembly, especially a legislative body. The speaker's official role is to moderate debate, make rulings on procedure, announce the results of votes, and the like. The speaker decides who may speak and has the powers to discipline members who break the procedures of the house.
Mixed member proportional representation	Mixed member proportional representation, also termed mixed-member proportional voting and commonly abbreviated to MMP, is an 'additional member' voting system used to elect representatives to numerous legislatures around the world. MMP is similar to other forms of proportional representation (PR) in that the overall total of party members in the elected body is intended to mirror the overall proportion of votes received; it differs by including a set of members elected by geographic constituency who are deducted from the party totals so as to maintain overall proportionality. Therefore, the additional party seats are compensatory: they top up the local results.
Presidential election	A presidential election is the election of any head of state whose official title is president. List of presidential elections - Presidential elections of Mexico - United States presidential election
Seat	Seats were territorial-administrative units in the medieval Kingdom of Hungary. The seats were autonomous regions within the Kingdom, and were independent from the feudal county system. Their autonomy was granted in return for the military services they provided to the Hungarian Kings.
Split-ticket voting	A split-ticket refers to a ballot on which the voter has chosen candidates from different political parties when multiple offices are being decided by a single election. Split-ticket voting is in contrast to straight-ticket voting in which a voter chooses candidates from the same political party for every office on the ballot. Often, states will hold elections for many different offices on the same day.

Chapter 10. Elections

Electoral college	An electoral college is a set of electors who are selected to elect a candidate to a particular office. Often these represent different organizations or entities, with each organization or entity represented by a particular number of electors or with votes weighted in a particular way. Many times, though, the electors are simply important people whose wisdom, ideally, would provide a better choice than a larger body.
Electoral district	An electoral district is a distinct territorial subdivision for holding a separate election for one or more seats in a legislative body. However not all political systems use separate districts to conduct elections; Israel and the Netherlands, for instance, conduct parliamentary elections as a single, nationwide entity. In contrast, the United Kingdom, France and many other nations elect each member of the legislature from their own individual district.
Articles of Confederation	The Articles of Confederation was the first constitution of the United States and specified how the Federal government was to operate, including adoption of an official name for the new nation, United States of America. The Second Continental Congress appointed a committee to draft the Articles in June 1776 and sent the draft to the states for ratification in November 1777. In practice, the Articles were in use beginning in 1777. The ratification process was completed in March 1781. Under the Articles, the states retained sovereignty over all governmental functions not specifically relinquished to the national government. On June 12, 1776, a day after appointing a committee to prepare a draft of the Declaration of Independence, the Second Continental Congress resolved to appoint a committee of thirteen to prepare a draft of a constitution for a confederate type of union. The last draft of the Articles was written in the summer of 1777 and the Second Continental Congress approved them for ratification by the States on November 15, 1777, after a year of debate.
Baker	Baker is the code-name for a series of training exercises conducted by the United States Army and several Asian countries which hosted the exercises. The purpose of the exercises is to practice and develop counter-narcotics operations.

Some of the operations in this series include:

- Baker Blade: Classified exercise.
- Baker Mint: Conducted by the US Army and Malaysia in 1997.
- Baker Mint 99-1: Conducted by the US Army and Malaysia in 1999. Trained on military intelligence and photo-surveillance.
- Baker Mint Lens 99: Conducted by the US Army and Malaysia in 1999.
- Baker Mondial V: Conducted by the US Army and Mongolia in 1997. Trained on medical procedures.
- Baker Mongoose II: Conducted by the US Army and Mongolia in 1995.
- Baker Piston Lens 2000: Conducted by the US Army and the Philippines in 2000.
- Baker Tepid: A series of eight exercises conducted by the US Army and Thailand.
- Baker Torch: A series of three exercises conducted by the US Army and Thailand from 1999 to 2001. Trained on border control.
- Baker Torch Lens: Conducted by the US Army and Thailand.

Baker v. Carr	Baker v. Carr, 369 U.S. 186 (1962), was a landmark United States Supreme Court case that retreated from the Court's political question doctrine, deciding that reapportionment (attempts to change the way voting districts are delineated) issues present justiciable questions, thus enabling federal courts to intervene in and to decide reapportionment cases. The defendants unsuccessfully argued that reapportionment of legislative districts is a "political question," and hence not a question that may be resolved by federal courts. Plaintiff Charles Baker was a Republican who lived in Shelby County, Tennessee, the county in which Memphis is located.
Commission	A commission is a physical document issued to certify the appointment of a commissioned officer by a sovereign power.

Chapter 10. Elections

	The more specific terms commissioning parchment or commissioning scroll are often used to avoid ambiguity, due to "commission" being a homonym which directs the individual in carrying out their duty regardless of what authority or responsibility they may have at any time. However the document is not usually in the form of a scroll and is more often printed on paper instead of parchment.
Balkan Federation	The Balkan Federation was a project about the creation of a Balkan federation, based mainly on left political ideas.
	The concept of a Balkan federation emerged at the late 19th century from among left political forces in the region. The central aim was to establish a new political unity: a common federal republic unifying the Balkan Peninsula on the basis of internationalism, social solidarity, and economic equality.
Connecticut Compromise	The Connecticut Compromise was an agreement between large and small states reached during the Constitutional Convention of 1787 that in part defined the legislative structure and representation that each state would have under the United States Constitution. It proposed a bicameral legislature, resulting in the current United States Senate and House of Representatives.
	Context
	On May 29, 1787, Edmund Randolph of the Virginia delegation proposed the creation of a bicameral legislature.
Constitutional convention	A constitutional convention is an informal and uncodified procedural agreement that is followed by the institutions of a state. In some states, notably those Commonwealth of Nations states which follow the Westminster system and whose political systems are derived from British constitutional law, most of the functions of government are guided by constitutional convention rather than by a formal written constitution. In these states, the actual distribution of power may be markedly different from those which are described in the formal constitutional documents.

Chapter 10. Elections

National Convention	During the French Revolution, the National Convention, in France, comprised the constitutional and legislative assembly which sat from 20 September 1792 to 26 October 1795. It held executive power in France during the first years of the French First Republic. It was succeeded by the Directory, commencing 2 November 1795. Prominent members of the original Convention included Maximilien Robespierre of the Jacobin Club, Jean-Paul Marat (affiliated with the Jacobins, though never a formal member), and Georges Danton of the Cordeliers.
Prison	A prison is a place in which people are physically confined and, usually, deprived of a range of personal freedoms. Imprisonment or incarceration is a legal penalty that may be imposed by the state for the commission of a crime. Other terms are penitentiary, correctional facility, and gaol (or jail).
Redistricting	Redistricting, a form of redistribution, is the process of drawing United States district lines. This often means changing electoral district and constituency boundaries in response to periodic census results. In 36 states, the state legislature has primary responsibility for creating a redistricting plan, in many cases subject to approval by the state governor.
Reform Party	The Reform Party is a political party in Singapore. It was founded in 2008 by the late Joshua Benjamin Jeyaretnam, and is currently headed by his son Kenneth Jeyaretnam, who succeeded him as party secretary-general after the elder Jeyaretnam died in 2008. As of 2009, the party has not participated in any general election, but is expected to contest the next Singaporean general election. History The Reform Party was the brainchild of lawyer and politician Joshua Benjamin Jeyaretnam, the first opposition candidate to be elected Member of Parliament to the Parliament of Singapore.
Majority-minority district	A majority-minority district is a United States congressional district in which the majority of the constituents in the district are racial or ethnic minorities (white non-Hispanics). Whether a district is majority-minority is usually decided by United States Census data. Majority-minority districts are often the result of racial gerrymandering.

Chapter 10. Elections

Census	A census is the procedure of systematically acquiring and recording information about the members of a given population. It is a regularly occurring and official count of a particular population. The term is used mostly in connection with national population and housing censuses; other common censuses include agriculture, business, and traffic censuses.
Gazette	A gazette is a newspaper. The word comes from gazzetta, a Venetian coin used to buy early Italian newspapers; the coin became a name for the papers themselves. The word was loaned into English to describe a newspaper.
Gerrymandering	In the process of setting electoral boundaries, rather than using uniform geographic standards, Gerrymandering is a practice of political corruption that attempts to establish a political advantage for a particular party or group by manipulating geographic boundaries to create partisan, incumbent-protected, and neutral districts. The resulting district is known as a gerrymander; however, that word can also refer to the process. Gerrymandering may be used to achieve desired electoral results for a particular party, or may be used to help or hinder a particular group of constituents, such as a political, racial, linguistic, religious or class group.
Identity	Identity is an umbrella term used throughout the social sciences to describe a person's conception and expression of their individuality or group affiliations (such as national identity and cultural identity). The term is used more specifically in psychology and sociology, including the two forms of social psychology. The term is also used with respect to place identity.
Party system	A party system is a concept in comparative political science concerning the system of government by political parties in a democratic country. The idea is that political parties have basic similarities: they control the government, have a stable base of mass popular support, and create internal mechanisms for controlling funding, information and nominations.

	The concept was originated by European scholars studying the United States, especially James Bryce and Moisey Ostrogorsky, and has been expanded to cover other democracies.
Political science	Political Science is a social science concerned with the theory and practice of politics and the analysis of political systems and political behavior. Political scientists "see themselves engaged in revealing the relationships underlying political events and conditions. And from these revelations they attempt to construct general principles about the way the world of politics work." Political science intersects with other fields; including public policy, national politics, economics, international relations, comparative politics, psychology, sociology, history, law, and political theory.
Mississippi	Mississippi is a U.S. state located in the Southern United States. Jackson is the state capital and largest city. The state is heavily forested outside of the Mississippi Delta area, and its catfish aquaculture farms produce the majority of farm-raised catfish consumed in the United States.
Affirmative action	Affirmative action refers to policies that take factors including "race, color, religion, sex or national origin" into consideration in order to benefit an underrepresented group at the expense of a majority group, usually as a means to counter the effects of a history of discrimination. The focus of such policies ranges from employment and education to public contracting and health programs. "Affirmative action" is action taken to increase the representation of women and minorities in areas of employment, education, and business from which they have been historically excluded.
Desegregation	Desegregation is the process of ending the separation of two groups usually referring to races. This is most commonly used in reference to the United States. Desegregation was long a focus of the American Civil Rights Movement, both before and after the United States Supreme Court's decision in Brown v. Board of Education, particularly desegregation of the school systems and the military .
Common Cause	Common Cause is an alliance of four republican political organisations in the Commonwealth of Nations seeking to remove the Monarchy in each realm and replace it with a Republic, with an elected Head of State.

Chapter 10. Elections

	As of May 2008, the four members are: - Republic in the United Kingdom - The Republican Movement of Aotearoa New Zealand - The Australian Republican Movement - Citizens for a Canadian Republic
League of Women Voters	The League of Women Voters is an American political organization founded in 1920 by Carrie Chapman Catt during the last meeting of the National American Woman Suffrage Association approximately six months before the Nineteenth Amendment to the United States Constitution gave women the right to vote. It began as a "mighty political experiment" aimed to help newly-enfranchised women exercise their responsibilities as voters. Originally, only women could join the league; but in 1973 the charter was modified to include men.
Citizenship	Citizenship is the state of being a citizen of a particular social, political, or national community. Citizenship status, under social contract theory, carries with it both rights and responsibilities. "Active citizenship" is the philosophy that citizens should work towards the betterment of their community through economic participation, public, volunteer work, and other such efforts to improve life for all citizens.
George Washington	George Washington is a public artwork that is a copy of an original bust created by French artist and neoclassical sculptor Jean Antoine Houdon, displayed inside of the Indiana Statehouse, which is located in Indianapolis, Indiana, USA. The bust is made of white plaster and its dimensions are 25x18x18 inches. Description This piece is a bust of the first President of the United States, George Washington. It is made of white plaster, and its dimensions are 25x18x18 inches.

Chapter 10. Elections

Internets	"Internets" is a Bushism-turned-catchphrase used humorously to portray the speaker as ignorant about the Internet or about technology in general, or as having a provincial or folksy attitude toward technology. Former United States President George W. Bush first used the word publicly during the 2000 election campaign. The term gained cachet as an Internet humor meme following Bush's use of the term in the second 2004 presidential election debate on October 8, 2004.
Louisiana	Louisiana was the name of an administrative district of the Viceroyalty of New Spain from 1764 to 1803 that represented territory west of the Mississippi River basin, plus New Orleans. Spain acquired the territory from France: see Louisiana. History The area, comprising what is now known as the Louisiana Purchase, was turned over to the French for a few days in 1803 before it, in turn, was turned over to the United States.
Majority	A majority, is a subset of a group consisting of more than half of the group. This should not be confused with a plurality, which is a subset having the largest number of parts. A plurality is not necessarily a majority, as the largest subset may be less than half of the entire group.
Plurality	In North American English, the term plurality, used in the context of voting, refers to the largest number of votes to be received by any candidate or referendum. It is contrasted with a majority, which is more than half of the votes. For example, in a multiple contested race, plurality is the candidate with the most votes, while in a majority election a candidate can only win if they also receive over half of the votes.
Two-round system	The two-round system is a voting system used to elect a single winner. Under the two round system, the voter casts a single vote for their chosen candidate. However, if no candidate receives an absolute majority of votes, then those candidates having less than a certain proportion of the votes, or all but the two candidates receiving the most votes, are eliminated, and a second round of voting occurs.

Chapter 10. Elections

Two-round system	The two-round system is a voting system used to elect a single winner. Under the two round system, the voter casts a single vote for their chosen candidate. However, if no candidate receives an absolute majority of votes, then those candidates having less than a certain proportion of the votes, or all but the two candidates receiving the most votes, are eliminated, and a second round of voting occurs.
Germany	Germany officially the Federal Republic of Germany, is a country in Western Europe. It is bordered to the north by the North Sea, Denmark, and the Baltic Sea; to the east by Poland and the Czech Republic; to the south by Austria and Switzerland; and to the west by France, Luxembourg, Belgium, and the Netherlands. The territory of Germany covers an area of 357,021 km^2 and is influenced by a temperate seasonal climate.
New Deal	The New Deal is a programme of active labour market policies introduced in the United Kingdom by the Labour government in 1998, initially funded by a one off £5bn windfall tax on privatised utility companies. The stated purpose is to reduce unemployment by providing training, subsidised employment and voluntary work to the unemployed. Spending on the New Deal was £1.3 billion in 2001.
Rescue	Rescue refers to operations that usually involve the saving of life, or prevention of injury. Tools used might include search dogs, search and rescue horses, helicopters, the "Jaws of Life", and other hydraulic cutting and spreading tools used to extricate individuals from wrecked vehicles. Rescue operations are sometimes supported by special vehicles such as fire department's or EMS Heavy rescue vehicle.
News conference	A news conference is a media event in which newsmakers invite journalists to hear them speak and, most often, ask questions. A joint press conference instead is held between two or more talking sides. Practice In a news conference, one or more speakers may make a statement, which may be followed by questions from reporters.

Chapter 10. Elections

Primary election	A primary election is an election in which voters select candidates for a subsequent election. Primary elections are one means by which a political party nominates candidates for the next general election. Primaries are common in the United States, where their origins are traced to the progressive movement.
Proportional representation	Proportional representation is a goal of voting systems. While some systems that pursue this goal (such as closed party list) can address other proportionality issues (gender, religion, ethnicity), and these advantages are often used to promote such variants, it is not a feature of Proportional representation as such to ensure an even split of men vs. women, ethnic or religious representation that resembles the population, or any other goal. As it is used in practice in politics, the only proportionality being respected is a close match between the percentage of votes that groups of candidates obtain in elections in representative democracy, and the percentage of seats they receive (e.g., in legislative assemblies).
Interest	Interest is a fee paid on borrowed assets. It is the price paid for the use of borrowed money, or, money earned by deposited funds. Assets that are sometimes lent with interest include money, shares, consumer goods through hire purchase, major assets such as aircraft, and even entire factories in finance lease arrangements.
Medicare	Medicare is a social insurance program administered by the United States government, providing health insurance coverage to people who are aged 65 and over, or who meet other special criteria. Medicare operates similar to a single-payer health care system, but the key difference is that its coverage only extends to 80% of any given medical cost; the remaining 20% of cost must be paid by other means, such as privately-held supplemental insurance, or paid by the patient. The program also funds residency training programs for the vast majority of physicians in the United States.
Alien	In law, an alien is a person in a country who is not a citizen of that country. Categorization

Chapter 10. Elections

Types of "alien" persons are:

- An alien who is legally permitted to remain in a country which is foreign to him or her. On specified terms, this kind of alien may be called a legal alien of that country.

Estate	An estate is the net worth of a person at any point in time. It is the sum of a person's assets - legal rights, interests and entitlements to property of any kind - less all liabilities at that time. The issue is of special legal significance on a question of bankruptcy and death of the person.
Initiative	In political science, the initiative provides a means by which a petition signed by a certain minimum number of registered voters can force a public vote (plebiscite) on a proposed statute, constitutional amendment, charter amendment or ordinance, or, in its minimal form, to simply oblige the executive or legislative bodies to consider the subject by submitting it to the order of the day. It is a form of direct democracy. The initiative may take the form of either the direct initiative or indirect initiative.
Real estate	Real estate is a legal term (in some jurisdictions, such as the United Kingdom, Canada, Australia, USA and The Bahamas) that encompasses land along with improvements to the land, such as buildings, fences, wells and other site improvements that are fixed in location--immovable. Real estate law is the body of regulations and legal codes which pertain to such matters under a particular jurisdiction and include things such as commercial and residential real property transactions. Real estate is often considered synonymous with real property (sometimes called realty), in contrast with personal property (sometimes called chattel or personalty under chattel law or personal property law).
Referendum	A referendum is a direct vote in which an entire electorate is asked to either accept or reject a particular proposal. This may result in the adoption of a new constitution, a constitutional amendment, a law, the recall of an elected official or simply a specific government policy. It is a form of direct democracy.
Decision	A decision, defined in Article 288 of the Treaty on the Functioning of the European Union (formerly Article 249 TEC), is one of the three binding instruments provided by secondary EU legislation. A decision is binding on the person or entity to which it is addressed. Decisions may be addressed to member states or individuals.

Chapter 10. Elections

Recall	Recall is a bugle call used to signals to soldiers that duties or drills are to cease, or to indicate that a period of relaxation should end. Outside of a military context, it is used to signal when a game should end, such as a game of capture the flag among scouts. History Like other bugle calls, "recall" is a short tune that originated as a military signal announcing scheduled and certain non-scheduled events on a military installation, battlefield, or ship.
Recall election	A recall election is a procedure by which voters can remove an elected official from office through a direct vote (plebiscite), initiated when sufficient voters sign a petition. Recall has a history dating back to the ancient Athenian democracy. During the American Revolution the Articles of Confederation stipulated that state legislatures might recall delegates from the continental congress.
Discrimination	Discrimination is the cognitive and sensory capacity or ability to see fine distinctions and perceive differences between objects, subjects, concepts and patterns, or possess exceptional development of the senses. Used in this way to identify exceptional discernment since the 17th century, the term begun to be used as an expression of derogatory racial prejudice from the 1830s Thomas D. Rice's performances as "Jim Crow". Since the American Civil War the term 'discrimination' generally evolved in American English usage as an understanding of prejudicial treatment of an individual based solely on their race, later generalized as membership in a certain socially undesirable group or social category.
Cold War	The Cold War was the continuing state of political conflict, military tension, proxy wars, and economic competition existing after World War II (1939-1945) between the Communist World - primarily the Soviet Union and its satellite states and allies - and the powers of the Western world, primarily the United States and its allies. Although the primary participants' military force never officially clashed directly, they expressed the conflict through military coalitions, strategic conventional force deployments, extensive aid to states deemed vulnerable, proxy wars, espionage, propaganda, conventional and nuclear arms races, appeals to neutral nations, rivalry at sports events, and technological competitions such as the Space Race.

Chapter 10. Elections

	Despite being allies against the Axis powers, the USSR and the US disagreed about political philosophy and the configuration of the post-war world while occupying most of Europe.
Youth	Youth is the time of life between childhood and adulthood (maturity). Definitions of the specific age range that constitutes youth vary. An individual's actual maturity may not correspond to their chronological age, as immature individuals could exist at all ages.
Conservative Party	The Conservative Party was a Brazilian political party of the imperial period, which was formed circa 1836 and ended with the proclamation of the Republic in 1889. This party arose mostly from the Coimbra bloc and also from members of the Restorationist Party (Partido Restaurador), also called the Caramuru Party; it called itself the Party of Order (Portuguese: partido de ordem) to distinguish itself from the liberal opposition, which they accused of disorder and anarchy, and both the party and its leadership were known as "saquarema" after the village of Saquarema, where the leadership had plantations and support.
Equal Employment Opportunity Commission	The U.S. Equal Employment Opportunity Commission is an independent federal law enforcement agency that enforces laws against workplace discrimination. The Equal Employment Opportunity Commission investigates discrimination complaints based on an individual's race, color, national origin, religion, sex, age, perceived intelligence, disability and retaliation for reporting and/or opposing a discriminatory practice. It is empowered to file discrimination suits against employers on behalf of alleged victims and to adjudicate claims of discrimination brought against federal agencies.
Liberals	Liberals is a free market liberal party in Finland. Founded in 1965 as a reunification of the People's Party of Finland and Liberal League. Originally named Liberal People's Party (Finnish: Liberaalinen Kansanpuolue), it restyled its name as Liberals in 2000.
Liberal Party	The Liberal Party was a Belgian political party that existed from 1846 until 1961, when it became the Party for Freedom and Progress, Partij voor Vrijheid en Vooruitgang/Parti de la Liberté et du Progrès or PVV-PLP, under the leadership of Omer Vanaudenhove. History The Liberal Party was founded in 1846 and as such was the first political party of Belgium. Walthère Frère-Orban wrote the first charter for the new party.

Chapter 10. Elections

Conservatism	Conservatism is a political and social philosophy that promotes the maintenance of traditional institutions and supports, at the most, minimal and gradual change in society. Some conservatives seek to preserve things as they are, emphasizing stability and continuity, while others oppose modernism and seek a return to the way things were. The first established use of the term in a political context was by François-René de Chateaubriand in 1819, following the French Revolution.
Liberalism	Liberalism is the belief in the importance of liberty and equal rights. Liberals espouse a wide array of views depending on their understanding of these principles, but most liberals support such fundamental ideas as constitutions, liberal democracy, free and fair elections, human rights, capitalism, free trade, and the separation of church and state. These ideas are widely accepted, even by political groups that do not openly profess a liberal ideological orientation.
Virginia	The Commonwealth of Virginia is a U.S. state on the Atlantic Coast of the Southern United States. Virginia is nicknamed the "Old Dominion" and sometimes the "Mother of Presidents" because it is the birthplace of eight U.S. presidents. The geography and climate of the state are shaped by the Blue Ridge Mountains and the Chesapeake Bay, which provide habitat for much of its flora and fauna.
Issue	In law, issue can mean several things: • In wills and trusts, a person's issue are his or her lineal descendants or offspring. These are distinguished from heirs, which can include other kin such as a brother, sister, mother, father, grandfather, uncle, aunt, nephew, niece, or cousin. • In corporations and business associations law, issue can refer to areas involving stocks. • In evidence as well as civil and criminal procedure, there are issues of fact. Issues of fact are rhetorically presented by statements of fact which are each put to a test: Is the statement true or false? Often, different parties have conflicting statements of fact.

Chapter 10. Elections

Exploitation	The term exploitation may carry two distinct meanings: - The act of using something for any purpose. In this case, exploit is a synonym for use. - The act of using something in an unjust or cruel manner. It is this meaning of exploitation which is discussed below. As unjust benefit In political economy, economics, and sociology, exploitation involves a persistent social relationship in which certain persons are being mistreated or unfairly used for the benefit of others.
Retrospective	Retrospective generally means to take a look back at events that already have taken place. For example, the term is used in medicine, describing a look back at a patient's medical history or lifestyle. Music Retrospective compilations are sometimes assembled from an artist's greatest hits.
Duncan Black	Duncan Black was a Scottish economist who laid the foundations of social choice theory. In particular he was responsible for unearthing the work of many early political scientists, including Charles Dodgson, and was responsible for the Black electoral system, a Condorcet method whereby, in the absence of a Condorcet winner (e.g. due to a cycle), the Borda winner is chosen. Black was born in Motherwell, Scotland, an industrial town south east of Glasgow, to a working class family.

Chapter 10. Elections

Terrorism	Terrorism is the systematic use of terror especially as a means of coercion. No universally agreed, legally binding, criminal law definition of terrorism currently exists. Common definitions of terrorism refer only to those violent acts which are intended to create fear (terror), are perpetrated for a religious, political or ideological goal, deliberately target or disregard the safety of non-combatants (civilians), and are committed by non-government agencies.
Ireland	Ireland is the third-largest island in Europe and the twentieth-largest island in the world. It lies to the northwest of continental Europe and is surrounded by hundreds of islands and islets. To the east of Ireland is Great Britain, separated from it by the Irish Sea.
Northern Ireland	Northern Ireland is one of the four countries of the United Kingdom. Situated in the north-east of the island of Ireland, it shares a border with the Republic of Ireland to the south and west. At the time of the 2001 UK Census, its population was 1,685,000, constituting about 30% of the island's total population and about 3% of the population of the United Kingdom.
Homosexuality	Homosexuality is romantic and/or sexual attraction or behavior among members of the same sex or gender. As a sexual orientation, homosexuality refers to "an enduring pattern of or disposition to experience sexual, affectional, or romantic attractions" primarily or exclusively to people of the same sex; "it also refers to an individual's sense of personal and social identity based on those attractions, behaviors expressing them, and membership in a community of others who share them."
	Homosexuality is one of the three main categories of sexual orientation, along with bisexuality and heterosexuality, within the heterosexual-homosexual continuum. The consensus of the behavioral and social sciences and the health and mental health professions is that homosexuality is a normal and positive variation in human sexual orientation, though many religious societies, including Catholicism, Mormonism, and Islam, and some psychological associations, such as NARTH, teach that homosexual activity is sinful or dysfunctional.
Private	A Private is a soldier of the lowest military rank (equivalent to NATO Rank Grades OR-1 to OR-3 depending on the force served in). The usage of "Private" dates from the 18th century, when the army of Napoleon Bonaparte first established the permanent rank of Soldat.

Chapter 10. Elections

	In modern military parlance, 'Private' is shortened to 'Pte' in the United Kingdom and other Commonwealth countries and to 'Pvt.' in the United States.
Democratic National Committee	The Democratic National Committee is the principal organization governing the United States Democratic Party on a day to day basis. While it is responsible for overseeing the process of writing a platform every four years, the Democratic National Committee's central focus is on campaign and political activity in support of Democratic Party candidates, and not on public policy. The Democratic National Committee was established at the 1848 Democratic National Convention.
Freedom	Freedom is a London-based anarchist newspaper published fortnightly by Freedom Press. The paper was started in 1886 by volunteers including Peter Kropotkin and Charlotte Wilson and continues to this day as an unpaid project. Originally, the subtitle was "A Journal of Anarchist Socialism." The title was changed to "A Journal of Anarchist Communism" in June 1889. Today it is unlabelled.
Restoration	The Restoration of the monarchy began in 1660 when the English, Scottish and Irish monarchies were all restored under Charles II after the republic that followed the Wars of the Three Kingdoms. The term Restoration may apply both to the actual event by which the monarchy was restored, and to the period immediately following the event. Caribbean Barbados, as a haven for refugees fleeting the English republic, had held for Charles II under Lord Willoughby until defeated by George Ayscue.
Canvassing	Canvassing is the systematic initiation of direct contact with a target group of individuals commonly used during political campaigns. A campaign team (and during elections a candidate) will knock on doors of private residences within a particular geographic area, engaging in face-to-face personal interaction with voters. Canvassing may also be performed by telephone, where it is referred to as telephone canvassing.

Chapter 10. Elections

Electoral Commission	An Electoral Commission is an election management body, in charge of overseeing the implementation of election procedures:
	
	- Australia: Australian Electoral Commission
	- Bangladesh: Bangladesh Election Commission
	- Belize: Belize Elections and Boundaries Commission
	- Brazil: Supreme Electoral Court (Brazil)
	- Colombia: National Electoral Council (Colombia)
	- Ghana: Electoral Commission of Ghana
	- Guyana:Guyana Elections Commission
	- Hong Kong: Electoral Affairs Commission
	- India: Election Commission of India
	- Iran: Guardian Council
	- Iraq: Independent High Electoral Commission
	- Kenya:
	    - Electoral Commission of Kenya (defunct)
	    - Interim Independent Electoral Commission
	- Liberia: National Election Commission (Liberia)
	- Malaysia: Election Commission of Malaysia
	- Mexico: Federal Electoral Institute
	- Nepal: Election Commission of Nepal
	- New Zealand: Electoral Commission
	- Pakistan: Election Commission of Pakistan
	- Poland: Panstwowa Komisja Wyborcza (National Electoral Commission)
	- Philippines: Commission on Elections (Philippines)
	- Thailand: Election Commission (Thailand)
	- Ukraine: Central Election Commission of Ukraine
	- United Kingdom: Electoral Commission
	- United States:
	    - Election Assistance Commission, administers Federal elections and establishing standards for State and local governments
	    - Electoral Commission created solely to resolve the disputed 1876 presidential election
	    - Federal Election Commission, regulates campaign finance legislation
	- Uruguay: Electoral Court
	- Zimbabwe: Zimbabwe Electoral Commission

Chapter 10. Elections

Federal Election Commission	The Federal Election Commission is an independent regulatory agency that was founded in 1975 by the United States Congress to regulate the campaign finance legislation in the United States. It was created in a provision of the 1975 amendment to the Federal Election Campaign Act. It describes its duties as "to disclose campaign finance information, to enforce the provisions of the law such as the limits and prohibitions on contributions, and to oversee the public funding of Presidential elections." Membership The Commission is made up of six members, who are appointed by the President of the United States and confirmed by the United States Senate.
Federal Election Campaign Act	The Federal Election Campaign Act of 1971 (Federal Election Campaign Act, Pub.L. 92-225, 86 Stat. 3, enacted February 7, 1972, 2 U.S.C. § 431 et seq). is a United States federal law which increased disclosure of contributions for federal campaigns. It was amended in 1974 to place legal limits on the campaign contributions. The amendment also created the Federal Election Commission (FEC).
Japan	Japan is an island nation in East Asia. Located in the Pacific Ocean, it lies to the east of the Sea of Japan, China, North Korea, South Korea and Russia, stretching from the Sea of Okhotsk in the north to the East China Sea and Taiwan in the south. The characters that make up Japan's name mean "sun-origin", which is why Japan is sometimes referred to as the "Land of the Rising Sun".
Regulation	Regulation is "controlling human or societal behavior by rules or restrictions." Regulation can take many forms: legal restrictions promulgated by a government authority, self-regulation by an industry such as through a trade association, social regulation co-regulation and market regulation. One can consider regulation as actions of conduct imposing sanctions (such as a fine). This action of administrative law, or implementing regulatory law, may be contrasted with statutory or case law.
Political action committee	In the United States, a political action committee, is the name commonly given to a private group, regardless of size, organized to elect political candidates or to advance the outcome of a political issue or legislation. Legally, what constitutes a "Political action committee" for purposes of regulation is a matter of state and federal law. Under the Federal Election Campaign Act, an organization becomes a "political committee" by receiving contributions or making expenditures in excess of $1,000 for the purpose of influencing a federal election.

Chapter 10. Elections

Reform Act	In the United Kingdom, Reform Act is a generic term used for legislation concerning electoral matters. It is most commonly used for laws passed to enfranchise new groups of voters and to redistribute seats in the British House of Commons. The periodic redrawing of constituency boundaries is now dealt with by a permanent Boundary Commission in each part of the United Kingdom, rather than by a Reform Act.
Bill	A bill is a proposed law under consideration by a legislature. A bill does not become law until it is passed by the legislature and, in most cases, approved by the executive. Once a bill has been enacted into law, it is called an act or a statute.
Buckley v. Valeo	Buckley v. Valeo, 424 U.S. 1 (1976), was a case in which the Supreme Court of the United States upheld a federal law which set limits on campaign contributions, but ruled that spending money to influence elections is a form of constitutionally protected free speech, and struck down portions of the law. The court also stated candidates can give unlimited amounts of money to their own campaigns. Facts In 1974, over the veto of President Gerald R. Ford, the Congress passed significant amendments to the Federal Election Campaign Act of 1971, creating the first comprehensive effort by the federal government to regulate campaign contributions and spending.
Independent	In politics, an independent is an individual not affiliated to any political party. Independents may hold a centrist viewpoint between those of major political parties, or they may have a viewpoint based on issues that they do not feel that any major party addresses. Other independent candidates are associated with a political party and may be former members of it, but choose not to stand under its label.
Democratic Party	The Democratic Party is a social democratic political party in Italy, that is the largest party of Italian centre-left and the second largest of the country.

Chapter 10. Elections

	It was founded on 14 October 2007 as a merger of various left-wing and centrist parties which were part of The Union in the 2006 general election. Several parties merged into the Democratic Party, however its bulk was formed by the Democrats of the Left and Democracy is Freedom - The Daisy.
Democrats	The Democrats is a centre-right political party in Brazil, considered the main in the right-wing spectrum. Despite its former name (Liberal Front Party), the party affiliates itself to the Centrist Democrat International, and the International Democrat Union. The name comes from its support to free market policies.
Pardon	A pardon is the forgiveness of a crime and the penalty associated with it. It is granted by a head of state, such as a monarch or president, or by a competent church authority. Commutation is an associated term, meaning the lessening of the penalty of the crime without forgiving the crime itself.
Southern Democrats	Southern Democrats are members of the U.S. Democratic Party who reside in the American South. In the early 19th century, they were the definitive pro-slavery wing of the party, opposed to both the anti-slavery Republicans (GOP) and the more liberal Northern Democrats.
	Eventually "Redemption" was finalized in the Compromise of 1877 and the Redeemers gained control throughout the South.
Family values	Family values are political and social beliefs that hold the nuclear family to be the essential ethical and moral unit of society. Familialism is the ideology that promotes the family and its values as an institution.
	Although the phrase is vague and has shifting meanings, it is most often associated with social and religious conservatives.

Chapter 10. Elections

Southern strategy	In American politics, the Southern strategy refers to the late-20th century Republican Party strategy of winning elections in Southern states by exploiting anti-African American racism among Southern white voters and appealing to states' rights. Though the "Solid South" had been a longtime Democratic Party stronghold in the century following the American Civil War, many Southern Democrats were alienated from the party following the African American Civil Rights Movement, the signing of the Civil Rights Act of 1964 by Democratic President Lyndon B. Johnson, and desegregation. The strategy was first adopted under future Republican President Richard Nixon in the late 1960s and continued through the latter decades of the 20th century under Presidents Ronald Reagan and George H. W. Bush.
Attack	In computer and computer networks an attack is any attempt to destroy, expose, alter, disable, steal or gain unauthorized access to or make unauthorized use of an asset. Definitions IETF Internet Engineering Task Force defines attack in RFC 2828 as: US Government CNSS Instruction No. 4009 dated 26 April 2010 by Committee on National Security Systems of United States of America defines an attack as: The increasing dependencies of modern society on information and computers networks (both in private and public sectors, including military) has led to new terms like cyber attack and Cyberwarfare. CNSS Instruction No. 4009 define a cyber attack as: Phenomenology

Chapter 10. Elections

An attack can be active or passive.

An attack can be perpetrated by an insider or from outside the organization;

> An "inside attack" is an attack initiated by an entity inside the security perimeter (an "insider"), i.e., an entity that is authorized to access system resources but uses them in a way not approved by those who granted the authorization.
> An "outside attack" is initiated from outside the perimeter, by an unauthorized or illegitimate user of the system (an "outsider").

Demographics — Demographics are the characteristics of a human population. These types of data are used widely in sociology, public policy, and marketing. Commonly used demographics include gender, race, age, income, disabilities, mobility (in terms of travel time to work or number of vehicles available), educational attainment, home ownership, employment status, and even location.

Public opinion — Public opinion is the aggregate of individual attitudes or beliefs held by the adult population. Public opinion can also be defined as the complex collection of opinions of many different people and the sum of all their views.

The principle approaches to the study of public opinion may be divided into 4 categories:

1. quantitative measurement of opinion distributions;
2. investigation of the internal relationships among the individual opinions that make up public opinion on an issue;
3. description or analysis of the public role of public opinion;
4. study both of the communication media that disseminate the ideas on which opinions are based and of the uses that propagandists and other manipulators make of these media.

Concepts of "public opinion"

Public opinion as a concept gained credence with the rise of "public" in the eighteenth century.

Chapter 10. Elections

Democratic-Republican Party	The Democratic-Republican Party or Republican Party was an American political party founded in the early 1790s by Thomas Jefferson and James Madison. Political scientists use the former name, while historians prefer the latter one; contemporaries generally called the party the "Republicans", along with many other names. It was formed first in Congress and then in every state to contest elections and oppose the programs of Treasury Secretary Alexander Hamilton.
Superdelegate	"Superdelegate" is an informal term commonly used for some of the delegates to the Democratic National Convention, the presidential nominating convention of the United States Democratic Party. Unlike most convention delegates, the superdelegates are not selected based on the party primaries and caucuses in each U.S. state, in which voters choose among candidates for the party's presidential nomination. Instead, most of the superdelegates are seated automatically, based solely on their status as current or former party leaders and elected officials ("PLEOs").
Bradley effect	The Bradley effect, less commonly called the Wilder effect, is a theory proposed to explain observed discrepancies between voter opinion polls and election outcomes in some US government elections where a white candidate and a non-white candidate run against each other. Instead of ascribing the results to flawed methodology on the part of the pollster, the theory proposes that some voters tend to tell pollsters that they are undecided or likely to vote for a black candidate, and yet, on election day, vote for the white opponent. It was named after Los Angeles Mayor Tom Bradley, an African-American who lost the 1982 California governor's race despite being ahead in voter polls going into the elections.

Chapter 10. Elections

Chapter 10. Elections

Chapter 11. Political Parties

Congress	A congress is a formal meeting of the representatives of different nations, constituent states, independent organizations (such as trade unions), or groups.
	The term was chosen for the United States Congress to emphasize the status of each state represented there as a self-governing unit. Subsequent to the use of congress by the U.S. legislature, the term has been incorrectly adopted by many states within unions, and by unitary nation-states in the Americas, to refer to their legislatures.
Equal Employment Opportunity Commission	The U.S. Equal Employment Opportunity Commission is an independent federal law enforcement agency that enforces laws against workplace discrimination. The Equal Employment Opportunity Commission investigates discrimination complaints based on an individual's race, color, national origin, religion, sex, age, perceived intelligence, disability and retaliation for reporting and/or opposing a discriminatory practice. It is empowered to file discrimination suits against employers on behalf of alleged victims and to adjudicate claims of discrimination brought against federal agencies.
Executive	Executive branch of government is the part of government that has sole authority and responsibility for the daily administration of the state bureaucracy. The division of power into separate branches of government is central to the democratic idea of the separation of powers.
	In many countries, the term "government" connotes only the executive branch.
Executive order	An executive order in the United States is an order issued by the President, the head of the executive branch of the federal government.
Party system	A party system is a concept in comparative political science concerning the system of government by political parties in a democratic country. The idea is that political parties have basic similarities: they control the government, have a stable base of mass popular support, and create internal mechanisms for controlling funding, information and nominations.

Chapter 11. Political Parties

	The concept was originated by European scholars studying the United States, especially James Bryce and Moisey Ostrogorsky, and has been expanded to cover other democracies.
Political Parties	Political Parties: A Sociological Study of the Oligarchical Tendencies of Modern Democracy is a book by sociologist Robert Michels, published in 1911, and first introducing the concept of iron law of oligarchy. It is considered one of the classics of sociology and political science.
	This work analyzes the power structures of organizations such as political parties and trade unions.
Presidency	The word presidency is often used to describe the administration or the executive, the collective administrative and governmental entity that exists around an office of president of a state or nation. It is also the governing authority of some churches.
	For example, in a republic with a presidential system of government, the presidency is the executive branch of government, and is personified by a single elected man or woman who holds the office of "president".
Federalist	The term federalist describes several political beliefs around the world. Also, it may refer to the concept of federalism or the type of government called a federation. In early United States history, the Federalist Party was one of the first political parties; its members or supporters called themselves Federalists.
Gerrymandering	In the process of setting electoral boundaries, rather than using uniform geographic standards, Gerrymandering is a practice of political corruption that attempts to establish a political advantage for a particular party or group by manipulating geographic boundaries to create partisan, incumbent-protected, and neutral districts. The resulting district is known as a gerrymander; however, that word can also refer to the process.

Chapter 11. Political Parties

	Gerrymandering may be used to achieve desired electoral results for a particular party, or may be used to help or hinder a particular group of constituents, such as a political, racial, linguistic, religious or class group.
Rationality	The term "rationality" is used differently in different disciplines.
	In philosophy, rationality is originally the exercise of reason, the way humans come to conclusions when considering things most deliberately. However, the term "rationality" tends to be used in the specialized discussions of economics, sociology, psychology and political science.
Redistricting	Redistricting, a form of redistribution, is the process of drawing United States district lines. This often means changing electoral district and constituency boundaries in response to periodic census results. In 36 states, the state legislature has primary responsibility for creating a redistricting plan, in many cases subject to approval by the state governor.
Two-party system	A two-party system is a system where two major political parties dominate voting in nearly all elections at every level of government. As a result, all, or nearly all, elected offices are members of one of the two major parties. Under a two-party system, one of the two parties typically holds a majority in the legislature and is usually referred to as the majority party while the other is the minority party.
Democrats	The Democrats is a centre-right political party in Brazil, considered the main in the right-wing spectrum. Despite its former name (Liberal Front Party), the party affiliates itself to the Centrist Democrat International, and the International Democrat Union. The name comes from its support to free market policies.
Progressive Republicans	The Progressive Republicans were a French parliamentary group in the Chamber of Deputies of France during the first half of the French Third Republic. The Progressives were in fact the most conservative members of the Chamber, and most later went on the form the Republican Federation.

Chapter 11. Political Parties

Southern Democrats	Southern Democrats are members of the U.S. Democratic Party who reside in the American South. In the early 19th century, they were the definitive pro-slavery wing of the party, opposed to both the anti-slavery Republicans (GOP) and the more liberal Northern Democrats. Eventually "Redemption" was finalized in the Compromise of 1877 and the Redeemers gained control throughout the South.
Electoral college	An electoral college is a set of electors who are selected to elect a candidate to a particular office. Often these represent different organizations or entities, with each organization or entity represented by a particular number of electors or with votes weighted in a particular way. Many times, though, the electors are simply important people whose wisdom, ideally, would provide a better choice than a larger body.
Conservative Party	The Conservative Party was a Brazilian political party of the imperial period, which was formed circa 1836 and ended with the proclamation of the Republic in 1889. This party arose mostly from the Coimbra bloc and also from members of the Restorationist Party (Partido Restaurador), also called the Caramuru Party; it called itself the Party of Order (Portuguese: partido de ordem) to distinguish itself from the liberal opposition, which they accused of disorder and anarchy, and both the party and its leadership were known as "saquarema" after the village of Saquarema, where the leadership had plantations and support.
GREEN	Green is the only green real estate designation for REALTORs approved by the National Association of Realtors (NAR). The program was developed in 2008 by the Real Estate Buyer's Agent Council of NAR, with administration transferred to the Green Resource Council. The course curriculum includes sustainable building practices, marketing, and rating systems (e.g., LEED and Energy Star).
Liberals	Liberals is a free market liberal party in Finland. Founded in 1965 as a reunification of the People's Party of Finland and Liberal League. Originally named Liberal People's Party (Finnish: Liberaalinen Kansanpuolue), it restyled its name as Liberals in 2000.

Chapter 11. Political Parties

Liberal Party	The Liberal Party was a Belgian political party that existed from 1846 until 1961, when it became the Party for Freedom and Progress, Partij voor Vrijheid en Vooruitgang/Parti de la Liberté et du Progrès or PVV-PLP, under the leadership of Omer Vanaudenhove. History The Liberal Party was founded in 1846 and as such was the first political party of Belgium. Walthère Frère-Orban wrote the first charter for the new party.
Conservatism	Conservatism is a political and social philosophy that promotes the maintenance of traditional institutions and supports, at the most, minimal and gradual change in society. Some conservatives seek to preserve things as they are, emphasizing stability and continuity, while others oppose modernism and seek a return to the way things were. The first established use of the term in a political context was by François-René de Chateaubriand in 1819, following the French Revolution.
Government	In the social sciences, the term government refers to the particular group of people, the administrative bureaucracy, who control a state at a given time, and the manner in which their governing organizations are structured. That is, governments are the means through which state power is employed. States are served by a continuous succession of different governments.
Liberalism	Liberalism is the belief in the importance of liberty and equal rights. Liberals espouse a wide array of views depending on their understanding of these principles, but most liberals support such fundamental ideas as constitutions, liberal democracy, free and fair elections, human rights, capitalism, free trade, and the separation of church and state. These ideas are widely accepted, even by political groups that do not openly profess a liberal ideological orientation.
Election	An election is a formal decision-making process by which a population chooses an individual to hold public office. Elections have been the usual mechanism by which modern representative democracy operates since the 17th century. Elections may fill offices in the legislature, sometimes in the executive and judiciary, and for regional and local government.
Interest	Interest is a fee paid on borrowed assets. It is the price paid for the use of borrowed money, or, money earned by deposited funds. Assets that are sometimes lent with interest include money, shares, consumer goods through hire purchase, major assets such as aircraft, and even entire factories in finance lease arrangements.

Chapter 11. Political Parties

Abortion	Abortion is the termination of a pregnancy by the removal or expulsion of a fetus or embryo from the uterus, resulting in or caused by its death. An abortion can occur spontaneously due to complications during pregnancy or can be induced, in humans and other species. In the context of human pregnancies, an abortion induced to preserve the health of the gravida (pregnant female) is termed a therapeutic abortion, while an abortion induced for any other reason is termed an elective abortion.
Election Day	Election Day refers to the day when general elections are held. In many countries, general elections are always held on a Sunday, to enable as many voters as possible to participate, while in other countries elections are always held on a weekday. However, some countries, or regions within a country, always make a weekday election day a public holiday, thus satisfying both demands.
Identity	Identity is an umbrella term used throughout the social sciences to describe a person's conception and expression of their individuality or group affiliations (such as national identity and cultural identity). The term is used more specifically in psychology and sociology, including the two forms of social psychology. The term is also used with respect to place identity.
Bailout	In economics, a bailout is an act of loaning or giving capital to an entity (a company, a country, or an individual) that is in danger of failing, in an attempt to save it from bankruptcy, insolvency, or total liquidation and ruin; or to allow a failing entity to fail gracefully without spreading contagion. Overview A bailout could be done for mere profit, as when a predatory investor resurrects a floundering company by buying its shares at fire-sale prices; for social improvement, as when, hypothetically speaking, a wealthy philanthropist reinvents an unprofitable fast food company into a non-profit food distribution network; or the bailout of a company might be seen as a necessity in order to prevent greater, socioeconomic failures: For example, the US government assumes transportation to be the backbone of America's general economic fluency, which maintains the nation's geopolitical power. As such, it is the policy of the US government to protect the biggest American companies responsible for transportation--airliners, petrol companies, etc.--from failure through subsidies and low-interest loans.

Chapter 11. Political Parties

Institution	An institution is any structure or mechanism of social order and cooperation governing the behavior of a set of individuals within a given human community. Institutions are identified with a social purpose and permanence, transcending individual human lives and intentions, and with the making and enforcing of rules governing cooperative human behavior. The term "institution" is commonly applied to customs and behavior patterns important to a society, as well as to particular formal organizations of government and public service.
Canada	Canada was the name of the French colony that once stretched along the St. Lawrence River; the other colonies of New France were Acadia, Louisiana and Newfoundland. Canada, the most developed colony of New France, was divided into three districts, each with its own government: Québec, Trois-Rivières, and Montréal. The governor of the district of Québec was also the governor-general of all of New France.
Candidate	A candidate is the prospective recipient of an award or honor or a person seeking or being considered for some kind of position; for example: ● to be elected to an office -- in this case a candidate selection procedure occurs. ● to receive membership in a group "Nomination" is part of the process of selecting a candidate for either election to an office, or the bestowing of an honor or award. "Presumptive nominee" is a term used when a person or organization believes that the nomination is inevitable. The act of being a candidate in a race is called a "candidacy." "Candidate" is a derivative of the Latin "candida" (white).
Impeachment	Impeachment is a formal process in which an official is accused of unlawful activity and the outcome of which, depending on the country, can lead to the removal of that official from office or other punishment. Medieval popular etymology also associated it (wrongly) with derivations from the Latin impetere (to attack). (In its more frequent and more technical usage, impeachment of a person in the role of a witness is the act of challenging the honesty or credibility of that person).

Chapter 11. Political Parties

Nomination	Nomination is part of the process of selecting a candidate for either election to an office, or the bestowing of an honor or award.
	In the context of elections for public office, a candidate who has been selected by a political party is normally said to be the nominee of that party. The party's selection (that is, the nomination) is typically accomplished either based on one or more primary elections or by means of a political party convention or caucus, according to the rules of the party and any applicable election laws.
Political campaign	A political campaign is an organized effort which seeks to influence the decision making process within a specific group. In democracies, political campaigns often refer to electoral campaigns, wherein representatives are chosen or referendums are decided.
	Campaign message
	The message of the campaign contains the ideas that the candidate wants to share with the voters.
National Convention	During the French Revolution, the National Convention, in France, comprised the constitutional and legislative assembly which sat from 20 September 1792 to 26 October 1795 . It held executive power in France during the first years of the French First Republic. It was succeeded by the Directory, commencing 2 November 1795. Prominent members of the original Convention included Maximilien Robespierre of the Jacobin Club, Jean-Paul Marat (affiliated with the Jacobins, though never a formal member), and Georges Danton of the Cordeliers.
Discrimination	Discrimination is the cognitive and sensory capacity or ability to see fine distinctions and perceive differences between objects, subjects, concepts and patterns, or possess exceptional development of the senses. Used in this way to identify exceptional discernment since the 17th century, the term begun to be used as an expression of derogatory racial prejudice from the 1830s Thomas D. Rice's performances as "Jim Crow".

Chapter 11. Political Parties

	Since the American Civil War the term 'discrimination' generally evolved in American English usage as an understanding of prejudicial treatment of an individual based solely on their race, later generalized as membership in a certain socially undesirable group or social category.
News conference	A news conference is a media event in which newsmakers invite journalists to hear them speak and, most often, ask questions. A joint press conference instead is held between two or more talking sides. Practice In a news conference, one or more speakers may make a statement, which may be followed by questions from reporters.
Primary election	A primary election is an election in which voters select candidates for a subsequent election. Primary elections are one means by which a political party nominates candidates for the next general election. Primaries are common in the United States, where their origins are traced to the progressive movement.
League of Women Voters	The League of Women Voters is an American political organization founded in 1920 by Carrie Chapman Catt during the last meeting of the National American Woman Suffrage Association approximately six months before the Nineteenth Amendment to the United States Constitution gave women the right to vote. It began as a "mighty political experiment" aimed to help newly-enfranchised women exercise their responsibilities as voters. Originally, only women could join the league; but in 1973 the charter was modified to include men.
Administration	Administration, as a legal concept, is a procedure under the insolvency laws of a number of common law jurisdictions. It functions as a rescue mechanism for insolvent companies and allows them to carry on running their business. The process - an alternative to liquidation - is often known as going into administration.
Closed primary	A closed primary is a type of direct primary limited to registered party members who have declared their party affiliation, in order to vote in the election. This system is opposed to an open primaries system, in which voters do not have to declare their party affiliation in order to vote in the primary.

Chapter 11. Political Parties

	The closed primary serves to encourage party unity and prevent members of other parties from voting for a candidate they don't support in order to disrupt the election results.
Open primary	An open primary is a primary election that does not require voters to be affiliated with a political party in order to vote for partisan candidates. In a traditional open primary, voters may select one party's ballot and vote for that party's nomination. As in a closed primary, the highest voted candidate in each party then proceeds to the runoff election.
Publics	Publics are small groups of people who follow one or more particular issue very closely. They are well informed about the issue(s) and also have a very strong opinion on it/them. They tend to know more about politics than the average person, and, therefore, exert more influence, because these people care so deeply about their cause(s) that they donate much time and money.
Public relations	Public relations is a field concerned with maintaining a public image for businesses, non-profit organizations or high-profile people, such as celebrities and politicians.
	An earlier definition of public relations, by The first World Assembly of Public Relations Associations held in Mexico City in August 1978, was "the art and social science of analyzing trends, predicting their consequences, counseling organizational leaders, and implementing planned programs of action, which will serve both the organization and the public interest."
	Others define it as the practice of managing communication between an organization and its publics. Public relations provides an organization or individual exposure to their audiences using topics of public interest and news items that provide a third-party endorsement and do not direct payment.
Americas	The Americas, are the lands of the western hemisphere, composed of numerous entities and regions variably defined by geography, politics, and culture.

Chapter 11. Political Parties

The Americas are frequently recognised to comprise two separate continents (North America and South America), particularly in English-speaking nations. The Americas may also be recognised to comprise a single continent, in Latin America and in some European nations.

Internets	"Internets" is a Bushism-turned-catchphrase used humorously to portray the speaker as ignorant about the Internet or about technology in general, or as having a provincial or folksy attitude toward technology. Former United States President George W. Bush first used the word publicly during the 2000 election campaign. The term gained cachet as an Internet humor meme following Bush's use of the term in the second 2004 presidential election debate on October 8, 2004.
Treaty	A treaty is an express agreement under international law entered into by actors in international law, namely sovereign states and international organizations. A treaty may also be known as: (international) agreement, protocol, covenant, convention, exchange of letters, etc. Regardless of the terminology, all of these international agreements under international law are equally treaties and the rules are the same.
Court	A court is a form of tribunal, often a governmental institution, with the authority to adjudicate legal disputes between parties and carry out the administration of justice in civil, criminal, and administrative matters in accordance with the rule of law. In both common law and civil law legal systems, courts are the central means for dispute resolution, and it is generally understood that all persons have an ability to bring their claims before a court. Similarly, the rights of those accused of a crime include the right to present a defense before a court.
Independent	In politics, an independent is an individual not affiliated to any political party. Independents may hold a centrist viewpoint between those of major political parties, or they may have a viewpoint based on issues that they do not feel that any major party addresses. Other independent candidates are associated with a political party and may be former members of it, but choose not to stand under its label.
Nonpartisan	In political science, nonpartisan denotes an election, event, organization or person in which there is no formally declared association with a political party affiliation.

Chapter 11. Political Parties

Some nonpartisan organizations are truly such; others are nominally nonpartisan but in fact are generally identifiable with a political party.

United States of America

In U.S. history, the Nonpartisan League was an influential socialist political movement, especially in the Upper Midwest, particularly during the 1910s and 1920s.

New Deal

The New Deal is a programme of active labour market policies introduced in the United Kingdom by the Labour government in 1998, initially funded by a one off £5bn windfall tax on privatised utility companies. The stated purpose is to reduce unemployment by providing training, subsidised employment and voluntary work to the unemployed. Spending on the New Deal was £1.3 billion in 2001.

Rights

Rights are legal, social, or ethical principles of freedom or entitlement; that is, rights are the fundamental normative rules about what is allowed of people or owed to people, according to some legal system, social convention, or ethical theory. Rights are of essential importance in such disciplines as law and ethics, especially theories of justice and deontology.

Rights are often considered fundamental to civilization, being regarded as established pillars of society and culture, and the history of social conflicts can be found in the history of each right and its development.

Chapter 11. Political Parties

Issue	In law, issue can mean several things: • In wills and trusts, a person's issue are his or her lineal descendants or offspring. These are distinguished from heirs, which can include other kin such as a brother, sister, mother, father, grandfather, uncle, aunt, nephew, niece, or cousin. • In corporations and business associations law, issue can refer to areas involving stocks. • In evidence as well as civil and criminal procedure, there are issues of fact. Issues of fact are rhetorically presented by statements of fact which are each put to a test: Is the statement true or false? Often, different parties have conflicting statements of fact.
Laissez-faire	In economics, laissez-faire describes an environment in which transactions between private parties are free from state intervention, including restrictive regulations, taxes, tariffs and enforced monopolies. The phrase laissez-faire is French and literally means "let do", but it broadly implies "let it be", or "leave it alone." Origins of the phrase According to historical legend, the phrase stems from a meeting in about 1680 between the powerful French finance minister Jean-Baptiste Colbert and a group of French businessmen led by a certain M. Le Gendre. When the eager mercantilist minister asked how the French state could be of service to the merchants and help promote their commerce, Le Gendre replied simply "Laissez-nous faire" ("Leave us be", lit.

Chapter 11. Political Parties

Opposition	In politics, the opposition comprises one or more political parties or other organized groups that are opposed to the government, party or group in political control of a city, region, state or country. The degree of opposition varies according to political conditions - for example, across authoritarian and liberal systems where opposition may be repressed or welcomed.
Poland	Poland officially the Republic of Poland - is a country in Central Europe bordered by Germany to the west; the Czech Republic and Slovakia to the south; Ukraine, Belarus and Lithuania to the east; and the Baltic Sea and Kaliningrad Oblast, a Russian exclave, to the north. The total area of Poland is 312,679 square kilometres (120,726 sq mi), making it the 69th largest country in the world and the 9th largest in Europe. Poland has a population of over 38 million people, which makes it the 34th most populous country in the world and the sixth most populous member of the European Union, being its most populous post-communist member.
New Democrats	In the politics of the United States, the New Democrats are an ideologically centrist faction within the Democratic Party that emerged after the victory of Republican George H. W. Bush in the 1988 presidential election. They are identified with more pragmatic and centrist social/cultural/pluralist positions and neoliberal fiscal values. They are represented by organizations such as the Democratic Leadership Council (DLC), the New Democrat Network, and the Senate and House New Democrat Coalitions.
Policy	A policy is typically described as a principle or rule to guide decisions and achieve rational outcome(s). The term is not normally used to denote what is actually done, this is normally referred to as either procedure or protocol. Whereas a policy will contain the 'what' and the 'why', procedures or protocols contain the 'what', the 'how', the 'where', and the 'when'.
Social security	Social security is primarily a social insurance program providing social protection, or protection against socially recognized conditions, including poverty, old age, disability, unemployment and others. Social security may refer to: • social insurance, where people receive benefits or services in recognition of contributions to an insurance scheme. These services typically include provision for retirement pensions, disability insurance, survivor benefits and unemployment insurance. • income maintenance--mainly the distribution of cash in the event of interruption of employment, including retirement, disability and unemployment • services provided by administrations responsible for social security.

Chapter 11. Political Parties

Speaker	The term speaker is a title often given to the presiding officer (chair) of a deliberative assembly, especially a legislative body. The speaker's official role is to moderate debate, make rulings on procedure, announce the results of votes, and the like. The speaker decides who may speak and has the powers to discipline members who break the procedures of the house.
Appointee	An appointee may be one of the following: • A member who is appointed to a position or office is called an appointee. In law, such a term is applied to one who is granted power of appointment of property. • An appointee was also a foot soldier in the French army, who, for long service and bravery, received more pay than other privates. • An appointee is the third most lower rank of the Italian Corps of Carabineers • An appointee is the third most lower rank of the Swiss Armed Forces • An appointee is also a person or organisation entrusted with managing the daily finances of vulnerable individuals in the UK.
Majority	A majority, is a subset of a group consisting of more than half of the group. This should not be confused with a plurality, which is a subset having the largest number of parts. A plurality is not necessarily a majority, as the largest subset may be less than half of the entire group.
Pledge	A pledge is a bailment or deposit of personal property to a creditor to secure repayment for some debt or engagement, The term is also used to denote the property which constitutes the security. Pledge is the ravi of Roman law, from which most of the modern law on the subject is derived. It differs from hypothecation and from the more usual mortgage in that the pledge is in the possession of the pledgee; it also differs from mortgage in being confined to personal property (rather than real property).

Chapter 11. Political Parties

Privatization	Privatization is the incidence or process of transferring ownership of a business, enterprise, agency or public service from the public sector (the state or government) to the private sector (businesses that operate for a private profit) or to private non-profit organizations. In a broader sense, privatization refers to transfer of any government function to the private sector - including governmental functions like revenue collection and law enforcement. The term "privatization" also has been used to describe two unrelated transactions.
Seniority	In finance, seniority refers to the order of repayment in the event of bankruptcy. Senior debt must be repaid before subordinated debt is repaid. Bonds that have the same seniority in a company's capital structure are described as being pari passu.
Terrorism	Terrorism is the systematic use of terror especially as a means of coercion. No universally agreed, legally binding, criminal law definition of terrorism currently exists. Common definitions of terrorism refer only to those violent acts which are intended to create fear (terror), are perpetrated for a religious, political or ideological goal, deliberately target or disregard the safety of non-combatants (civilians), and are committed by non-government agencies.
Ireland	Ireland is the third-largest island in Europe and the twentieth-largest island in the world. It lies to the northwest of continental Europe and is surrounded by hundreds of islands and islets. To the east of Ireland is Great Britain, separated from it by the Irish Sea.
Northern Ireland	Northern Ireland is one of the four countries of the United Kingdom. Situated in the north-east of the island of Ireland, it shares a border with the Republic of Ireland to the south and west. At the time of the 2001 UK Census, its population was 1,685,000, constituting about 30% of the island's total population and about 3% of the population of the United Kingdom.
Attack	In computer and computer networks an attack is any attempt to destroy, expose, alter, disable, steal or gain unauthorized access to or make unauthorized use of an asset. Definitions IETF

Chapter 11. Political Parties

Internet Engineering Task Force defines attack in RFC 2828 as:

US Government

CNSS Instruction No. 4009 dated 26 April 2010 by Committee on National Security Systems of United States of America defines an attack as:

The increasing dependencies of modern society on information and computers networks (both in private and public sectors, including military) has led to new terms like cyber attack and Cyberwarfare.

CNSS Instruction No. 4009 define a cyber attack as:

Phenomenology

An attack can be active or passive.

An attack can be perpetrated by an insider or from outside the organization;

> An "inside attack" is an attack initiated by an entity inside the security perimeter (an "insider"), i.e., an entity that is authorized to access system resources but uses them in a way not approved by those who granted the authorization.
> An "outside attack" is initiated from outside the perimeter, by an unauthorized or illegitimate user of the system (an "outsider").

Bipartisanship	Bipartisanship is a political situation, usually in the context of a two-party system such as the United States, in which opposing political parties find common ground through compromise. The adjective bipartisan can refer to any bill, act, resolution, or other political act in which both of the two major political parties agree about all or many parts of a political choice. Bipartisanship involves trying to find common ground, but there is debate whether the issues needing common ground are peripheral or central ones.

Chapter 11. Political Parties

Health care	Health or healthcare is the treatment and prevention of illness. Health care is delivered by professionals in medicine, dentistry, nursing, pharmacy and allied health.
	The social and political issues surrounding access to healthcare in the US have led to vigorous public debate and the almost colloquial use of terms such as health care health insurance (reimbursement of health care costs), and public health (the collective state and range of health in a population).
Homosexuality	Homosexuality is romantic and/or sexual attraction or behavior among members of the same sex or gender. As a sexual orientation, homosexuality refers to "an enduring pattern of or disposition to experience sexual, affectional, or romantic attractions" primarily or exclusively to people of the same sex; "it also refers to an individual's sense of personal and social identity based on those attractions, behaviors expressing them, and membership in a community of others who share them."
	Homosexuality is one of the three main categories of sexual orientation, along with bisexuality and heterosexuality, within the heterosexual-homosexual continuum. The consensus of the behavioral and social sciences and the health and mental health professions is that homosexuality is a normal and positive variation in human sexual orientation, though many religious societies, including Catholicism, Mormonism, and Islam, and some psychological associations, such as NARTH, teach that homosexual activity is sinful or dysfunctional.
Initiative	In political science, the initiative provides a means by which a petition signed by a certain minimum number of registered voters can force a public vote (plebiscite) on a proposed statute, constitutional amendment, charter amendment or ordinance, or, in its minimal form, to simply oblige the executive or legislative bodies to consider the subject by submitting it to the order of the day. It is a form of direct democracy.
	The initiative may take the form of either the direct initiative or indirect initiative.

Chapter 11. Political Parties

Caucus	A caucus is a meeting of supporters or members of a political party or movement, especially in the United States. As the use of the term has been expanded the exact definition has come to vary among political cultures. Origin of the term The origin of the word caucus is debated, but it is generally agreed that it first came into use in the English colonies of North America. A February 1763 entry in the diary of John Adams of Braintree, Massachusetts, is one of the earliest appearances of Caucas, already with its modern connotations of a "smoke-filled room" where candidates for public election are pre-selected in private This day learned that the Caucas Clubb meets at certain Times in the Garret of Tom Daws, the Adjutant of the Boston Regiment.
Democratic Party	The Democratic Party is a social democratic political party in Italy, that is the largest party of Italian centre-left and the second largest of the country. It was founded on 14 October 2007 as a merger of various left-wing and centrist parties which were part of The Union in the 2006 general election. Several parties merged into the Democratic Party, however its bulk was formed by the Democrats of the Left and Democracy is Freedom - The Daisy.
Activism	Activism consists of intentional action to bring about social, political, economic, or environmental change. This action is in support of, or opposition to, one side of an often controversial argument.

Chapter 11. Political Parties

	The word "activism" is used synonymously with protest or dissent, but activism can take a wide range of forms from writing letters to newspapers or politicians, political campaigning, economic activism such as boycotts or preferentially patronizing businesses, rallies, street marches, strikes, both sit-ins and hunger strikes, or even guerrilla tactics.
Independent Party	The Independent Party is a social democratic and christian humanist political party in Uruguay. The party is leadered by Pablo Mieres, who was presidential candidate in the 2004 national elections and in 2009. Aims Its goal is to build a third way away from the heterodox left-wing coalition Frente Amplio and the traditional parties Colorado Party and National Party.
Timor	Timor is an island at the southern end of Maritime Southeast Asia, north of the Timor Sea. It is divided between the independent state of East Timor, and West Timor, belonging to the Indonesian province of East Nusa Tenggara. The island's surface is 11,883 square miles (30,777 km^2).
National Convention	During the French Revolution, the National Convention, in France, comprised the constitutional and legislative assembly which sat from 20 September 1792 to 26 October 1795 . It held executive power in France during the first years of the French First Republic. It was succeeded by the Directory, commencing 2 November 1795. Prominent members of the original Convention included Maximilien Robespierre of the Jacobin Club, Jean-Paul Marat (affiliated with the Jacobins, though never a formal member), and Georges Danton of the Cordeliers.
Geneva	Geneva is the second-most-populous city in Switzerland (after Zürich) and is the most populous city of Romandie . Situated where the Rhône River exits Lake Geneva, it is the capital of the Republic and Canton of Geneva. While the municipality itself (ville de Genève) has a population (as of December 2009) of 189,313, the canton of Geneva has 457,628 residents (as of December 2009).

Chapter 11. Political Parties

Geneva Conventions	The Geneva Conventions comprise four treaties and three additional protocols that set the standards in international law for humanitarian treatment of the victims of war. The singular term Geneva Convention refers to the agreements of 1949, negotiated in the aftermath of World War II, updating the terms of the first three treaties and adding a fourth treaty. The language is extensive, with articles defining the basic rights of those captured during a military conflict, establishing protections for the wounded, and addressing protections for civilians in and around a war zone.
Voting	Voting is a method for a group such as a meeting or an electorate to make a decision or express an opinion--often following discussions, debates, or election campaigns. It is often found in democracies and republics. Reasons for voting In a representative government, voting commonly implies election: a way for an electorate to select among candidates for office.
Region	Region is most commonly found as a term used in terrestrial and astrophysics sciences, notably among the different sub-disciplines of Geography, studied by regional geographers. Regions consist of subregions that contain clusters of like areas that are distinctive by their uniformity of description based on a range of statistical data, for example demographic, and locales. In astrophysics some regions have science-specific terms such as galactic clusters.
Balance of power	In parliamentary politics, the term balance of power sometimes describes the pragmatic mechanism exercised by a minor political party or other grouping whose guaranteed support may enable an otherwise minority government to obtain and hold office. This can be achieved either by the formation of a coalition government or by an assurance that any motion of no confidence in the government would be defeated. A party or person may also hold a theoretical 'balance of power' in a chamber without any commitment to government, in which case both the government and opposition groupings may on occasion need to negotiate that party's legislative support.
Power	Power is a measure of an entity's ability to control its environment, including the behavior of other entities. The term authority is often used for power, perceived as legitimate by the social structure. Power can be seen as evil or unjust, but the exercise of power is accepted as endemic to humans as social beings.

Chapter 11. Political Parties

Hamilton	Hamilton is a former New Zealand Parliamentary electorate, which was replaced by Hamilton East and Hamilton West electorates. Population centres The electorate was mainly urban, covering the city of Hamilton. History The Hamilton electorate dates from 1922. In 1969 it was renamed Hamilton West.
Alexander Hamilton	Alexander Hamilton was a Scottish sea captain, privateer and merchant.
James Madison	James Madison, Jr. (March 16, 1751 - June 28, 1836) was an American politician and political philosopher who served as the fourth President of the United States (1809-1817) and is considered one of the Founding Fathers of the United States. He was the principal author of the United States Constitution, and is often called the "Father of the Constitution".
John G. Adams	John G. Adams was the US Army's counsel in the Army-McCarthy Hearings. He was an Army veteran of World War II, and he worked in Washington, DC for the Defense Department before he became the US Army general counsel in 1953. From 1953 to 1955 he was the chief legal adviser to Army Secretary Robert Ten Broeck Stevens. Publications - Adams, John G. (1983).

Chapter 11. Political Parties

Commission	A commission is a physical document issued to certify the appointment of a commissioned officer by a sovereign power.
	The more specific terms commissioning parchment or commissioning scroll are often used to avoid ambiguity, due to "commission" being a homonym which directs the individual in carrying out their duty regardless of what authority or responsibility they may have at any time. However the document is not usually in the form of a scroll and is more often printed on paper instead of parchment.
Whig Party	The Whig Party was a political party of the United States during the era of Jacksonian democracy. Considered integral to the Second Party System and operating from the early 1830s to the mid-1850s, the party was formed in opposition to the policies of President Andrew Jackson and his Democratic Party. In particular, the Whigs supported the supremacy of Congress over the presidency and favored a program of modernization and economic protectionism.
Era of Good Feelings	The Era of Good Feelings was a period in United States political history in which partisan bitterness abated. It lasted approximately 1816-1824, during the administration of U.S. President James Monroe, who deliberately downplayed partisanship.
	The phrase was coined by Benjamin Russell, in the Boston newspaper, Columbian Centinel, on July 12, 1817, following Monroe's good-will visit to Boston.
Henry Clay	Henry Clay, Sr. (April 12, 1777 - June 29, 1852), was a 19th-century American planter, statesman and orator who represented Kentucky in both the Senate and the House of Representatives, where he served as Speaker. He also served as Secretary of State from 1825 to 1829.
Henry	Saint Henry was a medieval Swedish clergyman. According to legends, he conquered Finland together with King Eric the Saint of Sweden and died as a martyr, becoming a central figure in the local Roman Catholic Church. However, the authenticity of the accounts of his life, ministry, and death are widely disputed.

Chapter 11. Political Parties

LINCOLN	Lincoln was a parliamentary electorate in the Canterbury region of New Zealand from 1881 to 1890.
	The electorate was represented by two Members of Parliament:
	- Arthur Pyne O'Callaghan (1881-89), and
	- Alfred Saunders (1889-90)
Missouri Compromise	The Missouri Compromise was an agreement passed in 1820 between the pro-slavery and anti-slavery factions in the United States Congress, involving primarily the regulation of slavery in the western territories. It prohibited slavery in the former Louisiana Territory north of the parallel 36° 30' north except within the boundaries of the proposed state of Missouri. Prior to the agreement, the House of Representatives had refused to accept this compromise and a conference committee was appointed.
Civil War	"Civil War" is a song by the hard rock band Guns N' Roses, which originally appeared on the 1990 album Nobody's Child: Romanian Angel Appeal. It is a protest song on war, referring to all war as 'civil war' and that it only "feeds the rich while it buries the poor." In the song, singer Axl Rose asks, "What's so civil about war, anyway?"
	"Civil War" was the brainchild of the Guns N' Roses artists Slash, Axl Rose, and Duff McKagan. Slash stated that the song was an instrumental he had written right before the band left for the Japanese leg of its Appetite for Destruction world tour.
George Washington	George Washington is a public artwork that is a copy of an original bust created by French artist and neoclassical sculptor Jean Antoine Houdon, displayed inside of the Indiana Statehouse, which is located in Indianapolis, Indiana, USA. The bust is made of white plaster and its dimensions are 25x18x18 inches.
	Description

Chapter 11. Political Parties

	This piece is a bust of the first President of the United States, George Washington. It is made of white plaster, and its dimensions are 25x18x18 inches.
Progressive Era	The Progressive Era in the United States was a period of social activism and reform that flourished from the 1890s to the 1920s. The main goal of the Progressive movement was purification of government, as Progressives tried to expose and undercut political machines and bosses. Many (but not all) Progressives supported prohibition in order to destroy the political power of local bosses based in saloons.
Tammany Hall	Tammany Hall, also known as the Society of St. Tammany, the Sons of St. Tammany, or the Columbian Order, was founded in 1786 and incorporated on May 12, 1789 as the Tammany Society. It was the Democratic Party political machine that played a major role in controlling New York City politics and helping immigrants, most notably the Irish, rise up in American politics from the 1790s to the 1960s. It controlled Democratic Party nominations and patronage in Manhattan from the mayoral victory of Fernando Wood in 1854 through the election of John P. O'Brien in 1932. Tammany Hall was permanently weakened by the election of Fiorello La Guardia on a "fusion" ticket of Republicans, reform-minded Democrats, and independents in 1934, and, despite a brief resurgence in the 1950s, it ceased to exist in the 1960s.
Free riding	Free riding is a term used in the stock-trading world to describe the practice of buying shares or other securities without actually having the capital to cover the trade. This is possible when recently bought or sold shares are unsettled, and therefore have not been paid for. Since stock transactions usually settle after three business days, a crafty trader can buy a stock and sell it the following day (or the same day), without ever having sufficient funds in the account.
Patronage	In public transportation, patronage is a type of forecasting or statistic for studying the average quantity of passengers ("patrons") carried per certain time in a mode of public transit system. The concept should not be confused with the maximum loading capacity of one particular vehicle or the whole transit system. The gathered or predicted ridership data is usually referred by transport planner to align the route and decide what kind of vehicle will be employed.

Chapter 11. Political Parties

William Jennings Bryan	William Jennings Bryan was an American politician in the late-19th and early-20th centuries. He was a dominant force in the liberal wing of the Democratic Party, standing three times as its candidate for President of the United States (1896, 1900 and 1908). He served in the United States Congress briefly as a Representative from Nebraska and was the 41st United States Secretary of State under President Woodrow Wilson, 1913-1916. Bryan was a devout Presbyterian, a supporter of popular democracy, an enemy of gold, banks and railroads, a leader of the silverite movement in the 1890s, a peace advocate, a prohibitionist, and an opponent of Darwinism on religious grounds.
Homeland	A homeland is the concept of the place (cultural geography) to which an ethnic group holds a long history and a deep cultural association with --the country in which a particular national identity began. As a common noun, it simply connotes the country of one's origin.
Homeland security	Homeland security is an umbrella term for security efforts to protect the United States against terrorist activity. The term arose following a reorganization of many U.S. government agencies in 2003 to form the United States Department of Homeland Security after the September 11 attacks, and may be used to refer to the actions of that department, the United States Senate Committee on Homeland Security and Governmental Affairs, or the United States House of Representatives Committee on Homeland Security. In the United States In the United States, the concept of "homeland security" extends and recombines responsibilities of government agencies and entities.
Election Committee	The Election Committee is an 800-member electoral college in the politics of Hong Kong.
Fourth Party	The "Fourth Party" was a label given to a quartet of British MPs, Lord Randolph Churchill, Henry Drummond Wolff, John Gorst and Arthur Balfour, in the 1880-1885 parliament. They attacked what they saw as the weakness of both the Liberal government and the Conservative opposition. Despite the label, they were all backbench members of the Conservative Party.

Chapter 11. Political Parties

Conscience	Conscience is an aptitude, faculty, intuition, or judgment of the intellect that distinguishes right from wrong. Moral evaluations of this type may reference values or norms (principles and rules). In psychological terms conscience is often described as leading to feelings of remorse when a human does things that go against his/her moral values, and to feelings of rectitude or integrity when actions conform to such norms.
Great Society	The Great Society was a set of domestic programs proposed or enacted in the United States on the initiative of President Lyndon B. Johnson. Two main goals of the Great Society social reforms were the elimination of poverty and racial injustice. New major spending programs that addressed education, medical care, urban problems, and transportation were launched during this period.
Pardon	A pardon is the forgiveness of a crime and the penalty associated with it. It is granted by a head of state, such as a monarch or president, or by a competent church authority. Commutation is an associated term, meaning the lessening of the penalty of the crime without forgiving the crime itself.
Society	A society is (1) a group of people related to each other through persistent relations such as social status, roles and social networks. (2) A large social grouping that shares the same geographical territory and is subject to the same political authority and dominant cultural expectations. Human societies are characterized by patterns of relationships between individuals sharing a distinctive culture and institutions.
Vietnam	Vietnam, officially the Socialist Republic of Vietnam is the easternmost country on the Indochina Peninsula in Southeast Asia. It is bordered by People's Republic of China (PRC) to the north, Laos to the northwest, Cambodia to the southwest, and the South China Sea, referred to as East Sea (Vietnamese: Bi?n Đông), to the east. With a population of over 86 million, Vietnam is the 13th most populous country in the world.
Civil rights movement	The civil rights movement was a worldwide political movement for equality before the law occurring between approximately 1950 and 1980. It was accompanied by much civil unrest and popular rebellion. The process was long and tenuous in many countries, and most of these movements did not fully achieve their goals although, the efforts of these movements did lead to improvements in the legal rights of previously oppressed groups of peoples. Civil rights movement in Northern Ireland

Chapter 11. Political Parties

	Northern Ireland is a province of the United Kingdom which has witnessed violence over many decades, mainly because of sectarian tensions between the Catholic and Protestant community, known as the Troubles.
Ideology	An ideology is a set of ideas that constitutes one's goals, expectations, and actions. An ideology can be thought of as a comprehensive vision, as a way of looking at things (compare worldview), as in common sense and several philosophical tendencies , or a set of ideas proposed by the dominant class of a society to all members of this society (a "received consciousness" or product of socialization). The main purpose behind an ideology is to offer either change in society, or adherence to a set of ideals where conformity already exists, through a normative thought process.
Southern strategy	In American politics, the Southern strategy refers to the late-20th century Republican Party strategy of winning elections in Southern states by exploiting anti-African American racism among Southern white voters and appealing to states' rights. Though the "Solid South" had been a longtime Democratic Party stronghold in the century following the American Civil War, many Southern Democrats were alienated from the party following the African American Civil Rights Movement, the signing of the Civil Rights Act of 1964 by Democratic President Lyndon B. Johnson, and desegregation. The strategy was first adopted under future Republican President Richard Nixon in the late 1960s and continued through the latter decades of the 20th century under Presidents Ronald Reagan and George H. W. Bush.
Progressive Party	The Progressive Party of Belgium was a progressive Liberal party which existed from 1887 until 1900. History After the defeat of the Liberal party in the general elections of 1884 the doctrinarian faction continued to dominate the Belgian Liberal party. However, the progressistes or radicals no longer wanted to toe the line.

Chapter 11. Political Parties

Democratic National Committee	The Democratic National Committee is the principal organization governing the United States Democratic Party on a day to day basis. While it is responsible for overseeing the process of writing a platform every four years, the Democratic National Committee's central focus is on campaign and political activity in support of Democratic Party candidates, and not on public policy. The Democratic National Committee was established at the 1848 Democratic National Convention.
Freedom	Freedom is a London-based anarchist newspaper published fortnightly by Freedom Press. The paper was started in 1886 by volunteers including Peter Kropotkin and Charlotte Wilson and continues to this day as an unpaid project. Originally, the subtitle was "A Journal of Anarchist Socialism." The title was changed to "A Journal of Anarchist Communism" in June 1889. Today it is unlabelled.
Restoration	The Restoration of the monarchy began in 1660 when the English, Scottish and Irish monarchies were all restored under Charles II after the republic that followed the Wars of the Three Kingdoms. The term Restoration may apply both to the actual event by which the monarchy was restored, and to the period immediately following the event. Caribbean Barbados, as a haven for refugees fleeing the English republic, had held for Charles II under Lord Willoughby until defeated by George Ayscue.
Ensign	Ensign is a junior rank of commissioned officer in the armed forces of some countries, normally in the infantry or navy. As the junior officer in an infantry regiment was traditionally the carrier of the ensign flag, the rank itself acquired the name. The Spanish alférez and Portuguese alferes is a junior officer rank below lieutenant associated with carrying the flag, and so is often translated as "ensign".
Precinct	A precinct is a space enclosed by the walls or other boundaries of a particular place or building, or by an arbitrary and imaginary line drawn around it. The term has several different uses. It can, for example, refer to a division of a police department in a large city (either to the area patrolled or to the police station itself).

Chapter 11. Political Parties

State	Many sovereign independent state are made up of a number of country subdivisions also called states. In some cases, such as the United States, the national government arose from a union of sovereign entities, which transferred some of their powers to the national government, while retaining the remainder of their sovereignty. These are sometimes called federal states.
Ward	In Australia, Canada, Monaco, New Zealand, South Africa, the United Kingdom, and the United States, a ward is an electoral district within a municipality used in local politics. Wards are usually named after neighbourhoods, thoroughfares, parishes, landmarks, geographical features and in some cases historical figures connected to the area. It is common in the United States for wards to simply be numbered.

Chapter 11. Political Parties

Chapter 11. Political Parties

Chapter 12. Groups and Interests

Internets	"Internets" is a Bushism-turned-catchphrase used humorously to portray the speaker as ignorant about the Internet or about technology in general, or as having a provincial or folksy attitude toward technology. Former United States President George W. Bush first used the word publicly during the 2000 election campaign. The term gained cachet as an Internet humor meme following Bush's use of the term in the second 2004 presidential election debate on October 8, 2004.
Interest	Interest is a fee paid on borrowed assets. It is the price paid for the use of borrowed money, or, money earned by deposited funds. Assets that are sometimes lent with interest include money, shares, consumer goods through hire purchase, major assets such as aircraft, and even entire factories in finance lease arrangements.
Regent	A regent is a person selected to act as head of state (ruling or not) because the ruler is a minor, not present, or debilitated. In a monarchy, a regent usually governs due to one of these reasons, but may also be elected to rule during the interregnum when the royal line has died out. This was the case in Finland and Hungary, where the royal line was considered extinct in the aftermath of World War I. In Iceland, the regent represented the King of Denmark as sovereign of Iceland until the country became a republic in 1944.
Social security	Social security is primarily a social insurance program providing social protection, or protection against socially recognized conditions, including poverty, old age, disability, unemployment and others. Social security may refer to: • social insurance, where people receive benefits or services in recognition of contributions to an insurance scheme. These services typically include provision for retirement pensions, disability insurance, survivor benefits and unemployment insurance. • income maintenance--mainly the distribution of cash in the event of interruption of employment, including retirement, disability and unemployment • services provided by administrations responsible for social security.

Chapter 12. Groups and Interests

Initiative	In political science, the initiative provides a means by which a petition signed by a certain minimum number of registered voters can force a public vote (plebiscite) on a proposed statute, constitutional amendment, charter amendment or ordinance, or, in its minimal form, to simply oblige the executive or legislative bodies to consider the subject by submitting it to the order of the day. It is a form of direct democracy. The initiative may take the form of either the direct initiative or indirect initiative.
Prescription	In law, prescription is the method of sovereignty transfer of a territory through international law analogous to the common law doctrine of adverse possession for private real-estate. Prescription involves the open encroachment by the new sovereign upon the territory in question for a prolonged period of time, acting as the sovereign, without protest or other contest by the original sovereign. This doctrine legalizes de jure the de facto transfer of sovereignty caused in part by the original sovereign's extended negligence and/or neglect of the area in question.
Regulation	Regulation is "controlling human or societal behavior by rules or restrictions." Regulation can take many forms: legal restrictions promulgated by a government authority, self-regulation by an industry such as through a trade association, social regulation co-regulation and market regulation. One can consider regulation as actions of conduct imposing sanctions (such as a fine). This action of administrative law, or implementing regulatory law, may be contrasted with statutory or case law.
Lobbying	Lobbying is the intention of influencing decisions made by legislators and officials in the government by individuals, other legislators, constituents, or advocacy groups. A lobbyist is a person who tries to influence legislation on behalf of a special interest or a member of a lobby. Governments often define and regulate organized group lobbying that has become influential.
Congress	A congress is a formal meeting of the representatives of different nations, constituent states, independent organizations (such as trade unions), or groups.

Chapter 12. Groups and Interests

	The term was chosen for the United States Congress to emphasize the status of each state represented there as a self-governing unit. Subsequent to the use of congress by the U.S. legislature, the term has been incorrectly adopted by many states within unions, and by unitary nation-states in the Americas, to refer to their legislatures.
George Washington	George Washington is a public artwork that is a copy of an original bust created by French artist and neoclassical sculptor Jean Antoine Houdon, displayed inside of the Indiana Statehouse, which is located in Indianapolis, Indiana, USA. The bust is made of white plaster and its dimensions are 25x18x18 inches. Description This piece is a bust of the first President of the United States, George Washington. It is made of white plaster, and its dimensions are 25x18x18 inches.
Pluralism	Classical pluralism Classical pluralism is the view that politics and decision making are located mostly in the framework of government, but that many non-governmental groups use their resources to exert influence. The central question for classical pluralism is how power and influence is distributed in a political process. Groups of individuals try to maximize their interests.
Political action committee	In the United States, a political action committee, is the name commonly given to a private group, regardless of size, organized to elect political candidates or to advance the outcome of a political issue or legislation. Legally, what constitutes a "Political action committee" for purposes of regulation is a matter of state and federal law. Under the Federal Election Campaign Act, an organization becomes a "political committee" by receiving contributions or making expenditures in excess of $1,000 for the purpose of influencing a federal election.

Chapter 12. Groups and Interests

Executive	Executive branch of government is the part of government that has sole authority and responsibility for the daily administration of the state bureaucracy. The division of power into separate branches of government is central to the democratic idea of the separation of powers. In many countries, the term "government" connotes only the executive branch.
Executive order	An executive order in the United States is an order issued by the President, the head of the executive branch of the federal government.
Afghanistan	Afghanistan officially the Islamic Republic of Afghanistan, is a landlocked and mountainous country in south-central Asia. It is bordered by Pakistan in the south and east, Iran in the west, Turkmenistan, Uzbekistan and Tajikistan in the north, and China in the far northeast. The territories now comprising Afghanistan have been an ancient focal point of the Silk Road and human migration.
Common Cause	Common Cause is an alliance of four republican political organisations in the Commonwealth of Nations seeking to remove the Monarchy in each realm and replace it with a Republic, with an elected Head of State. As of May 2008, the four members are: • Republic in the United Kingdom • The Republican Movement of Aotearoa New Zealand • The Australian Republican Movement • Citizens for a Canadian Republic
Community	A community is an administrative division found in Belgium, Canada, Greece, Iceland, Wales, and the League of Nations Class A mandates
Federation	A federation, is a type of sovereign state characterized by a union of partially self-governing states or regions united by a central (federal) government. In a federation, the self-governing status of the component states is typically constitutionally entrenched and may not be altered by a unilateral decision of the central government.

CLAM101

Chapter 12. Groups and Interests

	The form of government or constitutional structure found in a federation is known as federalism.
General	General, Finnish: kenraali is the highest officer's rank in Sweden and Finland. In Sweden, it is held by the supreme commander of the Swedish Armed Forces and the monarch. In Finland, it is held by the Chief of Defence.
Independent	In politics, an independent is an individual not affiliated to any political party. Independents may hold a centrist viewpoint between those of major political parties, or they may have a viewpoint based on issues that they do not feel that any major party addresses. Other independent candidates are associated with a political party and may be former members of it, but choose not to stand under its label.
Institution	An institution is any structure or mechanism of social order and cooperation governing the behavior of a set of individuals within a given human community. Institutions are identified with a social purpose and permanence, transcending individual human lives and intentions, and with the making and enforcing of rules governing cooperative human behavior. The term "institution" is commonly applied to customs and behavior patterns important to a society, as well as to particular formal organizations of government and public service.
Publics	Publics are small groups of people who follow one or more particular issue very closely. They are well informed about the issue(s) and also have a very strong opinion on it/them. They tend to know more about politics than the average person, and, therefore, exert more influence, because these people care so deeply about their cause(s) that they donate much time and money.
Public health	Public health is "the science and art of preventing disease, prolonging life and promoting health through the organized efforts and informed choices of society, organizations, public and private, communities and individuals" (1920, C.E.A. Winslow). It is concerned with threats to the overall health of a community based on population health analysis. The population in question can be as small as a handful of people or as large as all the inhabitants of several continents (for instance, in the case of a pandemic).

Chapter 12. Groups and Interests

Rights	Rights are legal, social, or ethical principles of freedom or entitlement; that is, rights are the fundamental normative rules about what is allowed of people or owed to people, according to some legal system, social convention, or ethical theory. Rights are of essential importance in such disciplines as law and ethics, especially theories of justice and deontology.
	Rights are often considered fundamental to civilization, being regarded as established pillars of society and culture, and the history of social conflicts can be found in the history of each right and its development.
Terrorism	Terrorism is the systematic use of terror especially as a means of coercion. No universally agreed, legally binding, criminal law definition of terrorism currently exists. Common definitions of terrorism refer only to those violent acts which are intended to create fear (terror), are perpetrated for a religious, political or ideological goal, deliberately target or disregard the safety of non-combatants (civilians), and are committed by non-government agencies.
Health care	Health or healthcare is the treatment and prevention of illness. Health care is delivered by professionals in medicine, dentistry, nursing, pharmacy and allied health.
	The social and political issues surrounding access to healthcare in the US have led to vigorous public debate and the almost colloquial use of terms such as health care health insurance (reimbursement of health care costs), and public health (the collective state and range of health in a population).
Christian right	The Christian right is a term used predominantly in the United States of America to describe right-wing Christian individuals and organizations characterized by their strong support of public polices of social conservatism. The Christian Right is a movement that has been difficult to define due to the heterogeneity of the movement. Although views are virtually unanimous on certain issues such as abortion, some contrasting viewpoints can be found among people who identify themselves as members of the Christian Right.

Chapter 12. Groups and Interests

Coalition	The Coalition in Australian politics refers to a group of centre-right parties that has existed in the form of a coalition agreement (on and off) since 1922. The Coalition partners are the Liberal Party of Australia (or its predecessors before 1945) and the National Party of Australia (known as the Australian Country Party from 1921-1975 and the National Country Party of Australia from 1975-1982). The Country Liberal Party in the Northern Territory and the Liberal National Party in Queensland are their equivalents in those states, while the National Party of Western Australia and The Nationals South Australia are not in any form of coalition and are separate parties. There is no National Party in the ACT or Tasmania.
Election	An election is a formal decision-making process by which a population chooses an individual to hold public office. Elections have been the usual mechanism by which modern representative democracy operates since the 17th century. Elections may fill offices in the legislature, sometimes in the executive and judiciary, and for regional and local government.
Policy	A policy is typically described as a principle or rule to guide decisions and achieve rational outcome(s). The term is not normally used to denote what is actually done, this is normally referred to as either procedure or protocol. Whereas a policy will contain the 'what' and the 'why', procedures or protocols contain the 'what', the 'how', the 'where', and the 'when'.
The Jukes family	The Jukes family was a New York hill family studied in the late 19th and early 20th centuries. The studies are part of a series of other family studies, including the Kallikaks, the Zeros and the Nams, that were often quoted as arguments in support of eugenics, though the original Jukes study, by Richard L. Dugdale, placed considerable emphasis on the environment as a determining factor in criminality, disease and poverty. Dugdale's study In 1874, sociologist Richard L. Dugdale, a member of the executive committee of the Prison Association of New York, was delegated to visit jails in upstate New York.
New Politics	New Politics is an independent socialist journal founded in 1961 and still published in the United States today. While it is inclusive of articles from a variety of left-of-center positions, the publication leans strongly toward a Third Camp, democratic Marxist perspective, placing it typically to the left of the liberal or social democratic views in the journal Dissent, although over the years a number of authors have published in both periodicals.

Chapter 12. Groups and Interests

	Julius and Phyllis Jacobson were the founders and longtime co-editors of the journal, which had a political center of gravity reflective of their youthful formative experience in the Independent Socialist League of the 1940s and 1950s.
Physicians for Social Responsibility	Physicians for Social Responsibility is the largest physician-led organization in the country working to protect the public from the threats of nuclear proliferation, climate change, and environmental toxins. Continuing its long and respected history of physician-led activism, PSR produces and disseminates its own publications, provides specialized training, offers written and oral testimony to congress, conducts media interviews, and delivers professional and public education. PSR's 50,000 members and e-activists, 30 state and local chapters, 39 student chapters, and 14 national staff form a nationwide network that effectively targets threats to global survival, specifically nuclear warfare, nuclear proliferation, global warming, and toxic degradation of the environment.
Rebellion	Rebellion is a refusal of obedience or order. It may, therefore, be seen as encompassing a range of behaviors from civil disobedience and mass nonviolent resistance, to violent and organized attempts to destroy an established authority such as a government. Those who participate in rebellions are known as "rebels".
State	Many sovereign independent state are made up of a number of country subdivisions also called states. In some cases, such as the United States, the national government arose from a union of sovereign entities, which transferred some of their powers to the national government, while retaining the remainder of their sovereignty. These are sometimes called federal states.
United States	The United States of America (also referred to as the United States, the U.S., the USA, or America) is a federal constitutional republic comprising fifty states and a federal district. The country is situated mostly in central North America, where its forty-eight contiguous states and Washington, D.C., the capital district, lie between the Pacific and Atlantic Oceans, bordered by Canada to the north and Mexico to the south. The state of Alaska is in the northwest of the continent, with Canada to the east and Russia to the west across the Bering Strait.
Vietnam	Vietnam, officially the Socialist Republic of Vietnam is the easternmost country on the Indochina Peninsula in Southeast Asia. It is bordered by People's Republic of China (PRC) to the north, Laos to the northwest, Cambodia to the southwest, and the South China Sea, referred to as East Sea (Vietnamese: Bi?n Đông), to the east. With a population of over 86 million, Vietnam is the 13th most populous country in the world.

Chapter 12. Groups and Interests

Court	A court is a form of tribunal, often a governmental institution, with the authority to adjudicate legal disputes between parties and carry out the administration of justice in civil, criminal, and administrative matters in accordance with the rule of law. In both common law and civil law legal systems, courts are the central means for dispute resolution, and it is generally understood that all persons have an ability to bring their claims before a court. Similarly, the rights of those accused of a crime include the right to present a defense before a court.
Appointee	An appointee may be one of the following: - A member who is appointed to a position or office is called an appointee. In law, such a term is applied to one who is granted power of appointment of property. - An appointee was also a foot soldier in the French army, who, for long service and bravery, received more pay than other privates. - An appointee is the third most lower rank of the Italian Corps of Carabineers - An appointee is the third most lower rank of the Swiss Armed Forces - An appointee is also a person or organisation entrusted with managing the daily finances of vulnerable individuals in the UK.
Federalist	The term federalist describes several political beliefs around the world. Also, it may refer to the concept of federalism or the type of government called a federation. In early United States history, the Federalist Party was one of the first political parties; its members or supporters called themselves Federalists.
American Revolution	The American Revolution was the political upheaval during the last half of the 18th century in which thirteen colonies in North America joined together to break free from the British Empire, combining to become the United States of America. They first rejected the authority of the Parliament of Great Britain to govern them from overseas without representation, and then expelled all royal officials. By 1774 each colony had established a Provincial Congress, or an equivalent governmental institution, to form individual self-governing states. The British responded by sending combat troops to re-impose direct rule.

Chapter 12. Groups and Interests

Medicare	Medicare is a social insurance program administered by the United States government, providing health insurance coverage to people who are aged 65 and over, or who meet other special criteria. Medicare operates similar to a single-payer health care system, but the key difference is that its coverage only extends to 80% of any given medical cost; the remaining 20% of cost must be paid by other means, such as privately-held supplemental insurance, or paid by the patient. The program also funds residency training programs for the vast majority of physicians in the United States.
Trusts	In Conflict of Laws, the Hague Convention on the Law Applicable to Trusts and on Their Recognition was concluded on 1 July 1985 and entered into force 1 January 1992. The Convention aims to harmonise not only the municipal law definitions of a trust both within the USA and outside the USA, but also the Conflict rules for resolving problems in the choice of the lex causae. Explanation Many states do not have a developed law of trusts, or the principles differ significantly between states. It was therefore necessary for the Hague Convention to define a trust to indicate the range of legal transactions regulated by the Convention and, perhaps more significantly, the range of applications not regulated.
Election Day	Election Day refers to the day when general elections are held. In many countries, general elections are always held on a Sunday, to enable as many voters as possible to participate, while in other countries elections are always held on a weekday. However, some countries, or regions within a country, always make a weekday election day a public holiday, thus satisfying both demands.

Chapter 12. Groups and Interests

Ideology	An ideology is a set of ideas that constitutes one's goals, expectations, and actions. An ideology can be thought of as a comprehensive vision, as a way of looking at things (compare worldview), as in common sense and several philosophical tendencies , or a set of ideas proposed by the dominant class of a society to all members of this society (a "received consciousness" or product of socialization). The main purpose behind an ideology is to offer either change in society, or adherence to a set of ideals where conformity already exists, through a normative thought process.
Republic	A republic is a state under a form of government in which the people, or some significant portion of them, retain supreme control over the government. The term is generally also understood to describe a state where most decisions are made with reference to established laws, rather than the discretion of a head of state, and therefore monarchy is today generally considered to be incompatible with being a republic. One common modern definition of a republic is a state without a monarch.
Political entrepreneur	The term Political entrepreneur may refer to any of the following: - someone (usually active in the fields of either politics or business) who founds a new political project, group, or political party - a businessman who seeks to gain profit through subsidies, protectionism, government contracts, or other such favorable arrangements with government(s) through political influence . - a political actor (not necessarily a politician) who seeks to further his or her own political career and popularity by pursuing the creation of policy that pleases the populace. Politician as a political entrepreneur In the field of business, entrepreneurship involves people taking a risk in order to create new business ventures, to gain advantage over a competitor, and to maximize profits. Traditionally entrepreneurs have been associated with the world of business, however the term is used in the political arena also. For example Choi Taewook in 2004 wrote:

Chapter 12. Groups and Interests

	A political entrepreneur refers to a political player who seeks to gain certain political and social benefits in return for providing the common goods that can be shared by an unorganized general public.
Attack	In computer and computer networks an attack is any attempt to destroy, expose, alter, disable, steal or gain unauthorized access to or make unauthorized use of an asset. Definitions IETF Internet Engineering Task Force defines attack in RFC 2828 as: US Government CNSS Instruction No. 4009 dated 26 April 2010 by Committee on National Security Systems of United States of America defines an attack as: The increasing dependencies of modern society on information and computers networks (both in private and public sectors, including military) has led to new terms like cyber attack and Cyberwarfare. CNSS Instruction No. 4009 define a cyber attack as: Phenomenology An attack can be active or passive.

Chapter 12. Groups and Interests

	An attack can be perpetrated by an insider or from outside the organization;
	An "inside attack" is an attack initiated by an entity inside the security perimeter (an "insider"), i.e., an entity that is authorized to access system resources but uses them in a way not approved by those who granted the authorization. An "outside attack" is initiated from outside the perimeter, by an unauthorized or illegitimate user of the system (an "outsider").
Corporation	In feudal Europe, corporations were aggregations of business interests in compact, usually with an explicit license from city, church, or national leaders. These functioned as effective monopolies for a particular good or labor.
	The term "corporation" was used as late as the 18th century in England to refer to such ventures as the East India Company or the Hudson's Bay Company: commercial organizations that operated under royal patent to have exclusive rights to a particular area of trade.
Gate	A gate is a point of entry to a space enclosed by walls, or a moderately sized opening in a fence. Gates may prevent or control entry or exit, or they may be merely decorative. Other terms for gate include yett and port.
Presidency	The word presidency is often used to describe the administration or the executive, the collective administrative and governmental entity that exists around an office of president of a state or nation. It is also the governing authority of some churches.
	For example, in a republic with a presidential system of government, the presidency is the executive branch of government, and is personified by a single elected man or woman who holds the office of "president".

Chapter 12. Groups and Interests

Environmental protection	Environmental protection is a practice of protecting the environment, on individual, organizational or governmental level, for the benefit of the natural environment and (or) humans. Due to the pressures of population and our technology the biophysical environment is being degraded, sometimes permanently. This has been recognized and governments began placing restraints on activities that caused environmental degradation.
Stakeholder	A corporate stakeholder is a party that can affect or be affected by the actions of the business as a whole. The stakeholder concept was first used in a 1963 internal memorandum at the Stanford Research institute. It defined stakeholders as "those groups without whose support the organization would cease to exist." The theory was later developed and championed by R. Edward Freeman in the 1980s.
Americas	The Americas, are the lands of the western hemisphere, composed of numerous entities and regions variably defined by geography, politics, and culture. The Americas are frequently recognised to comprise two separate continents (North America and South America), particularly in English-speaking nations. The Americas may also be recognised to comprise a single continent , in Latin America and in some European nations.
Eisenstadt v. Baird	Eisenstadt v. Baird, 405 U.S. 438 (1972), was an important United States Supreme Court case that established the right of unmarried people to possess contraception on the same basis as married couples and, by implication, the right of unmarried couples to engage in potentially nonprocreative sexual intercourse (though not the right of unmarried people to engage in any type of sexual intercourse). The Court struck down a Massachusetts law prohibiting the distribution of contraceptives to unmarried people, ruling that it violated the Equal Protection Clause of the Constitution. Case History William Baird was charged with a felony for distributing contraceptive foams during lectures on population control at Boston University.

Chapter 12. Groups and Interests

Griswold v. Connecticut	Griswold v. Connecticut, 381 U.S. 479 (1965), was a landmark case in which the Supreme Court of the United States ruled that the Constitution protected a right to privacy. The case involved a Connecticut law that prohibited the use of contraceptives. By a vote of 7-2, the Supreme Court invalidated the law on the grounds that it violated the "right to marital privacy".
Treaty	A treaty is an express agreement under international law entered into by actors in international law, namely sovereign states and international organizations. A treaty may also be known as: (international) agreement, protocol, covenant, convention, exchange of letters, etc. Regardless of the terminology, all of these international agreements under international law are equally treaties and the rules are the same.
Veteran	A veteran is a person who has had long service or experience in a particular occupation or field; " A veteran of ..." . This page refers to military veterans, i.e., a person who has served or is serving in the armed forces, and has direct exposure to acts of military conflict, commonly known as war veterans (although not all military conflicts, or areas in which armed combat takes place, are necessarily referred to as "wars"). Public attitude towards veterans Military veterans often receive special treatment in their respective countries due to the sacrifices they made during wars.
Abortion	Abortion is the termination of a pregnancy by the removal or expulsion of a fetus or embryo from the uterus, resulting in or caused by its death. An abortion can occur spontaneously due to complications during pregnancy or can be induced, in humans and other species. In the context of human pregnancies, an abortion induced to preserve the health of the gravida (pregnant female) is termed a therapeutic abortion, while an abortion induced for any other reason is termed an elective abortion.
Amicus curiae	An amicus curiae is someone, not a party to a case, who volunteers to offer information to assist a court in deciding a matter before it. The information provided may be a legal opinion in the form of a brief (which is called an amicus brief when offered by an amicus curiae), a testimony that has not been solicited by any of the parties, or a learned treatise on a matter that bears on the case. The decision on whether to admit the information lies at the discretion of the court.

Chapter 12. Groups and Interests

Advancement	Advancement is a common law doctrine of intestate succession that presumes that gifts given to a person's heir during that person's life are intended as an advance on what that heir would inherit upon the death of the parent. For example, suppose person P had two children, A and B. Suppose also that P had $100,000, and gave $20,000 to child A before P's death, leaving $80,000 in P's estate. If P died without a will, and A and B were P's only heirs, A and B would be entitled to split P's estate evenly.
Brown v. Board of Education	Brown v. Board of Education of Topeka, 347 U.S. 483 (1954), was a landmark decision of the United States Supreme Court that declared state laws establishing separate public schools for black and white students unconstitutional. The decision overturned the Plessy v. Ferguson decision of 1896 which allowed state-sponsored segregation. Handed down on May 17, 1954, the Warren Court's unanimous (9-0) decision stated that "separate educational facilities are inherently unequal." As a result, de jure racial segregation was ruled a violation of the Equal Protection Clause of the Fourteenth Amendment of the United States Constitution.
Colored	Colored in the U.S.A (also coloured in Canadian, British and Commonwealth spelling) is a term once widely regarded as a description of black people (i.e., persons of sub-Saharan African ancestry; members of the "Black race") and Native Americans. It should not be confused with the more recent term people of color, which attempts to describe all "non-white peoples", not just black people. Today it is generally no longer regarded as a politically correct term, however even that is debatable, due to its continued occasional appearance, most notably its use in the acronym NAACP. Carla Sims, communications director for the NAACP in Washington, D.C., said "The term 'colored' is not derogatory, [the NAACP] chose the word 'colored' because it was the most positive description commonly used at that time.
Commission	A commission is a physical document issued to certify the appointment of a commissioned officer by a sovereign power.

Chapter 12. Groups and Interests

	The more specific terms commissioning parchment or commissioning scroll are often used to avoid ambiguity, due to "commission" being a homonym which directs the individual in carrying out their duty regardless of what authority or responsibility they may have at any time. However the document is not usually in the form of a scroll and is more often printed on paper instead of parchment.
Rescue	Rescue refers to operations that usually involve the saving of life, or prevention of injury.
	Tools used might include search dogs, search and rescue horses, helicopters, the "Jaws of Life", and other hydraulic cutting and spreading tools used to extricate individuals from wrecked vehicles. Rescue operations are sometimes supported by special vehicles such as fire department's or EMS Heavy rescue vehicle.
Roe v. Wade	Roe v. Wade, 410 U.S. 113 (1973), was a landmark although controversial decision by the United States Supreme Court on the issue of abortion. The Court decided that a right to privacy under the due process clause in the Fourteenth Amendment to the United States Constitution extends to a woman's decision to have an abortion, but that right must be balanced against the state's two legitimate interests for regulating abortions: protecting prenatal life and protecting the mother's health. Saying that these state interests become stronger over the course of a pregnancy, the Court resolved this balancing test by tying state regulation of abortion to the mother's current trimester of pregnancy.
National Convention	During the French Revolution, the National Convention, in France, comprised the constitutional and legislative assembly which sat from 20 September 1792 to 26 October 1795 . It held executive power in France during the first years of the French First Republic. It was succeeded by the Directory, commencing 2 November 1795. Prominent members of the original Convention included Maximilien Robespierre of the Jacobin Club, Jean-Paul Marat (affiliated with the Jacobins, though never a formal member), and Georges Danton of the Cordeliers.
Discrimination	Discrimination is the cognitive and sensory capacity or ability to see fine distinctions and perceive differences between objects, subjects, concepts and patterns, or possess exceptional development of the senses. Used in this way to identify exceptional discernment since the 17th century, the term begun to be used as an expression of derogatory racial prejudice from the 1830s Thomas D. Rice's performances as "Jim Crow".

Chapter 12. Groups and Interests

	Since the American Civil War the term 'discrimination' generally evolved in American English usage as an understanding of prejudicial treatment of an individual based solely on their race, later generalized as membership in a certain socially undesirable group or social category.
Insurance	In law and economics, insurance is a form of risk management primarily used to hedge against the risk of a contingent, uncertain loss. Insurance is defined as the equitable transfer of the risk of a loss, from one entity to another, in exchange for payment. An insurer is a company selling the insurance; an insured, or policyholder, is the person or entity buying the insurance policy.
National Convention	During the French Revolution, the National Convention, in France, comprised the constitutional and legislative assembly which sat from 20 September 1792 to 26 October 1795 . It held executive power in France during the first years of the French First Republic. It was succeeded by the Directory, commencing 2 November 1795. Prominent members of the original Convention included Maximilien Robespierre of the Jacobin Club, Jean-Paul Marat (affiliated with the Jacobins, though never a formal member), and Georges Danton of the Cordeliers.
Grassroots	A grassroots movement (often referenced in the context of a political movement) is one driven by the politics of a community. The term implies that the creation of the movement and the group supporting it are natural and spontaneous, highlighting the differences between this and a movement that is orchestrated by traditional power structures. Grassroots movements are often at the local level, as many volunteers in the community give their time to support the local party, which can lead to helping the national party.
Martin Luther King, Jr.	Martin Luther King, Jr. was an American clergyman, activist, and prominent leader in the African American civil rights movement. He is best known for being an iconic figure in the advancement of civil rights in the United States and around the world, using nonviolent methods following the teachings of Mahatma Gandhi.
Martin Luther	Martin Luther is a public artwork by German artist Ernst Rietschel, located at Luther Place Memorial Church in Washington, D.C., United States. Martin Luther was originally surveyed as part of the Smithsonian's Save Outdoor Sculpture! survey in 1993. The monument is a bronze full length portrait dedicated to theologian Martin Luther. Description

Chapter 12. Groups and Interests

	Martin Luther stands dressed in long robes with his proper right leg moving slightly forward.
Reconciliation	Reconciliation is a legislative process of the United States Senate intended to allow consideration of a budget bill with debate limited to twenty hours under Senate Rules. Reconciliation also exists in the United States House of Representatives, but because the House regularly passes rules that constrain debate and amendment, the process has had a less significant impact on that body.
	A reconciliation instruction (Budget Reconciliation) is a provision in a budget resolution directing one or more committees to submit legislation changing existing law in order to bring spending, revenues, or the debt-limit into conformity with the budget resolution.
Strike	Strike is a 1925 silent film made in the Soviet Union by Sergei Eisenstein. It was Eisenstein's first full-length feature film, and he would go on to make The Battleship Potemkin later that year. It was acted by the Proletcult Theatre, and composed of six parts.
Administration	Administration, as a legal concept, is a procedure under the insolvency laws of a number of common law jurisdictions. It functions as a rescue mechanism for insolvent companies and allows them to carry on running their business. The process - an alternative to liquidation - is often known as going into administration.
Federal Election Campaign Act	The Federal Election Campaign Act of 1971 (Federal Election Campaign Act, Pub.L. 92-225, 86 Stat. 3, enacted February 7, 1972, 2 U.S.C. § 431 et seq). is a United States federal law which increased disclosure of contributions for federal campaigns. It was amended in 1974 to place legal limits on the campaign contributions. The amendment also created the Federal Election Commission (FEC).
Protest	A protest expresses a strong reaction of events or situations. The term protest usually now implies a reaction against something, while previously it could also mean a reaction for something. Protesters may organize a protest as a way of publicly and forcefully making their opinions heard in an attempt to influence public opinion or government policy, or may undertake direct action in an attempt to directly enact desired changes themselves.

Chapter 12. Groups and Interests

Democratic National Committee	The Democratic National Committee is the principal organization governing the United States Democratic Party on a day to day basis. While it is responsible for overseeing the process of writing a platform every four years, the Democratic National Committee's central focus is on campaign and political activity in support of Democratic Party candidates, and not on public policy. The Democratic National Committee was established at the 1848 Democratic National Convention.
Watergate scandal	The Watergate scandal was a 1970s United States political scandal resulting from the break-in to the Democratic National Committee headquarters at the Watergate office complex in Washington, D.C. Effects of the scandal ultimately led to the resignation of the President of the United States, Richard Nixon, on August 9, 1974, the first and only resignation of any U.S. President. It also resulted in the indictment, trial, conviction and incarceration of several Nixon administration officials.
	The affair began with the arrest of five men for breaking and entering into the Democratic National Committee headquarters at the Watergate complex on June 17, 1972. The FBI connected the payments to the burglars to a slush fund used by the 1972 Committee to Re-elect the President.
Buckley v. Valeo	Buckley v. Valeo, 424 U.S. 1 (1976), was a case in which the Supreme Court of the United States upheld a federal law which set limits on campaign contributions, but ruled that spending money to influence elections is a form of constitutionally protected free speech, and struck down portions of the law. The court also stated candidates can give unlimited amounts of money to their own campaigns.
	Facts
	In 1974, over the veto of President Gerald R. Ford, the Congress passed significant amendments to the Federal Election Campaign Act of 1971, creating the first comprehensive effort by the federal government to regulate campaign contributions and spending.

Chapter 12. Groups and Interests

Reform Act	In the United Kingdom, Reform Act is a generic term used for legislation concerning electoral matters. It is most commonly used for laws passed to enfranchise new groups of voters and to redistribute seats in the British House of Commons. The periodic redrawing of constituency boundaries is now dealt with by a permanent Boundary Commission in each part of the United Kingdom, rather than by a Reform Act.
Bill	A bill is a proposed law under consideration by a legislature. A bill does not become law until it is passed by the legislature and, in most cases, approved by the executive. Once a bill has been enacted into law, it is called an act or a statute.
Activism	Activism consists of intentional action to bring about social, political, economic, or environmental change. This action is in support of, or opposition to, one side of an often controversial argument.
	The word "activism" is used synonymously with protest or dissent, but activism can take a wide range of forms from writing letters to newspapers or politicians, political campaigning, economic activism such as boycotts or preferentially patronizing businesses, rallies, street marches, strikes, both sit-ins and hunger strikes, or even guerrilla tactics.
Political Parties	Political Parties: A Sociological Study of the Oligarchical Tendencies of Modern Democracy is a book by sociologist Robert Michels, published in 1911, and first introducing the concept of iron law of oligarchy. It is considered one of the classics of sociology and political science.
	This work analyzes the power structures of organizations such as political parties and trade unions.
GREEN	Green is the only green real estate designation for REALTORs approved by the National Association of Realtors (NAR). The program was developed in 2008 by the Real Estate Buyer's Agent Council of NAR, with administration transferred to the Green Resource Council.

Chapter 12. Groups and Interests

	The course curriculum includes sustainable building practices, marketing, and rating systems (e.g., LEED and Energy Star).
Desegregation	Desegregation is the process of ending the separation of two groups usually referring to races. This is most commonly used in reference to the United States. Desegregation was long a focus of the American Civil Rights Movement, both before and after the United States Supreme Court's decision in Brown v. Board of Education, particularly desegregation of the school systems and the military .
Trade union	A trade union is an organization of workers that have banded together to achieve common goals such as better working conditions. The trade union, through its leadership, bargains with the employer on behalf of union members (rank and file members) and negotiates labour contracts (collective bargaining) with employers. This may include the negotiation of wages, work rules, complaint procedures, rules governing hiring, firing and promotion of workers, benefits, workplace safety and policies.
Appropriation	In law and government, appropriation is the act of setting apart something for its application to a particular usage, to the exclusion of all other uses.
	It typically refers to the legislative designation of money for particular uses, in the context of a budget or spending bill.
	Ecclesiastical law
	In ecclesiastical law, appropriation is the perpetual annexation of an ecclesiastical benefice to the use of some spiritual corporation, either aggregate or sole.
Bill of rights	A bill of rights is a list of the most important rights of the citizens of a country. The purpose of these bills is to protect those rights against infringement by the government. The term "bill of rights" originates from England, where it referred to the Bill of Rights 1689. Bills of rights may be entrenched or unentrenched.

Chapter 12. Groups and Interests

Free riding	Free riding is a term used in the stock-trading world to describe the practice of buying shares or other securities without actually having the capital to cover the trade. This is possible when recently bought or sold shares are unsettled, and therefore have not been paid for. Since stock transactions usually settle after three business days, a crafty trader can buy a stock and sell it the following day (or the same day), without ever having sufficient funds in the account.
Public opinion	Public opinion is the aggregate of individual attitudes or beliefs held by the adult population. Public opinion can also be defined as the complex collection of opinions of many different people and the sum of all their views. The principle approaches to the study of public opinion may be divided into 4 categories: 1. quantitative measurement of opinion distributions; 2. investigation of the internal relationships among the individual opinions that make up public opinion on an issue; 3. description or analysis of the public role of public opinion; 4. study both of the communication media that disseminate the ideas on which opinions are based and of the uses that propagandists and other manipulators make of these media. Concepts of "public opinion" Public opinion as a concept gained credence with the rise of "public" in the eighteenth century.

Chapter 12. Groups and Interests

Chapter 12. Groups and Interests

Chapter 13. The Media

Congress	A congress is a formal meeting of the representatives of different nations, constituent states, independent organizations (such as trade unions), or groups.
	The term was chosen for the United States Congress to emphasize the status of each state represented there as a self-governing unit. Subsequent to the use of congress by the U.S. legislature, the term has been incorrectly adopted by many states within unions, and by unitary nation-states in the Americas, to refer to their legislatures.
Federalist	The term federalist describes several political beliefs around the world. Also, it may refer to the concept of federalism or the type of government called a federation. In early United States history, the Federalist Party was one of the first political parties; its members or supporters called themselves Federalists.
Internets	"Internets" is a Bushism-turned-catchphrase used humorously to portray the speaker as ignorant about the Internet or about technology in general, or as having a provincial or folksy attitude toward technology. Former United States President George W. Bush first used the word publicly during the 2000 election campaign. The term gained cachet as an Internet humor meme following Bush's use of the term in the second 2004 presidential election debate on October 8, 2004.
Virginia	The Commonwealth of Virginia is a U.S. state on the Atlantic Coast of the Southern United States. Virginia is nicknamed the "Old Dominion" and sometimes the "Mother of Presidents" because it is the birthplace of eight U.S. presidents. The geography and climate of the state are shaped by the Blue Ridge Mountains and the Chesapeake Bay, which provide habitat for much of its flora and fauna.
Germany	Germany officially the Federal Republic of Germany, is a country in Western Europe. It is bordered to the north by the North Sea, Denmark, and the Baltic Sea; to the east by Poland and the Czech Republic; to the south by Austria and Switzerland; and to the west by France, Luxembourg, Belgium, and the Netherlands. The territory of Germany covers an area of 357,021 km^2 and is influenced by a temperate seasonal climate.
Affair	Affair may refer to professional, personal, or public business matters or to a particular business or private activity of a temporary duration, as in family affair, a private affair, or a romantic affair.
	Political affair

Chapter 13. The Media

	Political affair may refer to the illicit or scandalous activities of public, such as the Watergate affair, or to a legally constituted government department, for example, the United Nations Department of Political Affairs.
	Romantic affair
	A romantic affair, also called an affair of the heart, may refer to sexual liaisons among unwed parties, or to various forms of nonmonogamy.
Publics	Publics are small groups of people who follow one or more particular issue very closely. They are well informed about the issue(s) and also have a very strong opinion on it/them. They tend to know more about politics than the average person, and, therefore, exert more influence, because these people care so deeply about their cause(s) that they donate much time and money.
Freedom	Freedom is a London-based anarchist newspaper published fortnightly by Freedom Press.
	The paper was started in 1886 by volunteers including Peter Kropotkin and Charlotte Wilson and continues to this day as an unpaid project. Originally, the subtitle was "A Journal of Anarchist Socialism." The title was changed to "A Journal of Anarchist Communism" in June 1889. Today it is unlabelled.
Medicare	Medicare is a social insurance program administered by the United States government, providing health insurance coverage to people who are aged 65 and over, or who meet other special criteria. Medicare operates similar to a single-payer health care system, but the key difference is that its coverage only extends to 80% of any given medical cost; the remaining 20% of cost must be paid by other means, such as privately-held supplemental insurance, or paid by the patient.
	The program also funds residency training programs for the vast majority of physicians in the United States.

Chapter 13. The Media

Censorship	Censorship is suppression of speech or other communication which may be considered objectionable, harmful, sensitive, or inconvenient to the general body of people as determined by a government, media outlet, or other controlling body. Rationale The rationale for censorship is different for various types of information censored: - Moral censorship is the removal of materials that are obscene or otherwise considered morally questionable. Pornography, for example, is often censored under this rationale, especially child pornography, which is illegal and censored in many jurisdictions in the world. - Military censorship is the process of keeping military intelligence and tactics confidential and away from the enemy.
Freedom of speech	Freedom of speech is the freedom to speak freely without censorship or limitation, or both. The synonymous term freedom of expression is sometimes used to indicate not only freedom of verbal speech but any act of seeking, receiving and imparting information or ideas, regardless of the medium used. In practice, the right to freedom of speech is not absolute in any country and the right is commonly subject to limitations, such as on "hate speech".
Commission	A commission is a physical document issued to certify the appointment of a commissioned officer by a sovereign power. The more specific terms commissioning parchment or commissioning scroll are often used to avoid ambiguity, due to "commission" being a homonym which directs the individual in carrying out their duty regardless of what authority or responsibility they may have at any time. However the document is not usually in the form of a scroll and is more often printed on paper instead of parchment.

Chapter 13. The Media

National Convention	During the French Revolution, the National Convention, in France, comprised the constitutional and legislative assembly which sat from 20 September 1792 to 26 October 1795 . It held executive power in France during the first years of the French First Republic. It was succeeded by the Directory, commencing 2 November 1795. Prominent members of the original Convention included Maximilien Robespierre of the Jacobin Club, Jean-Paul Marat (affiliated with the Jacobins, though never a formal member), and Georges Danton of the Cordeliers.
Federal Communications Commission	The Federal Communications Commission is an independent agency of the United States government, created, Congressional statute , and with the majority of its commissioners appointed by the current President. The Federal Communications Commission works towards six goals in the areas of broadband, competition, the spectrum, the media, public safety and homeland security, and modernizing the Federal Communications Commission.
	The Federal Communications Commission was established by the Communications Act of 1934 as the successor to the Federal Radio Commission and is charged with regulating all non-federal government use of the radio spectrum (including radio and television broadcasting), and all interstate telecommunications (wire, satellite and cable) as well as all international communications that originate or terminate in the United States. It is an important factor in U.S. telecommunication policy.
State	Many sovereign independent state are made up of a number of country subdivisions also called states. In some cases, such as the United States, the national government arose from a union of sovereign entities, which transferred some of their powers to the national government, while retaining the remainder of their sovereignty. These are sometimes called federal states.
Idea	In the most narrow sense, an idea is just whatever is before the mind when one thinks. Very often, ideas are construed as representational images; i.e. images of some object. In other contexts, ideas are taken to be concepts, although abstract concepts do not necessarily appear as images.
Marketplace of ideas	The "marketplace of ideas" is a rationale for freedom of expression based on an analogy to the economic concept of a free market. The "marketplace of ideas" belief holds that the truth or the best policy arises out of the competition of widely various ideas in free, transparent public discourse, an important part of liberal democracy. This concept is often applied to discussions of patent law as well as freedom of the press and the responsibilities of the media.

Chapter 13. The Media

Homeland	A homeland is the concept of the place (cultural geography) to which an ethnic group holds a long history and a deep cultural association with --the country in which a particular national identity began. As a common noun, it simply connotes the country of one's origin.
Homeland security	Homeland security is an umbrella term for security efforts to protect the United States against terrorist activity. The term arose following a reorganization of many U.S. government agencies in 2003 to form the United States Department of Homeland Security after the September 11 attacks, and may be used to refer to the actions of that department, the United States Senate Committee on Homeland Security and Governmental Affairs, or the United States House of Representatives Committee on Homeland Security. In the United States In the United States, the concept of "homeland security" extends and recombines responsibilities of government agencies and entities.
Regulation	Regulation is "controlling human or societal behavior by rules or restrictions." Regulation can take many forms: legal restrictions promulgated by a government authority, self-regulation by an industry such as through a trade association, social regulation co-regulation and market regulation. One can consider regulation as actions of conduct imposing sanctions (such as a fine). This action of administrative law, or implementing regulatory law, may be contrasted with statutory or case law.
Blog	A blog is a type of website or part of a website. Blogs are usually maintained by an individual with regular entries of commentary, descriptions of events, or other material such as graphics or video. Entries are commonly displayed in reverse-chronological order.
Desegregation	Desegregation is the process of ending the separation of two groups usually referring to races. This is most commonly used in reference to the United States. Desegregation was long a focus of the American Civil Rights Movement, both before and after the United States Supreme Court's decision in Brown v. Board of Education, particularly desegregation of the school systems and the military .

Chapter 13. The Media

Discrimination	Discrimination is the cognitive and sensory capacity or ability to see fine distinctions and perceive differences between objects, subjects, concepts and patterns, or possess exceptional development of the senses. Used in this way to identify exceptional discernment since the 17th century, the term begun to be used as an expression of derogatory racial prejudice from the 1830s Thomas D. Rice's performances as "Jim Crow".
	Since the American Civil War the term 'discrimination' generally evolved in American English usage as an understanding of prejudicial treatment of an individual based solely on their race, later generalized as membership in a certain socially undesirable group or social category.
News conference	A news conference is a media event in which newsmakers invite journalists to hear them speak and, most often, ask questions. A joint press conference instead is held between two or more talking sides.
	Practice
	In a news conference, one or more speakers may make a statement, which may be followed by questions from reporters.
Americas	The Americas, are the lands of the western hemisphere, composed of numerous entities and regions variably defined by geography, politics, and culture.
	The Americas are frequently recognised to comprise two separate continents (North America and South America), particularly in English-speaking nations. The Americas may also be recognised to comprise a single continent , in Latin America and in some European nations.
Ireland	

Chapter 13. The Media

	Ireland is the third-largest island in Europe and the twentieth-largest island in the world. It lies to the northwest of continental Europe and is surrounded by hundreds of islands and islets. To the east of Ireland is Great Britain, separated from it by the Irish Sea.
Northern Ireland	Northern Ireland is one of the four countries of the United Kingdom. Situated in the north-east of the island of Ireland, it shares a border with the Republic of Ireland to the south and west. At the time of the 2001 UK Census, its population was 1,685,000, constituting about 30% of the island's total population and about 3% of the population of the United Kingdom.
Social security	Social security is primarily a social insurance program providing social protection, or protection against socially recognized conditions, including poverty, old age, disability, unemployment and others. Social security may refer to: - social insurance, where people receive benefits or services in recognition of contributions to an insurance scheme. These services typically include provision for retirement pensions, disability insurance, survivor benefits and unemployment insurance. - income maintenance--mainly the distribution of cash in the event of interruption of employment, including retirement, disability and unemployment - services provided by administrations responsible for social security.
Trusts	In Conflict of Laws, the Hague Convention on the Law Applicable to Trusts and on Their Recognition was concluded on 1 July 1985 and entered into force 1 January 1992. The Convention aims to harmonise not only the municipal law definitions of a trust both within the USA and outside the USA, but also the Conflict rules for resolving problems in the choice of the lex causae. Explanation Many states do not have a developed law of trusts, or the principles differ significantly between states. It was therefore necessary for the Hague Convention to define a trust to indicate the range of legal transactions regulated by the Convention and, perhaps more significantly, the range of applications not regulated.

Chapter 13. The Media

Homosexuality	Homosexuality is romantic and/or sexual attraction or behavior among members of the same sex or gender. As a sexual orientation, homosexuality refers to "an enduring pattern of or disposition to experience sexual, affectional, or romantic attractions" primarily or exclusively to people of the same sex; "it also refers to an individual's sense of personal and social identity based on those attractions, behaviors expressing them, and membership in a community of others who share them."
	Homosexuality is one of the three main categories of sexual orientation, along with bisexuality and heterosexuality, within the heterosexual-homosexual continuum. The consensus of the behavioral and social sciences and the health and mental health professions is that homosexuality is a normal and positive variation in human sexual orientation, though many religious societies, including Catholicism, Mormonism, and Islam, and some psychological associations, such as NARTH, teach that homosexual activity is sinful or dysfunctional.
Globe	The whaleship Globe, of Nantucket, Massachusetts, was active between 1815 and 1828.
	The Globe Mutiny
	On Dec. 22, 1822, Globe, with a compliment of 21 men, set sail on a whaling expedition to the Pacific. According to testimony, "Six men ran away in the Sandwich Islands, and one was discharged." On Jan. 26, 1824, a mutiny occurred.
Herald	The Herald is a monthly magazine published in Karachi, Sindh, Pakistan. It is a political magazine owned by Pakistan Herald Publications Limited (PHPL), which also publishes the Dawn Group of Newspapers. It is considered to be a neutral magazine and produces many large or breaking stories.
Mountain	A mountain is a large landform that stretches above the surrounding land in a limited area usually in the form of a peak. A mountain is generally steeper than a hill. The adjective montane is used to describe mountainous areas and things associated with them.
San Francisco	"San Francisco" is a song, written by John Phillips of The Mamas ' the Papas, and sung by Scott McKenzie. It was written and released in 1967 to promote the Monterey Pop Festival.

Chapter 13. The Media

	The lyrics of the song tell the listeners, "If you're going to San Francisco, be sure to wear some flowers in your hair".
Tribune	Tribune is a democratic socialist weekly, currently a magazine though in the past more often a newspaper, published in London. It considers itself "A thorn in the side of all governments, constructively to Labour, unforgiving to Conservatives."
	Origins
	Tribune was set up in early 1937 by two left-wing Labour Party Members of Parliament (MPs), Stafford Cripps and George Strauss, to back the Unity Campaign, an attempt to secure an anti-fascist and anti-appeasement United Front between the Labour Party and socialist parties to its left which involved Cripps's (Labour-affiliated) Socialist League, the Independent Labour Party and the Communist Party of Great Britain (CP).
	The paper's first editor was William Mellor, and its journalists included Michael Foot and Barbara Betts (later Barbara Castle).
Florida	Florida is a state located in the Southeastern United States. It borders Alabama to the northwest and Georgia to the north. Much of the state's land mass is a large peninsula with the Gulf of Mexico to the west, the Atlantic Ocean to the east, and the Florida Straits and Carribean to the south.
Slate	A slate is a group of candidates that run in multi-seat or multi-position elections on a common platform.
	The common platform may be because the candidates are all members of a political party, have the same or similar policies, or some other reason.
	Elections that commonly have slates
	United States electoral college

Chapter 13. The Media

The United States presidential elections use an electoral college to determine the winner and the electors are chosen by popular vote in each state.

Foundation	A foundation in the United States is a type of charitable organization. However, the Internal Revenue Code distinguishes between private foundations (usually funded by an individual, family, or corporation) and public charities (community foundations and other nonprofit groups that raise money from the general public). Private foundations have more restrictions and fewer tax benefits than public charities like community foundations.
Activism	Activism consists of intentional action to bring about social, political, economic, or environmental change. This action is in support of, or opposition to, one side of an often controversial argument.
	The word "activism" is used synonymously with protest or dissent, but activism can take a wide range of forms from writing letters to newspapers or politicians, political campaigning, economic activism such as boycotts or preferentially patronizing businesses, rallies, street marches, strikes, both sit-ins and hunger strikes, or even guerrilla tactics.
Interest	Interest is a fee paid on borrowed assets. It is the price paid for the use of borrowed money, or, money earned by deposited funds. Assets that are sometimes lent with interest include money, shares, consumer goods through hire purchase, major assets such as aircraft, and even entire factories in finance lease arrangements.
Netroots	Netroots is a term coined in 2002 by Jerome Armstrong to describe political activism organized through blogs and other online media, including wikis and social network services. The word is a portmanteau of Internet and grassroots, reflecting the technological innovations that set netroots techniques apart from other forms of political participation. In the United States, the term is used mainly in left-leaning circles.
Creative Commons	Creative Commons is a non-profit organization headquartered in San Francisco, California, United States devoted to expanding the range of creative works available for others to build upon legally and to share. The organization has released several copyright-licenses known as Creative Commons licenses free of charge to the public. These licenses allow creators to communicate which rights they reserve, and which rights they waive for the benefit of recipients or other creators.

Chapter 13. The Media

Fairness Doctrine	The Fairness Doctrine was a policy of the United States Federal Communications Commission (FCC), introduced in 1949, that required the holders of broadcast licenses to both present controversial issues of public importance and to do so in a manner that was, in the Commission's view, honest, equitable and balanced. The 1949 Commission Report served as the foundation for the Fairness Doctrine since it had previously established two more forms of regulation onto broadcasters. These two duties were to provide adequate coverage to public issues and that coverage must be fair in reflecting opposing views.
Rights	Rights are legal, social, or ethical principles of freedom or entitlement; that is, rights are the fundamental normative rules about what is allowed of people or owed to people, according to some legal system, social convention, or ethical theory. Rights are of essential importance in such disciplines as law and ethics, especially theories of justice and deontology.
	Rights are often considered fundamental to civilization, being regarded as established pillars of society and culture, and the history of social conflicts can be found in the history of each right and its development.
Pentagon Papers	The Pentagon Papers, officially titled United States-Vietnam Relations, 1945-1967: A Study Prepared by the Department of Defense, was a top-secret United States Department of Defense history of the United States' political-military involvement in Vietnam from 1945 to 1967. The papers were first brought to the attention of the public on the front page of the New York Times in 1971
	Contents
	Secretary of Defense Robert McNamara created the Vietnam Study Task Force on June 17, 1967, for the purpose of writing an "encyclopedic history of the Vietnam War". The secretary's motivation for commissioning the study is unclear.

Chapter 13. The Media

United States	The United States of America (also referred to as the United States, the U.S., the USA, or America) is a federal constitutional republic comprising fifty states and a federal district. The country is situated mostly in central North America, where its forty-eight contiguous states and Washington, D.C., the capital district, lie between the Pacific and Atlantic Oceans, bordered by Canada to the north and Mexico to the south. The state of Alaska is in the northwest of the continent, with Canada to the east and Russia to the west across the Bering Strait.
Vietnam	Vietnam, officially the Socialist Republic of Vietnam is the easternmost country on the Indochina Peninsula in Southeast Asia. It is bordered by People's Republic of China (PRC) to the north, Laos to the northwest, Cambodia to the southwest, and the South China Sea, referred to as East Sea (Vietnamese: Bi?n Đông), to the east. With a population of over 86 million, Vietnam is the 13th most populous country in the world.
Attack	In computer and computer networks an attack is any attempt to destroy, expose, alter, disable, steal or gain unauthorized access to or make unauthorized use of an asset. Definitions IETF Internet Engineering Task Force defines attack in RFC 2828 as: US Government CNSS Instruction No. 4009 dated 26 April 2010 by Committee on National Security Systems of United States of America defines an attack as: The increasing dependencies of modern society on information and computers networks (both in private and public sectors, including military) has led to new terms like cyber attack and Cyberwarfare. CNSS Instruction No. 4009 define a cyber attack as: Phenomenology

Chapter 13. The Media

	An attack can be active or passive.
	An attack can be perpetrated by an insider or from outside the organization;
	An "inside attack" is an attack initiated by an entity inside the security perimeter (an "insider"), i.e., an entity that is authorized to access system resources but uses them in a way not approved by those who granted the authorization. An "outside attack" is initiated from outside the perimeter, by an unauthorized or illegitimate user of the system (an "outsider").
Freedom of the press	Freedom of the press is the freedom of communication and expression through vehicles including various electronic media and published materials. While such freedom mostly implies the absence of interference from an overreaching state, its preservation may be sought through constitutional or other legal protections.
	With respect to governmental information, any government may distinguish which materials are public or protected from disclosure to the public based on classification of information as sensitive, classified or secret and being otherwise protected from disclosure due to relevance of the information to protecting the national interest.
Prior restraint	In U.S. law, prior restraint is a form of censorship in which one is prevented, in advance, from communicating certain material, rather than made answerable afterwards. Prior restraint is particularly restrictive because it prevents the forbidden material from being heard or distributed at all. Other restrictions on expression provide sanctions only after the offending material has been communicated, such as suits for slander or libel.
Terrorism	Terrorism is the systematic use of terror especially as a means of coercion. No universally agreed, legally binding, criminal law definition of terrorism currently exists. Common definitions of terrorism refer only to those violent acts which are intended to create fear (terror), are perpetrated for a religious, political or ideological goal, deliberately target or disregard the safety of non-combatants (civilians), and are committed by non-government agencies.

Chapter 13. The Media

Monitor	Monitor, is a non-departmental public body in the United Kingdom. Its purpose is to regulate NHS Foundation Trusts or Foundation Hospitals - hospitals that have opted out of direct governmental control. The body was established under the Health and Social Care (Community Health and Standards) Act 2003.
General	General, Finnish: kenraali is the highest officer's rank in Sweden and Finland. In Sweden, it is held by the supreme commander of the Swedish Armed Forces and the monarch. In Finland, it is held by the Chief of Defence.
Cuba	The Republic of Cuba is an island country in the Caribbean. The nation of Cuba consists of the main island of Cuba, the Isla de la Juventud, and several archipelagos. Havana is the largest city in Cuba and the country's capital.
Forum	A forum was the public space in the middle of a Roman city. In addition to its standard function as a marketplace, a forum was a gathering place of great social significance, and often the scene of diverse activities, including political discussions and debates, rendezvous, meetings, et cetera. Modelled on the Roman Forum in Rome itself, several smaller or more specialised forums appeared throughout Rome's archaic history.
Frontier	A frontier is a political and geographical term referring to areas near or beyond a boundary. 'Frontier' was borrowed into English from French in the 15th century, with the meaning "borderland"--the region of a country that fronts on another country. The use of "frontier" to mean "a region at the edge of a settled area" is a special North American development.

Chapter 13. The Media

New Deal	The New Deal is a programme of active labour market policies introduced in the United Kingdom by the Labour government in 1998, initially funded by a one off £5bn windfall tax on privatised utility companies. The stated purpose is to reduce unemployment by providing training, subsidised employment and voluntary work to the unemployed. Spending on the New Deal was £1.3 billion in 2001.
New Frontier	The term New Frontier was used by John F. Kennedy in his acceptance speech in the 1960 United States presidential election to the Democratic National Convention at the Los Angeles Memorial Coliseum as the Democratic slogan to inspire America to support him. The phrase developed into a label for his administration's domestic and foreign programs. In the words of Robert D. Marcus: "Kennedy entered office with ambitions to eradicate poverty and to raise America's eyes to the stars through the space program".
Pardon	A pardon is the forgiveness of a crime and the penalty associated with it. It is granted by a head of state, such as a monarch or president, or by a competent church authority. Commutation is an associated term, meaning the lessening of the penalty of the crime without forgiving the crime itself.
Invasion	An invasion is a military offensive consisting of all, or large parts of the armed forces of one geopolitical entity aggressively entering territory controlled by another such entity, generally with the objective of either conquering, liberating or re-establishing control or authority over a territory, forcing the partition of a country, altering the established government or gaining concessions from said government, or a combination thereof. An invasion can be the cause of a war, be a part of a larger strategy to end a war, or it can constitute an entire war in itself. Due to the large scale of the operations associated with invasions, they are usually strategic in planning and execution.
New Politics	New Politics is an independent socialist journal founded in 1961 and still published in the United States today. While it is inclusive of articles from a variety of left-of-center positions, the publication leans strongly toward a Third Camp, democratic Marxist perspective, placing it typically to the left of the liberal or social democratic views in the journal Dissent, although over the years a number of authors have published in both periodicals.

Chapter 13. The Media

	Julius and Phyllis Jacobson were the founders and longtime co-editors of the journal, which had a political center of gravity reflective of their youthful formative experience in the Independent Socialist League of the 1940s and 1950s.
Press release	A press release, news release, media release, press statement or video release is a written or recorded communication directed at members of the news media for the purpose of announcing something claimed as having news value. Typically, they are mailed, faxed, or e-mailed to assignment editors at newspapers, magazines, radio stations, television stations, and/or television networks. Commercial press release distribution services are also used to distribute them.
Release	Release, founded in 1967 by Caroline Coon and Rufus Harris, is a UK agency that provides legal advice and arrange legal representation for young people charged with the possession of drugs. Today Release is the oldest independent drugs charity in the world and continues to provide a range of services dedicated to meeting the health, welfare and legal needs of drugs users and those who live and work with them. Mission and vision Release is the UK centre of expertise on drugs and drugs law providing free and confidential specialist advice to the public and professionals.
Authority	Authority means invention, advice, opinion, influence, or command. Essentially authority is imposed by superiors upon inferiors either by force of arms (structural authority) or by force of argument (sapiential authority). Usually authority has components of both compulsion and persuasion.
Federal Reserve System	The Federal Reserve System is the central banking system of the United States. It was created in 1913 with the enactment of the Federal Reserve Act, largely in response to a series of financial panics, particularly a severe panic in 1907. Over time, the roles and responsibilities of the Federal Reserve System have expanded and its structure has evolved. Events such as the Great Depression were major factors leading to changes in the system.

Chapter 13. The Media

Stamp Act	A stamp act is a law enacted by government that requires a tax to be paid on the transfer of certain documents. The stamp act was considered unfair by many people. Those that pay the tax receive an official stamp on their documents.
Left Behind	Left Behind is a series of 16 best-selling novels by Tim LaHaye and Jerry Jenkins, dealing with Christian dispensationalist End Times: pretribulation, premillennial, Christian eschatological viewpoint of the end of the world. The primary conflict of the series is the members of the Tribulation Force against the Global Community and its leader Nicolae Carpathia--the Antichrist. Left Behind is also the title of the first book in the series.
LINCOLN	Lincoln was a parliamentary electorate in the Canterbury region of New Zealand from 1881 to 1890. The electorate was represented by two Members of Parliament: - Arthur Pyne O'Callaghan (1881-89), and - Alfred Saunders (1889-90)
No Child Left Behind Act	The No Child Left Behind Act of 2001 is a United States Act of Congress concerning the education of children in public schools. NCLB was originally proposed by the administration of George W. Bush immediately after taking office. The bill, shepherded through the Senate by Senator Ted Kennedy, one of the bill's co-authors, received overwhelming bipartisan support in Congress.
Lobbying	Lobbying is the intention of influencing decisions made by legislators and officials in the government by individuals, other legislators, constituents, or advocacy groups. A lobbyist is a person who tries to influence legislation on behalf of a special interest or a member of a lobby. Governments often define and regulate organized group lobbying that has become influential.

Chapter 13. The Media

Leviathan	Leviathan, Forme and Power of a Common Wealth Ecclesiasticall and Civil, commonly called Leviathan, is a book written by Thomas Hobbes which was published in 1651. It is titled after the biblical Leviathan. The book concerns the structure of society and legitimate government, and is regarded as one of the earliest and most influential examples of social contract theory. The publisher was Andrew Crooke, partner in Andrew Crooke and William Cooke.
Corporate action	A corporate action is an event initiated by a public company that affects the securities (equity or debt) issued by the company. Some corporate actions such as a dividend (for equity securities) or coupon payment (for debt securities (bonds)) may have a direct financial impact on the shareholders or bondholders; another example is a call (early redemption) of a debt security. Other corporate actions such as stock split may have an indirect impact, as the increased liquidity of shares may cause the price of the stock to rise.
Caucus	A caucus is a meeting of supporters or members of a political party or movement, especially in the United States. As the use of the term has been expanded the exact definition has come to vary among political cultures. Origin of the term The origin of the word caucus is debated, but it is generally agreed that it first came into use in the English colonies of North America. A February 1763 entry in the diary of John Adams of Braintree, Massachusetts, is one of the earliest appearances of Caucas, already with its modern connotations of a "smoke-filled room" where candidates for public election are pre-selected in private This day learned that the Caucas Clubb meets at certain Times in the Garret of Tom Daws, the Adjutant of the Boston Regiment.
Democratic Party	The Democratic Party is a social democratic political party in Italy, that is the largest party of Italian centre-left and the second largest of the country.

Chapter 13. The Media

	It was founded on 14 October 2007 as a merger of various left-wing and centrist parties which were part of The Union in the 2006 general election. Several parties merged into the Democratic Party, however its bulk was formed by the Democrats of the Left and Democracy is Freedom - The Daisy.
Civil rights movement	The civil rights movement was a worldwide political movement for equality before the law occurring between approximately 1950 and 1980. It was accompanied by much civil unrest and popular rebellion. The process was long and tenuous in many countries, and most of these movements did not fully achieve their goals although, the efforts of these movements did lead to improvements in the legal rights of previously oppressed groups of peoples. Civil rights movement in Northern Ireland Northern Ireland is a province of the United Kingdom which has witnessed violence over many decades, mainly because of sectarian tensions between the Catholic and Protestant community, known as the Troubles.
Election	An election is a formal decision-making process by which a population chooses an individual to hold public office. Elections have been the usual mechanism by which modern representative democracy operates since the 17th century. Elections may fill offices in the legislature, sometimes in the executive and judiciary, and for regional and local government.
Election Day	Election Day refers to the day when general elections are held. In many countries, general elections are always held on a Sunday, to enable as many voters as possible to participate, while in other countries elections are always held on a weekday. However, some countries, or regions within a country, always make a weekday election day a public holiday, thus satisfying both demands.
Watergate scandal	The Watergate scandal was a 1970s United States political scandal resulting from the break-in to the Democratic National Committee headquarters at the Watergate office complex in Washington, D.C. Effects of the scandal ultimately led to the resignation of the President of the United States, Richard Nixon, on August 9, 1974, the first and only resignation of any U.S. President. It also resulted in the indictment, trial, conviction and incarceration of several Nixon administration officials.

Chapter 13. The Media

The affair began with the arrest of five men for breaking and entering into the Democratic National Committee headquarters at the Watergate complex on June 17, 1972. The FBI connected the payments to the burglars to a slush fund used by the 1972 Committee to Re-elect the President.

Chapter 13. The Media

Chapter 13. The Media

Chapter 14. Economic Policy

Court	A court is a form of tribunal, often a governmental institution, with the authority to adjudicate legal disputes between parties and carry out the administration of justice in civil, criminal, and administrative matters in accordance with the rule of law. In both common law and civil law legal systems, courts are the central means for dispute resolution, and it is generally understood that all persons have an ability to bring their claims before a court. Similarly, the rights of those accused of a crime include the right to present a defense before a court.
Self-determination	The right of nations to self-determination is the principle in international law, that nations have the right to freely choose their sovereignty and international political status with no external compulsion or external interference. The principle does not state how the decision is to be made, or what the outcome should be, be it independence, federation, protection, some form of autonomy or even full assimilation. Neither does it state what the delimitation between nations should be -- or even what constitutes a nation.
Social security	Social security is primarily a social insurance program providing social protection, or protection against socially recognized conditions, including poverty, old age, disability, unemployment and others. Social security may refer to: - social insurance, where people receive benefits or services in recognition of contributions to an insurance scheme. These services typically include provision for retirement pensions, disability insurance, survivor benefits and unemployment insurance. - income maintenance--mainly the distribution of cash in the event of interruption of employment, including retirement, disability and unemployment - services provided by administrations responsible for social security.
Timor	Timor is an island at the southern end of Maritime Southeast Asia, north of the Timor Sea. It is divided between the independent state of East Timor, and West Timor, belonging to the Indonesian province of East Nusa Tenggara. The island's surface is 11,883 square miles (30,777 km^2).
Free market	A free market is a market in which there is no economic intervention and regulation by the state, except to enforce private contracts and the ownership of property. It is the opposite of a controlled market, in which the state directly regulates how goods, services and labor may be used, priced, or distributed, rather than relying on the mechanism of private ownership. Advocates of a free market traditionally consider the term to imply that the means of production is under private, not state control as well.

Chapter 14. Economic Policy

Individualism	Individualism is the moral stance, political philosophy, ideology, or social outlook that stresses "the moral worth of the individual". Individualists promote the exercise of one's goals and desires and so independence and self-reliance while opposing most external interference upon one's own interests, whether by society, family or any other group or institution.
	Individualism makes the individual its focus and so it starts "with the fundamental premise that the human individual is of primary importance in the struggle for liberation." Classical liberalism (including libertarianism), existentialism and anarchism (especially individualist anarchism) are examples of movements that take the human individual as a central unit of analysis.
Market economy	A market economy is an economy based on the power of division of labor in which the prices of goods and services are determined in a free price system set by supply and demand.
	This is often contrasted with a planned economy, in which a central government can distribute services using a fixed price system. Market economies are also contrasted with mixed economy where the price system is not entirely free but under some government control or heavily regulated, which is sometimes combined with state-led economic planning that is not extensive enough to constitute a planned economy.
Property	Property is any physical or intangible entity that is owned by a person or jointly by a group of people. Depending on the nature of the property, an owner of property has the right to consume, sell, rent, mortgage, transfer, exchange or destroy their property, and/or to exclude others from doing these things. Important widely recognized types of property include real property personal property private property public property and intellectual property., although the latter is not always as widely recognized or enforced.
Policy	A policy is typically described as a principle or rule to guide decisions and achieve rational outcome(s). The term is not normally used to denote what is actually done, this is normally referred to as either procedure or protocol. Whereas a policy will contain the 'what' and the 'why', procedures or protocols contain the 'what', the 'how', the 'where', and the 'when'.

Chapter 14. Economic Policy

Publics	Publics are small groups of people who follow one or more particular issue very closely. They are well informed about the issue(s) and also have a very strong opinion on it/them. They tend to know more about politics than the average person, and, therefore, exert more influence, because these people care so deeply about their cause(s) that they donate much time and money.
Domestic policy	Domestic policy, presents decisions, laws, and programs made by the government which are directly related to issues in the country. Domestic policy is the set of laws and regulations that a government establishes within a nation's borders. It differs from foreign policy, which refers to the ways a government advances its interests in world politics.
Congress	A congress is a formal meeting of the representatives of different nations, constituent states, independent organizations (such as trade unions), or groups. The term was chosen for the United States Congress to emphasize the status of each state represented there as a self-governing unit. Subsequent to the use of congress by the U.S. legislature, the term has been incorrectly adopted by many states within unions, and by unitary nation-states in the Americas, to refer to their legislatures.
Continental Congress	The Continental Congress was a convention of delegates called together from the Thirteen Colonies that became the governing body of the United States during the American Revolution. The Congress met from 1774 to 1789 in three incarnations. The first call for a convention was made over issues of mounting taxation without representation in Parliament and because of the British blockade.
Stamp Act	A stamp act is a law enacted by government that requires a tax to be paid on the transfer of certain documents. The stamp act was considered unfair by many people. Those that pay the tax receive an official stamp on their documents.

Chapter 14. Economic Policy

Contract	In the Conflict of Laws, the validity of a contract with one or more foreign law elements will be decided by reference to the so-called "proper law" of the contract. History Until the middle of the 19th century, the courts applied the lex loci contractus or the law of the place where the contract was made to decide whether the given contract was valid. The apparent advantage of this approach was that the rule was easy to apply with certain and predictable outcomes.
Force	In the field of law, the word force has two main meanings: unlawful violence and lawful compulsion. "Forced entry" is an expression falling under the category of unlawful violence; "in force" or "forced sale" would be examples of expressions in the category of lawful compulsion. When something is said to have been done "by force", it usually implies that it was done by actual or threatened violence ("might"), not necessarily by legal authority ("right").
Labor force	Overview In economics, the people in the labor force is all the nonmilitary people who are officially employed or unemployed. Normally, the labor force of a country (or other geographic entity) consists of everyone of working age (typically above a certain age (around 14 to 16) and below retirement (around 65) who are participating workers, that is people actively employed or seeking employment. People not counted include students, retired people, stay-at-home parents, people in prisons or similar institutions, people employed in jobs or professions with unreported income, as well as discouraged workers who cannot find work.

Chapter 14. Economic Policy

Public good	In economics, a public good is a good that is nonrival and non-excludable. Non-rivalry means that consumption of the good by one individual does not reduce availability of the good for consumption by others; and non-excludability that no one can be effectively excluded from using the good. In the real world, there may be no such thing as an absolutely non-rivaled and non-excludable good; but economists think that some goods approximate the concept closely enough for the analysis to be economically useful.
Executive	Executive branch of government is the part of government that has sole authority and responsibility for the daily administration of the state bureaucracy. The division of power into separate branches of government is central to the democratic idea of the separation of powers. In many countries, the term "government" connotes only the executive branch.
Executive order	An executive order in the United States is an order issued by the President, the head of the executive branch of the federal government.
Medicare	Medicare is a social insurance program administered by the United States government, providing health insurance coverage to people who are aged 65 and over, or who meet other special criteria. Medicare operates similar to a single-payer health care system, but the key difference is that its coverage only extends to 80% of any given medical cost; the remaining 20% of cost must be paid by other means, such as privately-held supplemental insurance, or paid by the patient. The program also funds residency training programs for the vast majority of physicians in the United States.
State	Many sovereign independent state are made up of a number of country subdivisions also called states. In some cases, such as the United States, the national government arose from a union of sovereign entities, which transferred some of their powers to the national government, while retaining the remainder of their sovereignty. These are sometimes called federal states.

Chapter 14. Economic Policy

United States	The United States of America (also referred to as the United States, the U.S., the USA, or America) is a federal constitutional republic comprising fifty states and a federal district. The country is situated mostly in central North America, where its forty-eight contiguous states and Washington, D.C., the capital district, lie between the Pacific and Atlantic Oceans, bordered by Canada to the north and Mexico to the south. The state of Alaska is in the northwest of the continent, with Canada to the east and Russia to the west across the Bering Strait.
Asset	In information security, computer security and network security an Asset is any data, device, or other component of the environment that supports information-related activities. Assets generally include hardware (eg. servers and switches), software (eg.
Corporation	In feudal Europe, corporations were aggregations of business interests in compact, usually with an explicit license from city, church, or national leaders. These functioned as effective monopolies for a particular good or labor. The term "corporation" was used as late as the 18th century in England to refer to such ventures as the East India Company or the Hudson's Bay Company: commercial organizations that operated under royal patent to have exclusive rights to a particular area of trade.
General	General, Finnish: kenraali is the highest officer's rank in Sweden and Finland. In Sweden, it is held by the supreme commander of the Swedish Armed Forces and the monarch. In Finland, it is held by the Chief of Defence.
Tarpaulin	A tarpaulin, is a large sheet of strong, flexible, water-resistant or waterproof material, often cloth such as canvas or polyester coated with urethane, or made of plastics such as polyethylene. In some places such as Australia, and in military slang, a tarp may be known as a hootch. Tarpaulins often have reinforced grommets at the corners and along the sides to form attachment points for rope, allowing them to be tied down or suspended.
Bankruptcy	Bankruptcy is a legally declared inability or impairment of ability of an individual or organization to pay its creditors. Creditors may file a bankruptcy petition against a business or corporate debtor ("involuntary bankruptcy") in an effort to recoup a portion of what they are owed or initiate a restructuring. In the majority of cases, however, bankruptcy is initiated by the debtor (a "voluntary bankruptcy" that is filed by the insolvent individual or organization).

Chapter 14. Economic Policy

Stimulus	In economics, stimulus refers to attempts to use monetary or fiscal policy (or stabilization policy in general) to stimulate the economy. Recently "stimulus" has become particularly associated with Keynesian economics and the theory that government spending projects can generate economic growth in a recession. Stimulus can also refer to monetary policies like lowering interest rates and quantitative easing.
Administration	Administration, as a legal concept, is a procedure under the insolvency laws of a number of common law jurisdictions. It functions as a rescue mechanism for insolvent companies and allows them to carry on running their business. The process - an alternative to liquidation - is often known as going into administration.
Regent	A regent is a person selected to act as head of state (ruling or not) because the ruler is a minor, not present, or debilitated. In a monarchy, a regent usually governs due to one of these reasons, but may also be elected to rule during the interregnum when the royal line has died out. This was the case in Finland and Hungary, where the royal line was considered extinct in the aftermath of World War I. In Iceland, the regent represented the King of Denmark as sovereign of Iceland until the country became a republic in 1944.
Regulation	Regulation is "controlling human or societal behavior by rules or restrictions." Regulation can take many forms: legal restrictions promulgated by a government authority, self-regulation by an industry such as through a trade association, social regulation co-regulation and market regulation. One can consider regulation as actions of conduct imposing sanctions (such as a fine). This action of administrative law, or implementing regulatory law, may be contrasted with statutory or case law.
Canada	Canada was the name of the French colony that once stretched along the St. Lawrence River; the other colonies of New France were Acadia, Louisiana and Newfoundland. Canada, the most developed colony of New France, was divided into three districts, each with its own government: Québec, Trois-Rivières, and Montréal. The governor of the district of Québec was also the governor-general of all of New France.
Mandate	In politics, a mandate is the authority granted by a constituency to act as its representative.

Chapter 14. Economic Policy

	The concept of a government having a legitimate mandate to govern via the fair winning of a democratic election is a central idea of democracy. New governments who attempt to introduce policies that they did not make public during an election campaign are said to not have a legitimate mandate to implement such policies.
Monitor	Monitor, is a non-departmental public body in the United Kingdom. Its purpose is to regulate NHS Foundation Trusts or Foundation Hospitals - hospitals that have opted out of direct governmental control. The body was established under the Health and Social Care (Community Health and Standards) Act 2003.
Homosexuality	Homosexuality is romantic and/or sexual attraction or behavior among members of the same sex or gender. As a sexual orientation, homosexuality refers to "an enduring pattern of or disposition to experience sexual, affectional, or romantic attractions" primarily or exclusively to people of the same sex; "it also refers to an individual's sense of personal and social identity based on those attractions, behaviors expressing them, and membership in a community of others who share them."
	Homosexuality is one of the three main categories of sexual orientation, along with bisexuality and heterosexuality, within the heterosexual-homosexual continuum. The consensus of the behavioral and social sciences and the health and mental health professions is that homosexuality is a normal and positive variation in human sexual orientation, though many religious societies, including Catholicism, Mormonism, and Islam, and some psychological associations, such as NARTH, teach that homosexual activity is sinful or dysfunctional.
Terrorism	Terrorism is the systematic use of terror especially as a means of coercion. No universally agreed, legally binding, criminal law definition of terrorism currently exists. Common definitions of terrorism refer only to those violent acts which are intended to create fear (terror), are perpetrated for a religious, political or ideological goal, deliberately target or disregard the safety of non-combatants (civilians), and are committed by non-government agencies.
Commission	A commission is a physical document issued to certify the appointment of a commissioned officer by a sovereign power.

Chapter 14. Economic Policy

The more specific terms commissioning parchment or commissioning scroll are often used to avoid ambiguity, due to "commission" being a homonym which directs the individual in carrying out their duty regardless of what authority or responsibility they may have at any time. However the document is not usually in the form of a scroll and is more often printed on paper instead of parchment.

Foundation	A foundation in the United States is a type of charitable organization. However, the Internal Revenue Code distinguishes between private foundations (usually funded by an individual, family, or corporation) and public charities (community foundations and other nonprofit groups that raise money from the general public). Private foundations have more restrictions and fewer tax benefits than public charities like community foundations.
Internets	"Internets" is a Bushism-turned-catchphrase used humorously to portray the speaker as ignorant about the Internet or about technology in general, or as having a provincial or folksy attitude toward technology. Former United States President George W. Bush first used the word publicly during the 2000 election campaign. The term gained cachet as an Internet humor meme following Bush's use of the term in the second 2004 presidential election debate on October 8, 2004.
Keynesian economics	Keynesian economics is a macroeconomic theory based on the ideas of 20th century English economist John Maynard Keynes. Keynesian economics argues that private sector decisions sometimes lead to inefficient macroeconomic outcomes and therefore advocates active policy responses by the public sector, including monetary policy actions by the central bank and fiscal policy actions by the government to stabilize output over the business cycle. The theories forming the basis of Keynesian economics were first presented in The General Theory of Employment, Interest and Money, published in 1936; the interpretations of Keynes are contentious, and several schools of thought claim his legacy.
New Deal	The New Deal is a programme of active labour market policies introduced in the United Kingdom by the Labour government in 1998, initially funded by a one off £5bn windfall tax on privatised utility companies. The stated purpose is to reduce unemployment by providing training, subsidised employment and voluntary work to the unemployed. Spending on the New Deal was £1.3 billion in 2001.

Chapter 14. Economic Policy

Reform Act	In the United Kingdom, Reform Act is a generic term used for legislation concerning electoral matters. It is most commonly used for laws passed to enfranchise new groups of voters and to redistribute seats in the British House of Commons. The periodic redrawing of constituency boundaries is now dealt with by a permanent Boundary Commission in each part of the United Kingdom, rather than by a Reform Act.
Unfunded mandate	In United States law and politics, unfunded mandates are regulations or conditions for receiving grants that impose costs on state or local governments or private entities for which they are not reimbursed by the federal government. • Any one of many federal legislations such as the Clean Air Act, and the Clean Water Act that require programs to be sponsored by the governments of the states, without providing any funds for those programs. • The provisions in the Americans with Disabilities Act that require nearly all American business owners to make their business premises available to disabled customers without providing any funds for the cost of reconstruction or additional interior space. • The provisions in the Emergency Medical Treatment and Active Labor Act that require nearly all American emergency rooms to accept and stabilize any patient regardless of the patient's ability to pay, but do not provide adequate reimbursement for indigent patients.
Eminent domain	Eminent domain compulsory purchase (United Kingdom, New Zealand, Ireland), resumption/compulsory acquisition (Australia) or expropriation (South Africa and Canada) is an action of the state to seize a citizen's private property, expropriate property, or seize a citizen's rights in property with due monetary compensation, but without the owner's consent. The property is taken either for government use or by delegation to third parties who will devote it to public or civic use or, in some cases, economic development. The most common uses of property taken by eminent domain are for public utilities, highways, and railroads, however it may also be taken for reasons of public safety, such as in the case of Centralia, Pennsylvania.
Interest	Interest is a fee paid on borrowed assets. It is the price paid for the use of borrowed money, or, money earned by deposited funds. Assets that are sometimes lent with interest include money, shares, consumer goods through hire purchase, major assets such as aircraft, and even entire factories in finance lease arrangements.

Chapter 14. Economic Policy

Rates	Rates are a type of taxation system in the United Kingdom, and in places with systems deriving from the British one, the proceeds of which are used to fund local government. Some other countries have taxes with a more or less comparable role, for example France's taxe d'habitation. Rates by country Hong Kong In Hong Kong, rates on property is based on the nominal rental value of the property.
Federal Reserve System	The Federal Reserve System is the central banking system of the United States. It was created in 1913 with the enactment of the Federal Reserve Act, largely in response to a series of financial panics, particularly a severe panic in 1907. Over time, the roles and responsibilities of the Federal Reserve System have expanded and its structure has evolved. Events such as the Great Depression were major factors leading to changes in the system.
Redistricting	Redistricting, a form of redistribution, is the process of drawing United States district lines. This often means changing electoral district and constituency boundaries in response to periodic census results. In 36 states, the state legislature has primary responsibility for creating a redistricting plan, in many cases subject to approval by the state governor.
Tariff	A tariff is a tax levied on imports or exports. History Tariffs are usually associated with protectionism, a government's policy of controlling trade between nations to support the interests of its own citizens. For economic reasons, tariffs are usually imposed on imported goods.

Chapter 14. Economic Policy

Adjustment	In law, the term adjustment may appear in varied contexts, as a synonym for terms with unrelated definitions: General Definition Adjust: 1. To settle or to bring to a satisfactory state, so that the parties are agreed in the result; as, to adjust accounts. 2. When applied to a liquidated demand, the verb "adjust" has the same meaning as the word "settle" in the same connection, and means to pay the demand. When applied to an unliquidated demand, it means to ascertain the amount due or to settle. In the latter connection, to settle means to effect a mutual adjustment between the parties and to agree upon the balance. Common Uses General Debt - Debtor and creditor adjustment: As the term appears in an assignment for the benefit of creditors, "Creditor" means one who has a definite demand against the assignor, or a cause of action capable of adjustment and liquidation at trial. 6 Am J2d Assign for Crs § 109. - Adjustable Rate Loan: Loan arrangement which permits the lender to change the interest rate based on a specific factor such as the prime lending rate charged by banks. - Adjusting agency: In one sense, a collection agency; in another sense, an agency representing a debtor in making an arrangement with his creditors for the settlement of his obligations by modification of the indebtedness.
Ensign	Ensign is a junior rank of commissioned officer in the armed forces of some countries, normally in the infantry or navy. As the junior officer in an infantry regiment was traditionally the carrier of the ensign flag, the rank itself acquired the name. The Spanish alférez and Portuguese alferes is a junior officer rank below lieutenant associated with carrying the flag, and so is often translated as "ensign".

Chapter 14. Economic Policy

Rescue	Rescue refers to operations that usually involve the saving of life, or prevention of injury.
	Tools used might include search dogs, search and rescue horses, helicopters, the "Jaws of Life", and other hydraulic cutting and spreading tools used to extricate individuals from wrecked vehicles. Rescue operations are sometimes supported by special vehicles such as fire department's or EMS Heavy rescue vehicle.
Abortion	Abortion is the termination of a pregnancy by the removal or expulsion of a fetus or embryo from the uterus, resulting in or caused by its death. An abortion can occur spontaneously due to complications during pregnancy or can be induced, in humans and other species. In the context of human pregnancies, an abortion induced to preserve the health of the gravida (pregnant female) is termed a therapeutic abortion, while an abortion induced for any other reason is termed an elective abortion.
Attack	In computer and computer networks an attack is any attempt to destroy, expose, alter, disable, steal or gain unauthorized access to or make unauthorized use of an asset.
	Definitions
	IETF
	Internet Engineering Task Force defines attack in RFC 2828 as:
	US Government
	CNSS Instruction No. 4009 dated 26 April 2010 by Committee on National Security Systems of United States of America defines an attack as:
	The increasing dependencies of modern society on information and computers networks (both in private and public sectors, including military) has led to new terms like cyber attack and Cyberwarfare.

Chapter 14. Economic Policy

	CNSS Instruction No. 4009 define a cyber attack as:
	
	Phenomenology
	
	An attack can be active or passive.
	
	An attack can be perpetrated by an insider or from outside the organization;
	
	    An "inside attack" is an attack initiated by an entity inside the security perimeter (an "insider"), i.e., an entity that is authorized to access system resources but uses them in a way not approved by those who granted the authorization.
	    An "outside attack" is initiated from outside the perimeter, by an unauthorized or illegitimate user of the system (an "outsider").

Identity	Identity is an umbrella term used throughout the social sciences to describe a person's conception and expression of their individuality or group affiliations (such as national identity and cultural identity). The term is used more specifically in psychology and sociology, including the two forms of social psychology. The term is also used with respect to place identity.
Minimum wage	A minimum wage is the lowest hourly, daily or monthly wage that employers may legally pay to employees or workers. Equivalently, it is the lowest wage at which workers may sell their labor. Although minimum wage laws are in effect in a great many jurisdictions, there are differences of opinion about the benefits and drawbacks of a minimum wage.
Strike	Strike is a 1925 silent film made in the Soviet Union by Sergei Eisenstein. It was Eisenstein's first full-length feature film, and he would go on to make The Battleship Potemkin later that year. It was acted by the Proletcult Theatre, and composed of six parts.
Consumer product	A consumer product is generally any tangible personal property for sale and that is used for personal, family, or household for non-business purposes. The determination whether a good is a consumer product requires a factual finding, on a case-by-case basis. This basis will vary from one jurisdiction to another.

Chapter 14. Economic Policy

Recall	Recall is a bugle call used to signals to soldiers that duties or drills are to cease, or to indicate that a period of relaxation should end. Outside of a military context, it is used to signal when a game should end, such as a game of capture the flag among scouts. History Like other bugle calls, "recall" is a short tune that originated as a military signal announcing scheduled and certain non-scheduled events on a military installation, battlefield, or ship.
Capitalism	Capitalism is an economic system in which the means of production are privately owned and operated for a private profit; decisions regarding supply, demand, price, distribution, and investments are made by private actors in the free market; profit is distributed to owners who choose to invest in businesses, and wages are paid to workers employed by businesses and companies. There is no consensus on the precise definition of capitalism, nor how the term should be used as an analytical category. There is, however, little controversy that private ownership of the means of production, creation of goods or services for profit in a market, and prices and wages are elements of capitalism.
Laissez-faire	In economics, laissez-faire describes an environment in which transactions between private parties are free from state intervention, including restrictive regulations, taxes, tariffs and enforced monopolies. The phrase laissez-faire is French and literally means "let do", but it broadly implies "let it be", or "leave it alone." Origins of the phrase

Chapter 14. Economic Policy

	According to historical legend, the phrase stems from a meeting in about 1680 between the powerful French finance minister Jean-Baptiste Colbert and a group of French businessmen led by a certain M. Le Gendre. When the eager mercantilist minister asked how the French state could be of service to the merchants and help promote their commerce, Le Gendre replied simply "Laissez-nous faire" ("Leave us be", lit.
ARTHUR	ARTHUR is an abbreviation for mobile "Artillery Hunting Radar" system developed in Sweden. This field artillery acquisition radar was developed for the primary role as the core element of a brigade or division level counter battery sensor system. It can also be used for peace support operations.
Implementation	Implementation is the realization of an application, or execution of a plan, idea, model, design, specification, standard, algorithm, or policy. Computer Science In computer science, an implementation is a realization of a technical specification or algorithm as a program, software component, or other computer system through programming and deployment. Many implementations may exist for a given specification or standard.
Hamilton	Hamilton is a former New Zealand Parliamentary electorate, which was replaced by Hamilton East and Hamilton West electorates. Population centres The electorate was mainly urban, covering the city of Hamilton. History The Hamilton electorate dates from 1922. In 1969 it was renamed Hamilton West.

Chapter 14. Economic Policy

Alexander Hamilton	Alexander Hamilton was a Scottish sea captain, privateer and merchant.
Creative Commons	Creative Commons is a non-profit organization headquartered in San Francisco, California, United States devoted to expanding the range of creative works available for others to build upon legally and to share. The organization has released several copyright-licenses known as Creative Commons licenses free of charge to the public. These licenses allow creators to communicate which rights they reserve, and which rights they waive for the benefit of recipients or other creators.
Disabilities	Disabilities were legal restrictions and limitations placed on Jews in the Middle Ages. They included provisions requiring Jews to wear specific and identifying clothing such as the Jewish hat and the yellow badge, restricting Jews to certain cities and towns or in certain parts of towns (ghettos), and forbidding Jews to enter certain trades. Disabilities also included special taxes levied on Jews, exclusion from public life, and restraints on the performance of religious ceremonies.
Federal Reserve System	The Federal Reserve System is the central banking system of the United States. It was created in 1913 with the enactment of the Federal Reserve Act, largely in response to a series of financial panics, particularly a severe panic in 1907. Over time, the roles and responsibilities of the Federal Reserve System have expanded and its structure has evolved. Events such as the Great Depression were major factors leading to changes in the system.
Rights	Rights are legal, social, or ethical principles of freedom or entitlement; that is, rights are the fundamental normative rules about what is allowed of people or owed to people, according to some legal system, social convention, or ethical theory. Rights are of essential importance in such disciplines as law and ethics, especially theories of justice and deontology. Rights are often considered fundamental to civilization, being regarded as established pillars of society and culture, and the history of social conflicts can be found in the history of each right and its development.
Credit	Credit is the trust which allows one party to provide resources to another party where that second party does not reimburse the first party immediately (thereby generating a debt), but instead arranges either to repay or return those resources (or other materials of equal value) at a later date. The resources provided may be financial (e.g. granting a loan), or they may consist of goods or services (e.g. consumer credit). Credit encompasses any form of deferred payment.

Chapter 14. Economic Policy

Insurance	In law and economics, insurance is a form of risk management primarily used to hedge against the risk of a contingent, uncertain loss. Insurance is defined as the equitable transfer of the risk of a loss, from one entity to another, in exchange for payment. An insurer is a company selling the insurance; an insured, or policyholder, is the person or entity buying the insurance policy.
Senate	A senate is a deliberative assembly, often the upper house or chamber of a legislature or parliament. There have been many such bodies in history, since senate means the assembly of the eldest and wiser members of the society and ruling class. Two of the first official senates were the Spartan Gerousia (Γερουσ?α) and the Roman Senate.
Speaker	The term speaker is a title often given to the presiding officer (chair) of a deliberative assembly, especially a legislative body. The speaker's official role is to moderate debate, make rulings on procedure, announce the results of votes, and the like. The speaker decides who may speak and has the powers to discipline members who break the procedures of the house.
Hundred Days	The Hundred Days, marked the period between Emperor Napoleon I of France's return from exile on Elba to Paris on 20 March 1815 and the second restoration of King Louis XVIII on 8 July 1815 (a period of 111 days). This period saw the War of the Seventh Coalition, and includes the Waterloo Campaign and the Neapolitan War. The phrase les Cent Jours was first used by the prefect of Paris, Gaspard, comte de Chabrol, in his speech welcoming the King.
Bailout	In economics, a bailout is an act of loaning or giving capital to an entity (a company, a country, or an individual) that is in danger of failing, in an attempt to save it from bankruptcy, insolvency, or total liquidation and ruin; or to allow a failing entity to fail gracefully without spreading contagion. Overview

Chapter 14. Economic Policy

	A bailout could be done for mere profit, as when a predatory investor resurrects a floundering company by buying its shares at fire-sale prices; for social improvement, as when, hypothetically speaking, a wealthy philanthropist reinvents an unprofitable fast food company into a non-profit food distribution network; or the bailout of a company might be seen as a necessity in order to prevent greater, socioeconomic failures: For example, the US government assumes transportation to be the backbone of America's general economic fluency, which maintains the nation's geopolitical power. As such, it is the policy of the US government to protect the biggest American companies responsible for transportation--airliners, petrol companies, etc.--from failure through subsidies and low-interest loans.
Economic policy	Economic policy refers to the actions that governments take in the economic field. It covers the systems for setting interest rates and government budget as well as the labour market, national ownership, and many other areas of government interventions into the economy.
	Such policies are often influenced by international institutions like the International Monetary Fund or World Bank as well as political beliefs and the consequent policies of parties.
Excise	An excise is commonly understood to refer to an inland tax on the sale, or production for sale, of specific goods; or, more narrowly, as a tax on a good produced for sale, or sold, within a country. An excise tax is one levied on specific goods or commodities produced or sold within a country, or on licenses granted for specific activities. Excises are distinguished from customs duties, which are taxes on importation.
Government	In the social sciences, the term government refers to the particular group of people, the administrative bureaucracy, who control a state at a given time, and the manner in which their governing organizations are structured. That is, governments are the means through which state power is employed. States are served by a continuous succession of different governments.
Institution	An institution is any structure or mechanism of social order and cooperation governing the behavior of a set of individuals within a given human community. Institutions are identified with a social purpose and permanence, transcending individual human lives and intentions, and with the making and enforcing of rules governing cooperative human behavior.

Chapter 14. Economic Policy

	The term "institution" is commonly applied to customs and behavior patterns important to a society, as well as to particular formal organizations of government and public service.
Tax cut	A tax cut is a reduction in taxes. The immediate effects of a tax cut are a decrease in the real income of the government and an increase in the real income of those whose tax rate has been lowered. In the longer term, however, the loss of government income may be mitigated, depending on the response that tax-payers make.
Poland	Poland officially the Republic of Poland - is a country in Central Europe bordered by Germany to the west; the Czech Republic and Slovakia to the south; Ukraine, Belarus and Lithuania to the east; and the Baltic Sea and Kaliningrad Oblast, a Russian exclave, to the north. The total area of Poland is 312,679 square kilometres (120,726 sq mi), making it the 69th largest country in the world and the 9th largest in Europe. Poland has a population of over 38 million people, which makes it the 34th most populous country in the world and the sixth most populous member of the European Union, being its most populous post-communist member.
Progressive Republicans	The Progressive Republicans were a French parliamentary group in the Chamber of Deputies of France during the first half of the French Third Republic. The Progressives were in fact the most conservative members of the Chamber, and most later went on the form the Republican Federation.
Rebellion	Rebellion is a refusal of obedience or order. It may, therefore, be seen as encompassing a range of behaviors from civil disobedience and mass nonviolent resistance, to violent and organized attempts to destroy an established authority such as a government. Those who participate in rebellions are known as "rebels".
Loophole	A loophole is a weakness or exception that allows a system, such as a law or security, to be circumvented or otherwise avoided. Loopholes are searched for and used strategically in a variety of circumstances, including taxes, elections, politics, the criminal justice system, or in breaches of security.
	Historically, Arrow Slits were narrow vertical windows from which castle defenders launched arrows from a sheltered position.

Chapter 14. Economic Policy

Redistribution	The term redistribution is used in Australia to mean a redrawing of electoral boundaries. It is equivalent to the term redistricting in the United States.
	In the House of Representatives each State and Territory is divided into electoral divisions.
Sale	Sale was an ancient Greek city located in Thrace, located in the region between the river Nestos to the river Hebros.
Sales tax	A sales tax is a consumption tax charged at the point of purchase for certain goods and services. The tax amount is usually calculated by applying a percentage rate to the taxable price of a sale. A portion of the sale may be exempt from the calculation of tax, because sales tax laws usually contain a list of exemptions.
Tax law	Tax law is the codified system of laws that describes government levies on economic transactions, commonly called taxes. Major issues Primary taxation issues facing the governments world over include; - taxes on income and wealth (or estates) - taxation of capital gains Tax education from law schools In law schools, "tax law" is a sub-discipline and area of specialist study. Tax law specialists are often employed in consultative roles, and may also be involved in litigation.
Democrats	The Democrats is a centre-right political party in Brazil, considered the main in the right-wing spectrum. Despite its former name (Liberal Front Party), the party affiliates itself to the Centrist Democrat International, and the International Democrat Union. The name comes from its support to free market policies.

Chapter 14. Economic Policy

Southern Democrats	Southern Democrats are members of the U.S. Democratic Party who reside in the American South. In the early 19th century, they were the definitive pro-slavery wing of the party, opposed to both the anti-slavery Republicans (GOP) and the more liberal Northern Democrats. Eventually "Redemption" was finalized in the Compromise of 1877 and the Redeemers gained control throughout the South.
Deficit	A deficit is the amount by which a sum of money falls short of the required amount. Primary deficit, total deficit, and debt A government's deficit can be measured with or without including the interest it pays on its debt. The primary deficit is defined as the difference between current government spending and total current revenue from all types of taxes.
Government spending	Government spending is classified by economists into three main types. Government acquisition of goods and services for current use to directly satisfy individual or collective needs of the members of the community is classed as government final consumption expenditure. Government acquisition of goods and services intended to create future benefits, such as infrastructure investment or research spending, is classed as government investment (gross fixed capital formation), which usually is the largest part of the government gross capital formation.
Congressional Budget Office	The Congressional Budget Office is a federal agency within the legislative branch of the United States government. It is a government agency that provides economic data to Congress. The Congressional Budget Office was created as a nonpartisan agency by the Congressional Budget and Impoundment Control Act of 1974.
Office of Management and Budget	The Office of Management and Budget is a Cabinet-level office, and is the largest office within the Executive Office of the President of the United States (EOP).

Chapter 14. Economic Policy

The current OMB Director is Jacob Lew.

History

The Bureau of the Budget, OMB's predecessor, was established as a part of the Department of the Treasury by the Budget and Accounting Act of 1921, which was signed into law by President Warren G. Harding.

Discretionary spending	Discretionary spending is a spending category about which government planners can make choices. It refers to spending set on a yearly basis by decision of Congress and is part of fiscal policy. This spending is optional, in contrast to entitlement programs for which funding is mandatory.
Mandatory spending	In economics, mandatory spending is spending on certain programs that is mandated, or required, by existing law.
	In the United States, mandatory spending refers to budget authority and ensuing outlays provided in laws other than appropriations acts, including annually appropriated entitlements. For example, nearly three-fourths of USDA spending is classified as mandatory (or appropriated entitlement) spending, including the farm commodity price and income support programs, crop insurance, food stamps and child nutrition programs.
Justice	Justice was the weekly newspaper of the Social Democratic Federation (SDF) in the United Kingdom.
	The SDF had been known until January 1884 as the Democratic Federation. With the change of name, the organisation launched the paper.

Chapter 14. Economic Policy

Federal government	A federal government is the common government of a federation. The structure of federal governments varies from institution to institution. Based on a broad definition of a basic federal political system, there are two or more levels of government that exist within an established territory and govern through common institutions with overlapping or shared powers as prescribed by a constitution.
Power	Power is a measure of an entity's ability to control its environment, including the behavior of other entities. The term authority is often used for power, perceived as legitimate by the social structure. Power can be seen as evil or unjust, but the exercise of power is accepted as endemic to humans as social beings.
Environmental protection	Environmental protection is a practice of protecting the environment, on individual, organizational or governmental level, for the benefit of the natural environment and (or) humans. Due to the pressures of population and our technology the biophysical environment is being degraded, sometimes permanently. This has been recognized and governments began placing restraints on activities that caused environmental degradation.
Environmental Protection Agency	The Environmental Protection Agency (Irish: An Ghníomhaireacht um Chaomhnú Comhshaoil) has responsibilities for a wide range of licensing, enforcement, monitoring and assessment activities associated with environmental protection.
Federalist	The term federalist describes several political beliefs around the world. Also, it may refer to the concept of federalism or the type of government called a federation. In early United States history, the Federalist Party was one of the first political parties; its members or supporters called themselves Federalists.
Health administration	Health administration is the field relating to leadership, management, and administration of hospitals, hospital networks, and health care systems. Health care administrators are considered health care professionals.
	The discipline is known by many names, including health management, healthcare management, health systems management, health care systems management, and medical and health services management.

Chapter 14. Economic Policy

Desegregation	Desegregation is the process of ending the separation of two groups usually referring to races. This is most commonly used in reference to the United States. Desegregation was long a focus of the American Civil Rights Movement, both before and after the United States Supreme Court's decision in Brown v. Board of Education, particularly desegregation of the school systems and the military .
Discrimination	Discrimination is the cognitive and sensory capacity or ability to see fine distinctions and perceive differences between objects, subjects, concepts and patterns, or possess exceptional development of the senses. Used in this way to identify exceptional discernment since the 17th century, the term begun to be used as an expression of derogatory racial prejudice from the 1830s Thomas D. Rice's performances as "Jim Crow".
	Since the American Civil War the term 'discrimination' generally evolved in American English usage as an understanding of prejudicial treatment of an individual based solely on their race, later generalized as membership in a certain socially undesirable group or social category.
Trusts	In Conflict of Laws, the Hague Convention on the Law Applicable to Trusts and on Their Recognition was concluded on 1 July 1985 and entered into force 1 January 1992. The Convention aims to harmonise not only the municipal law definitions of a trust both within the USA and outside the USA, but also the Conflict rules for resolving problems in the choice of the lex causae.
	Explanation
	Many states do not have a developed law of trusts, or the principles differ significantly between states. It was therefore necessary for the Hague Convention to define a trust to indicate the range of legal transactions regulated by the Convention and, perhaps more significantly, the range of applications not regulated.

Chapter 14. Economic Policy

Enron	Enron Corporation (former NYSE ticker symbol ENE) was an American energy, commodities, and services company based in Houston, Texas. Before its bankruptcy in late 2001, Enron employed approximately 22,000 staff and was one of the world's leading electricity, natural gas, communications, and pulp and paper companies, with claimed revenues of nearly $101 billion in 2000. Fortune named Enron "America's Most Innovative Company" for six consecutive years. At the end of 2001, it was revealed that its reported financial condition was sustained substantially by institutionalized, systematic, and creatively planned accounting fraud, known as the "Enron scandal".
Deregulation	Deregulation is the removal or simplification of government rules and regulations that constrain the operation of market forces. Deregulation does not mean elimination of laws against fraud, but eliminating or reducing government control of how business is done, thereby moving toward a more laissez-faire, free market. It is different from liberalization, where more players enter in the market, but continues the regulation and guarantee of consumer rights and maximum and minimum prices.
Cold War	The Cold War was the continuing state of political conflict, military tension, proxy wars, and economic competition existing after World War II (1939-1945) between the Communist World - primarily the Soviet Union and its satellite states and allies - and the powers of the Western world, primarily the United States and its allies. Although the primary participants' military force never officially clashed directly, they expressed the conflict through military coalitions, strategic conventional force deployments, extensive aid to states deemed vulnerable, proxy wars, espionage, propaganda, conventional and nuclear arms races, appeals to neutral nations, rivalry at sports events, and technological competitions such as the Space Race. Despite being allies against the Axis powers, the USSR and the US disagreed about political philosophy and the configuration of the post-war world while occupying most of Europe.
Public health	Public health is "the science and art of preventing disease, prolonging life and promoting health through the organized efforts and informed choices of society, organizations, public and private, communities and individuals" (1920, C.E.A. Winslow). It is concerned with threats to the overall health of a community based on population health analysis. The population in question can be as small as a handful of people or as large as all the inhabitants of several continents (for instance, in the case of a pandemic).

Chapter 14. Economic Policy

Reconciliation	Reconciliation is a legislative process of the United States Senate intended to allow consideration of a budget bill with debate limited to twenty hours under Senate Rules. Reconciliation also exists in the United States House of Representatives, but because the House regularly passes rules that constrain debate and amendment, the process has had a less significant impact on that body. A reconciliation instruction (Budget Reconciliation) is a provision in a budget resolution directing one or more committees to submit legislation changing existing law in order to bring spending, revenues, or the debt-limit into conformity with the budget resolution.
Lobbying	Lobbying is the intention of influencing decisions made by legislators and officials in the government by individuals, other legislators, constituents, or advocacy groups. A lobbyist is a person who tries to influence legislation on behalf of a special interest or a member of a lobby. Governments often define and regulate organized group lobbying that has become influential.
Military budget	A military budget of an entity, most often a nation or a state, is the budget and financial resources dedicated to raising and maintaining armed forces for that entity. Military budgets reflect how much an entity perceives the likelihood of threats against it, or the amount of aggression it wishes to employ. It also provides an idea of how much finances could be provided for the upcoming year.
News conference	A news conference is a media event in which newsmakers invite journalists to hear them speak and, most often, ask questions. A joint press conference instead is held between two or more talking sides. Practice In a news conference, one or more speakers may make a statement, which may be followed by questions from reporters.
Public opinion	Public opinion is the aggregate of individual attitudes or beliefs held by the adult population. Public opinion can also be defined as the complex collection of opinions of many different people and the sum of all their views.

Chapter 14. Economic Policy

The principle approaches to the study of public opinion may be divided into 4 categories:

1. quantitative measurement of opinion distributions;
2. investigation of the internal relationships among the individual opinions that make up public opinion on an issue;
3. description or analysis of the public role of public opinion;
4. study both of the communication media that disseminate the ideas on which opinions are based and of the uses that propagandists and other manipulators make of these media.

Concepts of "public opinion"

Public opinion as a concept gained credence with the rise of "public" in the eighteenth century.

Earth Day	Earth Day is a day that is intended to inspire awareness and appreciation for the Earth's natural environment. Earth Day was founded by United States Senator Gaylord Nelson as an environmental teach-in first held on April 22, 1970. While this first Earth Day was focused on the United States, an organization launched by Denis Hayes, who was the original national coordinator in 1970, took it international in 1990 and organized events in 141 nations. Earth Day is now coordinated globally by the Earth Day Network, and is celebrated in more than 175 countries every year.
Environmental policy	Environmental policy is any [course of] action deliberately taken [or not taken] to manage human activities with a view to prevent, reduce, or mitigate harmful effects on nature and natural resources, and ensuring that man-made changes to the environment do not have harmful effects on humans.
	It is useful to consider that environmental policy comprises two major terms: environment and policy. Environment primarily refers to the ecological dimension (ecosystems), but can also take account of social dimension (quality of life) and an economic dimension (resource management).

Chapter 14. Economic Policy

Henry	Saint Henry was a medieval Swedish clergyman. According to legends, he conquered Finland together with King Eric the Saint of Sweden and died as a martyr, becoming a central figure in the local Roman Catholic Church. However, the authenticity of the accounts of his life, ministry, and death are widely disputed.
National Park Service	The National Park Service is the U.S. federal agency that manages all national parks, many national monuments, and other conservation and historical properties with various title designations. It was created on August 25, 1916, by Congress through the National Park Service Organic Act.
	It is an agency of the United States Department of the Interior, a federal executive department whose head, the Secretary of the Interior, is a Cabinet officer nominated by the President and confirmed by the Senate.
Global warming	Global warming is the increase in the average temperature of Earth's near-surface air and oceans since the mid-20th century and its projected continuation. According to the 2007 Fourth Assessment Report by the Intergovernmental Panel on Climate Change (IPCC), global surface temperature increased 0.74 ± 0.18 °C (1.33 ± 0.32 °F) during the 20th century.[A] Most of the observed temperature increase since the middle of the 20th century has been caused by increasing concentrations of greenhouse gases, which result from human activity such as the burning of fossil fuel and deforestation. Global dimming, a result of increasing concentrations of atmospheric aerosols that block sunlight from reaching the surface, has partially countered the effects of warming induced by greenhouse gases.
GREEN	Green is the only green real estate designation for REALTORs approved by the National Association of Realtors (NAR). The program was developed in 2008 by the Real Estate Buyer's Agent Council of NAR, with administration transferred to the Green Resource Council.
	The course curriculum includes sustainable building practices, marketing, and rating systems (e.g., LEED and Energy Star).
Nation	Nation has different meanings in different contexts. In worldwide diplomacy, nation can mean country or sovereign state. The United Nations, for instance, speaks of how it was founded after the Second World War with "51 countries" and currently has "192 member states".

Chapter 14. Economic Policy

United Nations	The United Nations are facilitating cooperation in international law, international security, economic development, social progress, human rights, and achievement of world peace. The United Nations was founded in 1945 after World War II to replace the League of Nations, to stop wars between countries, and to provide a platform for dialogue. It contains multiple subsidiary organizations to carry out its missions.
Impeachment	Impeachment is a formal process in which an official is accused of unlawful activity and the outcome of which, depending on the country, can lead to the removal of that official from office or other punishment. Medieval popular etymology also associated it (wrongly) with derivations from the Latin impetere (to attack). (In its more frequent and more technical usage, impeachment of a person in the role of a witness is the act of challenging the honesty or credibility of that person).
Arctic	The Arctic is a region located at the northern-most part of the Earth. It consists of the Arctic Ocean and all or parts of Canada, Russia, Greenland, the United states, Norway, Sweden, Finland and Iceland. The Arctic region consists of a vast, ice-covered ocean, surrounded by treeless permafrost.
Kyoto Protocol	The Kyoto Protocol is a protocol to the United Nations Framework Convention on Climate Change (UNFCCC or FCCC), aimed at fighting global warming. The UNFCCC is an international environmental treaty with the goal of achieving the "stabilization of greenhouse gas concentrations in the atmosphere at a level that would prevent dangerous anthropogenic interference with the climate system."
	The Protocol was initially adopted on 11 December 1997 in Kyoto, Japan, and entered into force on 16 February 2005. As of April 2010, 191 states have signed and ratified the protocol.
	Under the Protocol, 37 countries ("Annex I countries") commit themselves to a reduction of four greenhouse gases (GHG) (carbon dioxide, methane, nitrous oxide, sulphur hexafluoride) and two groups of gases (hydrofluorocarbons and perfluorocarbons) produced by them, and all member countries give general commitments.

Chapter 14. Economic Policy

Minutes	Minutes, are the instant written record of a meeting or hearing. They often give an overview of the structure of the meeting, starting with a list of those present, a statement of the various issues before the participants, and each of their responses thereto. They are often created at the moment of the hearing by a typist or court recorder at the meeting, who may record the meeting in shorthand, and then prepare the minutes and issue them to the participants afterwards.
Carbon tax	A carbon tax is an environmental tax that is levied on the carbon content of fuels. Carbon atoms are present in every fossil fuel (coal, petroleum, and natural gas) and are released as carbon dioxide (CO_2) when they are burnt. In contrast, non-combustion energy sources--wind, sunlight, hydropower, and nuclear--do not convert hydrocarbons to carbon dioxide.
Arabia	Arabia was a satrapy (province) of the Achaemenid Empire and later of the Sassanid Empire, by the name of Arabistan. Achaemenid Era Achaemenid Arabia corresponded to the lands between Egypt and Mesopotamia, known as Arabia Petraea. According to Herodotus, the Cambyses did not subdue the Arabs when he attacked Egypt in 525 BCE. His successor Darius the Great does not mention the Arabs in the Behistun inscription from the first years of his reign, but mentions them in later texts.
Hungary	Hungary, officially the Republic of Hungary is a landlocked country in Central Europe. It is situated in the Pannonian Basin and it is bordered by Slovakia to the north, Ukraine and Romania to the east, Serbia and Croatia to the south, Slovenia to the southwest and Austria to the west. The capital and largest city is Budapest.
Mountain	A mountain is a large landform that stretches above the surrounding land in a limited area usually in the form of a peak. A mountain is generally steeper than a hill. The adjective montane is used to describe mountainous areas and things associated with them.
Netherlands	More than one name is used to refer to the Netherlands, both in English and in other languages. Some of these names refer to different, but overlapping geographical, linguistic and political areas of the country. This is a common source of confusion for outsiders.

Chapter 14. Economic Policy

Saudi Arabia	The Kingdom of Saudi Arabia, commonly known as Saudi Arabia is the largest Arab country of the Middle East. It is bordered by Jordan and Iraq on the north and northeast, Kuwait, Qatar and the United Arab Emirates on the east, Oman on the southeast, and Yemen on the south. It is also connected to Bahrain by the King Fahd Causeway.
Controversy	Controversy is a state of prolonged public dispute or debate, usually concerning a matter of opinion. The word was coined from the Latin controversia, as a composite of controversus - "turned in an opposite direction," from contra - "against" - and vertere - to turn, or versus, hence, "to turn against."
	Perennial areas of controversy include history, religion, philosophy and politics. Other minor areas of controversy may include economics, science, finances, and race.
Farm	A farm is an area of land, including various structures, devoted primarily to the practice of producing and managing food (produce, grains, or livestock), fibres and, increasingly, fuel. It is the basic production facility in food production. Farms may be owned and operated by a single individual, family, community, corporation or a company.
Human rights	Human rights are "rights and freedoms to which all humans are entitled." Proponents of the concept usually assert that everyone is endowed with certain entitlements merely by reason of being human. Human rights are thus conceived in a universalist and egalitarian fashion. Such entitlements can exist as shared norms of actual human moralities, as justified moral norms or natural rights supported by strong reasons, or as legal rights either at a national level or within international law.
National security	National security is the requirement to maintain the survival of the nation-state through the use of economic, military and political power and the exercise of diplomacy. The concept developed mostly in the United States of America after World War II. Initially focusing on military might, it now encompasses a broad range of facets, all of which impinge on the military or economic security of the nation and the values espoused by the national society. Accordingly, in order to possess national security, a nation needs to possess economic security, energy security, environmental security, etc.
Homeland	A homeland is the concept of the place (cultural geography) to which an ethnic group holds a long history and a deep cultural association with --the country in which a particular national identity began. As a common noun, it simply connotes the country of one's origin.

Chapter 14. Economic Policy

Homeland security	Homeland security is an umbrella term for security efforts to protect the United States against terrorist activity. The term arose following a reorganization of many U.S. government agencies in 2003 to form the United States Department of Homeland Security after the September 11 attacks, and may be used to refer to the actions of that department, the United States Senate Committee on Homeland Security and Governmental Affairs, or the United States House of Representatives Committee on Homeland Security. In the United States In the United States, the concept of "homeland security" extends and recombines responsibilities of government agencies and entities.
Gerrymandering	In the process of setting electoral boundaries, rather than using uniform geographic standards, Gerrymandering is a practice of political corruption that attempts to establish a political advantage for a particular party or group by manipulating geographic boundaries to create partisan, incumbent-protected, and neutral districts. The resulting district is known as a gerrymander; however, that word can also refer to the process. Gerrymandering may be used to achieve desired electoral results for a particular party, or may be used to help or hinder a particular group of constituents, such as a political, racial, linguistic, religious or class group.
Liberals	Liberals is a free market liberal party in Finland. Founded in 1965 as a reunification of the People's Party of Finland and Liberal League. Originally named Liberal People's Party (Finnish: Liberaalinen Kansanpuolue), it restyled its name as Liberals in 2000.
Liberal Party	The Liberal Party was a Belgian political party that existed from 1846 until 1961, when it became the Party for Freedom and Progress, Partij voor Vrijheid en Vooruitgang/Parti de la Liberté et du Progrès or PVV-PLP, under the leadership of Omer Vanaudenhove. History

Chapter 14. Economic Policy

	The Liberal Party was founded in 1846 and as such was the first political party of Belgium. Walthère Frère-Orban wrote the first charter for the new party.
Break	In locksmithing, a break in the pins is a separation in one or more sections of the pin used to encode the lock for a specific key or set of keys in a master keying system.
Liberalism	Liberalism is the belief in the importance of liberty and equal rights. Liberals espouse a wide array of views depending on their understanding of these principles, but most liberals support such fundamental ideas as constitutions, liberal democracy, free and fair elections, human rights, capitalism, free trade, and the separation of church and state. These ideas are widely accepted, even by political groups that do not openly profess a liberal ideological orientation.
Conservative Party	The Conservative Party was a Brazilian political party of the imperial period, which was formed circa 1836 and ended with the proclamation of the Republic in 1889. This party arose mostly from the Coimbra bloc and also from members of the Restorationist Party (Partido Restaurador), also called the Caramuru Party; it called itself the Party of Order (Portuguese: partido de ordem) to distinguish itself from the liberal opposition, which they accused of disorder and anarchy, and both the party and its leadership were known as "saquarema" after the village of Saquarema, where the leadership had plantations and support.
Conservatism	Conservatism is a political and social philosophy that promotes the maintenance of traditional institutions and supports, at the most, minimal and gradual change in society. Some conservatives seek to preserve things as they are, emphasizing stability and continuity, while others oppose modernism and seek a return to the way things were. The first established use of the term in a political context was by François-René de Chateaubriand in 1819, following the French Revolution.

Chapter 14. Economic Policy

Chapter 14. Economic Policy

Chapter 15. Social Policy

Civil War	"Civil War" is a song by the hard rock band Guns N' Roses, which originally appeared on the 1990 album Nobody's Child: Romanian Angel Appeal. It is a protest song on war, referring to all war as 'civil war' and that it only "feeds the rich while it buries the poor." In the song, singer Axl Rose asks, "What's so civil about war, anyway?" "Civil War" was the brainchild of the Guns N' Roses artists Slash, Axl Rose, and Duff McKagan. Slash stated that the song was an instrumental he had written right before the band left for the Japanese leg of its Appetite for Destruction world tour.
Commission	A commission is a physical document issued to certify the appointment of a commissioned officer by a sovereign power. The more specific terms commissioning parchment or commissioning scroll are often used to avoid ambiguity, due to "commission" being a homonym which directs the individual in carrying out their duty regardless of what authority or responsibility they may have at any time. However the document is not usually in the form of a scroll and is more often printed on paper instead of parchment.
Court	A court is a form of tribunal, often a governmental institution, with the authority to adjudicate legal disputes between parties and carry out the administration of justice in civil, criminal, and administrative matters in accordance with the rule of law. In both common law and civil law legal systems, courts are the central means for dispute resolution, and it is generally understood that all persons have an ability to bring their claims before a court. Similarly, the rights of those accused of a crime include the right to present a defense before a court.
Mandate	In politics, a mandate is the authority granted by a constituency to act as its representative. The concept of a government having a legitimate mandate to govern via the fair winning of a democratic election is a central idea of democracy. New governments who attempt to introduce policies that they did not make public during an election campaign are said to not have a legitimate mandate to implement such policies.

Chapter 15. Social Policy

Patriot	Patriots was the name the peoples of the Spanish America, who rebelled against Spanish control during the Spanish American wars of independence, called themselves. They supported the principles of the Age of Enlightenment and sought to replace the existing governing structures with Juntas. At first they declared themselves loyal to Ferdinand VII, who was captive of Napoleon Bonaparte and who was seem as a supporter of the new ideals because of his conflict with his father, the absolutist Charles IV. However, when Ferdinand VII was restored to power and began the Absolutist Restauration, most patriots in South America decided to support independentism instead.
Reform Act	In the United Kingdom, Reform Act is a generic term used for legislation concerning electoral matters. It is most commonly used for laws passed to enfranchise new groups of voters and to redistribute seats in the British House of Commons. The periodic redrawing of constituency boundaries is now dealt with by a permanent Boundary Commission in each part of the United Kingdom, rather than by a Reform Act.
Rights	Rights are legal, social, or ethical principles of freedom or entitlement; that is, rights are the fundamental normative rules about what is allowed of people or owed to people, according to some legal system, social convention, or ethical theory. Rights are of essential importance in such disciplines as law and ethics, especially theories of justice and deontology.
	Rights are often considered fundamental to civilization, being regarded as established pillars of society and culture, and the history of social conflicts can be found in the history of each right and its development.
Self-determination	The right of nations to self-determination is the principle in international law, that nations have the right to freely choose their sovereignty and international political status with no external compulsion or external interference. The principle does not state how the decision is to be made, or what the outcome should be, be it independence, federation, protection, some form of autonomy or even full assimilation. Neither does it state what the delimitation between nations should be -- or even what constitutes a nation.

Chapter 15. Social Policy

Unfunded mandate	In United States law and politics, unfunded mandates are regulations or conditions for receiving grants that impose costs on state or local governments or private entities for which they are not reimbursed by the federal government. • Any one of many federal legislations such as the Clean Air Act, and the Clean Water Act that require programs to be sponsored by the governments of the states, without providing any funds for those programs. • The provisions in the Americans with Disabilities Act that require nearly all American business owners to make their business premises available to disabled customers without providing any funds for the cost of reconstruction or additional interior space. • The provisions in the Emergency Medical Treatment and Active Labor Act that require nearly all American emergency rooms to accept and stabilize any patient regardless of the patient's ability to pay, but do not provide adequate reimbursement for indigent patients.
Pension	In general, a pension is an arrangement to provide people with an income when they are no longer earning a regular income from employment. Pensions should not be confused with severance pay; the former is paid in regular installments, while the latter is paid in one lump sum. The terms retirement plan or superannuation refer to a pension granted upon retirement.
Frontier	A frontier is a political and geographical term referring to areas near or beyond a boundary. 'Frontier' was borrowed into English from French in the 15th century, with the meaning "borderland"--the region of a country that fronts on another country. The use of "frontier" to mean "a region at the edge of a settled area" is a special North American development.

Chapter 15. Social Policy

Individualism	Individualism is the moral stance, political philosophy, ideology, or social outlook that stresses "the moral worth of the individual". Individualists promote the exercise of one's goals and desires and so independence and self-reliance while opposing most external interference upon one's own interests, whether by society, family or any other group or institution. Individualism makes the individual its focus and so it starts "with the fundamental premise that the human individual is of primary importance in the struggle for liberation." Classical liberalism (including libertarianism), existentialism and anarchism (especially individualist anarchism) are examples of movements that take the human individual as a central unit of analysis.
Policy	A policy is typically described as a principle or rule to guide decisions and achieve rational outcome(s). The term is not normally used to denote what is actually done, this is normally referred to as either procedure or protocol. Whereas a policy will contain the 'what' and the 'why', procedures or protocols contain the 'what', the 'how', the 'where', and the 'when'.
Social policy	Social policy primarily refers to guidelines and interventions for the changing, maintenance or creation of living conditions that are conducive to human welfare. Thus, social policy is that part of public policy that has to do with social issues. The Malcolm Wiener Center for Social Policy at Harvard University describes it as "public policy and practice in the areas of health care, human services, criminal justice, inequality, education, and labor." Social policy often deals with issues which Rittle ' Webber (1973) called wicked problems.
Veteran	A veteran is a person who has had long service or experience in a particular occupation or field; " A veteran of ..." . This page refers to military veterans, i.e., a person who has served or is serving in the armed forces, and has direct exposure to acts of military conflict, commonly known as war veterans (although not all military conflicts, or areas in which armed combat takes place, are necessarily referred to as "wars"). Public attitude towards veterans Military veterans often receive special treatment in their respective countries due to the sacrifices they made during wars.

Chapter 15. Social Policy

Senate	A senate is a deliberative assembly, often the upper house or chamber of a legislature or parliament. There have been many such bodies in history, since senate means the assembly of the eldest and wiser members of the society and ruling class. Two of the first official senates were the Spartan Gerousia (Γερουσ?α) and the Roman Senate.
Social security	Social security is primarily a social insurance program providing social protection, or protection against socially recognized conditions, including poverty, old age, disability, unemployment and others. Social security may refer to: • social insurance, where people receive benefits or services in recognition of contributions to an insurance scheme. These services typically include provision for retirement pensions, disability insurance, survivor benefits and unemployment insurance. • income maintenance--mainly the distribution of cash in the event of interruption of employment, including retirement, disability and unemployment • services provided by administrations responsible for social security.
Commerce Clause	The Commerce Clause is an enumerated power listed in the United States Constitution (Article I, Section 8, Clause 3). The clause states that the United States Congress shall have power "To regulate Commerce with foreign Nations, and among the several States, and with the Indian Tribes". Courts and commentators have tended to discuss each of these three areas of commerce as a separate power granted to Congress.
Homosexuality	Homosexuality is romantic and/or sexual attraction or behavior among members of the same sex or gender. As a sexual orientation, homosexuality refers to "an enduring pattern of or disposition to experience sexual, affectional, or romantic attractions" primarily or exclusively to people of the same sex; "it also refers to an individual's sense of personal and social identity based on those attractions, behaviors expressing them, and membership in a community of others who share them."

Chapter 15. Social Policy

Homosexuality is one of the three main categories of sexual orientation, along with bisexuality and heterosexuality, within the heterosexual-homosexual continuum. The consensus of the behavioral and social sciences and the health and mental health professions is that homosexuality is a normal and positive variation in human sexual orientation, though many religious societies, including Catholicism, Mormonism, and Islam, and some psychological associations, such as NARTH, teach that homosexual activity is sinful or dysfunctional.

Initiative

In political science, the initiative provides a means by which a petition signed by a certain minimum number of registered voters can force a public vote (plebiscite) on a proposed statute, constitutional amendment, charter amendment or ordinance, or, in its minimal form, to simply oblige the executive or legislative bodies to consider the subject by submitting it to the order of the day. It is a form of direct democracy.

The initiative may take the form of either the direct initiative or indirect initiative.

Insurance

In law and economics, insurance is a form of risk management primarily used to hedge against the risk of a contingent, uncertain loss. Insurance is defined as the equitable transfer of the risk of a loss, from one entity to another, in exchange for payment. An insurer is a company selling the insurance; an insured, or policyholder, is the person or entity buying the insurance policy.

Minimum wage

A minimum wage is the lowest hourly, daily or monthly wage that employers may legally pay to employees or workers. Equivalently, it is the lowest wage at which workers may sell their labor. Although minimum wage laws are in effect in a great many jurisdictions, there are differences of opinion about the benefits and drawbacks of a minimum wage.

Americas

The Americas, are the lands of the western hemisphere, composed of numerous entities and regions variably defined by geography, politics, and culture.

The Americas are frequently recognised to comprise two separate continents (North America and South America), particularly in English-speaking nations. The Americas may also be recognised to comprise a single continent , in Latin America and in some European nations.

Chapter 15. Social Policy

Congress	A congress is a formal meeting of the representatives of different nations, constituent states, independent organizations (such as trade unions), or groups.
	The term was chosen for the United States Congress to emphasize the status of each state represented there as a self-governing unit. Subsequent to the use of congress by the U.S. legislature, the term has been incorrectly adopted by many states within unions, and by unitary nation-states in the Americas, to refer to their legislatures.
Contract	In the Conflict of Laws, the validity of a contract with one or more foreign law elements will be decided by reference to the so-called "proper law" of the contract.
	History
	Until the middle of the 19th century, the courts applied the lex loci contractus or the law of the place where the contract was made to decide whether the given contract was valid. The apparent advantage of this approach was that the rule was easy to apply with certain and predictable outcomes.
Force	In the field of law, the word force has two main meanings: unlawful violence and lawful compulsion. "Forced entry" is an expression falling under the category of unlawful violence; "in force" or "forced sale" would be examples of expressions in the category of lawful compulsion.
	When something is said to have been done "by force", it usually implies that it was done by actual or threatened violence ("might"), not necessarily by legal authority ("right").
Labor force	Overview
	In economics, the people in the labor force is all the nonmilitary people who are officially employed or unemployed.

	Normally, the labor force of a country (or other geographic entity) consists of everyone of working age (typically above a certain age (around 14 to 16) and below retirement (around 65) who are participating workers, that is people actively employed or seeking employment. People not counted include students, retired people, stay-at-home parents, people in prisons or similar institutions, people employed in jobs or professions with unreported income, as well as discouraged workers who cannot find work.
State	Many sovereign independent state are made up of a number of country subdivisions also called states. In some cases, such as the United States, the national government arose from a union of sovereign entities, which transferred some of their powers to the national government, while retaining the remainder of their sovereignty. These are sometimes called federal states.
Welfare state	A welfare state is a concept of government where the state plays the primary role in the protection and promotion of the economic and social well-being of its citizens. It is based on the principles of equality of opportunity, equitable distribution of wealth, and public responsibility for those unable to avail themselves of the minimal provisions for a good life. The general term may cover a variety of forms of economic and social organization.
Advancement	Advancement is a common law doctrine of intestate succession that presumes that gifts given to a person's heir during that person's life are intended as an advance on what that heir would inherit upon the death of the parent. For example, suppose person P had two children, A and B. Suppose also that P had $100,000, and gave $20,000 to child A before P's death, leaving $80,000 in P's estate. If P died without a will, and A and B were P's only heirs, A and B would be entitled to split P's estate evenly.
Brown v. Board of Education	Brown v. Board of Education of Topeka, 347 U.S. 483 (1954), was a landmark decision of the United States Supreme Court that declared state laws establishing separate public schools for black and white students unconstitutional. The decision overturned the Plessy v. Ferguson decision of 1896 which allowed state-sponsored segregation. Handed down on May 17, 1954, the Warren Court's unanimous (9-0) decision stated that "separate educational facilities are inherently unequal." As a result, de jure racial segregation was ruled a violation of the Equal Protection Clause of the Fourteenth Amendment of the United States Constitution.

Chapter 15. Social Policy

Caucus	A caucus is a meeting of supporters or members of a political party or movement, especially in the United States. As the use of the term has been expanded the exact definition has come to vary among political cultures. Origin of the term The origin of the word caucus is debated, but it is generally agreed that it first came into use in the English colonies of North America. A February 1763 entry in the diary of John Adams of Braintree, Massachusetts, is one of the earliest appearances of Caucas, already with its modern connotations of a "smoke-filled room" where candidates for public election are pre-selected in private This day learned that the Caucas Clubb meets at certain Times in the Garret of Tom Daws, the Adjutant of the Boston Regiment.
Colored	Colored in the U.S.A (also coloured in Canadian, British and Commonwealth spelling) is a term once widely regarded as a description of black people (i.e., persons of sub-Saharan African ancestry; members of the "Black race") and Native Americans. It should not be confused with the more recent term people of color, which attempts to describe all "non-white peoples", not just black people. Today it is generally no longer regarded as a politically correct term, however even that is debatable, due to its continued occasional appearance, most notably its use in the acronym NAACP. Carla Sims, communications director for the NAACP in Washington, D.C., said "The term 'colored' is not derogatory, [the NAACP] chose the word 'colored' because it was the most positive description commonly used at that time.

Chapter 15. Social Policy

Thurgood Marshall	Thurgood Marshall was an American jurist and the first African American to serve on the Supreme Court of the United States. Before becoming a judge, he was a lawyer who was best remembered for his high success rate in arguing before the Supreme Court and for the victory in Brown v. Board of Education. He was nominated to the court by President Lyndon Johnson in 1967.
Class Warfare	Class Warfare is a book of interviews with Noam Chomsky conducted by David Barsamian. It was first published in the UK by Pluto Press in 1996. Contents - Introduction - Looking Ahead: Tenth Anniversary Interview (an interview conducted ten years since Barsamian first interviewed Chomsky) - Rollback: The Return of Predatory Capitalism - History and Memory - The Federal Reserve Board - Take from the Needy and Give to the Greedy Influence Writer Rob Williams has stated that Class War was a major inspiration for his superhero comic book series Cla$$war.
Voting	Voting is a method for a group such as a meeting or an electorate to make a decision or express an opinion--often following discussions, debates, or election campaigns. It is often found in democracies and republics. Reasons for voting In a representative government, voting commonly implies election: a way for an electorate to select among candidates for office.

Chapter 15. Social Policy

Agenda	An agenda is a list of meeting activities in the order in which they are to be taken up, beginning with the call to order and ending with adjournment. It usually includes one or more specific items of business to be considered. It may, but is not required to, include specific times for one OR more activities.
Interest	Interest is a fee paid on borrowed assets. It is the price paid for the use of borrowed money, or, money earned by deposited funds. Assets that are sometimes lent with interest include money, shares, consumer goods through hire purchase, major assets such as aircraft, and even entire factories in finance lease arrangements.
Judiciary	The judiciary is the system of courts that interprets and applies the law in the name of the state. The judiciary also provides a mechanism for the resolution of disputes. Under the doctrine of the separation of powers, the judiciary generally does not make law (that is, in a plenary fashion, which is the responsibility of the legislature) or enforce law (which is the responsibility of the executive), but rather interprets law and applies it to the facts of each case.
Executive	Executive branch of government is the part of government that has sole authority and responsibility for the daily administration of the state bureaucracy. The division of power into separate branches of government is central to the democratic idea of the separation of powers. In many countries, the term "government" connotes only the executive branch.
Filibuster	A filibuster is a type of parliamentary procedure. Specifically, it is a form of obstruction in a legislature or other decision-making body whereby a lone member can elect to delay or entirely prevent a vote on a proposal. The term "filibuster" was first used in 1851. It was derived from the Spanish filibustero, which translates as "pirate" or "freebooter." This term had evolved from the French word flibustier, which itself evolved from the Dutch vrijbuiter (free outsider).

Chapter 15. Social Policy

Adjustment

In law, the term adjustment may appear in varied contexts, as a synonym for terms with unrelated definitions:

General Definition

Adjust:

1. To settle or to bring to a satisfactory state, so that the parties are agreed in the result; as, to adjust accounts.
2. When applied to a liquidated demand, the verb "adjust" has the same meaning as the word "settle" in the same connection, and means to pay the demand. When applied to an unliquidated demand, it means to ascertain the amount due or to settle. In the latter connection, to settle means to effect a mutual adjustment between the parties and to agree upon the balance.

Common Uses

General Debt

- Debtor and creditor adjustment: As the term appears in an assignment for the benefit of creditors, "Creditor" means one who has a definite demand against the assignor, or a cause of action capable of adjustment and liquidation at trial. 6 Am J2d Assign for Crs § 109.
- Adjustable Rate Loan: Loan arrangement which permits the lender to change the interest rate based on a specific factor such as the prime lending rate charged by banks.
- Adjusting agency: In one sense, a collection agency; in another sense, an agency representing a debtor in making an arrangement with his creditors for the settlement of his obligations by modification of the indebtedness.

Ensign

Ensign is a junior rank of commissioned officer in the armed forces of some countries, normally in the infantry or navy. As the junior officer in an infantry regiment was traditionally the carrier of the ensign flag, the rank itself acquired the name. The Spanish alférez and Portuguese alferes is a junior officer rank below lieutenant associated with carrying the flag, and so is often translated as "ensign".

Chapter 15. Social Policy

Freedom	Freedom is a London-based anarchist newspaper published fortnightly by Freedom Press.
	The paper was started in 1886 by volunteers including Peter Kropotkin and Charlotte Wilson and continues to this day as an unpaid project. Originally, the subtitle was "A Journal of Anarchist Socialism." The title was changed to "A Journal of Anarchist Communism" in June 1889. Today it is unlabelled.
Eminent domain	Eminent domain compulsory purchase (United Kingdom, New Zealand, Ireland), resumption/compulsory acquisition (Australia) or expropriation (South Africa and Canada) is an action of the state to seize a citizen's private property, expropriate property, or seize a citizen's rights in property with due monetary compensation, but without the owner's consent. The property is taken either for government use or by delegation to third parties who will devote it to public or civic use or, in some cases, economic development. The most common uses of property taken by eminent domain are for public utilities, highways, and railroads, however it may also be taken for reasons of public safety, such as in the case of Centralia, Pennsylvania.
International trade	International trade is exchange of capital, goods, and services across international borders or territories. In most countries, it represents a significant share of gross domestic product (GDP). While international trade has been present throughout much of history , its economic, social, and political importance has been on the rise in recent centuries.
Medicare	Medicare is a social insurance program administered by the United States government, providing health insurance coverage to people who are aged 65 and over, or who meet other special criteria. Medicare operates similar to a single-payer health care system, but the key difference is that its coverage only extends to 80% of any given medical cost; the remaining 20% of cost must be paid by other means, such as privately-held supplemental insurance, or paid by the patient.
	The program also funds residency training programs for the vast majority of physicians in the United States.

Chapter 15. Social Policy

Price index	A price index is a normalized average (typically a weighted average) of prices for a given class of goods or services in a given region, during a given interval of time. It is a statistic designed to help to compare how these prices, taken as a whole, differ between time periods or geographical locations. Price indices have several potential uses.
Foundation	A foundation in the United States is a type of charitable organization. However, the Internal Revenue Code distinguishes between private foundations (usually funded by an individual, family, or corporation) and public charities (community foundations and other nonprofit groups that raise money from the general public). Private foundations have more restrictions and fewer tax benefits than public charities like community foundations.
Impeachment	Impeachment is a formal process in which an official is accused of unlawful activity and the outcome of which, depending on the country, can lead to the removal of that official from office or other punishment. Medieval popular etymology also associated it (wrongly) with derivations from the Latin impetere (to attack). (In its more frequent and more technical usage, impeachment of a person in the role of a witness is the act of challenging the honesty or credibility of that person).
Implementation	Implementation is the realization of an application, or execution of a plan, idea, model, design, specification, standard, algorithm, or policy. Computer Science In computer science, an implementation is a realization of a technical specification or algorithm as a program, software component, or other computer system through programming and deployment. Many implementations may exist for a given specification or standard.

Chapter 15. Social Policy

Trusts	In Conflict of Laws, the Hague Convention on the Law Applicable to Trusts and on Their Recognition was concluded on 1 July 1985 and entered into force 1 January 1992. The Convention aims to harmonise not only the municipal law definitions of a trust both within the USA and outside the USA, but also the Conflict rules for resolving problems in the choice of the lex causae. Explanation Many states do not have a developed law of trusts, or the principles differ significantly between states. It was therefore necessary for the Hague Convention to define a trust to indicate the range of legal transactions regulated by the Convention and, perhaps more significantly, the range of applications not regulated.
Ownership society	Ownership society is a slogan for a model of society promoted by former United States President George W. Bush. It takes as lead values personal responsibility, economic liberty, and the owning of property. The ownership society discussed by Bush also extends to certain proposals of specific models of health care and social security.
Society	A society is (1) a group of people related to each other through persistent relations such as social status, roles and social networks. (2) A large social grouping that shares the same geographical territory and is subject to the same political authority and dominant cultural expectations. Human societies are characterized by patterns of relationships between individuals sharing a distinctive culture and institutions.
Disabilities	Disabilities were legal restrictions and limitations placed on Jews in the Middle Ages. They included provisions requiring Jews to wear specific and identifying clothing such as the Jewish hat and the yellow badge, restricting Jews to certain cities and towns or in certain parts of towns (ghettos), and forbidding Jews to enter certain trades. Disabilities also included special taxes levied on Jews, exclusion from public life, and restraints on the performance of religious ceremonies.

Chapter 15. Social Policy

Appointee	An appointee may be one of the following: • A member who is appointed to a position or office is called an appointee. In law, such a term is applied to one who is granted power of appointment of property. • An appointee was also a foot soldier in the French army, who, for long service and bravery, received more pay than other privates. • An appointee is the third most lower rank of the Italian Corps of Carabineers • An appointee is the third most lower rank of the Swiss Armed Forces • An appointee is also a person or organisation entrusted with managing the daily finances of vulnerable individuals in the UK.
Canada	Canada was the name of the French colony that once stretched along the St. Lawrence River; the other colonies of New France were Acadia, Louisiana and Newfoundland. Canada, the most developed colony of New France, was divided into three districts, each with its own government: Québec, Trois-Rivières, and Montréal. The governor of the district of Québec was also the governor-general of all of New France.
Medicaid	Medicaid is the United States health program for eligible individuals and families with low incomes and resources. It is a means tested program that is jointly funded by the state and federal governments, and is managed by the states. Among the groups of people served by Medicaid are certain eligible U.S. citizens and resident aliens, including low-income adults and their children, and people with certain disabilities.
Prescription	In law, prescription is the method of sovereignty transfer of a territory through international law analogous to the common law doctrine of adverse possession for private real-estate. Prescription involves the open encroachment by the new sovereign upon the territory in question for a prolonged period of time, acting as the sovereign, without protest or other contest by the original sovereign. This doctrine legalizes de jure the de facto transfer of sovereignty caused in part by the original sovereign's extended negligence and/or neglect of the area in question.

Chapter 15. Social Policy

Publics	Publics are small groups of people who follow one or more particular issue very closely. They are well informed about the issue(s) and also have a very strong opinion on it/them. They tend to know more about politics than the average person, and, therefore, exert more influence, because these people care so deeply about their cause(s) that they donate much time and money.
Supplemental Security Income	Supplemental Security Income is a United States government program that provides stipends to low-income persons who are either aged (65 or older), blind, or disabled. Although administered by the Social Security Administration, Supplemental Security Income is funded from the U.S. Treasury general funds, not the Social Security trust fund. Supplemental Security Income was created in 1974 to replace federal-state adult assistance programs that served the same purpose.
Reconciliation	Reconciliation is a legislative process of the United States Senate intended to allow consideration of a budget bill with debate limited to twenty hours under Senate Rules. Reconciliation also exists in the United States House of Representatives, but because the House regularly passes rules that constrain debate and amendment, the process has had a less significant impact on that body.
	A reconciliation instruction (Budget Reconciliation) is a provision in a budget resolution directing one or more committees to submit legislation changing existing law in order to bring spending, revenues, or the debt-limit into conformity with the budget resolution.
Entitlement	An entitlement is a guarantee of access to benefits based on established rights or by legislation. A "right" is itself an entitlement associated with a moral or social principle, such that an "entitlement" is a provision made in accordance with legal framework of a society. Typically, entitlements are laws based on concepts of principle ("rights") which are themselves based in concepts of social equality or enfranchisement.
Progressive Era	The Progressive Era in the United States was a period of social activism and reform that flourished from the 1890s to the 1920s. The main goal of the Progressive movement was purification of government, as Progressives tried to expose and undercut political machines and bosses. Many (but not all) Progressives supported prohibition in order to destroy the political power of local bosses based in saloons.

Chapter 15. Social Policy

Vietnam	Vietnam, officially the Socialist Republic of Vietnam is the easternmost country on the Indochina Peninsula in Southeast Asia. It is bordered by People's Republic of China (PRC) to the north, Laos to the northwest, Cambodia to the southwest, and the South China Sea, referred to as East Sea (Vietnamese: Bi?n Đông), to the east. With a population of over 86 million, Vietnam is the 13th most populous country in the world.
Gerrymandering	In the process of setting electoral boundaries, rather than using uniform geographic standards, Gerrymandering is a practice of political corruption that attempts to establish a political advantage for a particular party or group by manipulating geographic boundaries to create partisan, incumbent-protected, and neutral districts. The resulting district is known as a gerrymander; however, that word can also refer to the process. Gerrymandering may be used to achieve desired electoral results for a particular party, or may be used to help or hinder a particular group of constituents, such as a political, racial, linguistic, religious or class group.
Redistricting	Redistricting, a form of redistribution, is the process of drawing United States district lines. This often means changing electoral district and constituency boundaries in response to periodic census results. In 36 states, the state legislature has primary responsibility for creating a redistricting plan, in many cases subject to approval by the state governor.
Montreal Protocol	The Montreal Protocol on Substances That Deplete the Ozone Layer (a protocol to the Vienna Convention for the Protection of the Ozone Layer) is an international treaty designed to protect the ozone layer by phasing out the production of numerous substances believed to be responsible for ozone depletion. The treaty was opened for signature on September 16, 1987, and entered into force on January 1, 1989, followed by a first meeting in Helsinki, May 1989. Since then, it has undergone seven revisions, in 1990 (London), 1991 (Nairobi), 1992 (Copenhagen), 1993 (Bangkok), 1995 (Vienna), 1997 (Montreal), and 1999 (Beijing). It is believed that if the international agreement is adhered to, the ozone layer is expected to recover by 2050. Due to its widespread adoption and implementation it has been hailed as an example of exceptional international co-operation, with Kofi Annan quoted as saying that "perhaps the single most successful international agreement to date has been the Montreal Protocol".

Chapter 15. Social Policy

Minutes	Minutes, are the instant written record of a meeting or hearing. They often give an overview of the structure of the meeting, starting with a list of those present, a statement of the various issues before the participants, and each of their responses thereto. They are often created at the moment of the hearing by a typist or court recorder at the meeting, who may record the meeting in shorthand, and then prepare the minutes and issue them to the participants afterwards.
Moral hazard	Moral hazard occurs when a party insulated from risk behaves differently than it would behave if it were fully exposed to the risk. Moral hazard arises because an individual or institution does not take the full consequences and responsibilities of its actions, and therefore has a tendency to act less carefully than it otherwise would, leaving another party to hold some responsibility for the consequences of those actions. For example, a person with insurance against automobile theft may be less cautious about locking his or her car, because the negative consequences of vehicle theft are (partially) the responsibility of the insurance company.
Capitalism	Capitalism is an economic system in which the means of production are privately owned and operated for a private profit; decisions regarding supply, demand, price, distribution, and investments are made by private actors in the free market; profit is distributed to owners who choose to invest in businesses, and wages are paid to workers employed by businesses and companies. There is no consensus on the precise definition of capitalism, nor how the term should be used as an analytical category. There is, however, little controversy that private ownership of the means of production, creation of goods or services for profit in a market, and prices and wages are elements of capitalism.
Government	In the social sciences, the term government refers to the particular group of people, the administrative bureaucracy, who control a state at a given time, and the manner in which their governing organizations are structured. That is, governments are the means through which state power is employed. States are served by a continuous succession of different governments.

Chapter 15. Social Policy

Left Behind	Left Behind is a series of 16 best-selling novels by Tim LaHaye and Jerry Jenkins, dealing with Christian dispensationalist End Times: pretribulation, premillennial, Christian eschatological viewpoint of the end of the world. The primary conflict of the series is the members of the Tribulation Force against the Global Community and its leader Nicolae Carpathia--the Antichrist. Left Behind is also the title of the first book in the series.
Nation	Nation has different meanings in different contexts. In worldwide diplomacy, nation can mean country or sovereign state. The United Nations, for instance, speaks of how it was founded after the Second World War with "51 countries" and currently has "192 member states".
No Child Left Behind Act	The No Child Left Behind Act of 2001 is a United States Act of Congress concerning the education of children in public schools. NCLB was originally proposed by the administration of George W. Bush immediately after taking office. The bill, shepherded through the Senate by Senator Ted Kennedy, one of the bill's co-authors, received overwhelming bipartisan support in Congress.
Ordinance	Ordinance in Belgium refers to legislation passed by the Brussels Parliament in exercise of its regional competences and by the United Assembly of the Common Community Commission. In principle, ordinances have the same legal force as laws and decrees, however, the Federal Government has the authority to suspend ordinances which in its view could jeopardise the role of Brussels as the capital of Belgium or the international role of Brussels, sometimes seen as the "capital of the European Union".
Soviet	Soviet was a name used for several Russian political organizations. Examples include the Czar's Council of Ministers, which was called the "Soviet of Ministers"; a workers' local council in late Imperial Russia; and the Supreme Soviet of the Soviet Union. Etymology "Soviet" is derived from a Russian word signifying council, advice, harmony, concord.[trans 1] The word "sovietnik" means councillor.

Chapter 15. Social Policy

Soviet Union

The Union of Soviet Socialist Republics, informally known as the Soviet Union, was a constitutionally socialist state that existed on the territory of most of the former Russian Empire in Eurasia between 1922 and 1991.

The Soviet Union had a single-party political system dominated by the Communist Party until 1990. Although the USSR was nominally a union of Soviet republics (of which there were 15 after 1956) with the capital in Moscow, it was in actuality a highly centralized state with a planned economy.

The Soviet Union was founded in December 1922 when the Russian SFSR, which formed during the Russian Revolution of 1917 and emerged victorious in the ensuing Russian Civil War, unified with the Transcaucasian, Ukrainian and Belorussian SSRs.

Territory

In international politics, a territory is a non-sovereign geographic area which has come under the authority of another government; which has not been granted the powers of self-government normally devolved to secondary territorial divisions; or both.

Types of administrative and/or political territories include:

- Many types of legally administered territories, each of which is a non-sovereign geographic area that has come under the authority of another government with varying degrees of local governmental control.

- This can include federated states which share authority with a central government such as the Länder of Germany or the Counties of a state within one of the States of the United States (those states being another example themselves that were sovereign and ceded rights to a central federated government),

- or alternatively, an administrative district established by a central nation-state as with the Bundesländer of Austria (which are now a federation),

- or the subnational entities constituting a unitary state such as France.

Chapter 15. Social Policy

	For example, American Samoa, Guam and Puerto Rico are all territories of the government of the United States with varying local autonomy. Similarly, with regard to the Canadian provinces and territories, the major difference between a Canadian province and a Canadian territory is that the federal government has more direct control over the territories, while the provinces are run by provincial governments empowered by the constitution.
Education policy	Education policy refers to the collection of laws and rules that govern the operation of education systems.
	Education occurs in many forms for many purposes through many institutions. Examples include early childhood education, kindergarten through to 12th grade, two and four year colleges or universities, graduate and professional education, adult education and job training.
Governor	A governor is a governing official, usually the executive (at least nominally, to different degrees also politically and administratively) of a non-sovereign level of government, ranking under the head of state. In federations, a governor may be the title of each appointed or elected politician who governs a constituent state.
	In countries the heads of the constitutive states, provinces, communities and regions may be titled Governor, although this is less common in parliamentary systems such as in some European nations and many of their former colonies, which use titles such as President of the Regional Council in France and Minister-President in Germany, where in some states there are governorates as sub-state administrative regions.
Deficit	A deficit is the amount by which a sum of money falls short of the required amount.
	Primary deficit, total deficit, and debt

Chapter 15. Social Policy

	A government's deficit can be measured with or without including the interest it pays on its debt. The primary deficit is defined as the difference between current government spending and total current revenue from all types of taxes.
Contract with America	The Contract with America was a document released by the United States Republican Party during the 1994 Congressional election campaign. Written by Larry Huuinter, who was aided by Newt Gingrich, Robert Walker, Richard Armey, Bill Paxon, Tom DeLay, John Boehner and Jim Nussle, and in part using text from former President Ronald Reagan's 1985 State of the Union Address, the Contract detailed the actions the Republicans promised to take if they became the majority party in the United States House of Representatives for the first time in 40 years. Many of the Contract's policy ideas originated at The Heritage Foundation, a conservative think tank.
World War I	World War I or First World War (called at the time the Great War) was a major war centered on Europe that began in the summer of 1914. The fighting ended in November 1918. This conflict involved all of the world's great powers, assembled in two opposing alliances: the Allies (centred around the Triple Entente) and the Central Powers. More than 70 million military personnel, including 60 million Europeans, were mobilized in one of the largest wars in history. More than 9 million combatants were killed, due largely to great technological advances in firepower without corresponding advances in mobility.
Charter	A charter is the grant of authority or rights, stating that the granter formally recognizes the prerogative of the recipient to exercise the rights specified. It is implicit that the granter retains superiority (or sovereignty), and that the recipient admits a limited (or inferior) status within the relationship, and it is within that sense that charters were historically granted, and that sense is retained in modern usage of the term. Also, charter can simply be a document giving royal permission to start a colony.
Charter school	Charter schools in the United States are primary or secondary schools that receive public money (and like other schools, may also receive private donations) but are not subject to some of the rules, regulations, and statutes that apply to other public schools in exchange for some type of accountability for producing certain results, which are set forth in each school's charter. Charter schools are opened and attended by choice. While charter schools provide an alternative to other public schools, they are part of the public education system and are not allowed to charge tuition.

Chapter 15. Social Policy

Administration	Administration, as a legal concept, is a procedure under the insolvency laws of a number of common law jurisdictions. It functions as a rescue mechanism for insolvent companies and allows them to carry on running their business. The process - an alternative to liquidation - is often known as going into administration.
Consumer product	A consumer product is generally any tangible personal property for sale and that is used for personal, family, or household for non-business purposes. The determination whether a good is a consumer product requires a factual finding, on a case-by-case basis. This basis will vary from one jurisdiction to another.
Environmental protection	Environmental protection is a practice of protecting the environment, on individual, organizational or governmental level, for the benefit of the natural environment and (or) humans. Due to the pressures of population and our technology the biophysical environment is being degraded, sometimes permanently. This has been recognized and governments began placing restraints on activities that caused environmental degradation.
Environmental Protection Agency	The Environmental Protection Agency (Irish: An Ghníomhaireacht um Chaomhnú Comhshaoil) has responsibilities for a wide range of licensing, enforcement, monitoring and assessment activities associated with environmental protection.
Health administration	Health administration is the field relating to leadership, management, and administration of hospitals, hospital networks, and health care systems. Health care administrators are considered health care professionals.
	The discipline is known by many names, including health management, healthcare management, health systems management, health care systems management, and medical and health services management.
Public health	Public health is "the science and art of preventing disease, prolonging life and promoting health through the organized efforts and informed choices of society, organizations, public and private, communities and individuals" (1920, C.E.A. Winslow). It is concerned with threats to the overall health of a community based on population health analysis. The population in question can be as small as a handful of people or as large as all the inhabitants of several continents (for instance, in the case of a pandemic).

Chapter 15. Social Policy

Health care	Health or healthcare is the treatment and prevention of illness. Health care is delivered by professionals in medicine, dentistry, nursing, pharmacy and allied health. The social and political issues surrounding access to healthcare in the US have led to vigorous public debate and the almost colloquial use of terms such as health care health insurance (reimbursement of health care costs), and public health (the collective state and range of health in a population).
James Madison	James Madison, Jr. (March 16, 1751 - June 28, 1836) was an American politician and political philosopher who served as the fourth President of the United States (1809-1817) and is considered one of the Founding Fathers of the United States. He was the principal author of the United States Constitution, and is often called the "Father of the Constitution".
Feminization	In sociology, feminization is a shift in gender roles and sex roles in a society, group, or organization towards a focus upon the feminine. This is the opposite of a cultural focus upon masculinity. Scholar Ann Douglas chronicled the rise of what she describes as sentimental "feminization" of American mass culture in the 19th century, in which writers of both sexes underscored popular convictions about women's weaknesses, desires, and proper place in the world.
Corporation	In feudal Europe, corporations were aggregations of business interests in compact, usually with an explicit license from city, church, or national leaders. These functioned as effective monopolies for a particular good or labor.

The term "corporation" was used as late as the 18th century in England to refer to such ventures as the East India Company or the Hudson's Bay Company: commercial organizations that operated under royal patent to have exclusive rights to a particular area of trade.

Chapter 15. Social Policy

Chapter 15. Social Policy

Chapter 16. Foreign Policy

Foundation	A foundation in the United States is a type of charitable organization. However, the Internal Revenue Code distinguishes between private foundations (usually funded by an individual, family, or corporation) and public charities (community foundations and other nonprofit groups that raise money from the general public). Private foundations have more restrictions and fewer tax benefits than public charities like community foundations.
Foreign policy	A country's foreign policy, called the foreign relations policy, consists of self-interest strategies chosen by the state to safeguard its national interests and to achieve its goals within international relations milieu. The approaches are strategically employed to interact with other countries. In recent times, due to the deepening level of globalization and transnational activities, the states will also have to interact with non-state actors.
Interest	Interest is a fee paid on borrowed assets. It is the price paid for the use of borrowed money, or, money earned by deposited funds. Assets that are sometimes lent with interest include money, shares, consumer goods through hire purchase, major assets such as aircraft, and even entire factories in finance lease arrangements.
National interest	The national interest, often referred to by the French expression raison d'État, is a country's goals and ambitions whether economic, military, or cultural. The nation is an important one in international relations where pursuit of the national interest is the foundation of the realist school. The national interest of a state is multi-faceted.
National security	National security is the requirement to maintain the survival of the nation-state through the use of economic, military and political power and the exercise of diplomacy. The concept developed mostly in the United States of America after World War II. Initially focusing on military might, it now encompasses a broad range of facets, all of which impinge on the military or economic security of the nation and the values espoused by the national society. Accordingly, in order to possess national security, a nation needs to possess economic security, energy security, environmental security, etc.
Policy	A policy is typically described as a principle or rule to guide decisions and achieve rational outcome(s). The term is not normally used to denote what is actually done, this is normally referred to as either procedure or protocol. Whereas a policy will contain the 'what' and the 'why', procedures or protocols contain the 'what', the 'how', the 'where', and the 'when'.

Chapter 16. Foreign Policy

Germany	Germany officially the Federal Republic of Germany, is a country in Western Europe. It is bordered to the north by the North Sea, Denmark, and the Baltic Sea; to the east by Poland and the Czech Republic; to the south by Austria and Switzerland; and to the west by France, Luxembourg, Belgium, and the Netherlands. The territory of Germany covers an area of 357,021 km^2 and is influenced by a temperate seasonal climate.
Iran	Iran newspaper is the official newspaper of the government of the Islamic Republic of Iran. Iran is a daily newspaper. The Islamic Republic News Agency that publishes Iran, also publishes Iran Daily that is an English language daily newspaper, Alvefagh that is an Arabic newspaper, Irane varzeshi that is a sport daily newspaper, and Irane Sepid for blind people.
Justice	Justice was the weekly newspaper of the Social Democratic Federation (SDF) in the United Kingdom. The SDF had been known until January 1884 as the Democratic Federation. With the change of name, the organisation launched the paper.
North Korea	North Korea officially the Democratic People's Republic of Korea (DPRK; Chosongul: ??????????), is a country in East Asia, occupying the northern half of the Korean Peninsula. Its capital and largest city is Pyongyang. The Korean Demilitarized Zone serves as the buffer zone between North Korea and South Korea.
Vietnam	Vietnam, officially the Socialist Republic of Vietnam is the easternmost country on the Indochina Peninsula in Southeast Asia. It is bordered by People's Republic of China (PRC) to the north, Laos to the northwest, Cambodia to the southwest, and the South China Sea, referred to as East Sea (Vietnamese: Bi?n Đông), to the east. With a population of over 86 million, Vietnam is the 13th most populous country in the world.
Appeasement	The term appeasement is commonly understood to refer to a diplomatic policy aimed at avoiding war by making concessions to another power. It has been described as "...the policy of settling international quarrels by admitting and satisfying grievances through rational negotiation and compromise, thereby avoiding the resort to an armed conflict which would be expensive, bloody, and possibly dangerous." It was used by European democracies in the 1930s who wished to avoid war with the dictatorships of Germany and Italy, bearing in mind the horrors of the First World War.

The term is most often applied to the foreign policy of British Prime Minister Neville Chamberlain towards Nazi Germany between 1937 and 1939. His policies of avoiding war with Germany have been the subject of intense debate for seventy years among academics, politicians and diplomats.

Congress

A congress is a formal meeting of the representatives of different nations, constituent states, independent organizations (such as trade unions), or groups.

The term was chosen for the United States Congress to emphasize the status of each state represented there as a self-governing unit. Subsequent to the use of congress by the U.S. legislature, the term has been incorrectly adopted by many states within unions, and by unitary nation-states in the Americas, to refer to their legislatures.

Address

An address is a collection of information, presented in a mostly fixed format, used for describing the location of a building, apartment, or other structure or a plot of land, generally using political boundaries and street names as references, along with other identifiers such as house or apartment numbers. Some addresses also contain special codes to aid routing of mail and packages, such as a ZIP code or post code.

Functions

Addresses have several functions:

1. Providing a means of physically locating a building, especially in a city where there are many buildings and streets,
2. Identifying buildings as the end points of a postal system,
3. A social function: someone's address can have a profound effect on their social standing,
4. As parameters in statistics collection, especially in census-taking or the insurance industry.

History

Chapter 16. Foreign Policy

	Until the advent of modern postal systems, most houses and buildings were not numbered.
Bureaucracy	In the social sciences, a bureaucracy is a large organization characterized by hierarchy, fixed rules, impersonal relationships, rigid adherence to procedures, and a highly specialized division of labor. Development Modern bureaucracies arose as the government of states grew larger during the modern period, and especially following the Industrial Revolution. As the authors David Osborne and Ted Gaebler point out "It is hard to imagine today, but a hundred years ago bureaucracy meant something positive.
Redistricting	Redistricting, a form of redistribution, is the process of drawing United States district lines. This often means changing electoral district and constituency boundaries in response to periodic census results. In 36 states, the state legislature has primary responsibility for creating a redistricting plan, in many cases subject to approval by the state governor.
Soviet	Soviet was a name used for several Russian political organizations. Examples include the Czar's Council of Ministers, which was called the "Soviet of Ministers"; a workers' local council in late Imperial Russia; and the Supreme Soviet of the Soviet Union. Etymology "Soviet" is derived from a Russian word signifying council, advice, harmony, concord.[trans 1] The word "sovietnik" means councillor.

Chapter 16. Foreign Policy

Soviet Union	The Union of Soviet Socialist Republics, informally known as the Soviet Union, was a constitutionally socialist state that existed on the territory of most of the former Russian Empire in Eurasia between 1922 and 1991.
	The Soviet Union had a single-party political system dominated by the Communist Party until 1990. Although the USSR was nominally a union of Soviet republics (of which there were 15 after 1956) with the capital in Moscow, it was in actuality a highly centralized state with a planned economy.
	The Soviet Union was founded in December 1922 when the Russian SFSR, which formed during the Russian Revolution of 1917 and emerged victorious in the ensuing Russian Civil War, unified with the Transcaucasian, Ukrainian and Belorussian SSRs.
Attack	In computer and computer networks an attack is any attempt to destroy, expose, alter, disable, steal or gain unauthorized access to or make unauthorized use of an asset.
	Definitions
	IETF
	Internet Engineering Task Force defines attack in RFC 2828 as:
	US Government
	CNSS Instruction No. 4009 dated 26 April 2010 by Committee on National Security Systems of United States of America defines an attack as:
	The increasing dependencies of modern society on information and computers networks (both in private and public sectors, including military) has led to new terms like cyber attack and Cyberwarfare.

Chapter 16. Foreign Policy

CNSS Instruction No. 4009 define a cyber attack as:

Phenomenology

An attack can be active or passive.

An attack can be perpetrated by an insider or from outside the organization;

> An "inside attack" is an attack initiated by an entity inside the security perimeter (an "insider"), i.e., an entity that is authorized to access system resources but uses them in a way not approved by those who granted the authorization.
> An "outside attack" is initiated from outside the perimeter, by an unauthorized or illegitimate user of the system (an "outsider").

Chapter 16. Foreign Policy

Non-state actor	Non-state actors, in international relations, are actors on the international level which are not states. The admission of non-state actors into international relations theory is inherently a rebuke to the assumptions of realism and other "black box" theories of international relations, which argue that interactions between states are the main relationships of interest in studying international events.
	
	Types of non-state actors
	
	- Non-governmental organizations (NGOs)
	
	    These groups are typically considered a part of civil society.
	
	- Multinational Corporations (MNCs)
	
	- The International Media
	- Violent non-state actor
	    o Armed groups, including groups such as Al-Qaeda, Lashkar e Tayyaba, Jaish e Mohammed.
	    o Criminal organizations, for example drug cartels such as the Gulf Cartel.
	- Religious Groups
	
	- Transnational diaspora communities
	
	Most types of non-state actors would be considered part of civil society, though some function within the international market (e.g. MNCs and organized crime).

Terrorism	Terrorism is the systematic use of terror especially as a means of coercion. No universally agreed, legally binding, criminal law definition of terrorism currently exists. Common definitions of terrorism refer only to those violent acts which are intended to create fear (terror), are perpetrated for a religious, political or ideological goal, deliberately target or disregard the safety of non-combatants (civilians), and are committed by non-government agencies.

Chapter 16. Foreign Policy

Alliance	An alliance is an agreement or friendship between two or more parties, made in order to advance common goals and to secure common interests. Examples of alliances International relations In international relations, the Anglo-Portuguese Alliance, signed in 1373 between the Kingdom of England (succeeded by the United Kingdom) and Portugal, is the oldest alliance in the world which is still in force.
Caucus	A caucus is a meeting of supporters or members of a political party or movement, especially in the United States. As the use of the term has been expanded the exact definition has come to vary among political cultures. Origin of the term The origin of the word caucus is debated, but it is generally agreed that it first came into use in the English colonies of North America. A February 1763 entry in the diary of John Adams of Braintree, Massachusetts, is one of the earliest appearances of Caucas, already with its modern connotations of a "smoke-filled room" where candidates for public election are pre-selected in private This day learned that the Caucas Clubb meets at certain Times in the Garret of Tom Daws, the Adjutant of the Boston Regiment.

Chapter 16. Foreign Policy

Cold War	The Cold War was the continuing state of political conflict, military tension, proxy wars, and economic competition existing after World War II (1939-1945) between the Communist World - primarily the Soviet Union and its satellite states and allies - and the powers of the Western world, primarily the United States and its allies. Although the primary participants' military force never officially clashed directly, they expressed the conflict through military coalitions, strategic conventional force deployments, extensive aid to states deemed vulnerable, proxy wars, espionage, propaganda, conventional and nuclear arms races, appeals to neutral nations, rivalry at sports events, and technological competitions such as the Space Race. Despite being allies against the Axis powers, the USSR and the US disagreed about political philosophy and the configuration of the post-war world while occupying most of Europe.
Japan	Japan is an island nation in East Asia. Located in the Pacific Ocean, it lies to the east of the Sea of Japan, China, North Korea, South Korea and Russia, stretching from the Sea of Okhotsk in the north to the East China Sea and Taiwan in the south. The characters that make up Japan's name mean "sun-origin", which is why Japan is sometimes referred to as the "Land of the Rising Sun".
Woodrow Wilson	Thomas Woodrow Wilson was the 28th President of the United States from 1913 to 1921. A leader of the Progressive Movement, he served as President of Princeton University from 1902 to 1910, and then as the Governor of New Jersey from 1911 to 1913. With Theodore Roosevelt and William Howard Taft dividing the Republican Party vote, Wilson was elected President as a Democrat in 1912. He is the only U.S. President to hold a Ph.D. degree, which he obtained from Johns Hopkins University. In his first term, Wilson persuaded a Democratic Congress to pass the Federal Reserve Act, Federal Trade Commission Act, the Clayton Antitrust Act, the Federal Farm Loan Act and America's first-ever federal progressive income tax in the Revenue Act of 1913. Wilson brought many white Southerners into his administration, and tolerated their expansion of segregation in many federal agencies.

Chapter 16. Foreign Policy

	Narrowly re-elected in 1916, Wilson's second term centered on World War I. He based his re-election campaign around the slogan "he kept us out of war", but U.S. neutrality was challenged in early 1917 when the German government sent the Zimmermann Telegram to Mexico and proposed a military alliance in a war against the U.S., and began unrestricted submarine warfare, sinking, without warning, every American merchant ship its submarines could find.
World War I	World War I or First World War (called at the time the Great War) was a major war centered on Europe that began in the summer of 1914. The fighting ended in November 1918. This conflict involved all of the world's great powers, assembled in two opposing alliances: the Allies (centred around the Triple Entente) and the Central Powers. More than 70 million military personnel, including 60 million Europeans, were mobilized in one of the largest wars in history. More than 9 million combatants were killed, due largely to great technological advances in firepower without corresponding advances in mobility.
Deterrence	Deterrence is often contrasted with retributivism, which holds that punishment is a necessary consequence of a crime and should be calculated based on the gravity of the wrong done.
	Deterrence can be divided into three separate categories.
	Specific deterrence focuses on the individual in question.
Isolationism	Isolationism is a foreign policy adopted by a nation in which the country refuses to enter into any alliances, foreign trade or economic commitments, or international agreements, in hopes of focusing all of its resources into advancement within its own borders while remaining at peace with foreign countries by avoiding all entanglements of foreign agreements. In other words, it asserts both of the following: 1. Non-interventionism - Political rulers should avoid entangling alliances with other nations and avoid all wars not related to direct territorial self-defense. 2. Protectionism - There should be legal barriers to control trade and cultural exchange with people in other states.

Chapter 16. Foreign Policy

	"Isolationism" has always been a debated political topic. Whether or not a country should be or should not be isolationist affects both living standards and the ability of political rulers to benefit favored firms and industries.
Nuclear weapon	A nuclear weapon is an explosive device that derives its destructive force from nuclear reactions, either fission or a combination of fission and fusion. Both reactions release vast quantities of energy from relatively small amounts of matter. The first fission ("atomic") bomb test released the same amount of energy as approximately 20,000 tons of TNT. The first thermonuclear ("hydrogen") bomb test released the same amount of energy as approximately 10,000,000 tons of TNT. A modern thermonuclear weapon weighing little more than a thousand kilograms (2,200 pounds) can produce an explosion comparable to the detonation of more than a billion kilograms (2.2 billion pounds) of conventional high explosive.
News conference	A news conference is a media event in which newsmakers invite journalists to hear them speak and, most often, ask questions. A joint press conference instead is held between two or more talking sides. Practice In a news conference, one or more speakers may make a statement, which may be followed by questions from reporters.
Preventive war	A preventive war is a war initiated to prevent another party from attacking, when an attack by that party is not imminent or known to be planned. Preventive war aims to forestall a shift in the balance of power by strategically attacking before the balance of power has a chance to shift in the direction of the adversary. Preventive war is distinct from preemptive war, which is first strike when an attack is imminent.

Chapter 16. Foreign Policy

Weapon	A weapon is an instrument used with the aim of causing harm or death to human being -- and for inflicting damage upon civil or military infrastructure and life-sustaining natural resources. In essence, it is a tool made with the purpose of increasing the efficacy and efficiency of such activities as hunting, fighting, the committing of criminal acts, the preserving of law and order, and the waging of war in an offensive or defensive fashion. Weapons are employed individually or collectively and can be improvised or purpose-built, sometimes with great skill and ingenuity.
Commission	A commission is a physical document issued to certify the appointment of a commissioned officer by a sovereign power. The more specific terms commissioning parchment or commissioning scroll are often used to avoid ambiguity, due to "commission" being a homonym which directs the individual in carrying out their duty regardless of what authority or responsibility they may have at any time. However the document is not usually in the form of a scroll and is more often printed on paper instead of parchment.
Consumer product	A consumer product is generally any tangible personal property for sale and that is used for personal, family, or household for non-business purposes. The determination whether a good is a consumer product requires a factual finding, on a case-by-case basis. This basis will vary from one jurisdiction to another.
Adolf Hitler	Adolf Hitler was an Austrian-born German politician and the leader of the National Socialist German Workers Party, commonly known as the Nazi Party. He was Chancellor of Germany from 1933 to 1945, and served as head of state as Führer und Reichskanzler from 1934 to 1945.

Chapter 16. Foreign Policy

A decorated veteran of World War I, Hitler joined the precursor of the Nazi Party (DAP) in 1919, and became leader of NSDAP in 1921. He attempted a failed coup d'etat known as the Beer Hall Putsch, which occurred at the Bürgerbräukeller beer hall in Munich on November 8-9, 1923. Hitler was imprisoned for one year due to the failed coup, and wrote his memoir, "My Struggle", while imprisoned.

Nation

Nation has different meanings in different contexts. In worldwide diplomacy, nation can mean country or sovereign state. The United Nations, for instance, speaks of how it was founded after the Second World War with "51 countries" and currently has "192 member states".

Rogers Act

The Rogers Act of 1924, often referred to as the Foreign Service Act of 1924, is the legislation that merged the United States diplomatic and consular services into the United States Foreign Service. It defined a personnel system under which the United States Secretary of State is authorized to assign diplomats abroad.

History

Article II, section 2 of the U.S. Constitution authorized the President to appoint, by and with the advice and consent of the Senate, "Ambassadors, other public Ministers, and Consuls." From 1789 until 1924, the Diplomatic Service, which staffed U.S. Legations and Embassies, and the Consular Service, which was primarily responsible for promoting American commerce and assisting distressed American sailors, developed separately.

Containment

Containment was a United States policy using military, economic, and diplomatic strategies to stall the spread of communism, enhance America's security and influence abroad, and prevent a "domino effect". A component of the Cold War, this policy was a response to a series of moves by the Soviet Union to expand communist influence in Eastern Europe, China, Korea, and Vietnam. It represented a middle-ground position between détente and rollback.

Nation state

The nation state is a state that self-identifies as deriving its political legitimacy from serving as a sovereign entity for a country as a sovereign territorial unit. The state is a political and geopolitical entity; the nation is a cultural and/or ethnic entity. The term "nation-state" implies that the two geographically coincide, and this distinguishes the nation state from the other types of state, which historically preceded it.

Chapter 16. Foreign Policy

Rogue	A rogue is a vagrant person who wanders from place to place. Like a drifter, a rogue is an independent person who rejects conventional rules of society in favor of following their own personal goals and values. In modern English language, the term rogue is used pejoratively to describe a dishonest or unprincipled person whose behavior one disapproves of, but who is nonetheless likeable or attractive.
Rogue state	Rogue state is a controversial term applied by some international theorists to states they consider threatening to the world's peace. This means meeting certain criteria, such as being ruled by authoritarian regimes that severely restrict human rights, sponsor terrorism, and seek to proliferate weapons of mass destruction. The term is used most by the United States, though it has been applied by other countries.
State	Many sovereign independent state are made up of a number of country subdivisions also called states. In some cases, such as the United States, the national government arose from a union of sovereign entities, which transferred some of their powers to the national government, while retaining the remainder of their sovereignty. These are sometimes called federal states.
National Convention	During the French Revolution, the National Convention, in France, comprised the constitutional and legislative assembly which sat from 20 September 1792 to 26 October 1795 . It held executive power in France during the first years of the French First Republic. It was succeeded by the Directory, commencing 2 November 1795. Prominent members of the original Convention included Maximilien Robespierre of the Jacobin Club, Jean-Paul Marat (affiliated with the Jacobins, though never a formal member), and Georges Danton of the Cordeliers.
Outsourcing	Outsourcing or sub-servicing often refers to the process of contracting to a third-party. Overview A precise definition of outsourcing has yet to be agreed upon. Thus, the term is used inconsistently.

Chapter 16. Foreign Policy

Canada	Canada was the name of the French colony that once stretched along the St. Lawrence River; the other colonies of New France were Acadia, Louisiana and Newfoundland. Canada, the most developed colony of New France, was divided into three districts, each with its own government: Québec, Trois-Rivières, and Montréal. The governor of the district of Québec was also the governor-general of all of New France.
Ensign	Ensign is a junior rank of commissioned officer in the armed forces of some countries, normally in the infantry or navy. As the junior officer in an infantry regiment was traditionally the carrier of the ensign flag, the rank itself acquired the name. The Spanish alférez and Portuguese alferes is a junior officer rank below lieutenant associated with carrying the flag, and so is often translated as "ensign".
Free trade	Free trade is a system of trade policy that allows traders to act and or transact without interference from government. According to the law of comparative advantage the policy permits trading partners mutual gains from trade of goods and services. Under a free trade policy, prices are a reflection of true supply and demand, and are the sole determinant of resource allocation.
North American Free Trade Agreement	The North American Free Trade Agreement is an agreement signed by the governments of Canada, Mexico, and the United States, creating a trilateral trade bloc in North America. The agreement came into force on January 1, 1994. It superseded the Canada-United States Free Trade Agreement between the U.S. and Canada. In terms of combined purchasing power parity GDP of its members, as of 2007 the trade bloc is the largest in the world and second largest by nominal GDP comparison. The North American Free Trade Agreement has two supplements, the North American Agreement on Environmental Cooperation (NAAEC) and the North American Agreement on Labor Cooperation (NAALC).

Chapter 16. Foreign Policy

Rights	Rights are legal, social, or ethical principles of freedom or entitlement; that is, rights are the fundamental normative rules about what is allowed of people or owed to people, according to some legal system, social convention, or ethical theory. Rights are of essential importance in such disciplines as law and ethics, especially theories of justice and deontology. Rights are often considered fundamental to civilization, being regarded as established pillars of society and culture, and the history of social conflicts can be found in the history of each right and its development.
Human rights	Human rights are "rights and freedoms to which all humans are entitled." Proponents of the concept usually assert that everyone is endowed with certain entitlements merely by reason of being human. Human rights are thus conceived in a universalist and egalitarian fashion. Such entitlements can exist as shared norms of actual human moralities, as justified moral norms or natural rights supported by strong reasons, or as legal rights either at a national level or within international law.
Protest	A protest expresses a strong reaction of events or situations. The term protest usually now implies a reaction against something, while previously it could also mean a reaction for something. Protesters may organize a protest as a way of publicly and forcefully making their opinions heard in an attempt to influence public opinion or government policy, or may undertake direct action in an attempt to directly enact desired changes themselves.
Status	A person's status is a set of social conditions or relationships created and vested in an individual by an act of law rather than by the consensual acts of the parties, and it is in rem, i.e. these conditions must be recognised by the world. It is the qualities of universality and permanence that distinguish status from consensual relationships such as employment and agency. Hence, a person's status and its attributes are set by the law of the domicile if born in a common law state, or by the law of nationality if born in a civil law state and this status and its attendant capacities should be recognised wherever the person may later travel.
Tariff	A tariff is a tax levied on imports or exports. History

Chapter 16. Foreign Policy

Tariffs are usually associated with protectionism, a government's policy of controlling trade between nations to support the interests of its own citizens. For economic reasons, tariffs are usually imposed on imported goods.

Adjustment

In law, the term adjustment may appear in varied contexts, as a synonym for terms with unrelated definitions:

General Definition

Adjust:

1. To settle or to bring to a satisfactory state, so that the parties are agreed in the result; as, to adjust accounts.
2. When applied to a liquidated demand, the verb "adjust" has the same meaning as the word "settle" in the same connection, and means to pay the demand. When applied to an unliquidated demand, it means to ascertain the amount due or to settle. In the latter connection, to settle means to effect a mutual adjustment between the parties and to agree upon the balance.

Common Uses

General Debt

- Debtor and creditor adjustment: As the term appears in an assignment for the benefit of creditors, "Creditor" means one who has a definite demand against the assignor, or a cause of action capable of adjustment and liquidation at trial. 6 Am J2d Assign for Crs § 109.
- Adjustable Rate Loan: Loan arrangement which permits the lender to change the interest rate based on a specific factor such as the prime lending rate charged by banks.
- Adjusting agency: In one sense, a collection agency; in another sense, an agency representing a debtor in making an arrangement with his creditors for the settlement of his obligations by modification of the indebtedness.

Chapter 16. Foreign Policy

Exploitation	The term exploitation may carry two distinct meanings: - The act of using something for any purpose. In this case, exploit is a synonym for use. - The act of using something in an unjust or cruel manner. It is this meaning of exploitation which is discussed below. As unjust benefit In political economy, economics, and sociology, exploitation involves a persistent social relationship in which certain persons are being mistreated or unfairly used for the benefit of others.
Deficit	A deficit is the amount by which a sum of money falls short of the required amount. Primary deficit, total deficit, and debt A government's deficit can be measured with or without including the interest it pays on its debt. The primary deficit is defined as the difference between current government spending and total current revenue from all types of taxes.
Kyoto Protocol	The Kyoto Protocol is a protocol to the United Nations Framework Convention on Climate Change (UNFCCC or FCCC), aimed at fighting global warming. The UNFCCC is an international environmental treaty with the goal of achieving the "stabilization of greenhouse gas concentrations in the atmosphere at a level that would prevent dangerous anthropogenic interference with the climate system." The Protocol was initially adopted on 11 December 1997 in Kyoto, Japan, and entered into force on 16 February 2005. As of April 2010, 191 states have signed and ratified the protocol.

Chapter 16. Foreign Policy

	Under the Protocol, 37 countries ("Annex I countries") commit themselves to a reduction of four greenhouse gases (GHG) (carbon dioxide, methane, nitrous oxide, sulphur hexafluoride) and two groups of gases (hydrofluorocarbons and perfluorocarbons) produced by them, and all member countries give general commitments.
Montreal Protocol	The Montreal Protocol on Substances That Deplete the Ozone Layer (a protocol to the Vienna Convention for the Protection of the Ozone Layer) is an international treaty designed to protect the ozone layer by phasing out the production of numerous substances believed to be responsible for ozone depletion. The treaty was opened for signature on September 16, 1987, and entered into force on January 1, 1989, followed by a first meeting in Helsinki, May 1989. Since then, it has undergone seven revisions, in 1990 (London), 1991 (Nairobi), 1992 (Copenhagen), 1993 (Bangkok), 1995 (Vienna), 1997 (Montreal), and 1999 (Beijing). It is believed that if the international agreement is adhered to, the ozone layer is expected to recover by 2050. Due to its widespread adoption and implementation it has been hailed as an example of exceptional international co-operation, with Kofi Annan quoted as saying that "perhaps the single most successful international agreement to date has been the Montreal Protocol".
Minutes	Minutes, are the instant written record of a meeting or hearing. They often give an overview of the structure of the meeting, starting with a list of those present, a statement of the various issues before the participants, and each of their responses thereto. They are often created at the moment of the hearing by a typist or court recorder at the meeting, who may record the meeting in shorthand, and then prepare the minutes and issue them to the participants afterwards.
Arabia	Arabia was a satrapy (province) of the Achaemenid Empire and later of the Sassanid Empire, by the name of Arabistan. Achaemenid Era Achaemenid Arabia corresponded to the lands between Egypt and Mesopotamia, known as Arabia Petraea. According to Herodotus, the Cambyses did not subdue the Arabs when he attacked Egypt in 525 BCE. His successor Darius the Great does not mention the Arabs in the Behistun inscription from the first years of his reign, but mentions them in later texts.

Chapter 16. Foreign Policy

Convention on the Elimination of All Forms of Racial Discrimination	The International Convention on the Elimination of All Forms of Racial Discrimination is a United Nations convention. A second-generation human rights instrument, the Convention commits its members to the elimination of racial discrimination and the promotion of understanding among all races. Controversially, the Convention also requires its parties to outlaw hate speech and criminalize membership in racist organizations.
Covenant	A covenant, in its most general sense, is a solemn promise to engage in or refrain from a specified action. A covenant is a type of contract in which the covenantor makes a promise to a covenantee to do or not do some action. In real property law, the term real covenants is used for conditions tied to the use of land.
Democracy	Democracy is a political form of government in which governing power is derived from the people, by consensus (consensus democracy), by direct referendum (direct democracy), or by means of elected representatives of the people (representative democracy). The term comes from the Greek: δημοκρατ?α - (demokratía) "rule of the people", which was coined from δ?μος (dêmos) "people" and κρ?τος (Kratos) "power", in the middle of the 5th-4th century BC to denote the political systems then existing in some Greek city-states, notably Athens following a popular uprising in 508 BC. Even though there is no specific, universally accepted definition of 'democracy', equality and freedom have been identified as important characteristics of democracy since ancient times. These principles are reflected in all citizens being equal before the law and having equal access to power.
Democratic republic	A democratic republic is, at least in theory, a country which is both a republic and a democracy. In practice countries which describe themselves as democratic republics rarely hold free or fair elections and the term is sometimes used as a euphemism for a dictatorship.
Discrimination	Discrimination is the cognitive and sensory capacity or ability to see fine distinctions and perceive differences between objects, subjects, concepts and patterns, or possess exceptional development of the senses. Used in this way to identify exceptional discernment since the 17th century, the term begun to be used as an expression of derogatory racial prejudice from the 1830s Thomas D. Rice's performances as "Jim Crow".

Chapter 16. Foreign Policy

	Since the American Civil War the term 'discrimination' generally evolved in American English usage as an understanding of prejudicial treatment of an individual based solely on their race, later generalized as membership in a certain socially undesirable group or social category.
Freedom	Freedom is a London-based anarchist newspaper published fortnightly by Freedom Press.
	The paper was started in 1886 by volunteers including Peter Kropotkin and Charlotte Wilson and continues to this day as an unpaid project. Originally, the subtitle was "A Journal of Anarchist Socialism." The title was changed to "A Journal of Anarchist Communism" in June 1889. Today it is unlabelled.
International Covenant on Civil and Political Rights	The International Covenant on Civil and Political Rights is a multilateral treaty adopted by the United Nations General Assembly on December 16, 1966, and in force from March 23, 1976. It commits its parties to respect the civil and political rights of individuals, including the right to life, freedom of religion, freedom of speech, freedom of assembly, electoral rights and rights to due process and a fair trial. As of December 2010, the Covenant had 72 signatories and 167 parties.
	The ICCPR is part of the International Bill of Human Rights, along with the International Covenant on Economic, Social and Cultural Rights (ICESCR) and the Universal Declaration of Human Rights (UDHR).
Republic	A republic is a state under a form of government in which the people, or some significant portion of them, retain supreme control over the government. The term is generally also understood to describe a state where most decisions are made with reference to established laws, rather than the discretion of a head of state, and therefore monarchy is today generally considered to be incompatible with being a republic. One common modern definition of a republic is a state without a monarch.

Chapter 16. Foreign Policy

Saudi Arabia	The Kingdom of Saudi Arabia, commonly known as Saudi Arabia is the largest Arab country of the Middle East. It is bordered by Jordan and Iraq on the north and northeast, Kuwait, Qatar and the United Arab Emirates on the east, Oman on the southeast, and Yemen on the south. It is also connected to Bahrain by the King Fahd Causeway.
Timor	Timor is an island at the southern end of Maritime Southeast Asia, north of the Timor Sea. It is divided between the independent state of East Timor, and West Timor, belonging to the Indonesian province of East Nusa Tenggara. The island's surface is 11,883 square miles (30,777 km^2).
Torture	Torture, according to the United Nations Convention Against Torture is: Throughout history, torture has often been used as a method of political re-education, interrogation, punishment, and coercion. In addition to state-sponsored torture, individuals or groups may be motivated to inflict torture on others for similar reasons to those of a state; however, the motive for torture can also be for the sadistic gratification of the torturer, as in the Moors murders. Torture is prohibited under international law and the domestic laws of most countries in the 21st century.
Peacekeeping	Peacekeeping is defined by the United Nations as "a unique and dynamic instrument developed by the Organization as a way to help countries torn by conflict create the conditions for lasting peace". It is distinguished from both peacebuilding and peacemaking. Peacekeepers monitor and observe peace processes in post-conflict areas and assist ex-combatants in implementing the peace agreements they may have signed.
Amnesty	Amnesty is a legislative or executive act by which a state restores those who may have been guilty of an offense against it to the positions of innocent people. It includes more than pardon, in as much as it obliterates all legal remembrance of the offense. The word has the same root as amnesia.

Chapter 16. Foreign Policy

Community	A community is an administrative division found in Belgium, Canada, Greece, Iceland, Wales, and the League of Nations Class A mandates
Point	Points, sometimes also called a "discount point", are a form of pre-paid interest. One point equals one percent of the loan amount. By charging a borrower points, a lender effectively increases the yield on the loan above the amount of the stated interest rate.
Treaty	A treaty is an express agreement under international law entered into by actors in international law, namely sovereign states and international organizations. A treaty may also be known as: (international) agreement, protocol, covenant, convention, exchange of letters, etc. Regardless of the terminology, all of these international agreements under international law are equally treaties and the rules are the same.
Lobbying	Lobbying is the intention of influencing decisions made by legislators and officials in the government by individuals, other legislators, constituents, or advocacy groups. A lobbyist is a person who tries to influence legislation on behalf of a special interest or a member of a lobby. Governments often define and regulate organized group lobbying that has become influential.
Gate	A gate is a point of entry to a space enclosed by walls, or a moderately sized opening in a fence. Gates may prevent or control entry or exit, or they may be merely decorative. Other terms for gate include yett and port.
Homeland	A homeland is the concept of the place (cultural geography) to which an ethnic group holds a long history and a deep cultural association with --the country in which a particular national identity began. As a common noun, it simply connotes the country of one's origin.
Homeland security	Homeland security is an umbrella term for security efforts to protect the United States against terrorist activity. The term arose following a reorganization of many U.S. government agencies in 2003 to form the United States Department of Homeland Security after the September 11 attacks, and may be used to refer to the actions of that department, the United States Senate Committee on Homeland Security and Governmental Affairs, or the United States House of Representatives Committee on Homeland Security. In the United States In the United States, the concept of "homeland security" extends and recombines responsibilities of government agencies and entities.

Chapter 16. Foreign Policy

National Security Council	A National Security Council is usually an executive branch governmental body responsible for coordinating policy on national security issues and advising chief executives on matters related to national security. An National Security Council is often headed by a national security advisor and staffed with senior-level officials from military, diplomatic, intelligence, law enforcement and other governmental bodies. The functions and responsibilities of an National Security Council at the strategic state level are different from those of the United Nations Security Council, which is more of a diplomatic forum.
Security Council	The Security Council (?????? Anzen-Hosho-Kaigi?) of Japan is the nine-person national security council which advises the prime minister on national security and the military and deals with a wide spectrum of issues which indirectly affect Japan's broader interests, including basic national defense policy, the National Defense Program Outline, the outline on coordinating industrial production and other matters related to the National Defense Program Outline, including decisions on diplomatic initiatives and defense operations.
Affair	Affair may refer to professional, personal, or public business matters or to a particular business or private activity of a temporary duration, as in family affair, a private affair, or a romantic affair. Political affair Political affair may refer to the illicit or scandalous activities of public, such as the Watergate affair, or to a legally constituted government department, for example, the United Nations Department of Political Affairs. Romantic affair A romantic affair, also called an affair of the heart, may refer to sexual liaisons among unwed parties, or to various forms of nonmonogamy.
Citizenship	Citizenship is the state of being a citizen of a particular social, political, or national community.

Chapter 16. Foreign Policy

	Citizenship status, under social contract theory, carries with it both rights and responsibilities. "Active citizenship" is the philosophy that citizens should work towards the betterment of their community through economic participation, public, volunteer work, and other such efforts to improve life for all citizens.
Constitutional amendment	A constitutional amendment is a change to the constitution of a nation or a state. In jurisdictions with "rigid" or "entrenched" constitutions, amendments do not require a special procedure different from that used for enacting ordinary laws.
	Some constitutions do not have to be amended with the direct consent of the electorate in a referendum.
Naturalization	Naturalization is the acquisition of citizenship and nationality by somebody who was not a citizen or national of that country when he or she was born.
	In general, basic requirements for naturalization are that the applicant hold a legal status as a full-time resident for a minimum period of time and that the applicant promise to obey and uphold that country's laws, to which an oath or pledge of allegiance is sometimes added. Some countries also require that a naturalized national must renounce any other citizenship that they currently hold, forbidding dual citizenship, but whether this renunciation actually causes loss of the person's original citizenship will again depend on the laws of the countries involved.
Cabinet	In the European Commission, a cabinet is the personal office of a European Commissioner. The role of a cabinet is to give political guidance to its Commissioner, while technical preparation is handled by the DGs (the European Civil Service).
	Composition

Chapter 16. Foreign Policy

	The Commissioner's cabinets are seen as the real concentration of power within the Commission and consists of six members, but the exact membership faces restrictions.
Executive	Executive branch of government is the part of government that has sole authority and responsibility for the daily administration of the state bureaucracy. The division of power into separate branches of government is central to the democratic idea of the separation of powers. In many countries, the term "government" connotes only the executive branch.
Power	Power is a measure of an entity's ability to control its environment, including the behavior of other entities. The term authority is often used for power, perceived as legitimate by the social structure. Power can be seen as evil or unjust, but the exercise of power is accepted as endemic to humans as social beings.
Power of the purse	The power of the purse is the ability of one group to manipulate and control the actions of another group by withholding funding, or putting stipulations on the use of funds. The power of the purse can be used to save their money and positively (e.g. awarding extra funding to programs that reach certain benchmarks) or negatively (e.g. removing funding for a department or program, effectively eliminating it). The power of the purse is most often utilized by forces within a government that do not have direct executive power but have control over budgets and taxation.
Armed Services	Armed Services is a collective term that refers to the major organisational entities of national armed forces, so named because they service a combat need in a specific combat environment. In most states Armed Services include the Army also known as Land Force or Ground Force, Navy also know a Marine Defence Force, and Air Force. Some countries have a separate service for the Space Forces or Military Space Forces, and the Russian Federation also has the Strategic Missile Troops and the Airborne Troops as independent Armed Services.

Chapter 16. Foreign Policy

Foreign relations	Foreign relations refers to the ongoing management of relationships between a public policy administrative organisation of a state and other entities external to its authority or influence. The primary goal of such organisations is therefore to create, develop and manage foreign policy and therefore describes relationships as seen from the self-interested perspective of the state when viewing the international milieu.
	The term foreign evolved during the mid-13th century CE from ferren, foreyne "out of doors," based on the Old French forain "outer, external, outdoor; remote" reflecting the sense of "not in one's own land" first attested in the late 14th century CE. Spelling in English altered in the 17th century, perhaps by influence of reign and sovereign, both associated at the time with the most common office of monarch that determined foreign policy, a set of diplomatic goals that seeks to outline how a country will interact with other countries of the world.
Peace	Peace describes a society or a relationship that is operating harmoniously and without violent conflict. Peace is commonly understood as the absence of hostility, or the existence of healthy or newly healed interpersonal or international relationships, safety in matters of social or economic welfare, the acknowledgment of equality and fairness in political relationships. In international relations, peacetime is the absence of any war or conflict.
Peace Corps	The Peace Corps is an American volunteer program run by the United States Government, as well as a government agency of the same name. The mission of the Peace Corps includes three goals: providing technical assistance, helping people outside the United States to understand U.S. culture, and helping Americans understand the cultures of other countries. Generally, the work is related to social and economic development.
Commerce Clause	The Commerce Clause is an enumerated power listed in the United States Constitution (Article I, Section 8, Clause 3). The clause states that the United States Congress shall have power "To regulate Commerce with foreign Nations, and among the several States, and with the Indian Tribes". Courts and commentators have tended to discuss each of these three areas of commerce as a separate power granted to Congress.
Ireland	Ireland is the third-largest island in Europe and the twentieth-largest island in the world. It lies to the northwest of continental Europe and is surrounded by hundreds of islands and islets. To the east of Ireland is Great Britain, separated from it by the Irish Sea.

Chapter 16. Foreign Policy

Irish Republican Army	The Irish Republican Army (Irish: Óglaigh na hÉireann) was an Irish republican revolutionary military organisation. It was descended from the Irish Volunteers, an organisation established on 25 November 1913 that staged the Easter Rising in April 1916. In 1919, the Irish Republic that had been proclaimed during the Easter Rising was formally established by an elected assembly (Dáil Éireann), and the Irish Volunteers were recognised by Dáil Éireann as its legitimate army. Thereafter, the Irish Republican Army waged a guerrilla campaign against British rule in Ireland in the 1919-21 Irish War of Independence.
Northern Ireland	Northern Ireland is one of the four countries of the United Kingdom. Situated in the north-east of the island of Ireland, it shares a border with the Republic of Ireland to the south and west. At the time of the 2001 UK Census, its population was 1,685,000, constituting about 30% of the island's total population and about 3% of the population of the United Kingdom.
Rescue	Rescue refers to operations that usually involve the saving of life, or prevention of injury.
	Tools used might include search dogs, search and rescue horses, helicopters, the "Jaws of Life", and other hydraulic cutting and spreading tools used to extricate individuals from wrecked vehicles. Rescue operations are sometimes supported by special vehicles such as fire department's or EMS Heavy rescue vehicle.
Dual loyalty	In politics, dual loyalty is loyalty to two separate interests that potentially conflict with each other.
	A classic example of political dual loyalty is a person who is a dual citizen or who is an immigrant living in one country, although the term is sometimes used in connection with people that have religious, cultural or political ties to a political interest other than the country of their primary residence. As opposed to ethical dual loyalty, which is often a self-described situation, political dual loyalty typically appears as an attack or a pejorative accusation designed to target and discredit a particular person or group, and to call into question the loyalty of that group to the country where they reside.

Chapter 16. Foreign Policy

Intellectual property	Intellectual property is a term referring to a number of distinct types of creations of the mind for which property rights are recognized--and the corresponding fields of law. Under intellectual property law, owners are granted certain exclusive rights to a variety of intangible assets, such as musical, literary, and artistic works; discoveries and inventions; and words, phrases, symbols, and designs. Common types of intellectual property include copyrights, trademarks, patents, industrial design rights and trade secrets in some jurisdictions.
Property	Property is any physical or intangible entity that is owned by a person or jointly by a group of people. Depending on the nature of the property, an owner of property has the right to consume, sell, rent, mortgage, transfer, exchange or destroy their property, and/or to exclude others from doing these things. Important widely recognized types of property include real property personal property private property public property and intellectual property., although the latter is not always as widely recognized or enforced.
Property rights	A property right is the exclusive authority to determine how a resource is used, whether that resource is owned by government or by individuals. All economic goods have a property rights attribute. This attribute has four broad components: 1. the right to use the good 2. the right to earn income from the good 3. the right to transfer the good to others 4. the right to enforcement of property rights. The concept of property rights as used by economists and legal scholars are related but distinct.
Christian right	The Christian right is a term used predominantly in the United States of America to describe right-wing Christian individuals and organizations characterized by their strong support of public polices of social conservatism. The Christian Right is a movement that has been difficult to define due to the heterogeneity of the movement. Although views are virtually unanimous on certain issues such as abortion, some contrasting viewpoints can be found among people who identify themselves as members of the Christian Right.

Chapter 16. Foreign Policy

Coalition	The Coalition in Australian politics refers to a group of centre-right parties that has existed in the form of a coalition agreement (on and off) since 1922. The Coalition partners are the Liberal Party of Australia (or its predecessors before 1945) and the National Party of Australia (known as the Australian Country Party from 1921-1975 and the National Country Party of Australia from 1975-1982). The Country Liberal Party in the Northern Territory and the Liberal National Party in Queensland are their equivalents in those states, while the National Party of Western Australia and The Nationals South Australia are not in any form of coalition and are separate parties. There is no National Party in the ACT or Tasmania.
Corporation	In feudal Europe, corporations were aggregations of business interests in compact, usually with an explicit license from city, church, or national leaders. These functioned as effective monopolies for a particular good or labor.
	The term "corporation" was used as late as the 18th century in England to refer to such ventures as the East India Company or the Hudson's Bay Company: commercial organizations that operated under royal patent to have exclusive rights to a particular area of trade.
Court	A court is a form of tribunal, often a governmental institution, with the authority to adjudicate legal disputes between parties and carry out the administration of justice in civil, criminal, and administrative matters in accordance with the rule of law. In both common law and civil law legal systems, courts are the central means for dispute resolution, and it is generally understood that all persons have an ability to bring their claims before a court. Similarly, the rights of those accused of a crime include the right to present a defense before a court.
GREEN	Green is the only green real estate designation for REALTORs approved by the National Association of Realtors (NAR). The program was developed in 2008 by the Real Estate Buyer's Agent Council of NAR, with administration transferred to the Green Resource Council.
	The course curriculum includes sustainable building practices, marketing, and rating systems (e.g., LEED and Energy Star).

Chapter 16. Foreign Policy

United Nations	The United Nations are facilitating cooperation in international law, international security, economic development, social progress, human rights, and achievement of world peace. The United Nations was founded in 1945 after World War II to replace the League of Nations, to stop wars between countries, and to provide a platform for dialogue. It contains multiple subsidiary organizations to carry out its missions.
Diplomacy	Diplomacy is the art and practice of conducting negotiations between representatives of groups or states. It usually refers to international diplomacy, the conduct of international relations through the intercession of professional diplomats with regard to issues of peace-making, trade, war, economics, culture, environment and human rights. International treaties are usually negotiated by diplomats prior to endorsement by national politicians.
Iraq	Iraq; officially the Republic of Iraq is a country in Western Asia spanning most of the northwestern end of the Zagros mountain range, the eastern part of the Syrian Desert and the northern part of the Arabian Desert. Iraq is bordered by Jordan to the west, Syria to the northwest, Turkey to the north, Iran to the east, and Kuwait and Saudi Arabia to the south. Iraq has a narrow section of coastline measuring 58 km (35 miles) on the northern Persian Gulf.
Assembly	Assembly is a bugle call used to call in a group of soldiers or scouts. It is also sometimes referred to as "Fall in".
Charter	A charter is the grant of authority or rights, stating that the granter formally recognizes the prerogative of the recipient to exercise the rights specified. It is implicit that the granter retains superiority (or sovereignty), and that the recipient admits a limited (or inferior) status within the relationship, and it is within that sense that charters were historically granted, and that sense is retained in modern usage of the term. Also, charter can simply be a document giving royal permission to start a colony.
General	General, Finnish: kenraali is the highest officer's rank in Sweden and Finland. In Sweden, it is held by the supreme commander of the Swedish Armed Forces and the monarch. In Finland, it is held by the Chief of Defence.
Taliban	

Chapter 16. Foreign Policy

	The Taliban, alternative spelling Taleban, is an Islamist militia group that ruled large parts of Afghanistan from September 1996 onwards. Although in control of Afghanistan's capital (Kabul) and most of the country for five years, the Taliban's Islamic Emirate of Afghanistan gained diplomatic recognition from only three states: Pakistan, Saudi Arabia, and the United Arab Emirates. After the attacks of September 11 2001 the Taliban regime was overthrown by Operation Enduring Freedom.
United States	The United States of America (also referred to as the United States, the U.S., the USA, or America) is a federal constitutional republic comprising fifty states and a federal district. The country is situated mostly in central North America, where its forty-eight contiguous states and Washington, D.C., the capital district, lie between the Pacific and Atlantic Oceans, bordered by Canada to the north and Mexico to the south. The state of Alaska is in the northwest of the continent, with Canada to the east and Russia to the west across the Bering Strait.
Debt relief	Debt relief is the partial or total forgiveness of debt, or the slowing or stopping of debt growth, owed by individuals, corporations, or nations. Traditionally, from antiquity through the 19th century, it refers to domestic debts, particularly agricultural debts and freeing of debt slaves. In the late 20th century it came to refer primarily to Third World debt, which started exploding with the Latin American debt crisis (Mexico 1982, etc)..
Allegiance	An allegiance is a duty of fidelity said to be owed by a subject or a citizen to his/her state or sovereign. Etymology From Middle English ligeaunce . The al- prefix was probably added through confusion with another legal term, allegeance, an "allegation" .
Cuba	The Republic of Cuba is an island country in the Caribbean. The nation of Cuba consists of the main island of Cuba, the Isla de la Juventud, and several archipelagos. Havana is the largest city in Cuba and the country's capital.

Chapter 16. Foreign Policy

Egypt	The Roman province of Egypt was established in 30 BC after Octavian (the future emperor Augustus) defeated his rival Mark Antony, deposed his lover Queen Cleopatra VII and annexed the Ptolemaic kingdom of Egypt to the Roman Empire. The province encompassed most of modern-day Egypt except for the Sinai Peninsula (which would later be conquered by Trajan). Aegyptus was bordered by the provinces of Creta et Cyrenaica to the West and Judaea to the East.
Equity	Equity is the concept or idea of fairness in economics, particularly as to taxation or welfare economics. Overview Equity may be distinguished from economic efficiency in overall evaluation of social welfare. Although 'equity' has broader uses, it may be posed as a counterpart to economic inequality in yielding a "good" distribution of welfare.
Marshall Plan	The Marshall Plan was the large-scale economic program, 1947-51, of the United States for rebuilding and creating a stronger economic foundation for the countries of Europe. The initiative was named after Secretary of State George Marshall) and was largely the creation of State Department officials, especially William L. Clayton and George F. Kennan. Marshall spoke of urgent need to help the European recovery in his address at Harvard University in June 1947.
Pledge	A pledge is a bailment or deposit of personal property to a creditor to secure repayment for some debt or engagement, The term is also used to denote the property which constitutes the security. Pledge is the ravi of Roman law, from which most of the modern law on the subject is derived. It differs from hypothecation and from the more usual mortgage in that the pledge is in the possession of the pledgee; it also differs from mortgage in being confined to personal property (rather than real property).

Chapter 16. Foreign Policy

Social security	Social security is primarily a social insurance program providing social protection, or protection against socially recognized conditions, including poverty, old age, disability, unemployment and others. Social security may refer to: • social insurance, where people receive benefits or services in recognition of contributions to an insurance scheme. These services typically include provision for retirement pensions, disability insurance, survivor benefits and unemployment insurance. • income maintenance--mainly the distribution of cash in the event of interruption of employment, including retirement, disability and unemployment • services provided by administrations responsible for social security.
Collective security	Collective security can be understood as a security arrangement, regional or global, in which each state in the system accepts that the security of one is the concern of all, and agrees to join in a collective response to threats to, and breaches of, the peace. Collective security is more ambitious than systems of alliance security or collective defence in that it seeks to encompass the totality of states within a region or indeed globally, and to address a wide range of possible threats. While collective security is an idea with a long history, its implementation in practice has proved problematic.
Liberty	Liberty is the concept of ideological and political philosophy that identifies the condition to which an individual has the right to behave according to one's own personal responsibility and free will. The conception of liberty is influenced by ideals concerning the social contract as well as arguments that are concerned with the state of nature. Individualist and classical liberal conceptions of liberty relate to the freedom of the individual from outside compulsion or coercion and this is defined as negative liberty.
Ratification	Ratification is the approval by the principal of an act of its agent where the agent lacked authority to legally bind the principal. The term applies to private contract law, international treaties, and constitutionals in federations such as the United States and Canada. Private law

Chapter 16. Foreign Policy

	In contract law, the need for ratification can arise in two ways: Where the agent attempts to bind the principal despite lacking the authority to do so, and where the principal authorizes the agent to make an agreement, but reserves the right to approve it.
Sanctions	Sanctions are penalties or other means of enforcement used to provide incentives for obedience with the law, or with rules and regulations. Criminal sanctions can take the form of serious punishment, such as corporal or capital punishment, incarceration, or severe fines. Within the civil law context, sanctions are usually monetary fines, levied against a party to a lawsuit or his/her attorney, for violating rules of procedure, or for abusing the judicial process.
ANZUS	The Australia, New Zealand, United States Security Treaty (ANZUS is the military alliance which binds Australia and New Zealand and, separately, Australia and the United States to cooperate on defence matters in the Pacific Ocean area, though today the treaty is understood to relate to attacks in any area.

Treaty structure

The treaty was previously a full three-way defense pact, but following a dispute between New Zealand and the United States in 1984 over visiting rights for nuclear-armed or nuclear-powered ships of the US Navy to New Zealand ports, the treaty may have lapsed between the United States and New Zealand, although it remains separately in force between both those countries and Australia.

The Australia-US alliance under the ANZUS Treaty remains in full force. |
| Hungary | Hungary, officially the Republic of Hungary is a landlocked country in Central Europe. It is situated in the Pannonian Basin and it is bordered by Slovakia to the north, Ukraine and Romania to the east, Serbia and Croatia to the south, Slovenia to the southwest and Austria to the west. The capital and largest city is Budapest. |
| NATO | |

Chapter 16. Foreign Policy

The NATO (pronounced /'ne?to?/ NAY-toe; French: Organisation du traité de l'Atlantique Nord (OTAN)), also called the (North) Atlantic Alliance, is an intergovernmental military alliance based on the NATO was signed on 4 April 1949. The NATO headquarters are in Brussels, Belgium, and the organization constitutes a system of collective defence whereby its member states agree to mutual defense in response to an attack by any external party.

For its first few years, NATO was not much more than a political association. However, the Korean War galvanized the member states, and an integrated military structure was built up under the direction of two U.S. supreme commanders.

New Zealand	New Zealand is an island country in the south-western Pacific Ocean comprising two main landmasses (the North Island and the South Island), and numerous smaller islands, most notably Stewart Island/Rakiura and the Chatham Islands. The indigenous Maori language name for New Zealand is Aotearoa, commonly translated as land of the long white cloud. The Realm of New Zealand also includes the Cook Islands and Niue (self-governing but in free association); Tokelau; and the Ross Dependency (New Zealand's territorial claim in Antarctica).
Poland	Poland officially the Republic of Poland - is a country in Central Europe bordered by Germany to the west; the Czech Republic and Slovakia to the south; Ukraine, Belarus and Lithuania to the east; and the Baltic Sea and Kaliningrad Oblast, a Russian exclave, to the north. The total area of Poland is 312,679 square kilometres (120,726 sq mi), making it the 69th largest country in the world and the 9th largest in Europe. Poland has a population of over 38 million people, which makes it the 34th most populous country in the world and the sixth most populous member of the European Union, being its most populous post-communist member.
Warsaw Pact	The Warsaw Treaty (1955-91) is the informal name for the Treaty of Friendship, Cooperation and Mutual Assistance, commonly known as the Warsaw Pact, creating the Warsaw Treaty Organization. The treaty was a mutual defense treaty subscribed to by eight communist states in Eastern Europe. It was established at the USSR's initiative and realized on 14 May 1955, in Warsaw, Poland.

Chapter 16. Foreign Policy

Czech Republic	The Czech Republic (/ˈtʃɛk/ chek; Czech: Česká republika, pronounced ['tʃɛska ˈrɛpublɪka], short form Cesko ['tʃɛsko], sometimes referred to as Czechia in English, is a landlocked country in Central Europe. The country borders Poland to the northeast, Germany to the west and northwest, Austria to the south and Slovakia to the east. The Czech Republic has been a member of NATO since 1999 and of the European Union since 2004. The Czech Republic is also a member of the Organization for Security and Cooperation in Europe (OSCE).
Multilateralism	Multilateralism is a term in international relations that refers to multiple countries working in concert on a given issue.

International organizations, such as the United Nations (UN) and the World Trade Organization are multilateral in nature. The main proponents of multilateralism have traditionally been the middle powers such as Canada, Australia, Switzerland, the Benelux countries and the Nordic countries. |
Sudan	Sudan officially the Republic of Sudan, Arabic: ??????? ???????? Jumhuriyat al Sudan, is a country in northeastern Africa. It is the largest country in Africa and the Arab world, and tenth largest in the world by area. It is bordered by Egypt to the north, the Red Sea to the northeast, Eritrea and Ethiopia to the east, Kenya and Uganda to the southeast, the Democratic Republic of the Congo and the Central African Republic to the southwest, Chad to the west and Libya to the northwest. The world's longest river, the Nile, divides the country between east and west sides.
Emperor	An emperor is a (male) monarch, usually the sovereign ruler of an empire or another type of imperial realm. Empress, the female equivalent, may indicate an emperor's wife (empress consort) or a woman who rules in her own right (empress regnant). Emperors are generally recognized to be of a higher honor and rank than kings.
Napoleon I	Napoleon Bonaparte was a military and political leader of France and Emperor of the French as Napoleon I, whose actions shaped European politics in the early 19th century.

Chapter 16. Foreign Policy

	Napoleon was born in Corsica, France to parents of minor noble Italian ancestry and trained as an artillery officer in mainland France. Bonaparte rose to prominence under the French First Republic and led successful campaigns against the First and Second Coalitions arrayed against France.
Haiti	Haiti, officially the Republic of Haiti is a Caribbean country. It occupies the western, smaller portion of the island of Hispaniola, in the Greater Antillean archipelago, which it shares with the Dominican Republic. Ayiti (land of high mountains) was the indigenous Taíno or Amerindian name for the mountainous western side of the island.
Prussia	Prussia is a historical region in Central Europe extending from the south-eastern coast of the Baltic Sea to the Masurian Lake District. It is now divided between Poland, Russia, and Lithuania. The former German state of Prussia derived its name from the region.
Rebellion	Rebellion is a refusal of obedience or order. It may, therefore, be seen as encompassing a range of behaviors from civil disobedience and mass nonviolent resistance, to violent and organized attempts to destroy an established authority such as a government. Those who participate in rebellions are known as "rebels".
Americas	The Americas, are the lands of the western hemisphere, composed of numerous entities and regions variably defined by geography, politics, and culture.
	The Americas are frequently recognised to comprise two separate continents (North America and South America), particularly in English-speaking nations. The Americas may also be recognised to comprise a single continent , in Latin America and in some European nations.
Latin America	Latin America is a region of the Americas where Romance languages - particularly Spanish and Portuguese, and variably French - are primarily spoken. Latin America has an area of approximately 21,069,500 km² (7,880,000 sq mi), almost 3.9% of the Earth's surface or 14.1% of its land surface area. As of 2010, its population was estimated at more than 580 million and its combined GDP at 5.16 trillion United States dollars (6.27 trillion at PPP).

Chapter 16. Foreign Policy

Balkanization	Balkanization, is a pejorative geopolitical term originally used to describe the process of fragmentation or division of a region or state into smaller regions or states that are often hostile or non-cooperative with each other. The term has arisen from the conflicts in the 20th century Balkans. While what is now termed Balkanization has occurred throughout history, the term originally described the creation of smaller, ethnically diverse states following the breakup of the Ottoman Empire after World War I. The term is also used to describe other forms of disintegration, including, for instance, the subdivision of the Internet into separate enclaves, the division of subfields and the creation of new fields from sociology, and the breakdown of cooperative arrangements due to the rise of independent competitive entities engaged in "beggar thy neighbour" bidding wars.
International trade	International trade is exchange of capital, goods, and services across international borders or territories. In most countries, it represents a significant share of gross domestic product (GDP). While international trade has been present throughout much of history , its economic, social, and political importance has been on the rise in recent centuries.
Globalization	Globalisation (or globalization) describes the process by which regional economies, societies, and cultures have become integrated through a global network of political ideas through communication, transportation, and trade. The term is most closely associated with the term economic globalization: the integration of national economies into the international economy through trade, foreign direct investment, capital flows, migration, the spread of technology, and military presence. However, globalization is usually recognized as being driven by a combination of economic, technological, sociocultural, political, and biological factors.
Market economy	A market economy is an economy based on the power of division of labor in which the prices of goods and services are determined in a free price system set by supply and demand.

Chapter 16. Foreign Policy

	This is often contrasted with a planned economy, in which a central government can distribute services using a fixed price system. Market economies are also contrasted with mixed economy where the price system is not entirely free but under some government control or heavily regulated, which is sometimes combined with state-led economic planning that is not extensive enough to constitute a planned economy.
Self-determination	The right of nations to self-determination is the principle in international law, that nations have the right to freely choose their sovereignty and international political status with no external compulsion or external interference. The principle does not state how the decision is to be made, or what the outcome should be, be it independence, federation, protection, some form of autonomy or even full assimilation. Neither does it state what the delimitation between nations should be -- or even what constitutes a nation.
Capitalism	Capitalism is an economic system in which the means of production are privately owned and operated for a private profit; decisions regarding supply, demand, price, distribution, and investments are made by private actors in the free market; profit is distributed to owners who choose to invest in businesses, and wages are paid to workers employed by businesses and companies. There is no consensus on the precise definition of capitalism, nor how the term should be used as an analytical category. There is, however, little controversy that private ownership of the means of production, creation of goods or services for profit in a market, and prices and wages are elements of capitalism.
Democratization	Democratization is the transition to a more democratic political regime. It may be the transition from an authoritarian regime to a full democracy, a transition from an authoritarian political system to a semi-democracy or transition from a semi-authoritarian political system to a democratic political system. The outcome may be consolidated (as it was for example in the United Kingdom) or democratization may face frequent reversals (as it has faced for example in Argentina).
Military justice	Military justice is the body of laws and procedures governing members of the armed forces. Many states have separate and distinct bodies of law that govern the conduct of members of their armed forces. Some states use special judicial and other arrangements to enforce those laws, while others use civilian judicial systems.

Chapter 16. Foreign Policy

Unilateralism	Unilateralism is any doctrine or agenda that supports one-sided action. Such action may be in disregard for other parties, or as an expression of a commitment toward a direction which other parties may find agreeable. Unilateralism is a neologism, (used in all countries) coined to be an antonym for multilateralism --the doctrine which asserts the benefits of participation from as many parties as possible.
Conservative Party	The Conservative Party was a Brazilian political party of the imperial period, which was formed circa 1836 and ended with the proclamation of the Republic in 1889. This party arose mostly from the Coimbra bloc and also from members of the Restorationist Party (Partido Restaurador), also called the Caramuru Party; it called itself the Party of Order (Portuguese: partido de ordem) to distinguish itself from the liberal opposition, which they accused of disorder and anarchy, and both the party and its leadership were known as "saquarema" after the village of Saquarema, where the leadership had plantations and support.
Federalist	The term federalist describes several political beliefs around the world. Also, it may refer to the concept of federalism or the type of government called a federation. In early United States history, the Federalist Party was one of the first political parties; its members or supporters called themselves Federalists.
Henry	Saint Henry was a medieval Swedish clergyman. According to legends, he conquered Finland together with King Eric the Saint of Sweden and died as a martyr, becoming a central figure in the local Roman Catholic Church. However, the authenticity of the accounts of his life, ministry, and death are widely disputed.
Liberals	Liberals is a free market liberal party in Finland. Founded in 1965 as a reunification of the People's Party of Finland and Liberal League. Originally named Liberal People's Party (Finnish: Liberaalinen Kansanpuolue), it restyled its name as Liberals in 2000.
Liberal Party	The Liberal Party was a Belgian political party that existed from 1846 until 1961, when it became the Party for Freedom and Progress, Partij voor Vrijheid en Vooruitgang/Parti de la Liberté et du Progrès or PVV-PLP, under the leadership of Omer Vanaudenhove. History The Liberal Party was founded in 1846 and as such was the first political party of Belgium. Walthère Frère-Orban wrote the first charter for the new party.

Chapter 16. Foreign Policy

Conservatism	Conservatism is a political and social philosophy that promotes the maintenance of traditional institutions and supports, at the most, minimal and gradual change in society. Some conservatives seek to preserve things as they are, emphasizing stability and continuity, while others oppose modernism and seek a return to the way things were. The first established use of the term in a political context was by François-René de Chateaubriand in 1819, following the French Revolution.
Liberalism	Liberalism is the belief in the importance of liberty and equal rights. Liberals espouse a wide array of views depending on their understanding of these principles, but most liberals support such fundamental ideas as constitutions, liberal democracy, free and fair elections, human rights, capitalism, free trade, and the separation of church and state. These ideas are widely accepted, even by political groups that do not openly profess a liberal ideological orientation.
Detention	Detention is the process when a state, government or citizen lawfully holds a person by removing their freedom of liberty at that time. This can be due to (pending) criminal charges being raised against the individual as part of a prosecution or to protect a person or property. Being detained does not always result in being taken to a particular area (generally called a detention centre), either for interrogation, or as punishment for a crime .
Missouri Compromise	The Missouri Compromise was an agreement passed in 1820 between the pro-slavery and anti-slavery factions in the United States Congress, involving primarily the regulation of slavery in the western territories. It prohibited slavery in the former Louisiana Territory north of the parallel 36° 30' north except within the boundaries of the proposed state of Missouri. Prior to the agreement, the House of Representatives had refused to accept this compromise and a conference committee was appointed.
New Deal	The New Deal is a programme of active labour market policies introduced in the United Kingdom by the Labour government in 1998, initially funded by a one off £5bn windfall tax on privatised utility companies. The stated purpose is to reduce unemployment by providing training, subsidised employment and voluntary work to the unemployed. Spending on the New Deal was £1.3 billion in 2001.
Leviathan	Leviathan, Forme and Power of a Common Wealth Ecclesiasticall and Civil, commonly called Leviathan, is a book written by Thomas Hobbes which was published in 1651. It is titled after the biblical Leviathan. The book concerns the structure of society and legitimate government, and is regarded as one of the earliest and most influential examples of social contract theory. The publisher was Andrew Crooke, partner in Andrew Crooke and William Cooke.

Chapter 16. Foreign Policy

Corporate action	A corporate action is an event initiated by a public company that affects the securities (equity or debt) issued by the company. Some corporate actions such as a dividend (for equity securities) or coupon payment (for debt securities (bonds)) may have a direct financial impact on the shareholders or bondholders; another example is a call (early redemption) of a debt security. Other corporate actions such as stock split may have an indirect impact, as the increased liquidity of shares may cause the price of the stock to rise.
Democrats	The Democrats is a centre-right political party in Brazil, considered the main in the right-wing spectrum. Despite its former name (Liberal Front Party), the party affiliates itself to the Centrist Democrat International, and the International Democrat Union. The name comes from its support to free market policies.
New Democrats	In the politics of the United States, the New Democrats are an ideologically centrist faction within the Democratic Party that emerged after the victory of Republican George H. W. Bush in the 1988 presidential election. They are identified with more pragmatic and centrist social/cultural/pluralist positions and neoliberal fiscal values. They are represented by organizations such as the Democratic Leadership Council (DLC), the New Democrat Network, and the Senate and House New Democrat Coalitions.
Select committee	A select committee is a committee made up of a small number of parliamentary members appointed to deal with particular areas or issues originating in the Westminster system of parliamentary democracy. Select committees exist in the British Parliament, as well as in other parliaments based on the Westminster model, such as those in Australia and New Zealand. In the United Kingdom, Departmental Select Committees came into being in 1979, following the recommendations of a Procedure Select Committee, set up in 1976, which reported in 1978. It recommended the appointment of a series of select committees covering all the main departments of state, with wide terms of reference, and with power to appoint special advisers as the committees deemed appropriate.
Election	An election is a formal decision-making process by which a population chooses an individual to hold public office. Elections have been the usual mechanism by which modern representative democracy operates since the 17th century. Elections may fill offices in the legislature, sometimes in the executive and judiciary, and for regional and local government.

Chapter 16. Foreign Policy

Appointee	An appointee may be one of the following: • A member who is appointed to a position or office is called an appointee. In law, such a term is applied to one who is granted power of appointment of property. • An appointee was also a foot soldier in the French army, who, for long service and bravery, received more pay than other privates. • An appointee is the third most lower rank of the Italian Corps of Carabineers • An appointee is the third most lower rank of the Swiss Armed Forces • An appointee is also a person or organisation entrusted with managing the daily finances of vulnerable individuals in the UK.
Mandate	In politics, a mandate is the authority granted by a constituency to act as its representative. The concept of a government having a legitimate mandate to govern via the fair winning of a democratic election is a central idea of democracy. New governments who attempt to introduce policies that they did not make public during an election campaign are said to not have a legitimate mandate to implement such policies.
Reform Act	In the United Kingdom, Reform Act is a generic term used for legislation concerning electoral matters. It is most commonly used for laws passed to enfranchise new groups of voters and to redistribute seats in the British House of Commons. The periodic redrawing of constituency boundaries is now dealt with by a permanent Boundary Commission in each part of the United Kingdom, rather than by a Reform Act.

Chapter 16. Foreign Policy

Unfunded mandate	In United States law and politics, unfunded mandates are regulations or conditions for receiving grants that impose costs on state or local governments or private entities for which they are not reimbursed by the federal government. • Any one of many federal legislations such as the Clean Air Act, and the Clean Water Act that require programs to be sponsored by the governments of the states, without providing any funds for those programs. • The provisions in the Americans with Disabilities Act that require nearly all American business owners to make their business premises available to disabled customers without providing any funds for the cost of reconstruction or additional interior space. • The provisions in the Emergency Medical Treatment and Active Labor Act that require nearly all American emergency rooms to accept and stabilize any patient regardless of the patient's ability to pay, but do not provide adequate reimbursement for indigent patients.
Election Day	Election Day refers to the day when general elections are held. In many countries, general elections are always held on a Sunday, to enable as many voters as possible to participate, while in other countries elections are always held on a weekday. However, some countries, or regions within a country, always make a weekday election day a public holiday, thus satisfying both demands.
Voting	Voting is a method for a group such as a meeting or an electorate to make a decision or express an opinion--often following discussions, debates, or election campaigns. It is often found in democracies and republics. Reasons for voting In a representative government, voting commonly implies election: a way for an electorate to select among candidates for office.

Chapter 16. Foreign Policy

Gerrymandering	In the process of setting electoral boundaries, rather than using uniform geographic standards, Gerrymandering is a practice of political corruption that attempts to establish a political advantage for a particular party or group by manipulating geographic boundaries to create partisan, incumbent-protected, and neutral districts. The resulting district is known as a gerrymander; however, that word can also refer to the process. Gerrymandering may be used to achieve desired electoral results for a particular party, or may be used to help or hinder a particular group of constituents, such as a political, racial, linguistic, religious or class group.
Executive order	An executive order in the United States is an order issued by the President, the head of the executive branch of the federal government.

Chapter 16. Foreign Policy